Columbia Review
MCAT Practice Tests

Columbia Review
MCAT Practice Tests

Stephen D. Bresnick, M.D.
Attending Surgeon
Division of Plastic Surgery
University of Southern California School of Medicine
Los Angeles, California
Co-Director, Columbia Review
San Francisco, California

William H. Bresnick, M.D.
Attending Physician and Clinical Instructor
San Francisco General Hospital
University of California, San Francisco, School of Medicine
Co-Director, Columbia Review
San Francisco, California

Williams & Wilkins
A WAVERLY COMPANY

BALTIMORE • PHILADELPHIA • LONDON • PARIS • BANGKOK
HONG KONG • MUNICH • SYDNEY • TOKYO • WROCLAW

Editor: Elizabeth Nieginski
Manager, Development Editing: Julie A. Scardiglia
Managing Editor: Darrin Kiessling
Marketing Manager: Christopher Brenchley
Development Editor: Beth Goldner
Production Coordinator: Felecia R. Weber
Designer: Bi-Comp, Inc.
Illustration Planner: Felecia R. Weber
Cover Designer: Graphic World, Inc.
Typesetter: Bi-Comp, Inc.
Printer: The Mack Printing Group
Digitized Illustrations: Bi-Comp, Inc.
Binder: The Mack Printing Group

351 West Camden Street
Baltimore, Maryland 21201-2436 USA

Rose Tree Corporate Center
1400 North Providence Road
Building II, Suite 5025
Media, Pennsylvania 19063-2043 USA

Accurate indications, adverse reactions and dosage schedules for drugs are provided in this book, but it is possible that they may change. The reader is urged to review the package information data of the manufacturers of the medications mentioned.

Printed in the United States of America

First Edition

Library of Congress Cataloging-in-Publication Data

Bresnick, Stephen D.
    Columbia Review MCAT practice tests / Stephen Bresnick, William
H. Bresnick. — 1st ed.
        p.   cm.
    ISBN 0-683-18099-1
    1. Medical colleges—United States—Entrance examinations—Study
guides. I. Bresnick, William H. II. Columbia Review, Inc.
III. Title. IV. Title: MCAT practice tests.
    [DNLM: 1. Medicine—examination questions. 2. College Admission
Test.   W 18.2 B842cb 1997]
R838.5.B744   1997
610′.76—DC21
DNLM/DLC
for Library of Congress   97-6524
                                                                    CIP

The publishers have made every effort to trace the copyright holders for borrowed material. If they have inadvertently overlooked any, they will be pleased to make the necessary arrangements at the first opportunity.

To purchase additional copies of this book, call our customer service department at **(800) 638-0672** or fax orders to **(800) 447-8438.** For other book services, including chapter reprints and large quantity sales, ask for the Special Sales department.

Canadian customers should call **(800) 665-1148,** or fax **(800) 665-0103.** For all other calls originating outside of the United States, please call **(410) 528-4223** or fax us at **(410) 528-8550.**

Visit Williams & Wilkins on the Internet: **http://www.wwilkins.com** or contact our customer service department at **custserv@wwilkins.com.** Williams & Wilkins customer service representatives are available from 8:30 am to 6:00 pm, EST, Monday through Friday, for telephone access.

                                                            98 99 00
                                        2 3 4 5 6 7 8 9 10

CONTENTS

PREFACE

As a premedical student, the MCAT is the most important test that you will ever take. Serious and intense preparation is critical for MCAT success. This book is designed to be the most intensive MCAT practice test book available. It uses materials from the national leader in intensive MCAT preparation, **Columbia Review**, to provide **important strategies and the practice you need to ace the MCAT.**

Columbia Review is a national MCAT preparation program that specializes only in MCAT preparation and medical school admissions assistance. The physicians directing our MCAT program have over 25 years of combined experience preparing students for the MCAT and have served on medical school admission committees. At Columbia Review, we focus all of our attention on the MCAT; thus, we are able to provide a focused, detailed, and efficient review. The live version of our program offers more than 150 hours of classroom instruction. In addition to live classes, Columbia Review offers a home-study MCAT review program.

Columbia Review MCAT Practice Tests contains the finest MCAT practice testing material available. You deserve nothing less than the best!

FEATURES

- Outstanding MCAT preparation material from a top MCAT preparation company
- A detailed review of critical MCAT strategies
- Three full-length, high-quality practice MCAT tests (includes more than 650 practice questions)
- Detailed solutions and analyses for all questions
- Predicted MCAT scoring

We know that this book will be a critical part of your MCAT preparation. Be sure to look for the other Columbia Review MCAT titles:

Intensive Preparation for the MCAT
Verbal Reasoning Powerbuilder

Here's to intensive MCAT preparation and high MCAT scores!

Stephen D. Bresnick, M.D.
William H. Bresnick, M.D.

ACKNOWLEDGMENTS

The authors wish to thank the staff of the Columbia Review Intensive MCAT Preparation Course for their contributions. In addition, we thank Williams & Wilkins for their dedication in creating a great, high-quality book for MCAT practice testing. We especially acknowledge Beth Goldner, Elizabeth Nieginski, Kevin Thibodeau, and Tim Satterfield for their expertise and assistance with this important project.

REVIEW OF MCAT STRATEGIES

ACING THE MCAT

The MCAT is not a test of memorization. It is a test of reading comprehension, reasoning, and application of science to problem solving. As you begin your MCAT preparation, there are some basic strategies that you should keep in mind. This chapter will provide a quick review of key MCAT strategies.

Acing the MCAT requires strong basic skills, an understanding of key strategies, and an intensive MCAT preparation. A great way to think about MCAT success is to imagine a pyramid, as shown in Figure 1. At the base of the pyramid is your **baseline intelligence and ability.** Because you have done well in college and are very intelligent, most of you already possess this important foundation of the pyramid.

On the next level of the pyramid is your **ability to read and comprehend** information. Most of you are strong readers and already have what it takes to succeed. For others, English may be a second language. Some students have been science majors in college and have avoided reading-oriented course work. Perhaps these students are a little weak in reading skills. If reading is a problem for you, concentrate on building your reading ability. This is not an easy task, because reading is a skill that you develop over many years. A speed reading/reading comprehension program through your school may be of use. Columbia Review has also developed a special book, *Verbal Reasoning Powerbuilder* to help strengthen students' reading ability for the MCAT. This book is available through your college bookstore or through Williams and Wilkins (call 1-800-638-0672 to order).

The third level of the MCAT success pyramid is your **science knowledge.** You must know the basic sciences "cold" in order to maximize your MCAT success. Focus on conceptual understanding before spending much time memorizing material. If you just memorize science facts and do not understand them, you are bound to have a disaster!

The fourth level of the pyramid is **passage-solving skills.** As you know, the MCAT contains 31 passages. Twenty-two of these are in science, and nine are in verbal reasoning. Getting good at solving passages takes practice. Passage solving is a skill in itself that develops as you work through hundreds of practice passages.

The fifth level of the pyramid is an understanding of **timing and other important strategies.** To finish the MCAT in the normal time allocation, you must move quickly. It is very depressing to run out of time on the MCAT. Practice testing and timing drills will help you avoid making errors in timing. An understanding of important strategies and practice in applying these strategies will also boost your MCAT scores.

The final level of the pyramid is practice. You must practice applying your skills and science knowledge to solving MCAT-style questions. We recommend doing as many sample MCAT examinations as you can get your hands on! Practice, practice, practice!

All of the elements of this pyramid are important (see Figure 1). Ignoring any one of the important parts of the MCAT Success Pyramid will interfere with your acing of the MCAT. This book will be useful in helping you assess your mastery of science, work on your timing skills, and practice your strategic approach. Good luck!

STRATEGIES FOR APPROACHING THE MCAT

Before moving into specific strategies, the importance of relaxation cannot be overemphasized. **Relaxation is a key to success on the MCAT.** If you are too nervous, you will not be able to concentrate. It is normal to be moderately nervous about the MCAT. Actually, a reasonable amount of anxiety often increases concentration and performance. The key is to control this anxiety and nervousness. You will do this by knowing that **relaxation comes with confidence.** You will be confident and relaxed when you have prepared thoroughly for this test and have worked

1

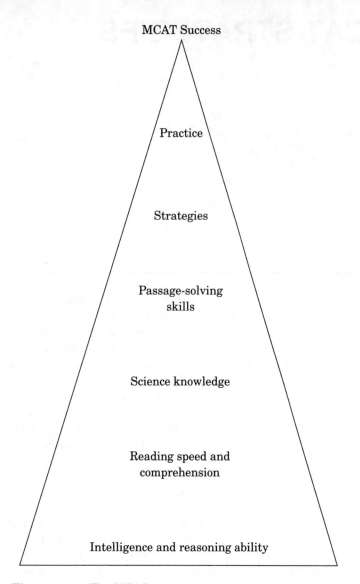

MCAT Success

Practice	Practice makes perfect!
Strategies	Strategic approach makes the difference! Timing, process of elimination, approach, and so on.
Passage-solving skills	Getting good at solving passages requires a great deal of practice!
Science knowledge	You must know your stuff! Physics, General Chemistry, Biology, and Organic Chemistry
Reading speed and comprehension	You have to be able to read quickly with good comprehension.
Intelligence and reasoning ability	Your baseline ability. You already have this!

Figure 1.   The MCAT success pyramid.

harder than your competitors. You must know the material well, and you must be good at solving MCAT-style passages.

Previewing Questions

Previewing is one of the most strategic things you can do when taking the MCAT. Previewing refers to overviewing the question stems before actually reading the passages. It is very strategic to read the question stems to Verbal Reasoning passages and Physical and Biological Sciences passages before actually reading the passages themselves. This is useful because it shows you in advance what the test writer is going to ask about. Previewing question stems allows you to focus on what is important when you read the passage. The specific previewing approaches for each section of the MCAT will be provided later in this chapter.

ANSWERING QUESTIONS

You do not have to answer questions in order. Most students solve MCAT questions in order. This is OK when the questions are not too difficult. However, if you approach a tough question in a passage and do not have much time to answer it, consider doing the easiest questions that go with that passage first. Then go back to the tough question later. **This is strategic, because it gives you extra time to think about a difficult question.** Frequently, you will have a better chance of answering the tough question correctly if you have had a minute or two to allow your subconscious mind to "stew on it."

Always keep in mind that questions are not arranged by the level of difficulty. The SAT is arranged this way, but the MCAT is not. Thus, there is no strategy for random guessing based on the position of the question on the test (early versus late questions). However, if you are short of time, it is strategic to do all of the easy questions in a passage set before spending time working on the harder questions. Your score on the MCAT is determined based on how many questions you answer correctly, not on which questions you answer.

Never leave questions blank. Be strategic about educated guessing. There is no penalty for guessing. Always answer every question. Your MCAT score is based on how many questions you answer correctly. If you have no idea of how to solve a specific question, see if you can eliminate at least one, or, if possible, two choices. This will greatly increase your chances of guessing the answer correctly. Sometimes the wording or tone of some choices does not match the question. These choices can frequently be eliminated.

Qualifying Words

Look for qualifying words in MCAT questions. A qualifying word is a word that places limits on the answer choice. These words give you clues as to what the likely answers are. For example, if you read an MCAT question that asked you what was the "best explanation" for something, you should realize that the incorrect choices might give correct, plausible explanations. However, you would want to evaluate each explanation to see which was best. You must be careful not to impulsively choose the first correct explanation you read. In this example, you would be looking for the BEST correct explanation. Other examples of qualifying words include *most likely, least, most plausible,* and so on.

On the MCAT, always look for qualifying words to give you clues to the most likely answer. In this book, you will have a great deal of practice in working through questions with qualifying words. The detailed solutions to the questions will point out these words and give you insight into how you can improve your MCAT scores by using qualifying word clues to arrive at the best answer.

Look for qualifying words in the answer choices to multiple-choice questions. Sometimes you will see that answer choices contain qualifying words that take into account that there are often exceptions to a statement. These answer choices are often the correct answer to a question. Words like *sometimes, probably,* or *some* are great examples of qualifying words that should make you evaluate that answer choice carefully. The author of the question has chosen these words for a reason!

Also pay attention to the wording of answer choices. When you see a relatively complicated answer choice, it should signal to you that the author of the question may have added qualifying clauses or phrases to make that answer choice complete and unequivocal. On the other hand, sometimes the author has added detail to an answer choice to make it seem complex and attractive. Don't be impulsive and just choose this answer; take the time to analyze it with some skepticism and added attention.

Look for absolutes in the answer choices to multiple-choice questions. As a general observation, absolute statements in the answer choices to MCAT questions are more likely incorrect than correct. These statements are frequently overgeneralizations. Absolute statements in answer choices are often easy to eliminate. This is because absolute statements are often easy to contradict. There are frequently exceptions to most absolute statements or rules. This is especially true in biological science.

Consider an example from a recent MCAT. A biology question tested the concept of the genetic code. The question asked which statement was true about the genetic code. An answer choice stated "RNA cannot be synthesized from DNA." Notice that this is an absolute statement. If you can think of only one exception to this statement, the answer choice is incorrect. If you study biology, you will remember that some viruses can transcribe DNA from RNA. Thus, this choice can be eliminated. Always see if you can eliminate possible answer choices that contain absolute statements or overstatements.

Brainstorming and Visual Aids

Use brainstorming techniques and visual aids to help figure out the hard questions. You can frequently come up with a plan for solving a question when you "jog" your memory. A good way of brainstorming is to quickly write down notes to yourself that stimulate your thinking. Also, try to draw diagrams to help you understand a description or complex process. If a passage describes a series of experiments, it is strategic to make a flow diagram to sketch out the steps of the experiment. These visual aids can really help you score better on the MCAT.

It is also very strategic to recopy in the margin of a passage any formulas or expressions given in the passage. When formulas are given in MCAT passages, you are often asked to algebraically manipulate them or apply them to solving problems. Frequently, having these expressions condensed in the margin to look at gives you an idea of how to approach or solve problems.

Suppose that on the MCAT you are asked to calculate the force on a particle. Under the stress of the test, you may find it difficult to get started in solving this question. A good way to proceed is to jot down all the expressions you know that allow you to calculate force on a particle (e.g., $F = ma$, $F = qvB$, and so on). You then can look at these formulas and see which one may be applicable to the specific question. This would be a good way to apply the brainstorming strategy.

Process of Elimination

Use the process of elimination on every question to arrive at the most likely answer. Remember that there may be several correct statements as answer choices to a question, yet one of the choices is the **best.** You are to select the **best statement or choice.** Being impulsive and quickly choosing the first correct statement you see is a big mistake. Always arrive at the best answer to every MCAT question by eliminating three answer choices and being left with the best answer choice. Using the process of elimination on every MCAT question will definitely increase your MCAT scores.

If you reach a question that is very difficult, and you have no idea of what the answer is, try to eliminate one or more choices. A random guess has a 25% chance of being correct. If you can correctly eliminate even one choice, your educated guess has a 33% chance of being correct. Two correct eliminations raises the odds to 50%. This sure beats leaving the question unanswered and having a 0% chance of getting the question correct!

Understand the Test Writers

It is very strategic to think like the test writers think. When the test writers make up questions with a single correct answer, they also compose three incorrect answer choices. We have done an analysis of the incorrect answer choices on MCAT examinations and have found a repetitive pattern for many of the questions!

There is some psychology behind the construction of incorrect answer choices. The three incorrect choices frequently seen on the MCAT include:

A "SEXY" ANSWER CHOICE

This answer choice is very attractive to the MCAT student. It is often close to being the best answer. Often, students who use the process of elimination will find that they are left with two choices: the "sexy" choice and the best choice. Usually, it requires careful reasoning or intensive study to be able to choose between these two choices. Sometimes the "sexy" choice is a little tricky. Test writers sometimes include key words or important phrases in "sexy" choices to make them appear more attractive.

A "FAIR" ANSWER CHOICE

This choice is not way off, but it just does not answer the question appropriately. Most students are able to eliminate this choice.

A "WAY-OUT" CHOICE

This choice is way off the mark. Students who choose this choice are either confused, careless, or do not know the material.

EXAMPLE AND ANALYSIS OF COMMON ANSWER CHOICE STRUCTURES

As you know, there are always four choices for every MCAT question. Suppose that the test writer wishes to make the best choice, and correct answer, choice B. The format of the answer choices could look like this:

A. Fair choice
B. Best choice
C. Sexy choice
D. Way-out choice

To understand this psychology, take a look at this sample question. This question is very similar to a question that has actually appeared on the MCAT:

Which of the following is the BEST description for the mechanism of thermoregulation in human skin?

A. The skin has the ability to maintain homeostasis.
B. The skin has autonomic nervous system innervation of glands and blood vessels.
C. The skin has an elaborate network of somatic nerve fibers that innervate and control precapillary sphincters and venous drainage and regulate blood flow.
D. The skin provides protection against dehydration.

The question asks you to find the best description for the mechanism of how the skin regulates body temperature. Remember that autonomic nerves innervate sweat glands and blood vessels in the skin. This is how thermoregulation occurs. Let's analyze each choice. We will start with the choices that are the easiest to eliminate.

Choice D is the "way-out" choice. This is the choice that is the farthest from answering the question. The skin does prevent dehydration, but this answer provides no mechanism for thermoregulation. Choice D makes a statement that does not appear related to the question being asked. Eliminate choice D.

Choice A is the "fair" choice. It does not adequately explain a mechanism for body temperature control. Although the test writer included a great word (homeostasis) in the answer choice, choice A just does not answer the question. Eliminate choice A.

Choice C is the "sexy" choice. The test writer has made this choice long, descriptive, and has included attractive wording, such as "elaborate network," "precapillary sphincters," and "regulate blood flow." This choice is very attractive to the student who does not really know the material well. The statement is incorrect, because autonomic fibers rather than somatic fibers innervate the blood vessels in the skin. "Sexy" choices are not really trick choices. They are often close to being true. Sometimes they are true statements that do not answer the question as well as the best choice does. In this example, wait to evaluate the last choice before eliminating this choice.

Choice B is the best choice. When you review biology, you will note that body temperature control occurs with sweat output from glands and vasodilatation/vasoconstriction from autonomic nerve fiber innervation. This choice gives a correct mechanism that addresses the question. Eliminate choice C and select choice B as the best choice.

Always Use Common Sense

This sounds obvious, but under the stress of the MCAT and the difficulty of some of the passages, many students lose sight of basic common sense. If you know the material and seem to understand a passage, an answer choice that seems the most logical is probably correct.

Changing Answer Choices

Do not change an answer unless you have a good reason to do so. Research has shown that if you are choosing between two or more answer choices, your first impression or educated guess has the best chance of being correct. Only change an answer to an educated guess if you:

1. On further thought, conclude that your educated guess is actually an incorrect choice
2. Remember something that changes the odds that your educated guess is correct. Perhaps an answer to a later question has given you new insight into a previous question
3. Identify a miscalculation that changes an answer
4. Realize that you misread the question. Perhaps you did not initially notice an important qualifying word such as *NOT, BEST,* or *LEAST.*

Transferring Answers

Transfer answers to the answer sheet in blocks after completing each passage. It is better to transfer answers in groups after solving each passage than transferring each answer independently. Group answer transfer saves about 15 seconds a passage. This translates into several minutes over the course of one part of the test. You may need every minute that you have. In addition, transferring answers in groups decreases the chance that you will accidentally misnumber your answers.

Always Keep Track of the Time

Test timing is one key to success. You have about 9 minutes for each verbal reasoning passage and about 8 minutes for each science passage. Go into the MCAT with a wristwatch that has a stopwatch mode. Every three passages or so, check the elapsed time. This allows you to make timing adjustments as you take the examination, and helps prevent you from not finishing the test. The three full-length practice tests in this book will give you opportunities to master test timing. Your goal is to finish the MCAT without sacrificing comprehension and performance. This will only come with practice.

STRATEGIES FOR SOLVING MCAT SCIENCE PASSAGES

Introduction to the Science Sections of the MCAT

As you know, passage-based questions will make up 80% of the questions asked on the Physical Sciences and Biological Sciences sections of the MCAT. Remember that on **each** of these two sections, there are a total of 77 questions. Sixty-two of these questions will be based on passages. The remaining 20% of the questions (15 questions) in each of these two sections will be independent, single-item multiple-choice questions. These are usually much easier to answer because they are less involved, more straightforward, and usually not based on data analysis.

The purpose of this section of the book is to present to you valuable information and strategies for improving your ability to tackle MCAT science passages. It is highly recommended that you read this section several times, master the information presented here, and practice these strategies on MCAT passages included in this book and on "real" MCAT tests. Your goal is to learn to think like the persons who write the passages and test questions. You want to familiarize yourself with the passage types, question types, and steps to follow in approaching passages.

Who writes MCAT passages? Believe it or not, **basic science college instructors and professors write MCAT passages and questions.** These test writers are biologists, chemists, and physicists, not physicians. It is important that you keep this in mind, because understanding where the test writers are coming from helps you understand their thought patterns.

As you are studying for the MCAT, do not spend too much time memorizing trivia. Focus on conceptual understanding and comprehension before memorization. Always keep in mind that the MCAT is more of a thinking test than a memorization test. For high MCAT scores, you will need to "know your stuff" in physics, general chemistry, biology, and organic chemistry. If you need a good MCAT preparation book to help you review this material, all the important information you need to know for the MCAT is included in *Columbia Review's Intensive Preparation for the MCAT.*

As we have discussed previously, obtaining high MCAT scores requires that you practice as many simulated MCAT passages as possible. Getting good at solving MCAT passages is an art in itself and requires a great deal of practice. **We suggest budgeting at least as much time solving passage problems in a science as you spend reviewing that science.** For example, if you take 30 hours to review physics carefully, try to spend at least this much time solving physics passages. You will find over 650 practice MCAT questions in this book. Eight hundred additional practice questions may be found in *Columbia Review's Intensive Preparation for the MCAT* (call Williams and Wilkins at 1-800-638-0672 to order). If you are interested in working through thousands of additional questions, Columbia Review has a **home-study course** available (call 1-800-300-PREP for more information).

Science Passages: Structure and Type

The Physical and Biological Sciences sections on the MCAT each present 11 passages. These passages describe a scientific problem for you to solve. You are not expected to have any detailed scientific and/or medical knowledge. All the information that you need to answer the question is either presented in the passage or is basic science information that you are responsible for and should know. Passages usually contain the following elements:

1. 200–300 words of descriptive information
2. A graph or table presenting data
3. Statements presenting results of experiments or data
4. A figure or experimental apparatus

You should know that some of the passages will be fairly long and wordy. This is especially true of biology passages. Strong reading comprehension skills help you to quickly read and understand these wordy passages.

There are four basic question formats that you will see in passage-based questions:

1. **Information presentation passages** look like textbook or journal articles. These passages often contain new information that you are *not* expected to know. They do require that you have background knowledge in basic science. The questions that accompany the passages test your understanding and evaluation of passages as well as your ability to manipulate the information given to solve problems.
2. **Problem-solving passages** present problems in science (physics, general chemistry, biology, and organic chemistry). These questions ask you to determine the probable causes of situations, events, or phenomena described. In addition, you are asked to select appropriate methods of solving the problems.
3. **Research study passages** give you the rationale, method, and results of research projects. The questions then ask you to interpret and understand the projects that were described. Data in the form of graphs and tables are often presented.
4. **Persuasive argument passages** present you with two viewpoints. The passages may express single viewpoints or two opposing points of view. Questions test your understanding of the arguments presented in the passages and ask you to evaluate the validity of the arguments. These are the least common passage type.

Types of Questions

The questions that follow MCAT passages fall into one of six categories. You should master this list of question types. Knowing the types of questions asked gives you a strategic advantage in knowing how to approach the questions. Once you learn to recognize certain types of questions, you will save yourself valuable time and be more efficient in solving them. Six basic types of questions commonly follow MCAT passages:

1. **Information recall.** These are questions that can be answered by directly drawing information from the passage. Believe it or not, many of these questions can be answered even if you do not know the science on which a passage is based! The test writers want to see if you can find information "buried" in a passage. These questions look a great deal like questions you would find in the Verbal Reasoning section.
2. **Data interpretation.** These questions see if you can interpret graphs, tables, and figures and make sense of the data presented in them. These are common MCAT questions. Most premedical students have difficulty answering these question types. The persons who have more experience with research and reading scientific papers are usually better at answering these types of questions. If this is your weakness, focus on practicing with every passage you can get your hands on!
3. **Simple calculation.** These questions test to see if you understand the basic concepts of the science being discussed. As a general rule, and specifically for help with this question type, do not memorize things as you prepare for the MCAT. Focus your efforts on **understanding** topics. This is your best preparation for this type of question.
4. **Conceptual understanding.** Questions that test your understanding of basic scientific principles are among the most common MCAT questions in the science sections. As a general rule, and specifically for help with this question type, do not simply memorize things as you study for the MCAT. Focus your efforts on **understanding** topics. This is your best preparation for this type of question.
5. **Application.** These questions ask you to apply concepts or principles given in a passage. You are often asked to apply the new idea or concept to a new situation. These questions test how flexible and creative a thinker you are.
6. **Evaluation.** These questions ask you to evaluate arguments and information provided. You may be asked to make conclusions from data or evaluate if conclusions are justified. These questions are usually linked to experimental data from which you are expected to be able to draw conclusions.

The Columbia Review Six-Step MCAT Passage Attack Method

The MCAT experts at Columbia Review have carefully evaluated MCAT science passages and studied the best ways to approach them. We have arrived at what most students find to be an effective, strategic technique for passage solving.

The first thing to keep in mind is **timing.** Recall that on both the Physical Sciences and Biological Sciences sections, you will have 11 passages to solve. Each passage has five to eight questions that follow the reading material, graph, or table. This gives you about **8 minutes per passage.** We suggest that you spend the 8 minutes on any passage with this approximate breakdown (Table 1).

Table 1. Allocating Your Time on a Science Passage

Previewing	30 seconds
Reading	2 minutes
Answering questions	5–5½ minutes

The second thing to keep in mind is **that any single MCAT question should take 1 minute or less to solve.** If a question appears very difficult or time-consuming to you, it usually means that either you do not know how to do the question or you are not approaching the question correctly. Stop for a minute and rethink your approach.

Another basic rule to remember is that **most MCAT questions that need a formula to solve require the use of only one formula.** It is unusual for you to need multiple different formulas to solve a problem. If you always remember that the test writers design questions to be answered in a minute or less, this will help you realize that the questions are generally not overly sophisticated and complex.

STEP 1

Quickly read the question stems of each multiple-choice question in the passage (15 seconds). This is a great strategy, because it allows you to see exactly what will be asked in advance before you even read the passage. After skimming the question stems, you will be able to focus on important information in the passages and find answers as you read. Focus on quickly grasping the topics being asked about, the direction of the questioning, and the tone of the questions. Do not waste time reading all the answer choices to questions at this stage. This slows you down and is inefficient. We also do not recommend trying to answer questions at this stage. This tends to make you lose concentration and speed.

STEP 2

Quickly look at any graph, table, or figure presented in the passage (15 seconds). If the author of the passage took the time to create a table or graph, you can predict that it will be important. It is rare that a graph or table is presented and not asked about. A graph, table, or figure often summarizes important information and may be the source for the main take-home message of the passage. Often, graphs and tables are self-explanatory and give you an overview of what is important. Thus, previewing graphs, tables, and figures can quickly give you an overview of important data and help you thoroughly understand the passage. In addition, looking at a graphic representation of data more than once improves overall understanding and retention of information. A 15-second preview followed by a longer, formal evaluation of the graph, table, or figure as you are reading the passage will give you two opportunities to master the data presented.

STEP 3

Read the passage (2 minutes). As you are reading, think about what type of passage it is and decide whether information presented is data, opinion, or fact. As you are reading the passage, **ask yourself if the passage is information presentation, problem solving, research study,** or **persuasive argument.** Having a "feel" for the passage type will give you an idea as to the tone of the likely answers.

Constantly ask yourself why the test writers provided the given information. If the information is data, think about its significance. If an opinion is presented, ask yourself if it is supported by the passage or data. If a fact is given, ask yourself if it is questionable or contradicted by the passage. Also, be sensitive to the tone of the passage. Always ask yourself: What is the author's attitude or opinion?

STEP 4

Identify important points, formulas, and data. Underline, circle, and make notes in the margins any time you come across important points, formulas, or data. You will know what is important because you have already read the question stems! Here are some general rules:

Most formulas given in a passage are used in answering questions. If you see a formula given in a passage, circle it and/or rewrite it in the margin.

Any quantitative relationship you see spelled-out in words should be written in symbols in the margin. Many students read right over these relationships unless they write them out and put them in the margin. For example, suppose that on the MCAT you were to see a statement in a physics passage that stated: the force experienced by a particle is equal to the product of the charge of the particle, the velocity of the particle, and the magnitude of the magnetic field that the particle is in. What would you do with this statement? You would write the relationship as a formula in the margin of the passage so that you would remember it and be ready to use it. You could write the statement like this: $F = qvB$.

You will frequently see the answers to information recall questions given in the text of a passage. Underline or circle these.

STEP 5

Start answering questions, and always think about the type of question you are being asked. Thinking about question type is a great strategy because it will help you in solving questions. It helps direct your time and effort effectively. For example, a very specific question that pertains to information discussed in the passage is most likely an information recall question. These questions have answers that are given in the passage. It would be wasting time to try to figure out or solve these questions.

By identifying the question type, you can most efficiently spend your time finding the answer in the passage. Once you know what type of question is being asked, you will know whether to spend time looking to provide direct recall, interpreting data, applying principles, and so on. Try to identify where in the passage a particular idea was developed. If you can, use associative reasoning to link various parts of the passage to various questions.

Also remember that working backward is helpful in answering questions. Frequently, you will be asked a question that you really do not know how to answer. Often, you can plug the choices back into the question and see one choice that fits the best. This strategy can help you identify correct answers and get you out of trouble!

STEP 6

Always use the process of elimination. You always arrive at an answer by eliminating three choices. Even if you think you know the answer, eliminate the other choices before choosing an answer. There are only four choices for each question. If you can eliminate a few possible choices, you have a much better chance of answering the question correctly. Eliminate a choice if it violates the concept presented, tone of the passage, information given, basic principles, and so on. You can eliminate choices that violate common sense or seem extreme. You can frequently eliminate choices that are simple manipulations of the numbers given in a problem. The test writers frequently put in answer choices like these to attract test takers who do not know the material. For calculation questions, be mindful of units. Looking at the units of the answer choices can frequently help you work backward to solve the problem and eliminate answer choices.

STRATEGIES FOR VERBAL REASONING

In this section, you will review some important, basic strategies for succeeding on the MCAT Verbal Reasoning section. This section provides only a brief introduction to important strategies. Many of these strategies, and others, are discussed in detail in the *Columbia Review's Intensive Preparation for the MCAT* and the *Columbia Review's Verbal Reasoning Powerbuilder*. We recommend working through this section now, and reviewing it several times as you work through Verbal Reasoning passages in this book. Some of these strategies are best understood once you have had a chance to practice Verbal Reasoning passages.

Before you begin working on practice Verbal Reasoning passages, it is important for you to have a mental game plan of how to approach the Verbal Reasoning test. These basic strategies are important to think about and master.

Motivation and Concentration

You must be totally motivated to do well on the Verbal Reasoning section. Make it a priority to work through this book and to practice verbal passages.

You must concentrate on your reading and not let any distractions affect you. Do not let your mind wander as you read. The biggest problem that you will face when reading MCAT passages is **maintaining your concentration.** Many of the passages are dry and uninteresting. It is natural for your concentration to wander when reading boring passages. Have you ever had your eyes move down a column of reading material while your mind was elsewhere? You must **concentrate deeply** and completely when reading MCAT Verbal Reasoning passages.

Have a Preplanned Approach

There are two basic ways to approach the Verbal Reasoning passages. Most students prefer the first technique described in the following text, in which question stems are previewed before the passage is read. Other students find this technique somewhat distracting and prefer to start reading the passage before answering questions. The best way to see which approach will work best for you is to try them both on some of the practice reading comprehension examinations. Here are the two approaches:

APPROACH 1

Skim the question stems, read the passage, and then carefully read the questions.

With this approach, you should read through the questions before reading the passage and underline stems, key phrases, main ideas, and important words like *except*, *only*, *always*, *inference*, and *conclusion*. Question stems are the parts of questions that ask you a specific thing or give you a task to perform. Make a mental picture of what the author is stressing or asking about. Spend no more than 15 to 20 seconds reading the question stems. Then, read the passage and keep an eye out for the key words and stems from the questions and mark (underline, circle, note in margins) the passage accordingly. Some students like to read the first and last sentences of each paragraph **before** actually reading the passage carefully.

Next, **reread each question carefully** and look back at the passage. Usually, the marks you made will bring you right back to the part of the passage where the topic of the question is discussed.

Consider trying this question stem reading technique. It is not necessary to read the answer choices. The purpose of question stem reading is to get an idea of what will be important in the passage. This strategy takes practice.

In a way, question stem previewing is a legal and ethical way of already knowing the questions before even reading the passage! Make sure that you spend only about a total of 15 to 20 seconds on question stem previewing. You need to skim only the question stems to gain an idea of the topics to be asked about. Then, when you begin reading the passage, you can identify key words, ideas, and concepts that were asked about in the questions.

This strategy helps many students with the Verbal Reasoning test. However, other students find that question stem previewing distracts them. Try this strategy for yourself to see if it helps. It you find question stem previewing too distracting, consider using approach 2.

APPROACH 2

Skim topic sentences, read the passage, and then answer the questions.

With this approach, you should start by skimming the topic sentences of each paragraph (first and last sentences) to preview the passage. This allows you to form a mental picture of the flow and main idea of the passage. Previewing topic sentences gives a great deal back to you compared with the few seconds of time it requires.

Next, read the passage, underlining or circling key ideas and main points, and making brief notes summarizing material in the margins. Feel free to read at a variable speed. Speed up if you understand or are familiar with the material. Slow down if the discussion gets complicated.

Next, read the questions and then refer back to your highlights and margin notes to answer the questions.

Whichever method you choose, you should practice reading selections and answering questions as much as possible. Practice will hone your comprehension skills and make your reading more time-efficient.

Read from a Distance

Do not get emotionally involved. Frequently MCAT passages will offer discussion on an issue or event. These passages may present a point of view. Even if you disagree with the points or opinions being expressed, try to remain neutral and only answer questions based on the facts or opinions expressed in the passage.

Common Sense and First Impressions

Always use common sense and go with your first impression. Although this advice seems obvious, many students lose sight of basic common sense under the stress of the Verbal Reasoning test. If you seem to understand the passage, an answer choice that seems most logical is probably correct. Your *first* logical impression is more often the correct one. This means that you should not change your mind about an answer to a question unless you have a good reason to. Also, **you do not have to do the passages in order!** Most students find it easiest to work through Verbal Reasoning passages in order. This minimizes disorganization. However, if you come across a passage that is very difficult for you, it may be strategic to skip it and do a passage which is easier. If you are going to skip around, it is very strategic to **work first on passages containing the most questions.** Remember, your score is determined by the number of questions you answer correctly.

Timing

You are severely punished for not finishing the Verbal Reasoning test. Your score is based on the number of questions that you answer correctly. There is no penalty for guessing and you should answer every question on the test. However, randomly guessing on questions that you do not have time to read and evaluate means that you will probably get only about 25% of these correct (4 choices per question). Since the Verbal Reasoning section is very competitive, having to guess on many questions means that most likely, you will not do well. Students often do not finish this section because they mismanage their time. We do not want this to happen to you!

The following are some simple strategies to get your timing in order:

1. **Start by looking at the last passage in the Verbal Reasoning test.** Since each passage is numbered, the number of the last passage will tell you how many total passages are on the exam. For example, if the last passage is number 9, there are 9 passages on the test. Most recently, there have been 9 passages on this section. Several years ago, there were 10 passages.
2. **Next, divide the number of passages into the total time allotted for the section.** You will be given 85

minutes total. Thus, divide 9 into 85 minutes. This gives about 9 minutes per passage, with about 4 minutes left over to either check your work or go back to solve any question that was difficult.

3. **Every three passages, you must check the time.** If by the end of the third passage, you are more than 27 minutes (three passages multiplied by 9 minutes per passage) into the test, you are working too slowly. Adjust your pace and speed up!

If you follow this simple approach, you will have the best chance of finishing the test. Because many of the other students will mismanage their time and not finish, this gives you an advantage.

Strategies for Reading the Passages

BE AN ACTIVE READER

Think as you read! Ask yourself questions about what you are reading. What is the main idea? Why is the author discussing a particular topic? What is the tone? What is emphasized in the passage? On the MCAT, never be a passive reader. If you are not thinking about what you are reading, you will have more difficulty with comprehension.

MAKE A MENTAL MAP OF THE PASSAGE

As you read the passage, make a mental picture of the layout of the passage. Think about how the author develops the ideas. It is a good idea to make a few notes in the margin next to each paragraph identifying the basic idea or theme of the paragraph. The mental map and notes that you make will help you rapidly find the answers to questions that follow the passage.

FOCUS ON THE TOPIC SENTENCES

The main idea and important take-home points in a passage are generally provided in the first and last sentences of each paragraph. Pay special attention to the topic sentences of the paragraphs as you read.

AS YOU READ, MARK THE TEXT, NOTING KEY WORDS, PHRASES, AND IDEAS

You are encouraged to write in the test booklet. Use the margins for short notations and comments. Circling and underlining are very useful. If you do not make useful marks on the Verbal Reasoning test, you are making a very big mistake!

ANSWERS COME FROM THE PASSAGE

Answers will be either directly stated or indirectly stated (implied). Because you may have previewed the question stems before reading the passage, you may be able to find the answers to questions as you read. Remember that the Verbal Reasoning test does not ask you questions from your knowledge base.

CHECK THE CITATION AT THE END OF THE PASSAGE

Many Verbal Reasoning passages are drawn from books, journals, and other published works. If a passage has been drawn from a previously published literary piece, an author citation, name of the piece, and date published will be provided. This information is very useful, because it gives you the title that the author assigned to the work. This frequently helps identify the answers to main idea questions.

Strategies for Answering the Questions

Understand how to strategically identify question types and approach them. There are six types of questions on the MCAT Verbal Reasoning test:

1. **Fact**
2. **Inference**
3. **Main idea**
4. **Tone**
5. **Application**
6. **Structure**

FACT QUESTIONS

Fact questions require you to report information that was specifically stated in the passage. Usually, the information is reworded or paraphrased in the answer choices. It is helpful to **go back to the passage** to find the information being asked about. If you made a **mental map** as you read, or made **strategic notes in the margins** of the paragraphs, it will be easy to find the answers to these questions.

Look for the following phrases that often appear in the stem of a fact question:

- According to the passage. . . .
- The author states, says, asserts, claims, or declares. . . .
- The passage states, says, asserts, claims, or declares. . . .
- According to the author. . . .

Traps to avoid

Trap: Reading your own ideas into the passage or into the question or answer. Remember to stick with the facts presented.

Trap: Looking for a complicated answer. Generally, fact questions are straightforward and relatively simple. Do not make your task more difficult by "reading into" possible choices and then confusing yourself.

Trap: Choosing answers that appear to be taken word-for-word from the passage.

INFERENCE QUESTIONS

Inference questions require you to understand what the passage implies rather than what is stated specifically. Look for questions that ask you to make **assumptions and to draw conclusions** on the basis of the facts stated in the passage. To answer an inference-type question correctly, you first must know the basic facts of the passage, then organize appropriate facts into principles and draw a conclusion from these principles that matches one of the answer choices.

Look for the following phrases that often appear in the stem of an inference question:

- The passage suggests or implies. . . .
- It is the author's opinion or view. . . .
- One can assume. . . .
- It is the purpose of. . . .
- One can conclude. . . .
- It can be deduced or reasonably inferred. . . .
- The author most likely believes. . . .
- Any question that requires you to give a reason for some statement or belief of the author.

Traps to avoid

Trap: Assuming that the answer can be found directly in the text. It is important to realize that although all of the necessary information to answer a question correctly is contained in the text, you must go one step beyond the facts and draw a conclusion *based* on the facts.

Trap: Inserting your own opinions. Although you must infer what the passage implies, you must do so on the basis of the materials given in the passage. Eliminate personal biases and focus on ideas and information in the passage.

MAIN IDEA QUESTIONS

Main idea questions ask you to **determine the central thesis** of the passage or key concept or assumption in the author's thinking. To answer these questions correctly, it is important that you (1) know the facts of the passage, (2) organize those facts into the basic principles of the text, (3) draw appropriate conclusions regarding the relationship or importance of the principles to each other, and (4) determine the central thought of the passage based on the relative importance of the principles contained in the passage.

Look for the following phrases that often appear in the stem of main idea questions:

- The passage is primarily concerned with. . . .
- The central idea. . . .
- If you were to sum up the passage. . . .
- The main thought. . . .
- . . . best describes the passage. . . .
- The primary point. . . .

Traps to avoid

Trap: Failing to include certain key facts in your decision-making process. One of the best ways to keep all of the facts of a passage in mind before attempting to answer a **main idea**–type question is to write in the margin next to each paragraph one or two key words that summarize the thought contained in that paragraph. Then, "add" up the words you wrote and think about a theme to link those words. Select the answer choice that most closely describes the theme supported by the key words.

Trap: Thinking that main idea–type questions are easy because, in a way, you are being asked to give a title to the passage. These questions are often difficult; but if you avoid flowery or stylistic answers and stick to the main concepts contained in the passage, you should (with practice) be able to select the correct answer most of the time. Also, remember to check to see if there is a citation at the end of the passage. A citation tells you the name of the article or book from which the passage was drawn. Frequently, looking at the citation title will help you arrive at the main idea.

TONE QUESTIONS

Tone questions ask you to describe or identify the author's attitude in the passage. These questions usually refer to the tone of the whole passage. Answer these questions by thinking about the feel of the passage. Is it positive, negative, or neutral? How does the author seem to feel about the topic? Your first impression of the author's attitude is most likely the correct passage tone.

Traps to avoid

Trap: Using your bias or attitude for the topic being discussed rather than the author's. It is critical that you think only about the author's opinion or feel for the topic.

APPLICATION QUESTIONS

Application questions ask you to take a concept or idea from the passage and apply it to a different situation. The key to answering these questions correctly is to understand the concept being described and **apply it, without significant change,** to the new situation. Try **thinking of an analogy or a simple example** of the concept to help you apply it to the new situation.

Traps to avoid

Trap: Taking a concept or idea that is presented in the passage and modifying it so that it does not "cleanly" apply to the new situation.

Structure Questions

Structure questions ask you to describe the meaning or significance of a particular portion of the passage. The best way to answer these questions is to think of your **mental map** of the passage. Your mental map and any notations that you have made in the passage margins give you clues as to where information or ideas are located.

Traps to avoid

Trap: If you do not make a mental map of the passage as you read, you frequently will forget where ideas are stressed or mentioned. It becomes time-consuming to randomly search the passage for answers. When you lose time on the MCAT, you frequently do not finish the test.

USE THE PROCESS OF ELIMINATION

Remember that an answer choice can be true and still be the wrong answer to a particular question. Your job is to find the **best answer** to each question. For the two types of questions on the Verbal Reasoning test, use the process of elimination strategies:

MULTIPLE-CHOICE QUESTIONS

There will be *four* choices following each question (answers A–D). **Always use the process of elimination in answering each question.** For example, if you eliminate one of the four choices, your chance of answering a question correctly based on educated guessing goes from 25% to 33%. If you are able to correctly eliminate two choices, your chance of answering the question based on educated guessing alone goes all the way up to 50%. Also, remember that, frequently, several answer choices are correct statements. However, one of the choices is **the best correct statement.** Always evaluate each choice to find which is best. If you are impulsive and do not evaluate each answer choice, you will often make an error and choose a correct statement that is not the best statement!

EXTENDED MULTIPLE-CHOICE QUESTIONS

In this format, recall that the question is usually followed by three statements: I, II, and III. You choose which of those statements are correct and then choose the right answer. **Evaluate each statement based on its own merit.** If one of the statements is false or does not appropriately answer the question, eliminate it. Once you eliminate the statement, eliminate the answer choices that have that statement as a correct statement answering the question. This way, you are using the statements to strategically eliminate possible answer choices. Remember that for each answer choice you eliminate, your odds of getting any one question correct improve dramatically.

LOOK FOR DISTRACTORS TO HELP ELIMINATE ANSWER CHOICES

Distractors are words or phrases in answer choices that are meant to lead you astray. The test writers use distractors to design incorrect answer choices. Always keep your eye out for distractors, because they provide a way of eliminating incorrect answer choices!

A good way to eliminate answer choices is to take each choice individually and try to object to it. Look to see if the choice makes a statement that is irrelevant to the passage or that overgeneralizes it. Also ask yourself if the answer choice makes a statement that is too strong or whether the tone of the answer choice conflicts with the tone of the passage.

Common **distractors** to find and eliminate as answer choices include:

1. **Choices that are outside the scope of the passage.** For example, if an answer choice to a question has little to do with the question or passage or appears to cover a peripheral topic, eliminate it. Also eliminate any answer choice that goes well beyond the coverage of the passage.

2. **Choices that are too strong or too weak in making a point or statement.** Some answer choices go too far and overstate a point from the passage. Other answer choices are too weak and do not sufficiently make a key point. Eliminate these types of choices.

3. **Choices that are too broad or overgeneralized.** The test writers frequently test your ability to identify overstatements and overassertions. If an answer choice makes too large a statement or is not specific enough, it is acting as a distractor and should be eliminated.

4. **Choices that make absolute statements.** Beware of answer choices that make emphatic statements. These answer choices are frequently incorrect. This is because a single exception is all that is needed to contradict the absolute statement. Remember that many of the passages on the MCAT cover nonscience areas and focus on discussion and inference. In these passage types, there is often an exception to almost any statement that can be made from the passage. In social science and humanities passages, rarely is there an instance in which an absolute statement is always true!

5. **Choices that copy language from the passage with distorted meaning.** A common trick of test writers is to use manipulated wording from the passage to draw the test taker into choosing an incorrect choice. Direct wording from a passage is rarely a correct answer choice. Often, the test writers modify a correct statement or idea from the passage and make it ambiguous or incorrect. This modified passage wording is then used as an answer choice. Always be suspicious of answer choices that appear to have phrases repeated from the passage. Evaluate the choices carefully and see if the context or meaning of the phrases from the passage has been changed.

6. **Choices that appear "sexy."** The test writers often choose words or phrases to put in answer choices that appear attractive and seductive. The answer choice may make a true statement, yet not directly answer the question being asked. The majority of MCAT students who fall for these incorrect answer choices are the impulsive students. Never be impulsive! Remem-

ber that no matter how good an answer choice sounds, it must be the best answer to the question being asked. Do not fall for phrasing that sounds good but does not really answer the question.

UNDERSTAND THE ANATOMY OF ANSWER CHOICES

The test writers frequently make up answer choices that have little to do with the passage. These answer choices are not contradicted by anything in the passage, yet they are not supported. **Always look for answer choices that do not appear to be supported.** Eliminate these. Also eliminate answer choices that are contradicted. Also keep in mind that the test writers rarely word correct answer choices with duplicate wording from the passage. Instead, **correct answer choices are frequently reworded to paraphrase the passage.** The test writers do this to see if you can process the meaning of answer choices.

Verbal Reasoning

Time: 85 minutes
Questions: 1–65

VERBAL REASONING

Passage I (Questions 1–8)

Watching a film by Jim Jarmusch is always a unique experience. His films have a look about them that few other directors have achieved. His characters are unusual people living on the desolate fringes of American life. Although Jarmusch sets his films in bleak urban landscapes, they nonetheless have a wry, quiet humor about them, and one can't help feeling warmly toward the characters by the end.

Jarmusch's works are characterized by two kinds of film shooting—panning across horizontal landscapes and a stuck view, motionless, inside a blank room. His second film, *Down By Law,* begins with a traveling shot of decrepit houses in New Orleans. His third film, and the first one done in color, *Mystery Train,* begins with two characters on a train to Memphis, with the brown, featureless Tennessee landscape running by outside, and continues by following the two characters walking purposefully through deserted streets, past boarded-up buildings, empty lots, and unsavory bars and restaurants.

The stark rooms in *Down By Law,* shot in overexposed black and white, convey perfectly the uncluttered emptiness of the main characters' lives. Cinematographer Robbie Muller achieves remarkable framing in these scenes. The parallel lines of sidewalk and curb, or the perpendiculars where ceilings meet walls, place the characters within artful diagonals and set lines of sight that converge at vanishing points somewhere off the side of the screen. The first half of Jarmusch's first endeavor, *Stranger Than Paradise,* takes place in the cramped, barely furnished apartment of the two male leading characters. The audience feels exactly the claustrophobia that takes hold of these men and then propels them on a road trip to Cleveland and then Florida. The same tone is conveyed through the film's sound design. These scenes are designed to capture all the echoes and ambient noise of bleak, white rooms, and Jarmusch gives us many long moments of silence and stillness in which to hear them.

Jarmusch draws out his scenes because his characters are people who have time on their hands. All of them are dreamers (often played by Jarmusch's regular John Lurie), who on the outside are thoroughly disaffected and cynical, but who on the inside retain hopes of miraculous improvements in their lives. One senses that Jarmusch's characters guard their dreams with their cynical attitudes because they have been laughed at and thwarted one too many times.

The main characters in *Down By Law,* Jack and Zach, characterize perfectly this theme in the final scene of the film. They have escaped from prison; they have found clothes to replace their prison uniforms; they bid a jocular goodbye (undercurrents of feeling of their friendship buried under macho coolness to each other); and they walk off in two directions on a forked road, with nothing visible but trees on either side. Jack and Zach have nothing in the world, and neither knows where his road will lead, but neither has a thing in the world to lose.

Each of Jarmusch's films also contains one or more foreign characters. These people arrive, from Italy, Japan, and Czechoslovakia, on the extreme fringes of American society; because they don't know any better, they mistake the fringes of society for the cultural mainstream. They display, without the veneers of defensiveness, the innocent hope and wonder still possible in the New World. One worries about the Japanese teenagers walking at night through what we know is a dubious neighborhood in Memphis, but in their innocence they are protected, and they have a perfectly enjoyable and memorable trip.

From M.G. Ross, *Jarmusch: An Original American Film-maker.* © 1995 by M.G. Ross.

16

GO ON TO THE NEXT PAGE.

1. To what does the phrase "the New World" refer to in the final paragraph?

    A. Japan
    B. The fringes of capitalistic society
    C. The Sun Belt
    D. America

2. Which of the following are embellished by the sound design?

    I.   The bleak, urban settings
    II. The desolation of the characters' lives
    III. The sense of time in the characters' lives

    A. I only
    B. I and III only
    C. I and III only
    D. I, II, and III

3. Which of the following are characteristics of the foreign characters in Jarmusch's films?

    I.   Optimism
    II. Callowness
    III. Ignorance

    A. I and II only
    B. II and III only
    C. I and III only
    D. I, II, and III

4. Which of the following descriptions is true of both the American and foreign characters?

    A. Both are cynical.
    B. Both are on the run from the law.
    C. Both are open and friendly.
    D. Both are hoping for a golden opportunity.

5. Given the information in the passage, what can you infer is the purpose of Jarmusch's panning shots?

    A. To demonstrate the opulence of American cities
    B. To convey the passage of time
    C. To show more of the same stark, decrepit locales
    D. To shift between several characters' stories

6. Which of the following would be an appropriate occupation for one of Jarmusch's American characters?

    I.   Teacher
    II. Professional gambler
    III. Unemployed person collecting welfare

    A. I only
    B. II only
    C. II and III only
    D. I, II, and III

7. Which of the following is not common to all three of Jarmusch's films?

    A. All take place, at least in part, in the American South.
    B. All leave one with warm feelings about the characters.
    C. All contain at least one disoriented character.
    D. All are shot in black and white.

8. Which of the following is implied by the scene description in the fifth paragraph?

    A. Jack and Zach are not Americans.
    B. Jack and Zach will soon find their fortunes.
    C. Jack and Zach were previously partners in crime.
    D. None of the above

Passage II (Questions 9–16)

Many believe that the debate over the moral permissibility of abortion turns on the issue of the right to life. Much of the argument on both sides centers on the determination of when life begins—whether at conception, birth, or sometime in between (e.g., after the first trimester or pregnancy). Opponents of abortion hope that by demonstrating that the unborn fetus is a person, they can show that an unborn fetus has a right to life and that abortion is murder. Advocates of abortion feel they must deny the fetus's personhood in order to answer this argument.

However, in her article "A Defense of Abortion," Judith Jarvis Thompson shows another way out for those who believe that abortion is morally permissible. She argues that the issue turns, not on the fetus's right to life, but on the woman's right to bodily autonomy. She shows that even if one considers the fetus a fully living human being from the moment of conception, one should still conclude that women have the right to terminate unwanted pregnancies.

Thompson argues this point by using an ingenious analogy. She poses the following situation to her readers: "You awake one morning to find yourself in a hospital bed, back to back with an unconscious, very famous violinist. It turns out that you have been kidnaped by the Society of Music Lovers. The famous violinist has been discovered to have a severe kidney disease, and you have been hooked up to this violinist so that he can use your kidneys. A doctor comes and explains the situation: although you have been attached to the violinist without your consent, if you detach yourself, the violinist will die. However, if you remain attached for 9 months, the violinist will be cured, and you will be free to go."

Thompson expects that our intuitions will match hers, that such a scenario is outrageously unjust, and that you clearly have the right to detach yourself. These intuitions are grounded in the basic right that every person has to decide what will happen in and to his or her body. Opponents of abortion grant this right, but claim that, morally, another individual's right to life outweighs our own right when the two come in conflict. Thompson's example is designed to show that this is not the case. The person attached to the violinist has every right not to consent to the 9-month stay in the hospital bed. The violinist does not have the right to use another's body without that person's consent, even if his life depends on it. The analogy to pregnancy should be clear. The claim is that even if the fetus is as fully fledged a human being as the famous violinist, a woman has the right to curtail the fetus's dependency on her body.

Thompson does not deny that it would be very *nice* of you to stay attached to the violinist anyway. This would be an act of charity similar to that performed by the Good Samaritan. It would be nice of you to stay attached if the violinist's cure took only an hour, rather than 9 months.

However, even in this case, the violinist would not have the *right* to the use of your kidneys. She points out that even if person A ought to do something for person B, it does not follow that person B has a *right against* person A to have that thing done for him or her. No laws require individuals to go out of their way to be Good Samaritans.

Thompson points out at the end of her article that she has only shown that a woman has the right to terminate an unwanted pregnancy; she has not shown that the woman has the right to guarantee the death of the fetus. Given the state of medical technology, termination of pregnancy and termination of the fetus's life go hand in hand, necessarily at the early stages of pregnancy, and very likely even in later stages. However, medical advances may make it necessary to draw the distinction between these two situations more sharply. In the future, courts may rule that women have the right to terminate any unwanted pregnancy, but that the state has the obligation to preserve and maintain the life of the fetus nevertheless.

From Judith Jarvis Thompson, *A Defense of Abortion.* © 1996 by J. Thompson.

9. As it is described in the passage, the violinist story is analogous with which of the following?

   I. Pregnancies due to rape
   II. Pregnancies in which the mother's health is endangered
   III. Pregnancies due to birth control failure

   A. I only
   B. II and III only
   C. I and III only
   D. I, II, and III

10. What is the distinction drawn in the final paragraph?

   A. Between the fetus's right to life and the mother's right to life
   B. Between the fetus's right to life and the fetus's right to autonomy
   C. Between the mother's right to autonomy and the mother's right to death of the fetus
   D. Between the fetus's right to death and the mother's right to the fetus' life

GO ON TO THE NEXT PAGE.

11. Why does Thompson make the sick person a famous violinist?

A. To make our intuitions pull more strongly for the right of the other person to detach himself or herself
B. To reflect the aesthetic, musical qualities of pregnancy
C. To incorporate the right-to-life argument that any unborn child may grow up to be an artistic genius, president, etc
D. To reflect her belief in the supreme value of all human life

12. Which of the following cases are NOT parallel to the violinist analogy?

I. Pregnancies of surrogate mothers
II. Pregnancies due to artificial insemination
III. Spontaneous miscarriages

A. I only
B. I and II only
C. III only
D. I, II, and III

13. What does Thompson mean by the phrase "person B has a *right against* person A," in the fifth paragraph?

A. The rights of person A take precedence over those of person B.
B. Person A has an obligation to do something for person B.
C. Person A can call for assistance in helping person B.
D. Person B has the right to dislike person A.

14. Which of the following would be the best title for this passage?

A. *A Defense of Thompson*
B. *A Woman's Place is in the Womb*
C. *Abortion and the Law*
D. *Right to Life vs. Right to Bodily Autonomy*

15. Thompson would advocate which of the following?

A. Mandatory organ donor programs
B. Good Samaritan laws
C. Laws requiring consent of the father before abortion
D. None of the above

16. If scientists could determine the exact point at which the fetus becomes a person, would this change Thompson's conclusion?

A. Yes, because a woman would then have the right to terminate the pregnancy before that point
B. No, because she has shown that even if the fetus is a person, a woman still has the right to terminate the pregnancy
C. No, because science could never determine this point
D. Yes, because this would then show that the fetus has a right to life

19

GO ON TO THE NEXT PAGE.

We will not start with postulates but with an investigation. Let us choose as its subject certain phenomena that are very common and very familiar but that have been very little examined, and that, because they can be observed in any healthy person, have nothing to do with illnesses. They are what are known as "parapraxes," to which everyone is liable. It may happen, for instance, that a person who intends to say something may use another word instead (a *slip of the tongue*), or he may do the same thing in writing, and may or may not notice what he has done. Or a person may read something, whether in print or manuscript, which is different from what is actually before his eyes (a *misreading*), or he may hear wrongly something that has been said to him (a *mishearing*) on the assumption, of course, that there is no organic disturbance of his powers of hearing. Another group of these phenomena has as its basis *forgetting*—not, however, a permanent forgetting, but only a temporary one. Thus, a person may be unable to get hold of a name that he nevertheless knows and recognizes at once, or he may forget to carry out an *intention*, although he remembers it later and has thus only forgotten it at that particular moment.

The most usual, and at the same time the most striking kind of slips of the tongue, however, are those in which one says the precise opposite of what one intended to say. Here, of course, we are very remote from relations between sounds and the effects of similarity; and instead we can appeal to the fact that contraries have a strong conceptual kinship with each other and stand in a particularly close psychological association with each other. There are historical examples of such occurrences. A president of the lower house of our parliament once opened the sitting with the words: "Gentlemen, I take notice that a full quorum of members is present and herewith declare the sitting *closed.*"

Any other familiar association can act in the same insidious fashion as a contrary one, and can emerge in quite unsuitable circumstances.

We must include among the causes of parapraxes not only relations between sounds and verbal similarity but the influence of word associations as well. But that is not all. In a number of cases, it seems impossible to explain a slip of the tongue unless we take into account something that had been said, or even merely thought, in an earlier sentence.

We have so far paid no attention whatever to the product of the slip considered by itself, without reference to its origin . . . we are bound in the end to find the courage to say that in a few examples what results from the slip of the tongue has a sense of its own: that the product of the slip of the tongue may perhaps itself have a right to be regarded as a completely valid physical act, pursuing an aim of its own, as a statement with context and significance . . . it seems now as though sometimes the faulty act was itself quite a *normal* act, which merely took the place of the other act, which was the one expected or intended.

We are told that a lady who was well-known for her energy remarked on one occasion: "My husband asked his doctor what diet he ought to follow; but the doctor told him he had no need to diet; he could eat and drink what I want." Here again, the slip of the tongue has an unmistakable other side to it: it was giving expression to a consistently planned program.

17. This passage implies that:

  A. behavioral theories are essential before accumulating empirical evidence.
  B. behavioral theories are often refuted by empirical evidence.
  C. Empirical evidence is useless without theories.
  D. Empirical evidence can be worthwhile without a theoretical base.

18. Following the logic of the passage, one may conclude that the President of the Lower House of Parliament felt that:

  A. as a full quorum of members was present, the meeting was quite normal.
  B. the Lower House of Parliament was wholly ineffectual.
  C. the Lower House of Parliament was unreceptive to change.
  D. the sitting of the Lower House of Parliament was closed to the public.

19. This passage could be titled:

  A. *The World of Parapraxes*
  B. *The Norm and Dysfunction in Language*
  C. *The Famous Freudian Slip*
  D. *Meaning What You Say*

20. From this passage, we can draw which of the following conclusions?

  I. Slips of the tongue usually have no greater or other meaning.
  II. One can be paranoid about one's tendency to mishear, misread, and forget.
  III. Often a slip of the tongue can have a sense of its own.
  IV. Asserting the opposite of what you mean can make you seem unreliable.

  A. II and III only
  B. III only
  C. I and IV only
  D. I, II, and IV only

GO ON TO THE NEXT PAGE.

21. Which of the following statements is NOT necessarily true?

    A. A permanent forgetting is much more serious than a temporary forgetting.

    B. The woman described in the last paragraph has a certain personal agenda for her husband.

    C. Contraries often have a strong attachment to each other.

    D. The common nature of parapraxes in healthy people leads us to believe that they have no relationship to mental illness.

22. If the faulty act or statement took the place of the intended act or statement, then we might speculate that:

    A. the main cause of parapraxes was the relationship between sounds and verbal similarity.

    B. the person who made the "slip" tends to be strongly influenced by word associations.

    C. there is really no such thing as "normal."

    D. the subconscious had ideas that the conscious mind had not acknowledged or had rejected.

23. Freud uses a variety of rhetorical strategies to make his points. The following are lists of these strategies. Each list offers an "order of importance" in terms of how these strategies help to support his thesis. Choose the list you find the most accurate.

    A. Anecdotes, definitions, italics

    B. Examples, catalogues, anecdotes

    C. Definitions, anecdotes, rhetorical questions

    D. Parapraxes, lists, italics

Passage IV (Questions 24–29)

There are certain things we don't want people to do in our society, and when people do them, society punishes them. But have you ever stopped to consider this peculiar practice? Why should incarceration be an appropriate response to criminal action?

Let's consider two possible motives for punishment: deterrence and retribution. If punishment is for deterrence, it is designed primarily to prevent crimes from being committed. If punishment is for retribution, that means it is for giving those who punish the satisfaction of getting back at the criminal.

Is our criminal justice and prison system designed for deterrence of crimes? Obviously, not for the person being punished—it is too late to deter that person. Does jailing those who have already committed a crime deter others from committing further crimes? First, how could you tell? How can you measure the number of crimes that are *not* committed every year? And then how could you tell that fear of punishment was the reason these uncommitted crimes were not committed? One could try to measure the changes in the rate of the performance of particular crimes when punishment, or more severe punishment, is instituted. If rates go down when punishment is stiffened, that might show deterrence. However, statistics show that this is not the case. As the old commonplace saying goes, no one ever commits a crime expecting to get caught. If punishment worked for deterrence, we would have far fewer crimes than we do.

What about retribution? This is a more plausible motivation for our existing system of criminal justice and punishment, because the purpose of the punishment is to have an effect specifically on the person who has committed the crime, and not on some other unspecified potential criminals. But is retribution very *nice*? Supposedly, our society has moved past the justice of, "An eye for an eye, a tooth for a tooth," and toward the justice of, "Turn the other cheek."

And if punishment is designed primarily for retribution, aren't we just punishing crime by committing another crime? This is most clearly the case with the death penalty, but even confinement in prison seems an uncharitable thing to do to anyone.

And whom could such a system benefit? The criminal certainly comes out worse: he or she must suffer additionally. Society at large does not benefit from reduced crime rates, because the crime in question has already happened, and as we have shown previously, the punishment of this criminal cannot be shown to prevent future crimes. Those who mete out the punishment may get some perverse satisfaction from exacting revenge on the criminal. But in our current system, those actually wronged by the crime do not get the satisfaction of meting out the punishment. It is all performed at a distance, in concrete fortresses set away from centers of civilization. It seems that neither deter-

GO ON TO THE NEXT PAGE.

rence nor retribution should be the motivation behind our current system of criminal punishment.

Adapted from Gerald Gates, *Problems with Our Criminal Justice System*. © 1997 by The Legal Reform Commission.

24. Which of the following does the author of this passage *fail* to consider in the third paragraph?

   I. Deterrence of the crime being punished
  II. Deterrence of future crimes by noncriminals
 III. Deterrence of future crimes by repeat offenders

   A. I only
   B. II only
   C. III only
   D. I, II, and III

25. The author's final argument against the deterrence hypothesis in the third paragraph might be said to have which of the following weaknesses?

   A. Sometimes criminals do get caught.
   B. The author never cites the statistics or gives the source.
   C. The author should also consider under what circumstances crime rates *rise*.
   D. The author needs to consider overall rates for all crimes.

26. Why is the author against the retribution hypothesis?

   I. Retribution is directed specifically against the criminal.
  II. Retribution is not very nice.
 III. Retribution is not effective for deterrence.

   A. I and III only
   B. II only
   C. III only
   D. None of the above

27. Which of the following motivations for punishment are *not* considered by the author?

   I. Revenge won by victims' families
  II. Rehabilitation of the criminal
 III. Preventing repeat offenses

   A. I only
   B. I and II only
   C. II and III only
   D. I and III only

28. What is the author's main argument in the passage?

   A. The reasons for our system of punishment are unclear.
   B. Punishment of criminals is not justified.
   C. Our system of punishment should be changed.
   D. Americans are soft on crime.

29. According to the argument in the fifth paragraph, why is incarceration like the death penalty?

   A. Both would be opposed by the Catholic church.
   B. Both give the satisfaction of revenge to the victims of crime.
   C. Both discourage the criminal from committing further crimes.
   D. Both amount to criminal violation of the rights of the prisoner.

GO ON TO THE NEXT PAGE.

Passage V (Questions 30–37)

It is common for Americans to think that the heroes of Greek tragedies bring their unfortunate ends on themselves. This is because we live in a society imbued with a traditional Christian moral framework, in which good deeds are rewarded, and bad deeds are punished. Our Calvinist legacy causes us to believe that when misfortune befalls someone, especially a fictional character, it is because that character previously sinned and deserves some kind of punishment.

One can certainly see this moral system operating in the popular fictional narratives that surround us. In Westerns, adventure films, police dramas, and romantic comedies, the villains invariably receive some kind of retribution by the end of the picture—loss of fortune, loss of the "romantic interest" in the story, loss of limb, or loss of life. Just as invariably, the heroes and heroines, although they may suffer many character-building trials along the way, usually win money, love, and the goodwill of the community in the final scene.

The Greeks had another value system. Their gods were not gods of judgment. Greek gods and goddesses were more like celestial "beautiful people." Their existences were filled with soap-opera intrigue—incest, clandestine sexual trysts, plots against each other, lavish parties, and contests of sport. The gods represented ideals of beauty, courage, and other virtues. However, they did not represent ideals for which human beings were supposed to aim. There was a "golden mean" that separated human beings from gods. No matter how virtuous a human being was in life, he or she had no hope of eventually being rewarded with a divine existence. Human beings who crossed the golden mean were said to display *hubris,* a kind of pride. Hubris could offend the gods, but it also made ordinary mortals rise above themselves to become heroic.

It is important to recognize that the tragic flaw is not an *action* that brings on a downfall, it is a *character trait.* Inevitability is a crucial component in any tragedy. This is what made it so gripping for the Greek audience. It can never be the case that the tragic figure could have done otherwise. Oedipus would not be Oedipus without his stubborn pursuit of the truth, and without his dedication to going the last mile to save his state. Given his personality, and given his station as a leader who is dedicated to ridding his town of its curse, he could not have abandoned the search for the source of that curse, even though it would turn out to be himself. In the end, Oedipus discovers information that he would rather not know, and must damn himself and throw himself out of his country to make things right. It is tempting for modern readers to think that Oedipus brings his downfall on himself, by pursuing the search after warnings have been given, and by having committed the sin of incest. However, Greek theatergoers would have know that they were watching the inevitable contradictions of the heroic life being played out before them.

Adapted from Laurence Heftel, *An Analysis of Greek Tragedies: Common Misunderstandings.* © 1994 by Viking Press.

---

30. Which of the following would be differences between the Calvinist god and the Greek gods?

   I. Legislative vs. lenient
   II. Punitive vs. disinterested
  III. Rewarding of outstanding behavior vs. disapproving of outstanding behavior

   A. I and II only
   B. I and III only
   C. II and III only
   D. I, II, and III

31. According to the author, how do Americans misinterpret the tragic flaw?

   A. They attribute it to the hero of the tragedy.
   B. They believe it is engendered by blameworthy behavior by the tragic hero.
   C. They believe it prevents the tragic hero from going to heaven.
   D. They believe it brings the hero's downfall.

32. How might someone display *hubris?*

   I. Undertaking a dangerous mission, believing oneself to be immortal
   II. Giving up one's fortune for someone in need
  III. Bragging about an athletic success

   A. I only
   B. I and II only
   C. I and III only
   D. III only

33. What is Oedipus' tragic flaw?

   A. Cursing the gods
   B. Killing his father and marrying his mother
   C. Stubbornness
   D. Impatience

34. Which of the following are differences between Greek tragic heroes and modern heroes, as they are described in the passage?

    I. Happy ending vs. sad ending
    II. Commit sin vs. free from sin
    III. Deserved vs. inevitable ending

    A. I only
    B. I and II only
    C. III only
    D. I and III only

35. Which of the following words best describes the author's aim in the passage?

    A. Chastising
    B. Revisionary
    C. Perfunctory
    D. Instructional

36. What might be the purpose of the warnings given to Oedipus?

    A. Foreshadowing events
    B. Giving Oedipus a chance to change his mind
    C. Illustrating the point of view of other characters
    D. Showing that the gods are getting ready to take revenge

37. Which of the following are possible tragic flaws?

    I. Political ambition
    II. Stealing
    III. Being too trusting

    A. I and II only
    B. II only
    C. I and III only
    D. III only

Passage VI (Questions 38–45)

Drawing hieroglyphs on papyrus required very considerable skill and patience. Writing with such highly detailed signs was ill-adapted to daily life and the speed required for certain tasks. So at about the same time as the hieroglyphic system came into existence, the scribes also developed a more flowing cursive script. It was called hieratic (from the Greek *hieros,* "sacred") or sacerdotal, because according to the Greek historian Herodotus (circa 424–485), from whom the term comes, this script was originally used by priests.

This cursive writing system contained the same elements as the hieroglyphic one (pictograms, phonograms, and determinates), but because these elements were often used in compounds, the signs gradually began to diverge from the original pictures.

By about 650 B.C., while both the hieroglyphic and cursive hieratic writing systems were still current, a third system—quicker, lighter, and more ligatured—appeared, which was read, like the hieratic, from right to left. This became known as demotic script—the writing of the people—and was to become the prevalent script in use in Egypt. On the famous Rosetta stone, from which Jean-François Champollion was able to decipher hieroglyphs, the same text is found written in hieroglyphs, demotic, and Greek. For a nonspecialist, it is extremely difficult to recognize the original hieroglyphs to which the individual demotic signs correspond.

Some traces of this ancient demotic script still persist today. Just as it was possible to discover numerous clues to the spoken language of the ancient Egyptians through the study of spoken Coptic, so some demotic signs have been retained in Coptic script. Hence, Champollion insisted that to understand hieroglyphs, it was essential to be able to read Coptic.

Although the Mesopotamian and Egyptian scripts have yielded up their secrets, the writing of ancient Crete remains a mystery. Around the second millennium B.C., cuneiform had reached its definitive form, and the Egyptian civilization was expanding vastly, leading to a proliferation of hieroglyphic inscriptions. At the same time, there developed in Crete, and doubtless also on the Greek mainland, a writing system that has long posed problems for scholars.

During the mid-19th century, the excavation of the ruined Cretan city of Knossos discovered a large collection of fragmentary inscriptions. These signs were engraved on seals of steatite (a soft, easily worked stone) or impressed on clay, as in the case of the famous Phaistos disk, which remains one of the greatest puzzles in the history of writing. In 1906 Italian archaeologists discovered this large clay disk, which was covered on both faces with 45 signs written in a spiral. So far, no one has been able to decipher them.

Meanwhile, on the other side of the world, in about 2000 B.C., the Chinese developed the writing system that

GO ON TO THE NEXT PAGE.

is still in use in China today. The Chinese writing system is unique; it was invented in about the second millennium B.C., codified around 1500 B.C., and systematized between 200 B.C. and 200 A.D.; it remains essentially unchanged today.

While hieroglyphs and cuneiform were supplanted by Arabic writing many centuries ago in Egypt and Mesopotamia, Chinese writing in contrast has effectively remained unaltered. Admittedly, the Chinese originally wrote with a brush and ink, while today they tend to write with a pen—even a ballpoint pen—and printing machinery and typewriters are equipped with characters that lack the thick downstrokes and the thin upstrokes that originally characterized handwritten Chinese characters. But with the exception of certain modifications made in the interest of simplicity, the Chinese writing system has remained very faithful to its original form.

38. The three types of writing in ancient Egypt were:

    A. hieroglyphic, Coptic, cuneiform.
    B. hieroglyphic, hieratic, demotic.
    C. pictogram, phonogram, determinates.
    D. Coptic, hieratic, demotic.

39. From the information in the passage, we can infer that:

    A. Coptic is still widely spoken and written.
    B. Coptic is still considered something of a "holy" language.
    C. Coptic is the modern-day version of hieroglyphics.
    D. the language of the people filtered into Coptic.

40. "On the famous Rosetta stone, from which Jean-François Champollion was able to decipher hieroglyphics, the same text is found written in hieroglyphs, demotic, and Greek." Based on this quote from the passage and the passage itself, which of the following assertions is supported?

    A. The text on the Rosetta stone was written by the people, for the people.
    B. The text on the Rosetta stone was composed by three different men.
    C. Demotic language and hieroglyphics are extremely close in symbol and meaning; the differences between them are when they developed and who used them.
    D. The demotic language grew to usurp the hieratic language.

41. The central thrust of this passage is:

    A. the modern interpretation of ancient alphabets and scripts.
    B. why certain language systems have managed to survive the ages relatively intact and others remain a mystery to us.
    C. the evolution of writing systems in the Far East.
    D. the development of writing systems in the Far and Middle East in ancient times.

42. The proliferation of hieroglyphics occurred because:

    A. papyrus was an easier material to work with than stone, and it was abundant.
    B. the demotic and hieratic writing systems were outgrowths of hieroglyphics.
    C. the second millennium B.C. was a time of growth for Egyptian civilization.
    D. such highly detailed signs were ill-adapted to daily life and the speed required for certain tasks.

43. According to the information in the passage, the Chinese writing system shares which of the following characteristics with the Egyptian writing system?

    A. They are both systems that employ signs, such as pictograms.
    B. Both were codified.
    C. Both remain essentially unaltered, even today.
    D. Both have made certain modifications in the interest of simplicity.

44. What conclusion might we be able to draw from the information in the passage about Egyptian society in the second millennium B.C?

    A. The priests and the common people had little to do with each other.
    B. Written communication was important in every caste of society.
    C. Egyptian society was considerably more democratic than other societies.
    D. Egyptian society was considerably more advanced than other societies.

45. Which of the following assertions would the findings of the excavation of the Cretan city of Knossos not support?

I. The writing of ancient Crete remains a mystery.
II. We have little insight into the ancient writing system that would serve as a template for modern-day Italian.
III. Stone and clay were cheap and easily worked materials.
IV. The Phaistos disk was found in several pieces.

A. I and III only
B. I, III, and IV only
C. II, III, and IV only
D. III and IV only

Passage VII (Questions 46–51)

The rain forest is being rapidly destroyed in many regions of the earth. Logging contributes to much of the clearing of the rain forest. A prime example of regional destruction of the rain forest is the logging that is occurring in the state of Sarawak on the island of Borneo. Sarawak is in the northwest of Borneo, and the rain forest occupies most of Sarawak's nearly 50,000 square miles. Borneo's rain forest currently contains 20,000 species of flowering plants, several thousand species of trees, hundreds of species of butterflies, 180 species of mammals, and over 100 kinds of fruiting trees, but logging is threatening the diversity of species. In addition, 24 ethnic groups dwell in the forests; most of these groups employ primitive agriculture, but some depend on hunting and gathering in the forest to survive. The effects of logging threaten not only the lifestyles but the very lives of these nomadic people.

The loggers argue that their methods are actually more beneficial to the rain forest than are the agricultural techniques of the native farmers. However, although the loggers cut select trees rather than clear-cutting the forest, even this method causes a great deal of damage. Bulldozers cut roads through the growth randomly, sometimes along the crests and sides of hills. This causes erosion during the daily rains, therefore polluting streams and making reseeding impossible. Each felled tree hits or topples up to 10 more when it falls. Separate crews go through the forest to clear away the cut trees, which causes even more disruption. Bulldozers have indiscriminately cut roads and logging camps out of native families' rice farms, on which these people formerly used crop rotation to preserve the land. Roads have even been cut through the burial ground of the Penan people.

The nomadic Penan people use the rain forest for shelter, and for food game and from plants. Western-style progress would not be completely without its benefits to these people; few live to the age of 50, because agricultural and medical development have been stultified by religious superstitions. But logging makes the transition to modernity uncomfortable, difficult, and perhaps impossible. First, cutting roads and the destruction of removing trees even selectively logged has disrupted the ecological system; many of the sago palms on which the Penan depend for most of their carbohydrates are gone, and wild game have been driven away. Penan men now have to hunt for days instead of hours to find game to feed their families, and sometimes their families go hungry. Second, the government has enacted laws against logging protests. Many Penan protesters have been detained for 2 weeks or more, and they are totally baffled by the country's Western court procedures, which are conducted in English, when their cases come to trial. The logging industry has taken away their livelihood, and has jailed and terrorized them for their assertions to get it back.

GO ON TO THE NEXT PAGE.

The worst heartbreak is that the high-quality, ancient hardwood from the rain forest is not being used, as it could be, for homes, or by master woodworkers for fine furniture. It is being turned into plywood. Because loggers do not have to pay for property rights, and labor is basically free, the price of Borneo's hardwood trees undercuts that of soft farmed woods such as pine that are usually used for plywood. Most of the wood is sold to Japanese companies to make molds for concrete, of which most of their buildings are constructed. These molds can be used up to three times, and are then sent to landfills or burned. In these fires, it is the future of the rain forest, and the lifestyles and lives of the native people of Sarawak, that are going up in smoke.

From Irene Rosenthal, *The Destruction of a Land and a People: Sarawak and Penan.* © 1995 by I. Rosenthal.

46. Which of the following is implied by the passage?

    A. Logging in the rain forest threatens diversity of plant species because it threatens the diversity of the inhabitants.

    B. Logging in the rain forest threatens the condition of the soil because it threatens the lives of the inhabitants.

    C. Logging in the rain forest threatens the lives of the inhabitants because it diminishes the diversity of plant species.

    D. Logging in the rain forest threatens Borneo's economy because it threatens the supply of trees to Japan.

47. Which of the following are effects of logging in Sarawak?

    I. Clear-cutting of forest areas
    II. Diminished food supply
    III. Soil erosion

    A. II only
    B. I and II only
    C. II and III only
    D. I, II, and III

48. Why does the author say that the future is "going up in smoke" in the last sentence?

    A. The author objects to the burning of industrial waste.

    B. The wood fueling the fire represents the Penan people's livelihood.

    C. The author advocates only domestic use of rain forest products.

    D. Loggers are clear-cutting and burning rain forest land.

49. Which of the following policies would be solutions to the problems cited by the author?

    I. Cessation of all logging in Sarawak
    II. Paying the Penan people a decent wage for their labor
    III. Conducting trials in the Penan people's native language

    A. I and III only
    B. II and III only
    C. III only
    D. None of the above

50. Why do Penan men now have to hunt for days instead of hours?

    A. Malnutrition makes them tire more easily.

    B. Falling trees have killed many rain forest game animals.

    C. Penan families are increasing in size.

    D. Rain forest game animals have been killed or frightened away by the logging.

51. Why are the Penan people's lives threatened?

    A. Dangerous conditions exist in the Sarawak jails.

    B. Ecological changes have reduced their food supply.

    C. They are unable to earn enough to pay for shelter.

    D. They are unable to make the transition to modern operations.

In the middle 1800s, efforts to create wholly new kinds of language gave way to projects that imitated real languages. None attracted much attention until 1879, when an energetic Catholic priest in Bavaria, Johann Martin Schleyer, published a scheme he called Volapuk. The idea is said to have occurred to him as he lay in bed one sleepless night. Unaware perhaps of previous efforts, and so working from scratch, he developed a system loosely based on the Germanic and Romance tongues. About 40 percent of the words were supposed to have come from English.

Volapuk struck fire because it was designed for ordinary people, rather than for well-educated intellectuals. Volapuk societies soon sprang up in many parts of Europe and America; books and magazines began to appear in the language, and some thousands of adherents began using it for correspondence.

But Volapuk was seriously flawed. It had a complicated grammar with endless verb forms. Words looked clumsy and sounded harsh, frequently having been altered and shortened so that they hardly resembled the natural forms they were derived from. There was also a problem with Father Schleyer's proprietary attitude. Only he and a few authorized academicians could create new words, modify grammar, or even approve officers in local clubs. It is said that at first he resisted including certain words in the language—like "jealousy"—out of religious motives.

When general assemblies of Volapukists were held in Friedrichshafen and Munich, delegates had trouble understanding one another, so they conversed mostly in German. There soon arose bitter quarrels among various factions; disillusion set in; and the movement was all but dead by 1900.

In Poland, one who observed Volapuk's course with special interest was a young physician named Ludovic Lazarus Zamenhof. As a boy growing up in Bialystok, he had been struck by the antipathy with which the borderland town's racial communities regarded each other. To Ludovic, it seemed that language was at least the mortar that kept the walls of misunderstanding in place.

Young Zamenhof's father and grandfather had been language teachers, and Ludovic was born with an unusual gift for languages. At school he excelled in German, French, Latin, and Greek. Hebrew and Yiddish he absorbed at synagogue and at his mother's knee. He was most comfortable with Russian, the language of the schools, for Poland was very much a part of the Russian empire. Later, he would learn Polish and some English.

By 1879, when Volapuk appeared, Ludovic had already drafted his own version of an international language and taught it to his friends during his last year of school. On looking further into the language, he decided Volapuk was too hard to learn and wouldn't really work. Even as he embarked on his medical career, he continued to labor over his project of a truly workable international language.

Zamenhof studied general medicine in Moscow and Warsaw, practiced for a time in Lithuania, and then went to Vienna for a course in ophthalmology. An incurable humanitarian, he ultimately went to the poorest district of Warsaw and set up practice as an ophthalmologist. Patients swarmed to his tiny rooms, but he charged so little—sometimes nothing at all—that he himself lived in frequent want. In 1887, Zamenhof married Clara Zilbernik, a sensitive young woman from Kaunas, Lithuania, who shared his idealistic and upbeat outlook. Later that year with Clara's support, he published his *International Language, Introduction and Complete Textbook*. It was an unpretentious gray booklet of only 40 pages, but one that would ultimately have a large impact. The book was signed by a pseudonym: Zamenhof was determined to put as much distance as possible between the work and its creator, and hence avoid the mistake of Volapuk's founder. For the same reason, in place of a copyright notice, he published a statement forever relinquishing all rights to the language.

The pseudonym Zamenhof used was "Esperanto," which means "One who hopes." Besides the "complete textbook," there was a basic word list of some 900 entries, and some sample texts, including translations from the Bible, a personal letter, and three short poems. The poems are especially interesting, because they demonstrate Zamenhof's conviction that, along with grammar and vocabulary, a particular style or character—a literary "soul," if you will—is also an essential part of any language.

52. None of the "universal languages" proposed have really taken off. From the information in this passage, which of the following conclusions can be drawn?

   A. In the development of any universal language, certain languages will be privileged.
   B. The founder of any such language has some sort of personal agenda.
   C. Language really is the mortar that keeps the walls of misunderstanding in place.
   D. Developing such a language is fraught with grammatical, syntactical, and political problems.

53. Volapuk struck fire because it was designed for ordinary people, rather than for well-educated intellectuals. Which of the following contradicts this idea?

A. Bitter quarrels arose among factions at the general assemblies of Volapukists.
B. Words looked clumsy and sounded harsh, frequently having been altered and shortened.
C. Only Father Schleyer and a chosen few could create new words and modify grammar.
D. Zamenhof decided that Volapuk was too hard to learn and really wouldn't work.

54. From the information in this passage, how would you characterize Father Schleyer and Zamenhof, respectively?

A. Zealous, peculiar
B. Gentle, tenacious
C. Possessive, optimistic
D. Protective, earnest

55. Suppose that Esperanto were now the second language spoken in the United States, displacing Spanish. What evidence from the passage would back up this growth spurt?

A. People in the 18th century were interested in new languages that imitated real languages.
B. The book did not have a flashy cover, but made a large impact.
C. Zamenhof had already taught the language to his friends during his last year of school.
D. Besides the complete textbook, Zamenhof published a word list and sample texts, including translations from the Bible and poetry.

56. What mistakes did Zamenhof want to avert?

A. The potential ego involved in being the founder of a language
B. The positivism involved in being the founder of a language
C. The previous experiences involved in being the founder of a language
D. Other strong personal commitments

57. Based on the information in the passage, which of the following might Zamenhof say a language does not necessarily need?

A. Various genres of creative writing
B. Spiritual and religious texts
C. An alphabet
D. A political manifesto

58. Which of the following does not support our perception of Zamenhof's selfless motivations?

A. His statement releasing all rights to the language
B. His choice to make the book cover gray
C. His naming of the language *Esperanto*
D. His charging patients so little

59. Which of the following made a less than significant contribution to Zamenhof's desire to found a universal language?

I. His comfort with German, French, Latin, Greek, Hebrew, and Yiddish
II. His observations of discord in Bialystock and border communities
III. His choice to study ophthalmology
IV. His marriage to Clara Zilbernik

A. I and III only
B. II, III, and IV only
C. III and IV only
D. I only

This year in the fashion world, the rage in fabric design has been bold squares of vivid colors, bordered with black. Dresses, jackets, shirts, and shorts have displayed variously sized rectangles of blue, hot pink, white, mustard, oranges, and reds. How many of the women sporting these fashions realize that the inspiration for their garments was one man's spiritual vision of the relationship between the human mind and all of physical reality? How many of the clothing designers take care to adhere to this man's strict aesthetic principles?

The man with the vision was Piet Mondrian, a Dutch painter who lived from 1872 to 1944. His career spanned the periods in which impressionism, cubism, and abstract painting held sway, and he was influenced by each of them in turn. His best work was done later in his career. Mondrian developed his own philosophy of painting, known as "neoplasticism." It used only primary colors (red, blue, and yellow) and "non-colors" (black, white, and gray). Composition was based on the juxtaposition of opposites, using only straight lines and 90-degree angles, to attain equilibrium and balance—but without symmetry. Mondrian's geometric paintings succeed at this remarkably well; no two boxes of color in a single painting are the same size, but perfect balance is nonetheless achieved in the composition. Mondrian's unfinished works, with myriad attempts at creating and crossing out the firm black boundary lines, show how difficult this is. Pictures of his studio show multisized rectangular pieces of paper stuck up on the wall to be used in studies; his final, unfinished picture is composed half of paint and half of these paper squares.

Mondrian began by painting impressionistic landscapes and still lifes, but he soon departed from this style. Impressionism was concerned with fleeting impressions and emotional responses to scenes, whereas Mondrian carried out extended studies of scenes and objects to find their pure formal essences. When viewing his work chronologically, one can first see trees become geometric shapes and then become crossed lines at right angles; then these lines give way to the flat squares of color for which the artist is best known.

Mondrian was influenced by the principles of theosophy, a religion and intellectual movement that arose out of 18th century Germany. Theosophy is hard to pin down or define, but one central concern is the relationship among rational mind, physical reality, and spiritual divinity. One of the main aims of theosophists was to find correspondences among these three realms. Mondrian describes his paintings as an intellectual exploration of the pure forms of nature, or a type of formalism. Although this is how Mondrian described his work, it is important to keep in mind that nature doesn't come in pure forms. Rather, the pure forms are the human being's view of nature, interpreted, analyzed, and organized by the rational mind.

There are several problems with the dresses that are based on Mondrian's work. First, the designers don't stick strictly to primary colors. Second, they frequently use symmetry, and get a kind of balance—but not a balance of opposites. Finally, they never achieve the same emotionally moving harmony between the various elements that Mondrian did in his painting. Although this fashion movement amounts to little short of sacrilege to the artist's vision and philosophies, Mondrian himself would probably be happy that people are wearing the designs, because this fashion style represents a kind of integration of his intellectual aesthetic philosophy and the life of the human body.

Adapted from G. Henry, *Mondrian: The Man and His Vision.* © 1996 Farrington Press.

60. Which phrase best describes Mondrian's painting style?

   A. Intellectual formalism
   B. Impressionism
   C. Post-plasticism
   D. Sacred ruminations

61. What is the most significant accomplishment of Mondrian's later paintings?

   A. They effect a synthesis between painting and sculpture, because the shape of the canvas reflects the image painted on it.
   B. They go beyond cubism to represent the pure elements of physical reality.
   C. They integrate images from popular culture into high art.
   D. They portray objects viewed from many angles at the same time.

62. What word best describes the attitude that the author displays toward the fashion industry in this essay?

   A. Nonchalant
   B. Bemused
   C. Conspiratorial
   D. Indignant

63. Which of the following are shortcomings of the fashion designers in adhering to the principles of neoplasticism, according to the author?

    I. Use of hot pink, mustard, and orange in the garments
    II. Juxtaposition of shapes at nonperpendicular angles
    III. Display of works of art on the human body

    A. I only
    B. I and II only
    C. II and III only
    D. I, II, and III

64. Which of the principles of neoplasticism is expressed in the use of only squares and rectangles?

    I. Use of primary colors
    II. Juxtaposition of opposites
    III. Achievement of equilibrium and balance

    A. II only
    B. I and III only
    C. II and III only
    D. None of the above

65. Mondrian can be best characterized as which of the following?

    A. Nineteenth-century painter
    B. Twentieth-century painter
    C. Impressionist
    D. Pure cubist

STOP. IF YOU FINISH BEFORE TIME IS CALLED, CHECK YOUR WORK. YOU MAY GO BACK TO ANY QUESTION IN THIS TEST BOOKLET.

Physical Sciences

Time: 100 minutes
Questions: 66–142

PHYSICAL SCIENCES

Directions: Most questions in the Physical Sciences test are organized into groups, each preceded by a descriptive passage. After studying the passage, select the one best answer to each question. Some questions are not based on a descriptive passage and are also independent of each other. You should also select the one best answer to these independent questions. A periodic table is provided for your use. You may consult it whenever you wish.

PERIODIC TABLE OF THE ELEMENTS

IA																	VIIIA
1 H 1.0	IIA											IIIA	IVA	VA	VIA	VII A	2 He 4.0
3 Li 6.9	4 Be 9.0											5 B 10.8	6 C 12.0	7 N 14.0	8 O 16.0	9 F 19.0	10 Ne 20.2
11 Na 23.0	12 Mg 24.3											13 Al 27.0	14 Si 28.1	15 P 31.0	16 S 32.1	17 Cl 35.5	18 Ar 39.9
19 K 39.1	20 Ca 40.1	21 Sc 45.0	22 Ti 47.9	23 V 50.9	24 Cr 52.0	25 Mn 54.9	26 Fe 55.8	27 Co 58.9	28 Ni 58.7	29 Cu 63.5	30 Zn 65.4	31 Ga 69.7	32 Ge 72.6	33 As 74.9	34 Se 79.0	35 Br 79.9	36 Kr 83.8
37 Rb 85.5	38 Sr 87.6	39 Y 88.9	40 Zr 91.2	41 Nb 92.9	42 Mo 95.9	43 Tc 98.0	44 Ru 101	45 Rh 102	46 Pd 106	47 Ag 108	48 Cd 112	49 In 115	50 Sn 119	51 Sb 122	52 Te 128	53 I 127	54 Xe 131
55 Cs 133	56 Ba 137	57 La 139	72 Hf 179	73 Ta 181	74 W 184	75 Re 186	76 Os 190	77 Ir 192	78 Pt 195	79 Au 197	80 Hg 201	81 Tl 204	82 Pb 207	83 Bi 208	84 Po 209	85 At 210	86 Rn 222
87 Fr 223	88 Ra 226	89 Ac 227															

58 Ce 140	59 Pr 141	60 Nd 144	61 Pm 145	62 Sm 150	63 Eu 152	64 Gd 157	65 Tb 159	66 Dy 163	67 Ho 165	68 Er 167	69 Tm 169	70 Yb 173	71 Lu 175
90 Th 232	91 Pa 231	92 U 238	93 Np 237	94 Pu 244	95 Am 243	96 Cm 247	97 Bk 247	98 Cf 251	99 Es 252	100 Fm 257	101 Md 258	102 No 259	103 Lr 260

GO ON TO THE NEXT PAGE.

A transducer is a machine that converts one form of energy into another form of energy. One form of transducer, a loudspeaker, is depicted below.

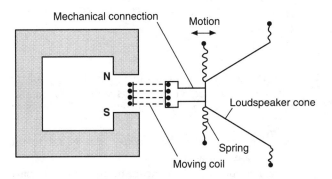

Figure 1.   Transducer.

A movable coil with N turns rests in a magnetic field. As a current passes through the wire, the electromagnetic force exerted on the coil is given by:

$$F = N a B i,$$

where N is the number of turns, a is the length of the wire in the magnetic field, B is the magnetic field strength, and i is the current through the wire.

The coil is in contact mechanically to a spring, which will restrain its motion. If one considers the displacement from equilibrium position to be x, and the spring constant k, then for a constant current, the displacement from equilibrium is given by:

$$x = N a B i / k,$$

which is true when the spring's restoring force equals the electromagnetic force on the coil. If the current varies with time sinusoidally, so will the equilibrium position of the speaker. Thus, the current introduced into the speaker wire is transduced into sound of the same frequency. It is also true that the frequency of the tone is determined only by the frequency of the input current sinusoid.

One final force is acting on the transducer, and that is a force of friction that opposes movement of the entire loudspeaker cone, etc. One way to incorporate this term is to add a friction term, f, which is a proportionality constant between the velocity of the system and the force of friction on it.

Faraday's law states that the voltage created by changing flux in a magnetic field is proportional to the number of turns multiplied by the change in flux per time. In this case, it represents a voltage drop across the path of the input current, and is approximated by the equation:

$$emf = (NBa)^2 / f$$

Assume that a speaker is typically driven by a 60-Hz alternating current source. Let B = 0.7 T, a = 30 cm, N = 350 turns, k = 25 N/m, and f = 667 N-sec/m.

66. Ignoring the contribution of friction, what is the maximum displacement from equilibrium for a loudspeaker driven by a 60-Hz, 1 mA (rms) sinusoidal current?

    A.   0.2 cm
    B.   0.4 cm
    C.   1.0 cm
    D.   2.0 cm

67. What describes the conversion of energy in the loudspeaker transducer described in the passage?

    A.   Electrical energy, potential energy, sound energy
    B.   Potential energy, kinetic energy, electrical energy
    C.   Electrical energy, kinetic energy, sound energy
    D.   Electrical energy, kinetic and potential energy, sound energy

68. A 60-Hz current is applied to the speaker and a constant tone is produced. If the magnetic field is reduced, the sound from the speaker should:

    A.   increase in pitch.
    B.   decrease in pitch.
    C.   increase in intensity.
    D.   decrease in intensity.

69. A speaker is powered by a 10-V (rms) voltage source. If the resistance of the battery is 2 Ω, the resistance of the coil is 6 Ω, what equivalent resistance (as determined by Faraday's law) will give the maximum power output across the speaker?

    A.   4 Ω
    B.   8 Ω
    C.   12 Ω
    D.   1 Ω

70. Which of the following will decrease the pitch of the sound produced by the loudspeaker?

    A.   Use of a spring with a higher spring constant
    B.   Placing the speaker under wire
    C.   Using the speaker on a 50-Hz AC outlet
    D.   Removing some of the 350 turns to the coil

PASSAGE II (Questions 71–75)

Each student in a chemistry class was given an unknown acid from a list of possible unknowns. Students were then asked to determine the identity of the unknown acid using only acid–base titrations. Table 1 provides information about each of the possible acids.

Table 1.   Characteristics of Unknown Acids

Acid	Formula	MW (g/mol)	Melting pt. (°C)	pK_a
Formic	HCOOH	46.03	8.2	3.77
Acetic	CH_3COOH	60.05	16.2	4.74
Propionic	CH_3CH_2COOH	74.08	−21.5	4.88
Oxalic	HOOCCOOH	90.04	101	3.14
				4.77

One student added 0.6 g of the assigned acid to 20.0 ml of water. The student then titrated the solution with 0.2 mol/L NaOH(aq) while noting the pH at 1-ml intervals with a pH meter. The results are shown in Figure 1.

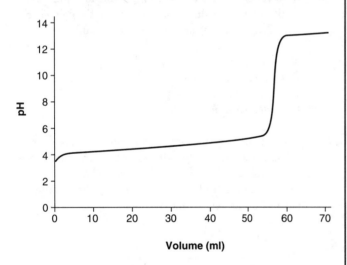

Figure 1.   Titration of an unknown acid.

Based on the titration curve, the student proposed that the unknown was neither formic nor oxalic acid.

71. What feature of the titration curve rules out formic acid?

    A. The pH at the equivalence point is not equal to the pK_a.
    B. The pH at the half-equivalence point is not equal to the pK_a.
    C. There is only one equivalence point.
    D. There are two equivalence points.

72. Consider the titration shown in Figure 1. The pH where the amount of added base is equivalent to the amount of unknown acid is closest to which of the following?

    A. 2
    B. 5
    C. 8
    D. 11

73. During the titration shown in Figure 1, which of the following was true when the pH was approximately 5?

    A. The amount of base added was equal to the amount of acid.
    B. The amount of the acid and its conjugate base were equal.
    C. The amount of the acid present was much greater than the amount of its conjugate base.
    D. The amount of the acid present was much less than the amount of its conjugate base.

74. Which pair of compounds from Table 1 best shows the effect of substituent effects on pK_a?

    A. Formic acid and oxalic acid
    B. Acetic acid and propionic acid
    C. Formic acid and acetic acid
    D. Acetic acid and oxalic acid

75. What was the unknown acid?

    A. Formic acid
    B. Acetic acid
    C. Propionic acid
    D. Oxalic acid

GO ON TO THE NEXT PAGE.

PASSAGE III (Questions 76–81)

In a study conducted by researchers, the healing, torsional strength, and elastic properties of bone transplants were investigated. Nonvascularized and vascularized tibial bone samples in cats were studied.

In the first experiment, a vertical incision was made on the surface of the right shin and two bone cuts were made through the tibia such that the vascular supply to the bone was severed. The segment of bone was removed and was immediately replaced in the wound bed. The left shin was prepared such that bone cuts were made and the vascular supply to the bone segment was not severed. The segment of bone was retained as a vascularized sample and replaced in the wound bed. In each experiment, the wounds were allowed to heal for variable periods.

Animals were sacrificed at intervals of 2 weeks, extending from 0 weeks to 18 weeks. Every 2 weeks, bone samples were removed from wound beds and the torque, strain, and stress of both vascularized and nonvascularized bone transplant samples were measured.

Three graphs are shown (Figure 1). Graph A shows maximum torque (percent of normal) plotted against time (weeks from experiment). Graph B shows strain plotted against time (weeks from experiment). Finally, graph C shows stress plotted against strain for a vascularized bone transplant sample at 10 weeks postexperiment.

76. The torque of specimens was measured by fixing the free ends of each bony sample and measuring the torque achieved by applying lateral rotation force in a clockwise direction. Which of the following would be important to know in making these torque measurements?

    A. Bone sample thickness
    B. Bone sample density
    C. Bone sample length
    D. Bone sample inertia

77. Which of the following are types of strain which may have been measured in these experiments?

    I. Tension
   II. Compression
  III. Shear

    A. I only
    B. I and II
    C. III only
    D. I, II, and III

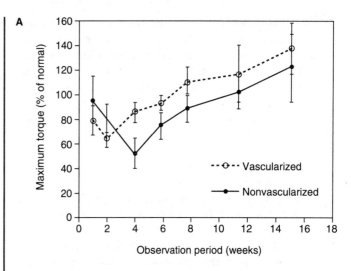

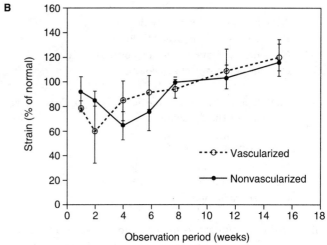

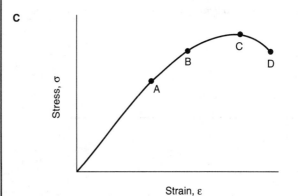

Figure 1. Graphs of Biomechanical Measurements.

78. A researcher evaluated the data presented in the passage. The conclusion reached by the researcher was as follows: At 7 weeks postexperiment, there appears to be a strain difference between vascularized and nonvascularized bone samples which is at least 10%. Based on your evaluation of the passage and the statement made by the researcher, you can best surmise that the statement is:

    A. supported by the data.
    B. contradicted by the data.
    C. neither supported nor contradicted by the data.
    D. both supported and contradicted by the data.

79. Consider point B on graph C. If the applied force is increased such that the strain increases, the object:

    A. becomes irreversibly deformed.
    B. will retain its original shape.
    C. fully resists due to tension strength.
    D. undergoes a phase change.

80. The slope of the linear portion of graph C is known as which of the following?

    A. Stiffness
    B. Bulk modulus
    C. Shear force
    D. Young's modulus

81. If the normal stress of bone samples is 10 N/m^2, the force associated with a vascularized bone sample of surface area 0.2 m^2 at 2 weeks from experiment is:

    A. 0.6 N.
    B. 1.0 N.
    C. 1.8 N.
    D. 2.0 N.

PASSAGE IV (Questions 82–87)

Semipermeable membranes are important in many chemical systems. Without such membranes, all substances would tend to diffuse down natural concentration gradients. By creating membranes with selective permeability, scientists and engineers can modify the concentration and composition of filtered fluids. In addition to those membranes which have been designed by scientists, many complex membranes with selective permeability are found in living cells.

There are several important membrane systems that are used in the chemical purification industry. For example, semipermeable membranes are commonly used in water purification systems. Extremely pure water can be produced by a process called reverse osmosis. Water filters operating on the reverse osmosis principle have two chambers separated by a semipermeable membrane. Pressure is exerted on the impure water on one side to force pure water through the membrane. Impurities, in the form of ions, may eventually collect on the "water-in" side of the apparatus. The accumulation of these impurities may be evaluated by various chemical assays. A diagram of a reverse osmosis filter system is shown in Figure 1.

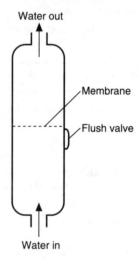

Figure 1.   Reverse osmosis filter system.

Reverse osmosis filter systems are water-intensive filters. This means that they waste a relatively large quantity of water in the purification process. This is due to the need to flush the increasingly impure water periodically.

GO ON TO THE NEXT PAGE.

Two different semipermeable filters were tested in the same reverse osmosis filter apparatus. Figure 2 shows the concentration of soluble ionic impurities forming on the "water-in" side of a reverse osmosis filter system with respect to time for the two filters. Filter effectiveness is measured by the ability of a filter to trap ionic impurities over time.

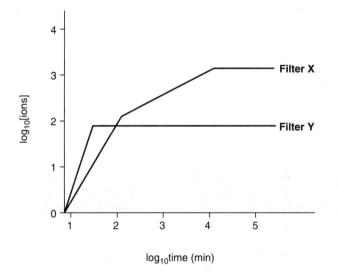

Figure 2. Concentration of ionic impurities versus time of filtering for filters X and Y.

82. Which of the following best describes reverse osmosis?

   A. Diffusion of water through a semipermeable membrane from high concentration to low
   B. Diffusion of water through a semipermeable membrane from low concentration to high
   C. Diffusion of water under pressure through a semipermeable membrane from high concentration to low
   D. Diffusion of water under pressure through a semipermeable membrane from low concentration to high

83. Which of the following statements best describes the data given in the passage for the reverse osmosis filter system?

   A. The accumulation rate of ionic impurities increases arithmetically over time for the two filters tested.
   B. Filter X concentrates ionic impurities more extensively than filter Y.
   C. The accumulation rate of ionic impurities for both tested filters is greatest after 24 hours of filtering.
   D. After 24 hours of filtering, filter X is more effective in filtering ion impurities than filter Y.

84. Purification of a very hard water supply requires much higher pressures than those for a soft water supply. The best explanation for this finding is that:

   A. hard water has a greater density.
   B. hard water has a greater concentration of particles.
   C. hard water has a greater concentration of volatile compounds.
   D. hard water is more viscous.

85. One source of well water was found to contain as its most significant impurity 32 ppm calcium chloride. A second source contained 48 ppm calcium sulfate. What comparison of the purification efficiency of these two water sources can be made?

   A. They will both be separated with equal efficiency.
   B. The water containing calcium sulfate will be separated less efficiently because of its higher concentration.
   C. The water containing calcium chloride will be separated less efficiently because of its greater concentration of ions.
   D. The water containing calcium sulfate will be separated more efficiently because of its greater concentration of ions.

86. In Figure 1, the flush valve is shown near the membrane. Why would one NOT expect the flush valve to be at the bottom of the impure water compartment?

   A. The appearance of the design does not necessitate it.
   B. The positioning of the flush valve is optimal for reducing leakage at high pressure.
   C. The positioning of the flush valve is optimal for decreasing the loss of the concentrated solution.
   D. The water entering the filter when the flush valve was open would simply flow out without removing the highly concentrated solution.

87. What would be the expected result if the pump providing the pressure were inoperative?

   A. No diffusion across the membrane would occur.
   B. Diffusion would occur in the same direction as when pressure is applied, but much more slowly.
   C. Diffusion would occur in the opposite direction as when pressure is applied.
   D. Diffusion would occur in both directions at the same rate.

39

GO ON TO THE NEXT PAGE.

88. What is the magnitude of the electric field at the center of a symmetric hollow sphere with a radius of 2 m and a surface charge of +2 mC?

    A. 0 N/C
    B. 1 N/C
    C. 2 N/C
    D. 4 N/C

89. An object is placed into a large beaker containing an unknown fluid. The object appears to float just below the fluid's surface. The object's buoyant force is determined by all of the following factors EXCEPT:

    A. the density of the fluid.
    B. the volume of the fluid.
    C. gravitational acceleration.
    D. the general size and shape of the object.

90. Which, if any, of the following statements are TRUE in regard to thermal relationships?

    A. One degree Fahrenheit change is more than one degree Celsius change.
    B. One unit Kelvin change equals one degree Fahrenheit change.
    C. Absolute zero corresponds to zero degrees Celsius.
    D. None of the above statements are true.

91. A concert listener standing 2 m away from the only speaker changes location so that she is now 8 m away from the speaker. In relative terms, how does the sound intensity at the second location compare to that at the first location?

    A. It is one-half.
    B. It is one-eighth.
    C. It is one-sixteenth.
    D. It is one-twenty-eighth.

PASSAGE V (Questions 92–97)

Metal corrosion has been estimated to have caused 80 billion dollars worth of damage in the United States in the mid-1980s. The chemical reactions involved in corrosion are complex, but involve a region of the metal surface acting as one electrode, where reaction 1 occurs.

Reaction 1

$$Fe(s) \rightarrow Fe^{+2}(aq) + 2e^-$$

Another region of the metal's surface acts as the other electrode, where reaction 2 occurs.

Reaction 2

$$O_2(g) + 4H^+(aq) + 4e^- \rightarrow 2H_2O(l)$$

The Fe^{+2} ions formed in reaction 1 can react with atmospheric oxygen to form hydrated iron(III) oxide according to reaction 3. The hydrated form of iron(III) oxide is commonly called rust.

Reaction 3

$$4Fe^{+2}(aq) + O_2(g) + (4 + 2x)H_2O(l)$$
$$\rightarrow 2Fe_2O_3 \cdot xH_2O(s) + 8H^+(aq)$$

Chemists have devised techniques to minimize the corrosion of metal. In one of these techniques, iron is protected against corrosion by coupling it to another metal which is more reactive when exposed to oxygen and water. Other techniques involve coating the surface of the metal with a protective layer. Resins, enamels, and water-based paints are common protective coatings for corrosion-prone metals.

92. Which of the following reaction types best describes reaction 1?

    A. Oxidation
    B. Sublimation
    C. Reduction
    D. Hydrolysis

93. It is well-known that some metals rust much more quickly in humid regions. In these cases, what is the role of water in producing corrosion?

    A. Water is needed to form the iron(III) oxide hydrate.
    B. Water is needed to dissolve the iron(II) cations formed in reaction 1.
    C. Water is needed to allow conduction from one electrode to another.
    D. Water is needed to allow conduction from one electrode to another and for iron(III) oxide hydrate formation.

GO ON TO THE NEXT PAGE.

94. Reaction 3 is best described as a(n):

 A. oxidation.
 B. sublimation.
 C. reduction.
 D. hydrolysis.

95. In cold climates, where salt is used to melt snow on the roads, automobiles rust much more quickly. What purpose does salt serve in corrosion?

 A. It makes the iron(II) cations more soluble.
 B. It lowers the pH, allowing the reaction to proceed more quickly.
 C. It makes the water more conductive.
 D. It makes the water less conductive.

96. What comparison can be made about the reduction potentials of iron and the coupled metal?

 A. The reduction potentials must be closely matched.
 B. The reduction potential of iron must be greater.
 C. The reduction potential of iron must be smaller.
 D. The reduction potentials are not important.

97. The overall reaction for the first step in the formation of rust is most likely:

 A. $Fe(s) + O_2(g) + 4H^+(aq) \rightarrow Fe^{+2}(aq) + 2H_2O(l)$.
 B. $2Fe(s) + O_2(g) + 4H^+(aq) \rightarrow 2Fe^{+2}(aq) + 2H_2O(l)$.
 C. $Fe(s) + 2O_2(g) + 8H^+(aq) \rightarrow Fe^{+2}(aq) + 4H_2O(l)$.
 D. $2Fe(s) + 2O_2(g) + 8H^+(aq) \rightarrow 2Fe^{+2}(aq) + 4H_2O(l)$.

PASSAGE VI (Questions 98–103)

The simple task of blowing a bubble or inflating a balloon requires that pressure be applied inside these objects. This pressure acts to distend the membrane of the bubble or balloon. The pressure depends on the stiffness of the membrane being inflated. This stiffness is the membrane tension.

Consider a spherical balloon. The spherical shape is maintained by a higher pressure inside the balloon than outside. Laplace's law, as applied to a spherical surface, describes the relation among the pressure difference, P; the radius of the sphere, r, and the tension of the membrane, T:

$$Pr = 2T.$$

Surface tension is due to attractive forces between molecules on the surface of a liquid. In bubbles formed by water, these forces are not dependent on the total surface area, but have a constant value irrespective of size. Because of this, for bubbles of different sizes, the internal pressure difference is expected to be inversely proportional to the radius. As an example, consider a soap bubble. Because it is composed of a double-layered membrane of soap molecules, the surface tension is twice that of a water bubble.

One can understand the microscopic factors behind surface tension by considering the boundary of a liquid and its vapor. Molecules deep to the surface experience attractive forces from all of their neighbors, lowering their potential energy. A molecule at the surface does not have as many neighbors. To achieve the lowest energy state, the molecules arrange themselves to have as many neighbors as possible by minimizing the surface area of the liquid–vapor interface.

Table 1 shows the surface tension measured for water at different temperatures.

Table 1. Surface Tension at Different Temperatures

Temperature in °C	Surface Tension in N/m
0	0.0756
20	0.0728
60	0.0662
100	0.0589

GO ON TO THE NEXT PAGE.

98. Based on information presented in the passage, the pressure difference of a soap bubble, compared to a water bubble of the same size, is:

A. one-half.
B. twice.
C. the same.
D. equal to atmospheric pressure.

99. For a sphere of radius 5 mm, the internal pressure is 1.33×10^4 N/m^2. The surface tension is:

A. 3.3 N/m.
B. 6.7 N/m.
C. 33 N/m.
D. 67 N/m.

100. Laplace's law can be used to consider the dynamics of contraction in the heart, where r reflects the size of the ventricular chamber, P represents the pressure at which the blood is ejected, and T is the muscular force necessary to achieve that pressure. Laplace's law indicates that the worst situation for a weak, failing heart would be:

A. enlarged ventricle with low blood pressure.
B. enlarged ventricle with high blood pressure.
C. shrunken ventricle with low blood pressure.
D. shrunken ventricle with high blood pressure.

101. The total force on the membrane of a sphere of radius 4 mm with a surface tension of 8×10^{-2} N/m is:

A. 0.004 N.
B. 0.008 N.
C. 0.016 N.
D. 0.032 N.

102. One method for measuring surface tension is the use of a capillary tube, a narrow-gauge glass tube. The force drawing the liquid up the tube is given by the surface tension, T, multiplied by the perimeter of the tube's inner diameter—reflecting the amount of liquid in contact with the capillary tube's walls. The column will rise until the force drawing the liquid up the tube equals the weight of the column of liquid. Assuming the following variables, the formula for the maximum height of rise is given by:

T = surface tension
r = inner diameter of the capillary tube
h = height the liquid ascends
d = density of the liquid
g = acceleration due to gravity

A. h = 2T/rdg.
B. h = T/pr^{2}dg.
C. h = T/rdg.
D. h = pr^{2}T/rg.

103. Based on the data presented in the table, the trend shown is best explained by:

A. decreased density at higher temperatures.
B. decreased vapor pressure at higher temperatures.
C. increased surface area at the boundary at higher temperatures.
D. decreased intermolecular forces due to increased molecular motion and intermolecular distances at higher temperatures.

42

GO ON TO THE NEXT PAGE.

It has long been known that unsupported objects tend to fall toward the ground. As the distance dropped increases, the speed at impact tends to increase. This is attributed to an acceleration caused by gravity. This acceleration is due to the gravitational attraction of the earth. Early philosophers and scientists studied gravitational properties. The prominent Greek philosopher Aristotle taught students that heavy objects fall faster than light objects. More than 1,000 years later, Galileo performed a series of experiments on objects rolling down smooth inclines, attempting to demonstrate basic principles of gravitational acceleration. He showed that the distance an object travels when in free fall varies as time squared.

A physics student studied the properties of gravity by conducting an experiment. A glass cylinder was constructed as shown in Figure 1. The cylinder was sealed to the environment except for a hollow glass rod which opened into the cylinder. The hollow rod communicated with the air. Hanging from a massless string within the cylinder is a coin (shaded) which has a mass of 0.1 kg. Also hanging from a massless string is a crumpled piece of paper (unshaded).

Experiment 1

Both strings are cut simultaneously. The objects fall and hit the bottom of the container.

Experiment 2

The open end of the cylinder is connected to a pump and all the air in the container is pumped out. The strings are cut simultaneously. The objects fall and hit the bottom of the container (Figure 1).

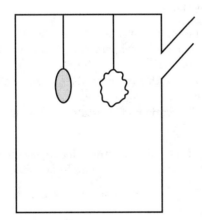

Figure 1.   Glass cylinder.

104. Consider experiment 1. Which object will hit the bottom of the cylinder first?

   A.   The coin
   B.   The paper
   C.   Neither, as both will hit the bottom simultaneously
   D.   Not enough information to determine

105. Consider experiment 2. Which object will strike the bottom of the cylinder first?

   A.   The coin
   B.   The paper
   C.   Neither, as both will hit the bottom simultaneously
   D.   Not enough information to determine

106. When the hollow rod is open to air in experiment one, the gravitational acceleration for the objects:

   A.   is constant.
   B.   decreases.
   C.   increases.
   D.   cannot be determined.

107. If the coin is dropped from a height of 50 cm from rest, how long does it take to strike the bottom of the container?

   A.   0.1 sec
   B.   0.3 sec
   C.   1.0 sec
   D.   3.2 sec

108. Consider the coin hanging from the massless string, as described in experiment 1. In reference to the coin, which of the following quantities would have a positive numeric value?

   A.   Kinetic energy
   B.   Potential energy
   C.   Momentum
   D.   Impulse

43

GO ON TO THE NEXT PAGE.

Two different methods for determining the amount of dissolved solids in a water sample were compared by researchers. Each method offered specific advantages and differed from the other method in number of steps and technique. After the recovery of dissolved solids in a water sample, the two methods were carefully analyzed. The details of the methods are described below.

Method 1

A 2-liter sample of water was heated in a flask until the remaining liquid could be transferred to a clean, dry, weighed evaporating dish. The dish was then heated over a water bath until almost dry and transferred to an oven at 100°C. The dish was heated until successive weighings matched to the third decimal place.

Method 2 (Figure 1)

A clean, dry platinum dish was weighed and filled with ½ inch of distilled water. A 500-ml volumetric flask was filled to the mark with water from the sample. The flask was fitted with a small glass cover and inverted with its mouth under the surface of the water in the platinum dish, as shown in Figure 1. The glass cover was removed and rinsed with distilled water. These rinsings were added to the water in the platinum dish. The apparatus was heated over water until nearly dry and transferred to an oven at 105°C. The dish was heated until successive weighings matched to the third decimal place.

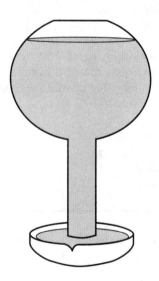

Figure 1. Apparatus used in method 2.

109. What was the likely effect of the difference in oven temperatures of the two methods?

    A. The higher temperature used in method 2 likely resulted in more complete removal of the water and more accurate results.

    B. The cooler temperature used in method 1 likely resulted in less decomposition of solid and more accurate results.

    C. The temperature difference most likely affected only the time needed to reach complete dryness and did not affect results.

    D. The temperature difference most likely had no effect.

110. Which of the following would tend to produce dissolved solid weights in excess of the true value by method 1?

    A. Incomplete drying of the dish at beginning of experiment

    B. Observation of crystals on the walls of the dish

    C. Observation of crystals on the walls of the flask

    D. Incomplete evaporation of the water in the oven

111. Which of the following would tend to produce dissolved solid weights in excess of the true value by method 2?

    A. Incomplete drying of the dish at beginning of experiment

    B. Rinsing of glass cover neglected

    C. Observation of crystals on the walls of the flask

    D. Incomplete evaporation of the water in the oven

112. Which of the following would tend to produce dissolved solid weights less than the true value by both methods?

    A. Incomplete drying of the flasks before trials

    B. Incomplete evaporation of the water in the oven

    C. Observation of crystals on the walls of the dishes

    D. Observation of crystals on the walls of the flasks

113. Which of the following would have the smallest effect on the accuracy of the results from method 2?

    A. Using water from the sample to rinse the glass cover

    B. Leaving the glass cover in the dish until evaporation is complete

    C. Spilling water from the volumetric flask while inverting it

    D. Spilling water from the dish while inverting the volumetric flask

GO ON TO THE NEXT PAGE.

Questions 114 through 118 are not based on a descriptive passage.

114. Two unknown inorganic species react as given below. Determine the overall reaction order using the experimental initial rate data obtained from experiments.

$$X + Y \rightarrow Z$$

Table 1. Reaction of Unknown Inorganic Species

Run	[X] (mol/L)	[Y] (mol/L)	Rate of Z Formation (mmol/L/min)
1	0.5	0.5	0.6
2	1.0	0.5	2.4
3	0.5	1.0	1.2

- **A.** 2
- **B.** 3
- **C.** 4
- **D.** 5

115. Given the following data, calculate the heat of formation for ethanol.

I. $C_2H_5OH + 3O_2 \rightarrow 2CO_2 + 3H_2O$
$$\Delta H = -327.0 \text{ kcal/mol}$$

II. $H_2O \rightarrow H_2 + \frac{1}{2}O_2 \qquad \Delta H = 68.3 \text{ kcal/mol}$

III. $C + O_2 \rightarrow CO_2 \qquad \Delta H = -94.1 \text{ kcal/mol}$

- **A.** -66.1 kcal
- **B.** $+67.2$ kcal
- **C.** $+66.21$ kcal
- **D.** -67.2 kcal

116. An object initially at rest is dropped from a height h. The ratio of its velocity after it has fallen one-half of the distance to the ground to the final velocity when it reaches the ground is:

- **A.** 0.25.
- **B.** 0.50.
- **C.** 0.71.
- **D.** 0.87.

117. Which of the following is responsible for the changes found in ionization energy when moving down a column in the periodic table?

- **A.** Increasing nuclear attraction for electrons
- **B.** Increased shielding of electrons and larger atomic or ionic radii
- **C.** Increased shielding of electrons and increasing nuclear attraction for electrons
- **D.** Increasing nuclear attraction for electrons and larger atomic or ionic nuclei

118. A student dissolves 2.0 g of NaCl in 100 g of water. What is the boiling point for the solution produced? Note that the solvent constant (k_b) for water is 0.52 kg °C/mol.

- **A.** 100.18°C
- **B.** 100.36°C
- **C.** 100.72°C
- **D.** 101.24°C

GO ON TO THE NEXT PAGE.

A d'Arsonval galvanometer is a simple electric meter that can be used to make a voltage or current measuring device. A typical construction is depicted in Figure 1. A wire loop is placed inside a magnetic field. The magnetic field is formed by two curved pole pieces and an iron insert, giving a fairly uniform field. As current flows through the loop inside the magnetic field, the loop will experience a force on each end. This force is determined by the magnetic field strength, the length of the wire inside the field, and the current through the wire loop.

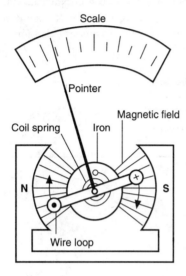

Figure 1. A galvanometer.

The magnetic field strength and length of the wire are fixed on construction, so the only variable is the current in the wire, and the resulting force on the wire loop is directly proportional to the current. In addition, the meter is made so that as the pointer is rotated, a coil spring is twisted, giving a restoring force. The coil will turn until the torque on the wire loop is balanced by the restoring force of the spring.

Recall that the force on a current carrying wire in a magnetic field is given by:

$$F = BIL,$$

where F is the force (N), B is the magnetic field strength (T), I is the current (A), and L is the length of the coil (m).

Assume the following values: field strength of 0.3 T; 0.015-m length of coil turned 40 times around itself; the radius of the coil from the center axis where the pointer is out to either end is 0.010; and the wire turns through one radian with a current of 0.001 A.

119. The torque on the wire loop from a 0.001-A current is:

   A. 1.2×10^{-5} Nm.
   B. 1.2×10^{-6} Nm.
   C. 2.4×10^{-6} Nm.
   D. 3.6×10^{-6} Nm.

120. To measure voltage, a galvanometer can be connected in series to a shunt resistor. In this way, a known current through the galvanometer will correspond to a known voltage decrease across the terminals of the voltage meter, which is proportional to the shunt resistance. To give a meter that reads 0 to 1 volt, from our galvanometer that gave a full-scale deflection at 1 mA, what must the shunt resistance be?

   A.   100 Ω
   B.   1,000 Ω
   C.   9, 998 Ω
   D.   10,000 Ω

121. A galvanometer has fallen out of calibration. Which of the following would LEAST likely lead to a reduced reading?

   A.   An overstretched coil spring
   B.   A bent pointer
   C.   A decreased current
   D.   A decreased magnetic field

122. All of the following lead to a more sensitive galvanometer (i.e., a full-scale deflection at a lower current) EXCEPT:

   A.   using more turns in the coil.
   B.   using a restoring spring with a higher spring constant.
   C.   using a higher strength magnetic field.
   D.   using a longer wire loop.

123. The force on one side of the wire loop described in the passage with a current of 0.00025 A is:

   A.   0.000001 N.
   B.   0.00025 N.
   C.   0.000045 N.
   D.   0.00015 N.

124. Based on the data provided in question 120, once built, the easiest way to change the voltage range of a galvanometer is to:

   A.   change the pointer length.
   B.   change the shunt resistance.
   C.   change the magnetic field strength.
   D.   change the number of times the coil is turned.

PASSAGE X (Questions 125–130)

Metal cations can be separated into groups based on the types of precipitation reactions which they undergo. Table 1 indicates the different cations grouped according to their precipitation reactions and the reagent which can be used.

Table 1. Metal Cation Precipitation Reactions

Group	Cation	Reagent	Insoluble Compound
1	Ag^+	HCl	AgCl
	Hg_2^{2+}		Hg_2Cl_2
	Pb^{2+}		$PbCl_2$
2	Bi^{3+}	H_2S in acid	Bi_2S_3
	Cd^{2+}		CdS
	Cu^{2+}		CuS
	Sn^{2+}		SnS
3	Al^{3+}	H_2S in base	$Al(OH)_3$
	Co^{2+}		CoS
	Cr^{3+}		$Cr(OH)_3$
	Fe^{2+}		FeS
	Mn^{2+}		MnS
	Ni^{2+}		NiS
	Zn^{2+}		ZnS
4	Ba^{2+}	Na_2CO_3	$BaCO_3$
	Ca^{2+}		$CaCO_3$
	Sr^{2+}		$SrCO^3$
5	K^+	none	none
	Na^+		none
	NH_4^+		none

The separation of a mixture of cations requires that the groups be separated in the order given in the table. For example, addition of H_2S in acidic solution to a mixture containing both group 1 and 2 cations would result in precipitation of all of them.

After separation of cations into groups based on their precipitation reactions, they can be further separated from cations in the same group. Alternatively, tests can be performed for some ions even in the presence of others. Such tests are called spot tests.

125. Which of the following equilibria represents the reaction occurring during the precipitation of Cd^{2+}?

   A. $Cd^{2+} + 2HCl \rightleftharpoons CdCl_2 + 2H^+$
   B. $Cd^{2+} + H_2S \rightleftharpoons CdS + 2H^+$
   C. $Cd^{2+} + HCl \rightleftharpoons CdCl + H^+$
   D. $Cd^{2+} + 2H_2S \rightleftharpoons CdS_2 + 4H^+$

126. What comparison can be made between the K_{sp} for CuS and Al_2S_3?

   A. K_{sp} for CuS $<$ K_{sp} for Al_2S_3
   B. K_{sp} for CuS $=$ K_{sp} for Al_2S_3
   C. K_{sp} for CuS $>$ K_{sp} for Al_2S_3
   D. No comparison can be made

127. What effect does base have on the equilibria between the group 3 cations and their precipitates?

   A. It increases the value of the K_{sp}.
   B. It decreases the value of the K_{sp}.
   C. It pulls the equilibrium to the left by reacting with the hydronium ions from the hydrogen sulfide.
   D. It pulls the equilibrium to the right by reacting with the hydronium ions from the hydrogen sulfide.

128. Why does Al^{3+} precipitate as the hydroxide rather than the sulfide?

   A. The concentration of hydroxide is greater than the concentration of sulfide.
   B. The concentration of sulfide is greater than that of hydroxide.
   C. The K_{sp} for the hydroxide is smaller.
   D. The K_{sp} for the hydroxide is larger.

129. Based on Table 1, what can be concluded about the solubility of chloride salts?

   A. Chloride salts are generally soluble.
   B. Chloride salts are the least soluble of any salt in general.
   C. Chloride salts have varying solubilities compared to sulfide salts.
   D. Chlorides do not form salts.

130. If the addition of HCl did not result in the complete precipitation of the group 1 cations, what problem would be observed?

   A. The group 1 cations would be incorrectly determined.
   B. The group 2 cations would show false positives.
   C. The group 2 cations would show false negatives.
   D. The group 3 cations would be incorrectly determined.

Each of the four containers shown below is filled with an identical fluid (Figure 1). Four different fluids are used to fill the containers in four separate experiments. For example, in the first experiment, pure water is used to fill all the containers. After a series of appropriate measurements are made, the containers are drained, cleaned, and ethanol is used to fill the containers. Once measurements are made with the containers filled with ethanol, the next fluid, glycerin, is tested.

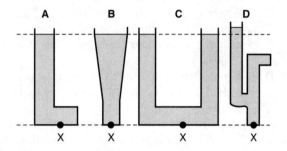

Figure 1. Four containers filled with identical fluids.

The density values of fluids may vary from one another. The density values of the four fluids evaluated in this experiment were determined experimentally, and are listed in the table below. The density measurements were performed at the indicated temperature (degrees Celsius) as shown in Table 1.

Table 1. Density Values for Several Fluids

Fluid	Density (kg/m³)	Temperature (°C)
Pure water	1000	0
Ethanol	791	20
Glycerin	1260	0
Blood plasma	1026	0

131. In which container is point "X" subjected to the most pressure?

    A. A
    B. B
    C. C
    D. D

132. An object is submerged in a fluid. It experiences an upward force that is equal to which of the following?

    A. The weight of the fluid displaced
    B. The volume of the fluid displaced
    C. The weight of the object
    D. The volume of the object

133. A sphere lies on the bottom of container "B" and is 5 m below the surface. If the fluid is pure water and the sphere has a density of 1,000 kg/m³, the pressure exerted on the sphere is closest to which of the following? (Assume standard atmospheric conditions. 1 atm pressure is 1×10^5 Pa.)

    A. 5.0×10^6 Pa
    B. 5.0×10^5 Pa
    C. 1.5×10^5 Pa
    D. 1.0×10^5 Pa

134. Which of the following forces is most responsible for the surface tension exhibited by the fluid at the surface of the containers?

    A. Adhesion
    B. Stress
    C. Cohesion
    D. Strain

135. Suppose that a 10-cm³ cube of mass 21 kg is submerged in container "B" of fluid density 0.2 kg/cm³. The cube is tied by a string to point "X" shown in the diagram and is buoyed upwards such that the string is pulled taut. The tension in the string would be closest to:

    A. 4 N.
    B. 6 N.
    C. 8 N.
    D. 10 N.

136. A cube of density 0.5 kg/cm³ floats on the surface of each of the liquids listed in Table 1 at 0°C. Which fluid would allow the greatest proportion of the cube to be exposed above the surface of the liquid?

    A. Pure water
    B. Ethanol
    C. Glycerin
    D. Plasma

GO ON TO THE NEXT PAGE.

137. Which compound is both a Lewis base and a Brønsted-Lowrey base?

    A. BH_3

    B. $Ca(OH)_2$

    C. NO_3^-

    D. NH_3

138. A communication satellite is placed into a perfect circular orbit many kilometers above the earth's surface. Which of the following statements is NOT true if the satellite is moving with constant velocity?

    A. The satellite is moving with constant speed.

    B. The satellite is always accelerating.

    C. The satellite has no net force in space.

    D. More than one of the above statements is NOT true.

139. Which of the following statements best explains why H_2O has an unusually high boiling point when compared with H_2S?

    A. H_2O molecules pack into a more ordered structure than H_2S molecules.

    B. Van der Waals forces are especially important.

    C. London forces are especially important.

    D. Hydrogen bonding is especially important.

140. An element with an atomic number of 4 and an atomic mass of 7 undergoes radioactive decay by electron capture. Which of the following represents the atomic number and mass of the resulting nucleus?

    A. Atomic number 3, atomic mass 7

    B. Atomic number 3, atomic mass 6

    C. Atomic number 4, atomic mass 7

    D. Atomic number 4, atomic mass 6

141. How long will it take a cyclist, starting from rest and accelerating uniformly at 5.0 m/s^2, to travel a distance of 10 m?

    A. 1 sec

    B. 2 sec

    C. 3 sec

    D. 4 sec

142. Determine the energy change per mole for the following chemical reaction.

$$2O_2 + CH_4 \rightarrow CO_2 + 2H_2O$$

Bond	Bond Dissociation Energy (kJ/mol)
C−C	340
C−H	420
O=O	490
O−H	460
C=O	720

    A. $+1920 \text{ kJ}$

    B. $+620 \text{ kJ}$

    C. -1920 kJ

    D. -620 kJ

STOP. IF YOU FINISH BEFORE TIME IS CALLED, CHECK YOUR WORK. YOU MAY GO BACK TO ANY QUESTION IN THIS TEST BOOKLET.

STOP.

Writing Sample

Time: 60 minutes total;
30 minutes per essay, each separately timed.

WRITING SAMPLE

Directions: You will be given 30 minutes to complete Essay Topic 1. Once time is called, you MUST stop working on this essay. Please draw a line below the last sentence in your essay to mark your stopping point. You will then have 30 minutes to complete Essay Topic 2. You may NOT work on Essay Topic 1 during the second 30-minute period that is allotted for Essay Topic 2. Use black ink, and do NOT skip lines between sentences. Illegible essays will not be scored.

52

GO ON TO THE NEXT PAGE.

ESSAY TOPIC 1

Consider this statement:

A nation should not interfere in the affairs of another nation.

Write a unified essay in which you perform the following tasks: Explain what you think this statement means. Describe a specific situation in which it would be acceptable for one nation to intrude into the affairs of another. Discuss what you think determines whether a nation should or should not seek to influence the actions of another.

ESSAY TOPIC 2

Consider this statement:

Education is a better teacher than experience.

Write a unified essay in which you perform the following tasks. Explain what you think this statement means. Describe a specific situation in which experience would be superior to the training or knowledge provided through education. Discuss what you think determines whether experience or education is superior in guiding an individual.

GO ON TO THE NEXT PAGE.

Biological Sciences

Time: 100 minutes
Questions: 143–219

BIOLOGICAL SCIENCES

Directions: Most questions in the Biological Sciences test are organized into groups, each preceded by a descriptive passage. After studying the passage, select the one best answer to each question. Some questions are not based on a descriptive passage and are also independent of each other. You should also select the one best answer to these independent questions. A periodic table is provided for your use. You may consult it whenever you wish.

PERIODIC TABLE OF THE ELEMENTS

IA																	VIIIA
1 H 1.0	IIA											IIIA	IVA	VA	VIA	VII A	2 He 4.0
3 Li 6.9	4 Be 9.0											5 B 10.8	6 C 12.0	7 N 14.0	8 O 16.0	9 F 19.0	10 Ne 20.2
11 Na 23.0	12 Mg 24.3											13 Al 27.0	14 Si 28.1	15 P 31.0	16 S 32.1	17 Cl 35.5	18 Ar 39.9
19 K 39.1	20 Ca 40.1	21 Sc 45.0	22 Ti 47.9	23 V 50.9	24 Cr 52.0	25 Mn 54.9	26 Fe 55.8	27 Co 58.9	28 Ni 58.7	29 Cu 63.5	30 Zn 65.4	31 Ga 69.7	32 Ge 72.6	33 As 74.9	34 Se 79.0	35 Br 79.9	36 Kr 83.8
37 Rb 85.5	38 Sr 87.6	39 Y 88.9	40 Zr 91.2	41 Nb 92.9	42 Mo 95.9	43 Tc 98.0	44 Ru 101	45 Rh 102	46 Pd 106	47 Ag 108	48 Cd 112	49 In 115	50 Sn 119	51 Sb 122	52 Te 128	53 I 127	54 Xe 131
55 Cs 133	56 Ba 137	57 La 139	72 Hf 179	73 Ta 181	74 W 184	75 Re 186	76 Os 190	77 Ir 192	78 Pt 195	79 Au 197	80 Hg 201	81 Tl 204	82 Pb 207	83 Bi 208	84 Po 209	85 At 210	86 Rn 222
87 Fr 223	88 Ra 226	89 Ac 227															

58 Ce 140	59 Pr 141	60 Nd 144	61 Pm 145	62 Sm 150	63 Eu 152	64 Gd 157	65 Tb 159	66 Dy 163	67 Ho 165	68 Er 167	69 Tm 169	70 Yb 173	71 Lu 175
90 Th 232	91 Pa 231	92 U 238	93 Np 237	94 Pu 244	95 Am 243	96 Cm 247	97 Bk 247	98 Cf 251	99 Es 252	100 Fm 257	101 Md 258	102 No 259	103 Lr 260

GO ON TO THE NEXT PAGE.

Passage I (Questions 143–149)

Drug-receptor theory is central to the field of pharmacology. A receptor can be thought of as a specialized target macromolecule that binds a drug and mediates its effect. Targets for drugs can be enzymes, nucleic acids, intracellular receptors, membrane-bound receptors, and other sites that have yet to be identified. There are even drugs such as anesthetic gases that are thought to act via nonspecific physical interactions with cell membranes.

The understanding of drug-receptor theory is drawn in part from studies of enzyme kinetics. A molecule of drug binds to its target receptor, forming a drug-receptor complex that elicits a biological response. The magnitude of the response depends on the concentration of drug at the receptor sites. This relationship is expressed graphically in a concentration–effect (CE) curve that displays drug effect on the y-axis and drug concentration on the x-axis. An example of a CE curve is shown in Figure 1. This curve illustrates plots for four different drugs, A through D. Assume that drugs A through D work at the same receptor.

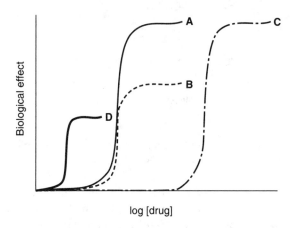

Figure 1. A CE curve for drugs A, B, C, and D.

The strength of a drug can be described by two parameters: efficacy and potency. Efficacy is the efficiency with which the drug-receptor complex produces a biological response. Efficacy is the maximal velocity for an enzyme-catalyzed reaction and is reflected by the height of the CE curve. If two drugs acting on the same receptor differ in efficacy, then the less efficacious drug is a partial agonist. Potency is a measure of how much drug is required to elicit a response and it is usually expressed as EC_{50}—the concentration of drug that gives 50% of that drug's maximal response.

143. According to the passage, what is the mechanism of anesthetic gases?

   A. Unknown
   B. Binding to intracellular receptor
   C. Binding to enzyme
   D. Interaction with cell membranes

144. Steroid drugs are lipophilic drugs that bind to intracellular proteins. A researcher treats a sample of cells with a transcription inhibitor. How would steroid drug effects be altered in cells treated with the transcription inhibitor?

   A. Drug effects would be increased.
   B. Drug effects would be decreased.
   C. There would be no change.
   D. There would be a transitory increase in drug effect, followed by a decrease in drug effect.

145. Formation of the drug-receptor complex is most analogous to which of the following?

   A. Substrate binding to allosteric site of enzyme
   B. Drug binding to membrane-bound receptor
   C. Substrate binding to active site of enzyme
   D. Hormones binding to one another

146. Based on the graph shown in Figure 1 and information given in the passage, drugs A and B both have:

   A. the same efficacy and the same potency.
   B. different efficacy and the same potency.
   C. the same efficacy and different potency.
   D. different efficacy and different potency.

147. Based on information given in the passage, EC_{50} can be defined on a CE curve as which of the following?

   A. A point on y-axis
   B. A point on x-axis
   C. The slope of the curve
   D. The height of the curve

148. A student makes four statements to summarize the relationships between drug potency and efficacy. Which statement is FALSE?

   A. A lower EC_{50} means greater potency.
   B. A higher efficacy means potentially greater biological response.
   C. Two drugs that differ in potency can be equally efficacious.
   D. Given a drug's potency, one can determine its efficacy.

149. Based on the data shown for drugs A through D in the graph, and information presented in the passage, which of the following statements is TRUE?

   A. D is less potent than C.
   B. A is less efficacious than D.
   C. A and C differ in efficacy.
   D. B is a partial agonist compared with C.

57

GO ON TO THE NEXT PAGE.

Passage II (Questions 150–155)

Aromatic ring systems do not undergo the electrophilic addition reactions that are typical of alkenes. Reactions that regenerate the aromaticity of the ring system are considerably more favorable. Aromaticity is regenerated when substitution, rather than addition reactions occur. One mechanism by which aromatic systems react is called electrophilic aromatic substitution. This mechanism is shown for a Friedel-Crafts reaction in Figure 1.

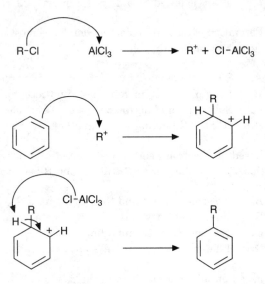

Figure 1. Friedel-Crafts reaction.

When a Friedel-Crafts reaction is performed on a series of substrates, an important trend is observed. Those substrates that have electron-withdrawing substituents tend to react slower than benzene and end up with meta-disubstituted products. Substrates that have electron-donating substituents tend to react more quickly than benzene and end up with orthodisubstituted and paradisubstituted products. Figure 2 summarizes some results

Substrate	Major product	Rate
		1.3×10^5
NO_2	NO_2	5.3×10^2
		1.9×10^5
OH	OH	4.8×10^7

Figure 2. Results of various Friedel-Crafts reactions.

obtained in a series of Friedel-Crafts reactions among various aromatic compounds, ethyl chloride, and $AlCl_3$.

150. Which of the following would be the major product of the reaction between methylbenzene and propyl chloride with aluminum trichloride present?

A. $CH(CH_3)_2$

B. $CH_2CH_2CH_3$

C. $CH_2CH_2CH_3$

D. $CH(CH_3)_2$

151. Why are electrophilic addition reactions not common with aromatic substrates?

A.   Aromatic substrates do not have a great enough reactivity to react with electrophiles.
B.   Aromatic substrates are more reactive toward nucleophiles.
C.   Aromatic substrates are so stable that they do not undergo reactions that do not result in aromatic products.
D.   Aromatic substrates are so unstable that they react before exposure to the electrophilic species.

GO ON TO THE NEXT PAGE.

152. Which of the following structures best shows why a nitro substituent disfavors electrophilic attack at the para position?

A.

B.

C.

D.

153. Which of the entries in the table can be classified as deactivated?

A. The first entry
B. The second entry
C. The third entry
D. The fourth entry

154. Which of the following products could NOT be made by a Friedel-Crafts reaction on a substituted benzene?

A.

B.

C.

D.

155. Which of the following structures could perform a Friedel-Crafts reaction?

A.

B.

C.

D.

Passage III (Questions 156–160)

The liver is a large, multifunctional organ located in the right upper abdominal quadrant of the abdomen. One of the liver's functions is to serve as a detoxification center. Because ingested material often contains toxins, blood from the gastrointestinal system is delivered, via the portal vein, to the liver before entering the systemic circulation. After blood is filtered by the liver, it is channeled into the hepatic veins. The hepatic veins drain into the inferior vena cava, which in turn, delivers blood back to the right atrium. This vascular arrangement permits the removal of toxins before they can damage cells in organs outside the liver. However, in some disease states, blood can bypass the portal vein and enter the systemic circulation without passing through the liver. Diseases that cause increased resistance to blood flow in the liver are collectively known as portal hypertensive diseases. The increased resistance to blood flow in the liver is most commonly caused by alcoholism and hepatitis. Both of these conditions cause extensive scarring within the liver. This scarring interferes with normal blood vessel anatomy and increases vascular resistance.

The liver is also responsible for the uptake and excretion of circulating bilirubin, a product of heme catabolism. Carrier-mediated uptake of bilirubin from the blood is accomplished by ligandins, a family of proteins found in liver cells. Bilirubin is then chemically modified in the liver to increase its polarity, followed by active secretion in the bile and excretion with the feces. Serum bilirubin levels are routinely tested to help assess liver function. Normal values range between 0.2 and 1.5 mg/dl.

Three patients who have presumed liver disease are evaluated. Blood samples are drawn and bilirubin levels are assessed. Figure 1 presents the bilirubin levels of the four patients evaluated.

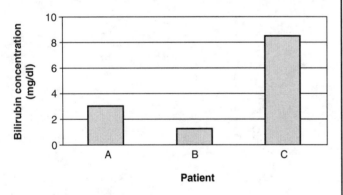

Figure 1. Bilirubin concentration of patients A, B, and C.

156. Propranolol, a drug used to treat a variety of conditions, is efficiently inactivated by the liver. According to the passage, which of the following would result in the highest systemic blood levels of propranolol?

 A. 80 mg taken orally
 B. 80 mg injected directly in the portal vein
 C. 80 mg injected in an arm vein
 D. A, B, and C will give the same blood level

157. Proteins essential to carrier-mediated uptake in the liver are known as:

 A. hepatic proteins.
 B. bilirubins.
 C. portal carriers.
 D. ligandins.

158. Heart failure occurs when part of the heart loses its ability to pump blood and, therefore, becomes an area of increased resistance. Based on information provided in the passage, which of the following would one expect to impair liver function the most?

 A. Failure of right side of the heart
 B. Failure of left side of the heart
 C. Aortic stenosis (narrowing of the aorta)
 D. None of the above, as heart failure will not affect the liver

159. Hemolytic anemia is a blood disorder characterized by massive destruction of erythrocytes and caused by many prescribed drugs. Which patient is more likely afflicted by this condition?

 A. Patient A
 B. Patient B
 C. Patient C
 D. None of the above (All patients A through C are equally likely to be afflicted.)

160. Fetal circulation is geared towards bypassing structures not yet needed because of the placenta. Which anatomic feature allows blood to bypass the fetal liver?

 A. Ductus venosus
 B. Ductus arteriosus
 C. Foramen magnum
 D. Foramen ovale

GO ON TO THE NEXT PAGE.

Passage IV (Questions 161–165)

Excessive concentrations of chemicals in the work-place can be a hazard to the health and safety of workers in chemical plants. Monitoring the air concentrations of the chemicals used in chemical plants is an important task. One common method for collecting these air samples is by drawing a known volume of air through a tube containing a substance that absorbs organic compounds. The organic compounds can then be extracted from the substance and analyzed. The apparatus for collecting these air samples is shown below in Figure 1.

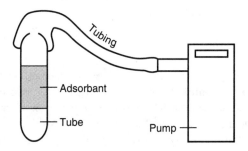

Figure 1. Apparatus for collecting air samples in chemical plants.

The analysis of these air sample extracts is commonly performed using gas chromatography. Standard solutions are used to construct a standard curve of concentration versus peak area. The concentrations of the unknown samples can then be calculated. Shown below are a chromatogram from the analysis of an air sample from a polystyrene plant (Figure 2). The sample contains at least

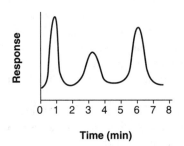

Figure 2. Chromatogram for the analysis of butadiene and styrene.

butadiene and styrene. Standard curves are shown for both butadiene and styrene (Figure 3). Of note, butadiene is a smaller molecule than styrene.

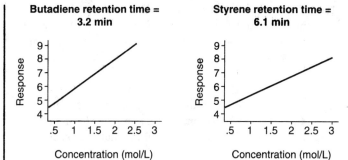

Figure 3. Standard curves for butadiene and styrene.

161. Which of the following mistakes would result in the greatest underestimation of the air concentration of styrene?

    A. Pump pulling more air than expected through the tube and addition of less styrene than measured in the standard solutions

    B. Pump pulling less air than expected through the tube and addition of less styrene than measured in the standard solutions

    C. Pump pulling more air than expected through tube and addition of more styrene than measured in the standard solutions

    D. Pump pulling less air than expected through tube and addition of more styrene than measured in the standard solutions

162. The most reasonable explanation for the presence of three peaks in the chromatogram shown in the passage is:

    A. butadiene decomposed on exposure to the heated column and produced two peaks.

    B. an unsuspected compound was present in the sample.

    C. styrene decomposed on exposure to the heated column and produced two peaks.

    D. styrene and butadiene reacted to form three different products.

163. Why does butadiene have a shorter retention time than styrene?

    A. Butadiene is smaller than styrene, so the intramolecular forces between butadiene and the column coating are not strong.

    B. Styrene is considerably more polar than butadiene and is attracted to the polar column.

    C. Styrene is considerably less polar than butadiene and is attracted to the nonpolar column.

    D. Butadiene is larger than styrene, so the intramolecular forces between butadiene and the carrier gas are very strong.

61

GO ON TO THE NEXT PAGE.

164. If an unknown sample showed a response of 7 at 3.2 minutes and a response of 8 at 6.1 minutes, what concentrations of styrene and butadiene were present?

    A.   1.5 mol/L styrene and 1.5 mol/L butadiene
    B.   1.5 mol/L butadiene and 2.5 mol/L styrene
    C.   1.5 mol/L styrene and 2.5 mol/L butadiene
    D.   1.9 mol/L butadiene and 1.7 mol/L styrene

165. Why is it important to know the volume of air pulled through the pump when collecting an air sample?

    A.   Without an accurate volume, the sample cannot be extracted.
    B.   Without an accurate volume, the extracted sample cannot be analyzed by gas chromatography.
    C.   Without an accurate volume, the standard curve cannot be calculated.
    D.   Without an accurate volume, the calculated concentration for the extract cannot be converted to an air concentration.

Questions 166 through 169 are NOT based on a descriptive passage.

---

166. Why do alcohols have boiling points much higher than hydrocarbons of similar molecular weight?

    A.   Alcohols have greater van der Waals attraction forces.
    B.   Alcohol molecules have greater molecular symmetry.
    C.   Hydrogen bonds must be broken in the process of volatilization.
    D.   Alcohols must overcome greater ionic forces in the process of volatilization.

167. In cattle, a specific locus on chromosome 9 codes for horn (dominant), or hornless (recessive) characteristics. A locus on chromosome 6 codes for short hair (dominant) or long hair (recessive). A dihybrid cross of horned, short-hair cattle produces which of the following ratios?

    A.   1 horned, long hair: 1 hornless, short hair
    B.   3 horned, short hair: 1 hornless, long hair
    C.   9 horned, short hair: 1 hornless, short hair
    D.   9 horned, long hair: 1 hornless, short hair

168. Which of the following is NOT true regarding the chemistry of carbon–carbon double-bonded compounds?

    A.   The double bond of alkenes acts to stabilize carbonium ions on adjacent carbons.
    B.   The double bond attracts electrophiles.
    C.   The double bond acts to stabilize free radicals on adjacent carbons.
    D.   The double bond attracts nucleophiles.

169. A common medical problem is the blockage of bile flow from the gallbladder to the intestine by a gallstone. One result of this is:

    A.   protein malabsorption.
    B.   fat malabsorption.
    C.   carbohydrate malabsorption.
    D.   water-soluble vitamin malabsorption.

GO ON TO THE NEXT PAGE.

Passage V (Questions 170–175)

It has long been known that cardiovascular exercise slows the resting heart rate and increases the volume of blood (stroke volume) pumped from the heart with each beat. However, the mechanism of this phenomenon was not recognized until researchers gained a better understanding of the autonomic nervous system. It was found that the SA node of the heart has an endogenous pacing rate of 100 beats/min. There is a continuous parasympathetic tone delivered to the SA node, which slows the resting heart rate for most individuals to about 70 beats/min. For athletes, the stroke volume and force of the heart beat are greater than for the general population. Greater stroke volume and contraction force are associated with parasympathetic activation and an increased tone at the SA node. This results in the slower heart rates found in many athletes.

The Study

The effects of 1 year of exercise training on cardiorespiratory fitness, muscle strength, and cholesterol levels were studied. Two hundred twenty-four men between the ages of 60 and 65 volunteered for the study. Half of the men exercised aerobically at 70% maximal heart rate for one-half hour, four times a week. The remaining men were sedentary. Assume that men in the two different groups were similar in all other ways. Six different variables were measured: maximum oxygen consumption, maximal heart rate, blood cholesterol level, grip strength, skinfold thickness, and body weight. These data are summarized in Table 1. A measure of metabolic rate was also determined. It was found that the resting metabolic rate was greater in exercising men than in sedentary men.

170. If muscle samples of exercising men and sedentary men were compared at the microscopic level, which of the following would be expected to be increased in exercising men?

  A. Golgi apparatus
  B. Lysosomes
  C. Smooth endoplasmic reticulum
  D. Mitochondria

171. Based on the results of this study, one could conclude which of the following?

  A. The exercise schedule used was not effective in decreasing the maximal heart rate of exercising men.
  B. Blood cholesterol levels do not appear to decrease with the exercise schedule used in this study.
  C. The maximum oxygen consumption of exercising men increased by more than 20 L per hour.
  D. After 1 year of exercise, it appears that the men in the 60- to 65-year-old age-group have lower heart rates and greater heart volumes than sedentary men.

172. Which of the following statements is best supported by the results of the study?

  A. The results of this study support the contention that exercise programs may prolong longevity.
  B. The results of this study refute the contention that exercise programs may prolong longevity.
  C. The results of this study do not support or refute the contention that exercise programs may prolong longevity.
  D. The results of this study both support and refute the contention that exercise programs may prolong longevity.

Table 1. The Effect of Exercise Training on Various Criteria (mean values)

Variable	Exercising Men		Sedentary Men	
	Baseline	1 Year	Baseline	1 Year
Maximum O_2 consumption (L/min)	2.36	2.60	2.35	2.41
Maximum heart rate (beats/min)	160.1	155.2	155.5	155.6
Blood cholesterol levels (mg%)	233.9	242.6	223.3	230.5
Grip strength (N)	43.0	43.8	44.7	44.2
Skinfold thickness (mm)	102.4	103.5	105.1	109.2
Weight (kg)	78.5	78.1	78.6	80.0

GO ON TO THE NEXT PAGE.

173. Which of the following substances mediate the para-sympathetic effect at the SA node?

    A. Dopamine
    B. Norepinephrine
    C. Epinephrine
    D. Acetylcholine

174. Based on information presented in the passage, which of the following would be reduced in exercising men?

    A. Cortisol levels
    B. Epinephrine levels
    C. Growth hormone levels
    D. Thyroid-stimulating hormone levels

175. The percent increase of maximum oxygen consumption (L/min) for exercising men at their baseline compared with that after 1 year of exercise training is closest to which of the following?

    A. 5%
    B. 8%
    C. 10%
    D. 12%

Passage VI (Questions 176–180)

DNA polymerases are a class of enzymes that make a complementary copy of a strand of DNA. The new DNA strand is synthesized by addition of one nucleotide at a time to the chain. The new nucleotide is chosen by its ability to form hydrogen bonds with the base on the template strand. A nucleotide triphosphate is shown below in Figure 1.

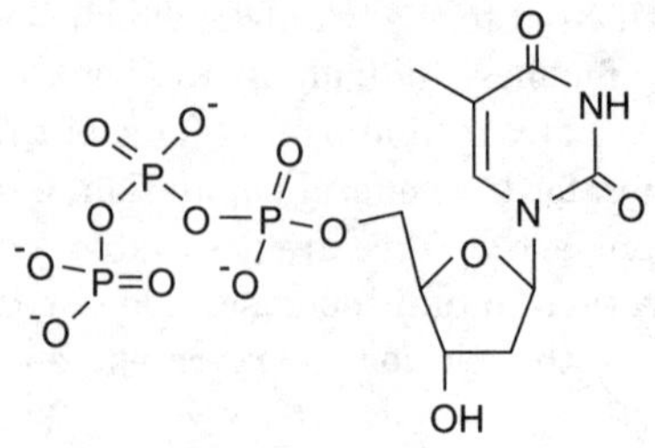

Figure 1. The structure of a nucleotide triphosphate.

The mechanism of DNA polymerase involves the nucleotide and the lengthening DNA chain in a bimolecular reaction. The mechanism of DNA polymerase action is shown in Figure 2.

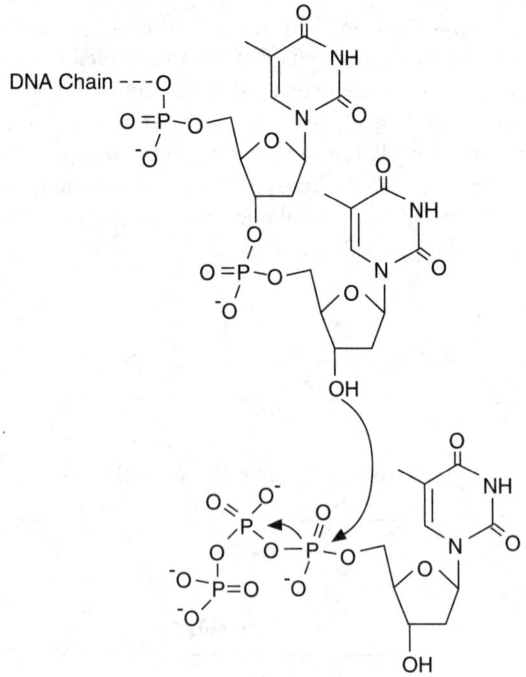

Figure 2. The mechanism of DNA polymerase action.

Reverse transcriptase is an enzyme that can use a strand of RNA as a template for DNA synthesis. This enzyme is found only in a class of viruses known as retroviruses. Retroviruses, such as the human immunodeficiency

GO ON TO THE NEXT PAGE.

virus (HIV), carry their genetic information as RNA rather than DNA. Many inhibitors of reverse transcriptase are used as treatments for diseases caused by retroviruses. Some of these inhibitors are nucleoside analogs that are phosphorylated by cellular enzymes before becoming active. One such inhibitor used in the treatment of HIV is azidothymidine (AZT), shown below in Figure 3.

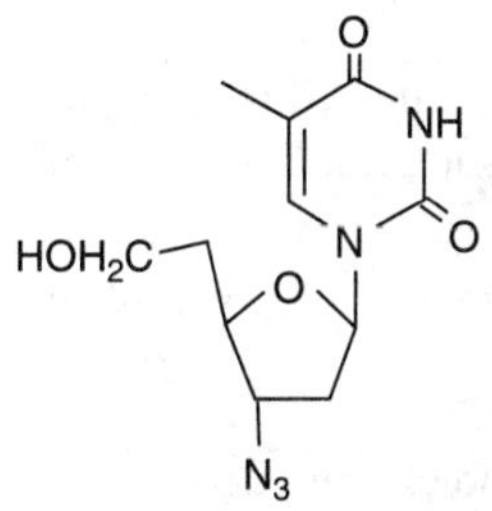

Figure 3. The structure of AZT.

176. The mechanism of DNA polymerase best resembles:

    A. S_N1.
    B. S_N2.
    C.   E1.
    D.   E2.

177. Which of the following is the most plausible mechanism for the chemical reaction catalyzed by reverse transcriptase?

    A.   It has no leaving group, so it could simply occupy the space in the enzyme where the nucleotide needs to bind.
    B.   It has no nucleophile, so it could simply occupy the space in the enzyme where the nucleotide needs to bind.
    C.   It has no leaving group, so it could not incorporate a new nucleotide in the DNA chain.
    D.   It has no nucleophile, so it could not incorporate a new nucleotide in the DNA chain.

178. Why does DNA polymerase need a nucleotide triphosphate?

    A.   The triphosphate acts as the nucleophile.
    B.   The diphosphate acts as the nucleophile.
    C.   The triphosphate acts as the leaving group.
    D.   The diphosphate acts as the leaving group.

179. The sugar component of the nucleotide shown in the passage has which of the following configurations?

    A.   Alpha furanose
    B.   Beta furanose
    C.   Alpha pyranose
    D.   Beta pyranose

180. Which of the following reasons best explains why specific inhibitors of reverse transcriptase are useful in treating retroviruses?

    A.   Reverse transcriptase is the only important enzyme that viruses have.
    B.   Reverse transcriptase does not have an analogous enzyme in the human body.
    C.   They are really easy to make.
    D.   Reverse transcriptase is needed to generate the genetic information of retroviruses.

Parkinson's disease (PD) is a progressive neurological disorder of muscle movement, characterized by resting tremor, muscular rigidity, slowness in initiating and performing voluntary movements, and gait abnormalities. Although the cause of PD is largely unknown, the disease does correlate with a loss of dopaminergic neurons in the substantia nigra, a part of the brain's basal ganglia system. Dopaminergic neurons are nerve cells that use dopamine as their primary neurotransmitter. The basal ganglia are a group of brain structures involved in motor control. Basal ganglia dysfunction has been implicated in a variety of disorders, including schizophrenia and Huntington's disease.

Drug therapy for PD is aimed at restoring levels of dopamine in the basal ganglia. Dopamine itself cannot cross into the brain from blood vessels, but its immediate precursor levodopa (L-dopa) readily enters the brain and is converted by the enzyme *dopa decarboxylase* into dopamine. Large doses of L-dopa are required because of peripheral conversion to dopamine. Excess dopamine in the peripheral circulation outside the brain causes nausea, vomiting, low blood pressure, and even cardiac rhythm disturbances. This problem can be attenuated with carbidopa, an inhibitor of *dopa decarboxylase* that does not cross into the brain from blood vessels.

Secondary parkinsonism, symptoms of PD in a patient without the disease, can occur as a result of medical treatment. For example, antipsychotic drugs block dopamine neurotransmission in the brain. Therefore, drug therapy for schizophrenia often results in parkinsonian movement abnormalities. PD-like symptoms in a young adult may indicate intravenous drug abuse. MPPP, an illicit, narcotic drug, can easily and accidentally change to MPTP, which selectively destroys dopaminergic neurons in the substantia nigra.

181. Based on information presented in the passage, which of the following diseases is NOT associated with basal ganglia dysfunction?

    A. Huntington's disease
    B. Epilepsy
    C. Schizophrenia
    D. Parkinson's disease

182. Nausea due to drug therapy of PD is most likely the result of which of the following?

    A. Peripheral *dopa decarboxylase* inhibition
    B. Excess dopamine in the brain
    C. Peripheral conversion of L-dopa to dopamine
    D. Substantia nigra degeneration

183. The release of prolactin, a pituitary hormone that stimulates milk production, is inhibited by dopamine. What effect would antipsychotic medication have on milk production?

    A. Increased milk due to dopamine-enhancing effect
    B. Decreased milk due to dopamine-enhancing effect
    C. Increased milk due to dopamine-blocking effect
    D. Decreased milk due to dopamine-blocking effect

184. What role does carbidopa play in the drug therapy of PD?

    A. Blockade of *dopa decarboxylase* in the brain
    B. Increases peripheral dopamine neurotransmission
    C. Increases central nervous system (CNS) dopamine levels after L-dopa administration
    D. Serves as substrate for dopamine synthesis

185. Which of the following drugs would NOT be useful in PD?

    A. A drug that mimics actions of dopamine
    B. A drug that prevents the breakdown of dopamine
    C. A drug that increases dopamine levels in neurons
    D. A drug that blocks dopamine neurotransmission

186. A rare form of PD shows autosomal dominant patterns of heritability. If both parents are heterozygous for PD, what percent of their children will be likely to develop PD?

    A. 50%
    B. 25%
    C. 75%
    D. All children will inherit the PD gene

GO ON TO THE NEXT PAGE.

Passage VIII (Questions 187–191)

Reactions of organic compounds with inorganic salts are common in the preparation of functionalized products. These reactions suffer from a simple problem, that of solubility. Most organic compounds are soluble in nonpolar solvents, and inorganic salts are not. The inorganic salts are very water-soluble, and most organic compounds are not. Even for those organic compounds soluble in water, reactions with solvated ions are very slow. Phase-transfer catalysts solve this problem. Phase-transfer catalysts help to transfer the organic salt from the aqueous phase to the organic phase so that a reaction can occur. One class of phase-transfer catalyst is the crown ethers. Shown in Figure 1 is 18-crown-6, one example of a crown ether.

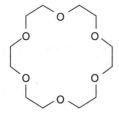

Figure 1.   The structure of 18-crown ether.

Crown ethers can form a complex with cations. Crown ethers with different ring sizes will accommodate different-sized cations in the oxygen-lined cavity. This serves to shield the cation from the organic solvent.

187. Which of the following reactions might require a phase-transfer catalyst?

- **A.** A nucleophilic substitution reaction with ethyl magnesium bromide acting as the nucleophile
- **B.** A Diels-Alder reaction between butadiene and ethylene
- **C.** An oxidation of ethylene using potassium permanganate as the oxidizing agent
- **D.** An elimination reaction of 2-chlorobutane using sodium ethoxide as the base

188. Which of the following compounds might serve as a phase-transfer catalyst analogous to 18-crown-6?

A.
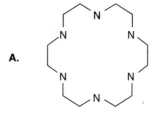

B.

C.
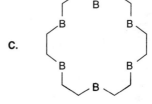

D.
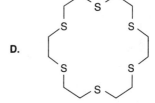

189. What type of bond is formed between 18-crown-6 and a potassium ion?

- **A.** Ionic
- **B.** Polar covalent
- **C.** Nonpolar covalent
- **D.** Coordinate covalent

190. Reactions between water-soluble organic compounds and anions in water are slow because:

- **A.** water solvates the organic compound and the anion cannot get close enough to react.
- **B.** water solvates the anion and the organic compound cannot get close enough to react.
- **C.** the anion will precipitate because of its lower solubility in the presence of an organic compound.
- **D.** the organic compound will precipitate because of its lower solubility in the presence of an anion.

67

GO ON TO THE NEXT PAGE.

191. Which of the following might serve as a phase-transfer catalyst for anions in a manner analogous to that of 18-crown-6 for cations?

A.

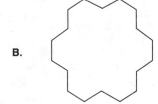

B.

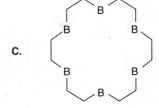

C.

D.

192. A researcher is interested in interfering with the development of the heart in an amphibian embryo. Drug A affects the induction of ectoderm from the underlying mesoderm. Drug B blocks the differentiation of mesoderm during gastrulation. Drug C interferes with the invagination process of gastrulation such that the endoderm layer does not form normally. Which drug would be best to accomplish the researcher's goals?

A. Drug A
B. Drug B
C. Drug C
D. Drug B or C, followed by drug A

193. Which of the following molecules is the most acidic?

1   2   3

A. 1
B. 2
C. 3
D. None of the above, as 2 and 3 have similar acidities.

194. Osteocytes are most associated with which of the following states of bone?

A. Formation
B. Resorption
C. Maintenance
D. Conversion into cartilage

195. Which of the following processes does NOT occur in intracellular organelles?

A. Oxidative phosphorylation
B. Krebs cycle
C. Electron transport
D. Glycolysis

GO ON TO THE NEXT PAGE.

196. Which of the following is the correct IUPAC name for the compound below?

A. 3-Bromo-4-ethyl-1-nitrobenzene
B. 1-Ethyl-2-bromo-4-nitrobenzene
C. 2-Bromo-4-nitrotoluene
D. 2-Bromo-1-ethyl-4-nitrobenzene

Passage IX (Questions 197–203)

Mimicry is said to occur when one organism evolves a resemblance to another. The organism imitated is the model and the organism performing the imitation is the mimic. When the mimic benefits at the expense of other organisms, it is known as aggressive mimicry. Müllerian mimicry occurs when the model and the mimic are both distasteful to predators. Protective mimicry is also common. Here, an edible organism mimics a distasteful or dangerous one. A toxic organism that advertises its poisonousness is called aposematic. Protective mimicry involving an aposematic mimic is called batesian mimicry after Henry W. Bates, the English naturalist who first described it in 1862.

A well-known example of mimicry can be found in coral reef-dwelling fish. The coral reef-dwelling saber-toothed blenny of the genus *Aspidontus* shows a remarkable resemblance to the common cleaner wrasse, *Labroides dimidiatus*. *Labroides* exhibit a cleaning behavior, in which they clean and eat debris and parasites from the surface of larger fish. *Labroides* approach a larger fish, perform a ritual dance, and are accepted as useful partners. The mimic *Aspidontus* dances in a manner similar to that of *Labroides;* however, it then proceeds to bite and feed from the tissue of the larger fish. After such violent acts, the blenny need not flee because a reciprocative attack from the injured fish is inhibited by the blenny's cleaner wrasse appearance.

A second classic example of mimicry can be found in moths and butterflies. In an experiment to investigate mimicry, biology researchers studied day-flying moths.

The Experiment

1. Day-flying moths (*Callosamia promethea*) were divided into two groups, equal in number.
2. One group was painted to resemble the toxic *Battus philenor* and the other to resemble the yellow and black form of the edible tiger swallowtail.
3. Both groups of moths were released simultaneously. Table 1 presents data on the number of moths recaptured from each group for the first 5 days of this 7-day experiment.

Table 1.   Number of Moths Recaptured Over 5 Days

Day of Experiment	0	1	2	3	4	5	Total
Toxic painted	54	26	12	4	2	2	100
Tiger painted	54	7	3	5	3	3	75

GO ON TO THE NEXT PAGE.

197. A poisonous organism that evolves a classic appearance which is easily recognized by predators exhibits which of the following?

    A. aggressive mimicry
    B. protective mimicry
    C. aposematic mimicry
    D. commensalism

198. Based on the data in the passage, the toxic-painted day-moth exemplifies which of the following?

    A. Batesian mimicry
    B. Müllerian mimicry
    C. commensalism
    D. aggressive mimicry

199. Based on information provided in the passage, the behavior of *Aspidontus* best exemplifies:

    A. batesian mimicry.
    B. self-mimicry.
    C. protective mimicry.
    D. aggressive mimicry.

200. What do the results of the release–recapture experiment imply?

    A. *B. philenor* has longer survival compared with the tiger swallowtail.
    B. The tiger swallowtail has longer survival compared with *B. philenor*.
    C. Nothing, because the results on day 1 were not significant.
    D. Aggressive mimicry benefits the toxic swallowtail.

201. Which of the following would confound interpretation of the release–recapture experiment?

    A. Painting interfered with flight of one group but not the other.
    B. Birds ate one group of moths but not the other.
    C. Both **A** and **B** are correct.
    D. Neither **A** nor **B** is correct.

202. A mutant mouse that resembles a miniature cat survives longer than other mice. The miniature cat–mouse reproduces successfully with normal mice and the genes for cat resemblance increase in subsequent generations of mice. This is an example of:

    A. speciation.
    B. increased fitness.
    C. chemical evolution.
    D. aggressive mimicry.

203. Two species of butterflies resemble each other. Both species of butterflies are distasteful to birds. A bird that consumes any member of either species will avoid the other species in the future. This behavior is best described by:

    A. Batesian mimicry.
    B. aggressive mimicry.
    C. Müllerian mimicry.
    D. protective mimicry.

GO ON TO THE NEXT PAGE.

Passage X (Questions 204–208)

The sexually transmitted disease syphilis is caused by a coiled spirochete known as *Treponema pallidum.* These bacteria, although too small to be seen with light microscopy, can be visualized by darkfield microscopy, which is an important diagnostic tool. Darkfield microscopy involves a special substage condenser that throws light across rather than through the field. Only light that is reflected or refracted by an object in the field reaches the eye.

Transmission occurs when the spirochete penetrates intact mucous membranes or abraded skin and multiplies locally, producing the primary skin lesion known as chancre. These skin lesions are infectious and present a risk for health care workers. Spread via the blood stream can lead to secondary symptoms including rash, fever, and hepatitis. Syphilis can, at this point, enter a latent phase marked by positive serologic tests and the absence of clinical symptoms. After a latency period of up to 10 years, 40% of syphilis cases progress to the tertiary stage, known for its CNS and cardiovascular manifestations.

Serologic testing forms the cornerstone for diagnosis. Two types of tests are available: reaginic tests [Venereal Disease Research Laboratory (VDRL) test, rapid plasma reagin (RPR)], which measure antibody to cardiolipin, a nontreponemal antigen; and treponemal tests [*T. pallidum* hemagglutination assay (TPHA), fluorescent treponemal antibody-absorbed (FTA-abs)], which are specific for treponemal antigens. Although the former group of tests is sensitive, it is known to give many false-positive results, an observation explained by the numerous conditions giving rise to anticardiolipin antibodies (Lyme disease, malaria, pregnancy, measles). Treponemal tests remain positive for life, whereas nontreponemal tests revert after the symptoms resolve. A collection of patients who had syphilis were studied and divided into three groups depending on the stage of syphilis they demonstrated. There were an equal number of people in each group: primary stage, secondary stage, and tertiary stage. VDRL, RPR, and TPHA tests were conducted on each patient of the group. The results of these tests are shown in Figure 1.

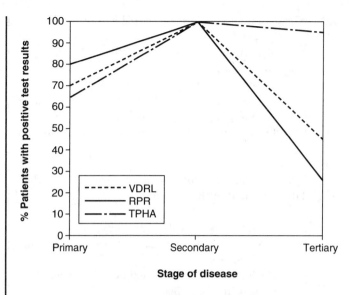

Figure 1. Percent of patients testing positive for syphilis versus stage of the disease.

204. Under the microscope, the organism responsible for syphilis would have what appearance?

    A. Rod shape
    B. Cocci shape
    C. Corkscrew shape
    D. Cylindrical shape

205. Based on information given in the passage, darkfield microscopy will result in which of the following patterns?

    A. Dark object and light background
    B. Dark object and darker background
    C. Light object and dark background
    D. The inability to visualize objects visible through light microscopy

206. A 40-year-old man tests positive by VDRL but has no symptoms of syphilis. Which of the following conditions is NOT possible?

    A. Latent syphilis
    B. False positive
    C. Lyme disease
    D. Tertiary syphilis

207. Which statement is best supported by the passage?

    A. If TPHA is positive and VDRL is negative, it must be a false positive.

    B. Sixty percent of syphilis cases resolve after 1° or 2° stages.

    C. Cardiolipin protein is found on *T. pallidum*.

    D. TPHA is most likely to give a positive result in 1° syphilis.

208. What serologic conclusions can be drawn from the data presented in the passage?

    A. 2° syphilis is difficult to diagnose.

    B. Production of treponemal antibodies decreases in 2° syphilis.

    C. Production of anticardiolipin antibodies increases in 3° syphilis.

    D. Production of anticardiolipin antibodies decreases in 3° syphilis.

Passage XI (Questions 209–214)

The search for new pharmaceuticals has led synthetic organic chemists toward larger and larger target molecules. To make such large molecules, the ability to form bonds between carbon atoms is becoming increasingly more important. One type of reaction that forms bonds between carbon atoms involves the use of reagents with nucleophilic carbon atoms. The greatest drawback in the use of nucleophilic carbon atoms is their strongly basic nature. This explains why Grignard's reagents produce significant yields only in aprotic solvents.

Grignard's reagents (R-MgX) are one type of reagent containing a nucleophilic carbon atom. This carbon atom will attack any electropositive atom, such as the carbon of a carbonyl, shown in Figure 1.

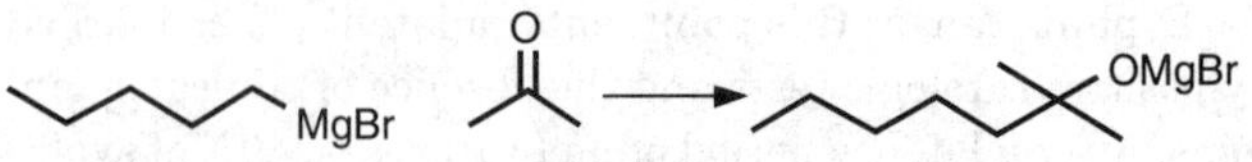

Figure 1. Reaction of Grignard's reagent.

Grignard's reagents are commonly used to make alcohols from ketones, aldehydes, and esters via hydrolysis of the resulting salt. Figure 2 summarizes results from a series of Grignard's reactions.

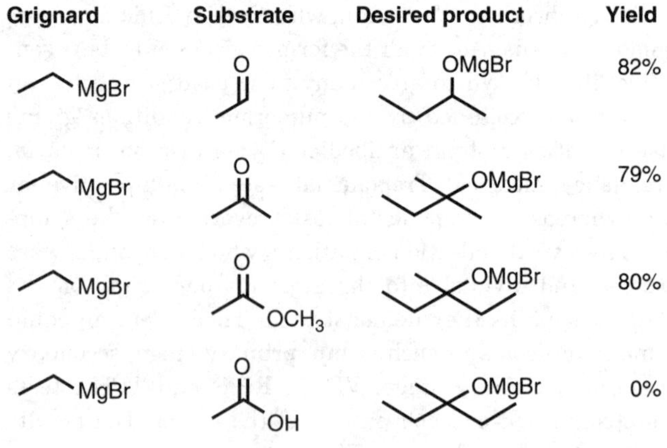

Grignard	Substrate	Desired product	Yield
			82%
			79%
			80%
			0%

Figure 2. The results of various Grignard's reactions.

209. What reagent would be used to convert the products from the table to the corresponding alcohols?

    A. Water

    B. An oxidizing agent

    C. A reducing agent

    D. Oxygen

GO ON TO THE NEXT PAGE.

210. Which of the following conclusions best explains the 0% yield for the last reaction in the table?

    A. The substrate molecule does not have an electrophilic carbon atom.
    B. Grignard's reagent is unreactive.
    C. The substrate has an acidic hydrogen atom.
    D. Grignard's reagent has an acidic hydrogen atom.

211. In 2-chloropropanol, which atom would be attacked first by Grignard's reagent?

    A.

    B.

    C.

    D.

212. Which of the following mechanistic steps accurately explains why two Grignard's reagent molecules react with each ester molecule?

    A.

    B.

    C.

    D.

213. Which of the following solvents would be appropriate for Grignard's reaction?

    A. CH_3CH_2OH
    B. H_2O
    C. CH_3CO_2H
    D. $CH_3CH_2OCH_2CH_3$

214. Which of the following compounds would NOT produce an alcohol on addition of Grignard's reagent followed by hydrolysis?

    A.

    B.

    C.

    D.

73

GO ON TO THE NEXT PAGE.

Questions 215 through 219 are NOT based on a descriptive passage.

215. Glucose and fructose belong to which groups, respectively?

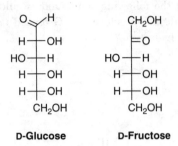

D-Glucose   **D-Fructose**

    A. Aldotriose and aldopentose
    B. Ketohexose and aldopentose
    C. Ketohexose and ketohexose
    D. Aldohexose and ketohexose

216. A biologist conducts an experiment in which the dorsal lip of the blastopore from an early frog embryo is inserted under the ectoderm on the ventral surface of a second early embryo. Which of the following would be expected of the host embryo?

    A. It will die in reaction to the foreign tissue.
    B. It will develop a second primitive streak.
    C. It will develop a second neural groove.
    D. It will develop an extra pair of legs.

217. Which of the following is the best explanation for why the genetic code is considered degenerate?

    A. One codon can code for several amino acids.
    B. Codons code for amino acids.
    C. Amino acids may form a large variety of possible proteins.
    D. Most amino acids have several codons.

218. The acid-catalyzed dehydration mechanism for alcohols is best described as a(n):

    A. E1.
    B. E2.
    C. S_N1.
    D. S_N2.

219. Exchange of fluid and nutrients across the capillary wall is dependent on two carefully balanced forces, i.e., hydrostatic and oncotic pressures. If hydrostatic pressure far exceeds oncotic pressure, one would expect which of the following?

    A. An increase in intravascular volume
    B. An increase in interstitial volume
    C. A decrease in interstitial volume
    D. A and C

STOP. IF YOU FINISH BEFORE TIME IS CALLED, CHECK YOUR WORK. YOU MAY GO BACK TO ANY QUESTION IN THIS TEST BOOKLET.

ANSWERS AND EXPLANATIONS TO TEST 1

Verbal Reasoning

1. D   You are asked to infer the meaning of words from the passage. Evaluate the content of the final paragraph. Note that the final paragraph describes the characters' optimism on reaching America.

2. D   This question is easy to answer if you skimmed the question stems before reading the passage. This strategy will allow you to look for the paragraph that describes the key words "sound design." The third paragraph describes the film's sound design. The passage describes that the sound design uses echoes and long silences.

3. D   Analyze each of the statements based on its own merit. Statement I is true because the foreign characters in Jarmusch's films have positive hopes. Statement II, or callowness, is a true statement because of the unworldliness of the foreign characters. Statement III, or ignorance, is also true because the characters don't know that the fringes of American society aren't the mainstream. Because all three statements are true, choice D is the best choice.

4. D   Paragraph four states that Jarmusch's characters retain hopes for life improvements and opportunities. Paragraph six describes the foreign characters, and their hope and wonder. To answer this question, use the process of elimination. Choice A is incorrect because there are no cynical descriptions provided for the characters. Choice B is not supported anywhere in the passage. Choice C may be true, but it is not directly stated or supported. Choice D is the best choice by the process of elimination.

5. C   Choice A is incorrect because Jarmusch's work does not focus on the opulent. Choices B and D are incorrect because the author never mentions these techniques in the passage. Choice C is supported by the second paragraph.

6. C   Evaluate each statement carefully. Statement I would not be appropriate for one of Jarmusch's characters because teaching careers require selflessness, dedication, and more energy than the described characters possess. Statement II is reasonable because gamblers are always hoping for a big break; this hope is similar to the feelings of the characters described in the passage. Statement III is also reasonable because unemployed people often have time on their hands, and are dealing with negative issues and often bleak circumstances.

7. D   Use the process of elimination to evaluate each choice. Choices A, B, and C are statements describing elements that are common to all three films. Choice D is not common to all three films because *Mystery Train* was filmed in color (see paragraph two).

8. D   Jack and Zach display the tough exteriors of Jarmusch's American characters. There is no implication that Jack and Zach are not Americans, so choice A is incorrect. The author never says they were in jail for the same crime (they're not), so choice C can be eliminated. Choice B is not supported by the passage because there is no guarantee that Jack and Zach will find their fortunes after the end of the film.

9. D Evaluate each statement on its own merit. Statements I and III can be considered analogous (although not identical) because these pregnancies are generally not desired and unplanned (analogous with the kidnaping). Statement II is reasonable, because pregnancies in which the mother's health is endangered require the woman to limit her mobility. This could require that the mother would sometimes have to stay in bed for months; this is directly analogous to the violinist story.

10. C Use the process of elimination to evaluate each statement. Quickly reread the final paragraph to get the gist of what is important. Note that the final paragraph addresses the mother's right to autonomy and the implications of fetal death. Choice C best describes the content of the final paragraph.

11. C Choice A is incorrect, because it does not appear to relate to the question being asked. Choice B is a nonsensical choice because pregnancy and music are related nowhere in the passage. Choice D does not clearly explain why the famous violinist was the chosen party. In addition, note that Thompson's opponents argue for the supreme value of all human life. Choice C is the best choice. Thompson is trying to grant the highest value possible to the dependent being's life, in order to show that the woman would still have a right to detach herself.

12. D To answer this question, carefully evaluate the statements. Note that in statements I and II, the pregnancy begins with voluntary consent of the mother. This is not parallel to the violinist analogy. In statement III, the termination happens involuntarily, with no decision on the part of the mother. This is also not parallel to the analogy. Thus, statements I, II, and III do not parallel the violinist analogy. This makes choice D the best choice.

13. B In the example, the violinist is person B. Person B's right against person A would be the violinist's right to compel the other person to stay attached and let him use his or her kidneys. This is best described in choice B. Choices A, C, and D are permutations of the correct relationship, constructed to confuse you.

14. D The title of this passage is given in the citation at the end of the passage. The title "A Defense of Abortion" indicates that Thompson is pro-choice. However, the body of the passage really describes the issue of bodily autonomy versus the right to life. Choice D is the best choice because the first two paragraphs show that the main topic of the passage is the conflict between the right to life and the right to bodily autonomy. Choice A is incorrect because Thompson is not being defended in the passage. Choice B is nonsensical. Choice C is not supported by the passage because the legal issues that relate to abortion are not discussed.

15. D Choice A is incorrect because mandatory organ donor programs would violate people's rights to bodily autonomy. Choice B does not support Thompson's basic belief systems described in the passage. Thompson believes that people cannot be compelled to perform charitable acts (see the fifth paragraph). Choice C cannot be supported from information given in the passage because Thompson never mentions the father's rights. Because choices A, B, and C do not support a stand that Thompson would advocate, the best choice is D (none of the aforementioned).

16. B The main argument that Thompson makes in this passage is nicely described in choice B. Thompson's main argument is that the personhood of the fetus makes no difference to the permissibility of abortion. This point is echoed throughout the passage.

---

17. D This passage provides a number of examples and anecdotes (empirical evidence). The first sentence of paragraph one proposes "an investigation." This answer, as well, does not assert that such evidence absolutely does not need a theoretical base, but that such evidence "can be worthwhile." Choice A is contradicted by the first sentence: postulates are theories, and the discussion that follows begins not with postulates, but with an investigation. Therefore, we do not need the postulates in order to investigate or gather information. The "refutation" or contradiction stated in B is not stated anywhere in this passage. And if empirical evidence were useless without theory (C), the passage would have no reason for existing. So this choice also contradicts the first sentence.

18. C The president was "opening" the meeting of the lower house of parliament, and in using the word "closed" (italicized in the passage), in light of a discussion of slips in which "one says the precise opposite of what one intended to say," we can infer that the lower house was not "open" to change; therefore, it was unreceptive. Choices A and D have nothing to do with the issue of parapraxes, and this question refers specifically to "the logic of the passage." Choice B is too extreme; the president may feel frustrated with the lower house, but we have no reason to believe that he finds them ineffectual.

19. C Although this passage briefly reviews the types of parapraxes (which would point to A), it focuses on the verbal slip of the tongue in all but the first paragraph. Choice B makes no sense, because this passage does not judge these occurrences as normal or dysfunctional. Choice D is both too colloquial and casual for a title, and does not encompass the various anecdotes and types of evidence offered in the passage.

20. B This answer (like most multiple-multiples) is best figured out by the process of elimination. We can eliminate statement I because it contradicts the information throughout the passage, which asserts that slips of the tongue are not wholly harmless. Therefore, C and D can be ruled out. We are left with A and B. Statement II also has no support in the passage, and is contradicted by the information in paragraph one. Therefore, choice B, containing only statement III, is correct.

21. A The key to the question is to look for the false statement, and not the true statement. Try to mentally eliminate the statement "necessarily." Although we may believe, based on our own knowledge, that a permanent forgetting is more serious than a temporary forgetting, the passage says no such thing. Choice B would seem to be true, according to the woman's slip of the tongue, implying that she would choose to control what her husband eats and drinks. Choice C would also seem true, as directly supported in paragraph two. Choice D is flatly stated to be true in the first two sentences of the passage.

22. D The terms "faulty act" and "intended" act are used in the fifth paragraph. Wrong choices: these words have no relationship to the connections between sounds and verbal similarity, and are not influenced by word associations, both of which are mentioned in paragraph four, which make A and B invalid. The statement in the fifth paragraph asserts that the faulty act can be "quite a normal act," which invalidates choice C ("there is really no such thing as 'normal' ").

23. A Choice D can be immediately eliminated because "parapraxes" are a psychological term used in the essay, and not a rhetorical strategy or "writing trick." Although there are plenty of definitions in paragraph one, they are not the dominant writing strategy, which would eliminate choice C. Examples or anecdotes run throughout the essay, but are similar strategies (anecdotes being stories, which could be considered one type of example), which makes choice B questionable. Choice A contains three strategies that all exist within the passage, in decreasing proportions.

24. C Answer this question by first skimming the third paragraph. Statements I and II are considered in the third paragraph. Statement III is not supported by information in the third paragraph of the passage. The author never considers that incarcerated criminals can't very well commit further crimes. Thus, the best choice is C (statement III only).

25. B The author's argument depends on the fact that crime rates go down when punishments are increased, but facts need to be supported with evidence. This makes choice B a very reasonable choice. Now consider the other choices. Choices A, C, and D are not as good as choice B because these choices do not directly affect the argument. Always be sure that a choice answers or addresses the question being asked.

26. B   The answer to this question is covered in paragraph four. The fact that retribution is more directed is a good point, and the author considers retribution and deterrence separately. Statements I and III are not supported or discussed in paragraph four. Statement II is supported and discussed.

27. C   The author considers compensation for families in the final paragraph. Compensation is not stated outright, but is inferred. However, there is enough information to eliminate statement I. Statements II and III are not considered by the author of this passage. This makes choice C (II and III only) the best choice.

28. A   The author's main purpose in this passage is to explore the reasons for punishment. Throughout the passage, it is evident that the author believes that the reasons for punishment are not clear. The first paragraph says the author is exploring the motivations for our system of punishment, not its justification or efficacy.

29. D   Use the process of elimination to evaluate each choice. First, skim the argument in the fourth paragraph. Note that the author discusses the death penalty in the fifth paragraph. The death penalty is described as "punishing crime by committing another crime." This helps support choice D, which suggests that incarceration and the death penalty both amount to punishing crime by committing another crime (criminal violation of the rights of the prisoner).

PASSAGE V

30. D   Based on information given in the passage, the Calvinist (i.e., Protestant, Christian) god sets laws for human beings to follow, and doles out punishments and rewards. The Greek gods set no laws, and were disinterested in human behavior unless it threatened to become godlike. Statements I, II, and III describe differences between Calvinist gods and Greek gods.

31. B   The first paragraph emphasizes that Americans believe that the heroes of Greek tragedies bring their own unfortunate end upon themselves. The fourth paragraph also indicates that modern readers are tempted to believe that the tragic hero does something wrong to bring about the tragedy. Choice B best describes this misinterpretation.

32. A   Hubris is the form of pride displayed when a human being crosses the golden mean. This term is described in the third paragraph. Statement I is an action that would display hubris. Statement II describes charity; this is not a demonstration of hubris. Analysis of statement III requires more subtle evaluation. Statement III is an example of grandiose behavior, which is different than the pride associated with a great accomplishment.

33. C   Tragic flaws must be a character trait; Oedipus' tragic flaw is that he stubbornly sticks to his search. Choice B is incorrect because the act of incest is not the tragic flaw; a tragic flaw cannot be an action. This is thoroughly discussed in the fourth paragraph. Choice A is incorrect because Oedipus does not curse the gods. Choice D is not supported, because the author never mentions patience.

34. A   The passage describes Greek tragic heroes and modern heroes. The passage points out that tragic heroes cannot commit sins without any divine rules to follow. Statement I states the difference between these two types of heroes: Modern heroes have happy endings, whereas Greek tragic heroes have sad endings. This is pointed out in the second and fourth paragraphs. Statements II and III are not differences supported by the passage. The best answer to this question is choice A (statement I only).

35. D   The author wants to point out a common mistake in the interpretation of modern versus Greek tragic heroes. Choice A is incorrect because there is no negative, chastising language in the passage. Choice B is false; the passage is not revisionary because it does not go against a received view. Choice C is not supported because the passage is not indifferent or apathetic.

36. A   Choice A is correct by the process of elimination. The warnings given to Oedipus allow the reader to have insight into the dilemma that Oedipus is in. Choice B is incorrect because Oedipus can't change his fate. Choice C can be eliminated because other characters are never mentioned in the passage. Choice D is incorrect because the passage indicates that the gods are not vengeful gods.

37. C Recall that the fourth paragraph indicates that the tragic flaw is NOT an action that brings on a downfall; it is a character trait. Stealing is an action, not a character trait. Eliminate statement II. Statements I and III (ambition and being too trusting) are more like character traits than actions. Thus, choice C is best (statements I and III).

---

38. B Choice B is correct because it is supported by information in paragraph three. We do not know enough information about Coptic from this passage to include it in this list, which eliminates A and D. Choice C comprises the three elements contained in hieroglyphics and cursive writing, as described in paragraph two, and hieroglyphics is only one type of ancient Egyptian writing, which thereby eliminates C.

39. D In paragraph four, we are told that "demotic signs have been retained in Coptic script." In paragraph three, we are told that demotic script was "the writing of the people." Therefore, we can infer that Coptic contains some of "the language of the people." We have no way of knowing, from the information in the passage, whether Coptic is widely spoken and written, which thereby eliminates choice A. We also have no indication that Coptic was ever a holy language (sacred languages being mentioned only in paragraph one, with no near references to Coptic), which eliminates choice B. And although it is tempting to choose choice C, particularly because Champollion insisted that "to understand hieroglyphs, it was essential to be able to read Coptic" (paragraph four), we cannot draw the conclusion that Coptic is modern-day hieroglyphics.

40. D Paragraph four offers considerable evidence that the spoken language or language of the people has in various ways survived, if only in traces. Also, the hieratic cursive is not one of the three languages on the Rosetta stone, which implies that the demotic script in some way usurped the hieratic script. Wrong choices: Choice A and its "democratic language" sound more like the Declaration of Independence than the Rosetta stone. One might feel inclined toward B simply because there are three languages on the Rosetta stone; that does not mean, however, that there were three different writers. Scribes (mentioned in paragraph 1) were the primary writers in ancient civilizations. Choice C has no support in the passage; in fact, hieroglyphics and hieratic writing had more in common, as stated in paragraph two.

41. D Choice A is far too general because it does not pinpoint specific cultures, which the passage does. Choice B, similarly, does not target specific cultures, and the passage does not thoroughly examine the evolution of languages as much as their ancient development. Choice C is too limited in that it points only to the Far East, and the passage spends a good deal of time on European and Middle Eastern "turf."

42. C Choice C is correct because it is directly supported by paragraph five. We might be inclined to choose A because it "sounds" as though it would make sense, but the passage tells us nothing about the relative ease of working with papyrus (in fact, paragraph 1 would lead us to believe otherwise). The hieratic system did not develop out of hieroglyphics, which invalidates choice B. And the information in D, which refers to working on papyrus, is drawn from paragraph one.

43. B Both Egyptian and Chinese writing systems were formally organized with rules and regulations, which constitutes being "codified." Choice A would seem to be partially correct, but it would be misleading to say that the Egyptian system employed signs to a dominant degree; at least, we could not determine this according to the passage. The first sentence of the final paragraph contradicts choice C (hieroglyphs and cuneiform were supplanted. . . .). And choice D refers directly and exclusively to the Chinese writing system (see the final paragraph).

44. B The passage points out that there were three different types of scripts, one particularly "of the people" (paragraph three), which would indicate that written communication was seen as essential, or at least helpful. Although paragraph one talks about hieratic language being originally used by priests, it tells us nothing about the politics of Egyptian society, which invalidates choices A and C. Choice D can be ruled out by the paragraphs that discuss the evolution of the Chinese writing system, which seemed to occur around the same time as the Egyptian system, and is commensurately complex.

45. C   At the end of paragraph five, we are told that a writing system developed in Crete "has long posed problems for scholars." Therefore, statement I is true, and in this question, we are looking for responses that are not true (not support). Therefore, any response with statement I as part of it can be eliminated, which leaves choices C and D. Although we are told in paragraph six that "fragmentary inscriptions" were discovered, we are not told that the Phaistos disk was in pieces. Therefore, statement IV should be a part of the answer. The key piece is statement III. Although we learn in paragraph six that steatite was a soft, easily worked stone, and we may wish to infer this about clay, we are not told that clay was easily worked, nor that either material was cheap. Therefore, statements II, III, and IV were not supported in the passage.

PASSAGE VII

46. C   The passage is informative/expository with a biased, argumentative slant. The author clearly appears in favor of the Penan people and repeatedly points out the destructive activities of loggers. In every instance in which a Penan ritual is discussed, the negative influence of logging activities on Penan activities and culture is emphasized. Keep the author's tone in mind when answering the questions. As you read this passage, remember to make a mental map of the flow of information contained in each paragraph. The first paragraph provides the answer to the first question. The species of plants and animals are discussed in the third paragraph, as is the threat to the diversity of these species. By inference, you can support choice C. By decreasing the number of plant species, you would expect some threat to people who are dependent on plants and animals for food. Choice A is incorrect because it transposes the correct relationship between plant species and inhabitants. Choice B is wrong because the soil is not emphasized in the passage. Choice D can be eliminated because Borneo's economy is not discussed in the passage.

47. C   To answer a multiple-multiple choice question, remember to evaluate each statement independently. Statement I is not supported because in the second sentence of the second paragraph, it is stated that loggers selectively cut trees rather than clear-cutting forests. This allows you to eliminate choices B and D. Statement II is supported by the third paragraph. Statement III is supported by the discussion of erosion in the second paragraph. This makes choice C correct.

48. B   This is a simple inference question. These questions require you to understand what the passage implies rather than what is stated specifically. To answer an inference-type question correctly, think about the attitudes and principles discussed in the passage. Draw a conclusion from these principles that matches one of the answer choices. In this passage, the last sentence uses the analogy of burning to describe the destruction of the lives and lifestyle of the Sarawak native people. This is supported by choice B. Choices A and D are factual choices that do not describe the life changes of the people. Choice C is not supported by the passage.

49. A   Evaluate each statement on its own merit. Statement I is supported by the logic presented in the passage; a cessation of logging would be expected to improve the problems cited by the author. This eliminates choices B, C, and D, which do not have statement I as an option. Statement III is supported by the fourth paragraph. Conducting trials in a way that the native people can comprehend would be expected to be an improvement to the current situation. Statement II is not well supported. The issue of wages and their effect on the Penan people is not discussed in the passage.

50. D This question is fact-based. Remember that fact questions require you to report information that was specifically stated in the passage. It is helpful to go back to the passage to find the information being asked about. If you made a mental map as you read, or made strategic notes in the margins of the paragraphs, it will be easy to find the answers to these questions. The answer is found in the fourth paragraph. The Penan men have to hunt for days instead of hours because the wild game have been driven away by logging and disruption of the ecological system.

51. B Use the process of elimination to answer this question. Choice A is not a supported statement because jail conditions are not discussed. Choice B is a true statement, which is supported by many parts of the passage. Choice C is not supported because paragraph four states that the Penan people use the rain forest for shelter. Choice D is a tricky choice. It is true that the Penan people are not a modern civilization. However, to decide whether choice B or D better addresses the question and the passage as a whole, think about the author's tone and bias. Is the problem the loggers impinging on the Penan people, or the Penan people not going with the flow of modern times? The passage stresses the effects of the loggers on the native people. The ecological changes leading to real threats to the Penan people are stressed. Choice B is the best choice.

PASSAGE VIII

52. D Although choice D is a generalization (as are the other choices), it is the least absolute, and supported by evidence about the development of Volapuk in paragraphs three, four, and five. We might want to choose choice A because of basic common sense, but it does not follow from the information in the passage. The word "any" is also a giveaway in that it indicates a generalization that cannot be supported. Choice B also contains the telltale "any," and we could be tricked into choosing this option, because Father Schleyer, the founder of Volapuk, had a type of personal agenda. Still, this does not mean that any founder would be of a similar ilk. Choice C comes directly from paragraph five, and is a paraphrase of Ludovic's beliefs, not a conclusion that we can draw.

53. C Choice C, because it refers to the "chosen few" who were allowed to amend Volapuk, contradicts the idea of a language for "ordinary people." Choice A "talks" about political dissension between people who spoke Volapuk, but we have no idea if this dissension was between intellectuals and nonintellectuals. Choice B refers to the visual and aural aspects of the language, with no reference to who spoke or developed it. Choice D jumps down to Zamenhof's issues with Volapuk, which have nothing to do with who spoke or developed it, and for whom.

54. C Information in paragraph three, particularly the word "proprietary," would lead us to describe Schleyer as "possessive." Information in paragraph eight, particularly the words "idealistic" and "upbeat," would lead us to describe Zamenhof as "optimistic." And although we may think of Schleyer as zealous and Zamenhof as peculiar (A), those assessments really would be more on the basis of personal feelings than on the information in the passage. It is unlikely that we would describe Schleyer as "gentle" (even if he is a Catholic priest), or as simply "protective," after reading paragraph three, which eliminates choices B and D. Similarly, Zamenhof, although energetic, could not be described as "tenacious," which has negative, argumentative overtones; and "earnest" simply does not say enough.

55. B The first part of this sentence is something of a red herring; that is, it can mislead you. But the second part, that the book of Esperanto had "a large impact," is the only phrase among the four choices that would lead toward the possibility of the rapid growth of the language. Choice A, directly from paragraph one, is tempting. But the fact that people were "interested" in these imitation languages is not strong enough to lead toward the possibility of Esperanto supplanting Spanish. The fact that Zamenhof taught Esperanto to his friends (paragraph seven) is charming, but would have no great impact. Choice D, from the final paragraph, is a testimony to Zamenhof's dedication to Esperanto, but in no way indicates that the language would really "take off."

56. A   Information in paragraph eight supports the assertion that Zamenhof wanted to avoid "ego traps." "Zamenhof was determined to put as much distance as possible between the work and its creator. . . he published a statement forever relinquishing all rights to the language." Choice B makes no sense because we have no idea what "positivism" is from the information provided in this passage. Choice C can be ruled out because Zamenhof had no previous experience in founding a language. Choice D is invalid because we are told, in paragraph eight, that Zamenhof chooses to get married, which certainly is a strong, personal commitment.

57. D   Again, information in paragraphs eight and nine leads us to believe that Zamenhof wanted to avoid the mistakes of Volapuk, among them Father Schleyer's religious motives and the factionalization of Volapukists. Also, in paragraph five, we learn that Zamenhof is particularly wary of language's power to keep "the walls of misunderstanding in place," in reference to Bialystok's racial antipathies. He wanted to make language apolitical, rather than political. A manifesto is a kind of speech or declaration in which a political party or faction puts forth its beliefs. The easiest way at this answer, however, is by the process of elimination. In the last paragraph, we learn that Zamenhof published translations from the Bible (eliminates choice B) and three short poems (eliminates choice A). Choice C can be eliminated simply because all of the aforementioned are clearly impossible without an alphabet.

58. B   Clearly, the color of the book cover has nothing to do with Zamenhof's selflessness. Choice A shows that Zamenhof is not in search of credit or fame. Choice C displays his optimism and hope for the world. Choice D shows his kindheartedness toward poor people.

59. C   The key to answering this question correctly is to note the words "less than significant contribution," which mean "an insignificant" or unimportant contribution. We would expect to be asked the reverse. Choice C asserts that statements III and IV were relatively unrelated to Zamenhof's desire to found a universal language. Note that Zamenhof chose to marry Clara Zilbernik in 1887, considerably after Zamenhof had drafted his own version of an international language. Therefore, the correct choice must include statement IV. In considering statement II, we must acknowledge that his observation of discord in his homeland did seem to contribute to his desire to create an international language (see paragraph five). Therefore, choice B can be eliminated. We can easily discern that his choice to study ophthalmology did not have much to do with his creation of an international language, which makes statement III work for our answer. Finally, his familiarity with several other languages would seem to contribute to his love of language and his desire to unify language and people through language.

PASSAGE IX

60. A   The fourth paragraph discusses Mondrian's description of his own work. The passage uses the term "formalism." One can imply from the passage that formalism is the concentration on essential elements such as color, shape, and line. Choice B is incorrect based on information given in the second paragraph. Choice C is false because Mondrian developed a style of painting known as "neoplasticism," not "post-plasticism." Choice D is neither supported nor contradicted.

61. B   Choice A is incorrect because the author never mentions the shape of Mondrian's canvasses. Choice C describes the paintings of modern painters, such as Andy Warhol; the author says that Mondrian's paintings have influence in the other direction. Choice D describes cubism, a precursor to Mondrian's paintings. Mondrian tried to get a single, essential point of view. His later works are best described by choice B.

62. D   It is clear from the final paragraph that the author of the passage is angry with the fashion industry for the abuse of Mondrian's work. Choices A and B describe neutral feelings, so they can be eliminated. Choice C suggests that the author is in league with the fashion industry; this is clearly opposite to the message of the final paragraph. Choice D, indignant, means angry or irate. This best describes the attitude of the author toward the fashion industry.

63. A The final paragraph indicates that the fashion designers frequently do not use primary colors in their designs. Statement I lists colors that are not primary colors. Thus, statement I is a true statement. The author never says that the designers use nonperpendicular angles, and in the final paragraph the author says that Mondrian would approve of displaying works of art on the body. Paragraph two supports statements II and III as elements that do follow the principles of neoplasticism. Thus, statements II and III can be eliminated as choices. Choice A, or (statement I only), is the best answer.

64. C Paragraph two discusses the principles of neoplasticism. The juxtaposition of opposites and achievement of equilibrium and balance were important components when squares and rectangles were used by Mondrian. The use of primary colors was not restricted to only square and rectangle use. Note that the question stem is restrictive and uses the word "only."

65. B Based on information given in the passage, you can surmise that Mondrian was 28 at the turn of the century. In paragraph two, the author says that Mondrian's most significant paintings were done in the later part of his career. This would place most of his work in the 20th century.

Physical Sciences

This is an information-presentation passage (physics) in which you are introduced to how a loudspeaker works. The passage at first appears complicated. It gives several formulas that you are expected to follow and apply. Several conceptual questions are posed based on information presented in the passage and your knowledge of sound and electromagnetism. Several of the questions may be answered directly from descriptive information given in the passage.

66. B The first question in this passage is a relatively straightforward plug-in type problem. Use the given equation: $x = NABi/k$. You are asked for the maximum displacement, or (x). You are given a frequency of 60 Hz, and a 1-mA rms current. To solve this problem, you must remember that an rms current of 1 mA has a peak current of $\sqrt{2}$ mA or about 1.4 mA. This is because Irms = Imax/$\sqrt{2}$r, or Imax = (Irms)($\sqrt{2}$). Thus, $x = (350)(0.7T)(0.3m)(1.4 \times 10^{-3} A)/(25 N/m) = 0.4$ cm.

67. D Energy conversion questions are commonly asked on the MCAT. In this question, an electrical current is transformed into kinetic energy. The kinetic energy provides movement and helps store potential energy in the spring. Next, the mechanical energy is transformed in sound energy.

68. D Choices A and B can be eliminated based on a phrase given in the passage. The passage states that "the frequency of the tone is determined by the frequency of the sinusoid, which remains unchanged." Remember that tone means pitch. Thus, the tone (pitch) should remain unchanged, and will not cause an increase or decrease in pitch. The second equation given in the passage, $x = NABi/k$, shows that a decreased magnetic field will decrease the maximum displacement, x. A decrease in maximum displacement will decrease the intensity of the sound.

69. B This question may appear difficult, but it is actually straightforward. The maximum power output will be achieved when the internal resistance of the speaker is matched. Just add the resistance of the battery (2 Ω) to the resistance of the coil (6 Ω). This gives 8 Ω. An 8-Ω equivalent resistance will match the 8-Ω internal resistance to give the maximum power output.

70. C Solve this question by the process of elimination. Recall that the passage stated that the frequency of the input current sinusoid will directly affect the pitch of the loudspeaker. Look carefully at the choices. Choice A is incorrect because the spring constant does not affect the pitch of the sound produced. Choice B does not make sense. Choice D can be eliminated because the number of turns (N) does not change the pitch of sound. Choice C is best by the process of elimination. Modifying the frequency of the current could decrease pitch.

This is a problem-solving passage (general chemistry) that covers acid–base titrations. A table describing various acids is given, as well as a titration curve. Basic conceptual questions and simple calculation questions are posed.

71. B The pH when half the acid has reacted to form its conjugate base is always equal to the pK_a. The titration curve indicates that the unknown acid should have a pK_a between 4 and 5 (the middle region of the plateau on the graph). Based on information presented in the table, formic acid has a pK_a less than 4.

72. C The equivalence point is the point at which the amount of added base equals the amount of unknown acid. This is the point of steep ascent in the titration curve. For this titration, the pH was around 8 when this occurred.

73. B At the half-equivalence point, half of the acid has been converted to its conjugate base. A pH of approximately 5 occurs at about 25 ml, which is halfway to the 50-ml equivalence point.

74. C The two compounds that differ only in the substituent attached to the COOH group are formic acid (substituent = H) and acetic acid (substituent = CH_3). The other choices have either a substituent difference in addition to some other difference or, in the case of acetic and propionic acid, only a size difference.

75. B The passage states that the student ruled out formic and oxalic acid (choices A and D). However, choices B and C cannot really be distinguished based on pK_a alone. The identity of the unknown acid can be found by calculating its molecular weight. Begin solving this problem by calculating the number of moles of NaOH added to the 0.6 g of acid. 0.05 L NaOH · 0.2 mol/L = 0.01 mol NaOH added. In a titration, an equal number of moles of acid should be present. This means there was 0.01 mol of the original acid. Because the original acid weighed 0.6 g, the molecular weight of the acid is 0.6 g/0.01 mol = 60 g/mol. Only acetic acid has a molecular weight close to this value.

This is a research study passage (physics) in which quantitative data from research experiments are presented. The design of the experiments is outlined and three different plots are drawn. It is important to follow the explanation of the experiments in this passage carefully. Pay attention to the meaning of each plot and its implications.

76. C This question is just testing your understanding of torque. Torque is equal to force times a lever arm. The lever arm refers to the perpendicular distance from the applied force to the axis of rotation. The thickness, density, and inertia of the sample are irrelevant for measuring torque. Thus, choices A, B, and D may be eliminated.

77. D Strain often refers to the fractional change in length of a substance. There are three major types of strain: tension, compression, and shear. These are unitless quantities. Because the three statements give the three types of strain, the best answer is choice D (I, II, and III).

78. B This is a data interpretation question. Look at the plot of graph B. Analysis shows that the difference at 7 weeks between vascularized and nonvascularized samples is less than 10%. Furthermore, the error bars on the graphs cross in this region, which implies the standard deviations of each graph overlap. This often means that the data points are not significantly different from one another.

79. A Point A is known as the linear limit. Point B is the elastic limit of the substance. Following the curve up to point B will result in elastic deformation. The substance will return to its original shape. When the stress and strain are such that point B is exceeded, the substance will undergo permanent deformation. Point C is known as the ultimate tension strength, and D is the fracture point.

80. D On the MCAT, you are expected to know that Young's modulus is the ratio of stretching stress to stretching strain. This corresponds to the linear portion of graph C. Choice A is incorrect because stiffness is a descriptive term rather than a quantitative relationship. Choice B is incorrect, as bulk modulus is the ratio of volume stress to volume strain. Choice C may be eliminated because shear force is a force associated with shearing and is not shown on any of the graphs.

81. D This is a simple calculation question. Stress = Force per unit area, or F/a. Thus, $10 \text{ N/m}^2 = F/(0.2 \text{m}^2) = 2.0 \text{ N}$.

This is an information-presentation passage (general chemistry) that introduces you to membranes and chemical purification. A diagram of a filter system is shown. In addition, a log–log graph is presented, showing a comparison of two different filters. Care should be taken when interpreting the values from the graph. Do not forget that the graph is in log values. The questions in this passage are primarily conceptual, based on colligative properties and your understanding of the figures.

82. C This question is best answered by the process of elimination. Evaluate each answer choice. Do not forget to read all the choices. Note that choice C is best supported by the passage. A and C differ only by the addition of the phrase "under pressure."

83. D Answer this question by evaluating the validity of each answer choice. The choices describe data which are summarized in the graph. Choice A is incorrect because the graph shows a log-log plot. These types of plots appear arithmetic, but they actually contain exponential data. Choice B is an overstatement. You do not know what happens to the ability of the filters to concentrate impurities over a long term. The graph shows only a limited period. Watch for incorrect choices like this on the MCAT. Whenever an emphatic statement is made, think of an example that contradicts it. If you can think of a contradiction, eliminate the choice. Now look at choices C and D. Each of these statements discusses 24 hours. Calculate how many minutes are in 24 hours: (24 hrs)(60 min/hr) = 1440 min. Now look at the x-axis. Which exponentials does 1440 most closely fit between? Recall that 10^3 = 1000 and 10^4 = 10,000. This means that 1440 most closely sits near the "3" on the $\log_{10}$ time coordinate. At this location, notice that the slope for filter X is increasing and filter Y is constant. This analysis helps eliminate choice C, which suggests that the accumulation rate is increasing for both filters. Choice D is best supported because filter X traps a higher concentration of ions compared with filter Y.

84. B This osmosis system shows a classic example of the colligative properties. The pressure needed to prevent pure water from diluting a solution on the other side of a membrane is solely dependent on the concentration of the particles in solution without regard for their identity.

85. A The important consideration in this question is the concentration of particles in solution. Calcium chloride dissociates to form three particles, so the concentration of particles would be 96 ppm. Calcium sulfate dissociates to form two particles so the concentration of particles would be 96 ppm also. This means that the purification efficiencies would be equal.

86. D To maintain efficiency, the highly concentrated solution that builds up during filter operation must be flushed. Think about the choices. Choice A is incorrect because it does not offer a reasonable explanation for the design. Choice B is not supported by the passage. Choices C and D must be carefully reasoned. Choice D is the better choice. The best arrangement for the valve is near the membrane, where the incoming water will force the concentrated solution out the valve.

87. C If the pump providing the pressure were inoperative, simple osmosis would occur. Choice A is incorrect because osmosis occurs naturally. Choices B and D are incorrect because osmosis occurs to allow water to diffuse down its concentration gradient. Choice C is the best choice. In the absence of pressure, water will flow across a membrane toward the more highly solute-concentrated side.

88. A   This question tests your conceptual understanding of electric fields. Recall that the direction of the electric field at a point can be determined by placing a small, positive test charge at that point in space. The direction the positive test charge is moved will show you the direction of the E-field acting at that point. In this question, the point in question is in the center of a hollow, symmetric sphere. In this shape, which is a hollow conductor, the net E-field is zero. This is because a small, positive test charge does not move if placed at the center of this shape.

89. D   The MCAT holds you responsible for understanding buoyant forces. Recall that buoyant force = $F_B = V\rho g$, where V is the volume of fluid displaced by the object, ρ is the density of the fluid, and g is the acceleration of gravity. Buoyant force is equal to the weight of the fluid displaced by the object. The general size and shape of the object are irrelevant.

90. D   Use the process of elimination to review each answer choice. Choice A is incorrect. Recall that for the Fahrenheit scale, water freezes at 32° and boils at 212°. The degree scale between freezing and boiling is 180°. In the Celsius scale, water freezes at 0° and boils at 100°. The degree scale between freezing and boiling is 100 degrees. Thus, each degree on the Fahrenheit scale means less than a degree on the Celsius scale. Choice B is also incorrect. A unit Kelvin change equals a unit of Celsius change, not Fahrenheit change. Finally, choice C is incorrect. Absolute zero is defined as 0 Kelvin. In terms of degrees Celsius, absolute zero is $-273°C$. Thus, choice D is the best choice by the process of elimination.

91. C   Remember that sound intensity falls off as $1/r^2$, in which r is the distance from the sound source. In this question, a distance of 2 m would correspond to a sound intensity ratio of $\frac{1}{2}^2$ or $\frac{1}{4}$. At 8 m, the sound intensity ratio would correspond to $\frac{1}{8}^2$ or $\frac{1}{64}$. Thus, the sound intensity at the new location compared with the original location = $(\frac{1}{64})/(\frac{1}{4}) = \frac{1}{16}$.

This is an information presentation passage (general chemistry). The oxidation–reduction chemistry of iron and rust is presented. Three reactions that outline the process are shown. Questions emphasize your understanding of redox, equation balancing, and conceptual principles.

92. A   This is a simple conceptual question. Simply look at the equation given for reaction 1. In reaction 1, the electrons are shown on the right side of the equation. The loss of electrons is an oxidation reaction. Remember the mnemonic: AN OX RED CAT. Oxidation occurs at the anode and involves the anion. Reduction occurs at the cathode and involves the cation.

93. D   Remember that redox reactions need a way to transfer electrons and ions from the anode cell to the cathode cell. In this case the two "cells" are not compartmentalized but the movement of charged particles is still needed. Also notice that the passage provides a clue in answering this question. Notice that water appears in equation 3 as necessary for formation of iron (III) oxide hydrate, or rust.

94. A   The addition of oxygen (or the loss of electrons) is the mark of an oxidation reaction. Both occur here as iron (II) loses electrons and gains oxygen to become iron (III). Choice B is incorrect because sublimation refers to a solid becoming a gas. Choice D may also be eliminated because hydrolysis reactions refer to reactions in which water is used to break bonds.

95. C   This question is testing your basic understanding of chemistry. Look for the most reasonable choice after evaluating each. Choice A describes iron (II) cations, which are not discussed in the passage. Based on information presented in the passage, iron (III) is associated with rust. Thus, choice A is difficult to support. Choice B may be eliminated because salt addition does not generally have a direct effect on changing pH. However, salts of acids and bases may help act as buffers. Choice C is the best choice and most logically follows the reasoning of the question. Pure water is not very conductive due to the small concentration of ions. The addition of salts greatly increases water's ability to conduct electricity.

96. B   The passage refers to coupling as a technique in which iron is coupled to another metal which is more reactive when exposed to oxygen and water. Now use inference to answer this question. To be more reactive to air and water, you should expect that the coupled metal must be more easily oxidized than iron. Something that is easily oxidized has a low reduction potential.

97. B   Look to see which reaction shows the oxidation of iron producing iron ions and water. See which reaction is balanced. Choices A, C, and D are incorrect because they are not balanced for charge. Choice B is balanced for atoms and charge. To make the electrons transferred equal, reaction 1 must be multiplied by 2 before adding it to reaction 2.

This is an information-presentation passage (physics) that presents the relationships among pressure, radius, and tension of spherical shapes. A single formula is introduced, and a table providing temperature values and surface tension values is given.

98. B   The answer to this question is given directly in the passage. The passage states that because a soap bubble is composed of a double-layered membrane of soap molecules, the surface tension is twice that of a water bubble.

99. C   This is a simple calculation question.

$$T = Pr/2$$
$$T = (1.33 \times 10^4 \, N/m^2)(5 \times 10^{-3} \, m)/2 = 33 \, N/m$$

100. B   This is an example of an application question. The Laplace's law, as discussed in the passage, is being applied to the conditions of a human heart. Again, use the formula given in the passage and solve for T: $T = P r /2$. To keep T small, you want P and r as small as possible—high blood pressure (P) and large ventricular chamber (r) are the worst combination, and the answer to this question. Note that the other choices are incorrect because their combination of (P) and (r) values leads to a lesser T value than choice B.

101. B   This is a simple calculation question. The pressure is given by $P = 2T/r$. The total pressure is P times the surface area of a sphere, $4\pi r^2$. The result is thus: Total P $= 8\pi Tr = 8\pi(8 \times 10^{-2} \, N/m)(4 \times 10^{-3} \, m) = 0.008 \, N$.

102. A   To solve this question, think about the two forces described. The two forces are the tension pulling the liquid up: $F_{up} = T(2\pi r)$, and the weight of a column of liquid pulling down, $F_{down} = mg = dVg = d(h\pi r^2)g$. Set these equations equal and solve for h. Solving, $T(2\pi r) = d(h\pi r^2)g$, for h gives answer A, $h = 2T/rdg$.

103. D   This is a data interpretation question. Look at the table carefully. Notice that as the temperature increases, the surface tension decreases. At higher temperature, because of the increased random motion of the molecules, molecules are further apart and have decreased intermolecular forces. This is the best explanation. Density may change with temperature, but not to the extent found in the table (answer A). Vapor pressure actually increases with temperature (answer B). There should not be as large a change in the surface area of the boundary as noticed in the table (answer C).

This is a problem-solving passage that appears similar to a research study passage. It is primarily testing you on your understanding of Newtonian physics rather than on the quantitative results of experiments. Remember that problem-solving passages are generally straightforward, and require less interpretation and struggle than other types of passages. Most of the questions are either conceptual or simple calculation types.

104. A   This is a conceptual question. Air resistance creates a force resisting the gravitational force attracting objects to the bottom of the container. The paper has a greater surface area than the coin for air resistance to act on; thus, the coin strikes first.

105. C This is the second conceptual question in this passage series. Recall that in a vacuum, gravitational acceleration is the same for all falling objects no matter what their size, weight, and composition.

106. A A third conceptual question is posed. Remember that gravitational acceleration is constant and does not change as objects fall. However, speed does change as an object falls.

107. B This is a simple calculation question. To find the time required to strike the ground, use the key kinematic equation: $y - y_o = (v_o)(t) - 0.5(g)(t^2)$. This becomes:

$$(0\text{ m} - 0.5\text{ m}) = (0)(t) - 0.5(10)(t^2)$$
$$t^2 = 0.1$$
$$t = 0.32\text{ sec.}$$

108. D This conceptual question tests your understanding of basic energy and momentum principles. Kinetic energy $= \frac{1}{2}mv^2$, and requires a positive velocity to have a positive value. Potential energy $= mgh$, and may have a positive value at rest. Both momentum and impulse require a positive velocity vector to have positive values. Momentum $= mv$ and Impulse $= Ft = \Delta mv$.

PASSAGE VIII

This is a research study passage (general chemistry) that tests your ability to follow and **compare** two different experimental methods. The questions are entirely conceptual and based on the meaning of experimental steps and procedures. Outlining the methods in the margin of the passage helps you keep the steps in mind.

109. C This question is testing your understanding of the described experimental methods. Evaluate the two methods carefully. Because the samples were checked to see that they had reached a constant weight, there was no effect of the drying temperature difference on the results. The hotter oven would dry the sample a little more quickly.

110. D Because the samples needed to be completely dry, water vapor from the water bath would certainly skew the results. An oven would not have this problem. Choice A is incorrect because weighings are performed at the end of the experiment. Choice B is incorrect because the exact location of the crystals in the dish is irrelevant. Choices C is incorrect because crystals on the walls of the flask would tend to produce weights less than the true value.

111. D If the water were not completely evaporated at the end of the experiment, the measured weight would be more than the actual weight. This would result in overestimation of the true value.

112. D This question asks the opposite of questions 110 and 111. You are looking for a mechanism that would explain weights less than the true value by both methods. Evaluate each choice. Choice A is incorrect because incompletely dry flasks before the trials would not change final weights. Choice B may be eliminated because incomplete evaporation of water in the oven would tend to exceed the true value. Observation of crystals on the walls of the dishes would not give weights any less than the true value. However, if crystals were observed on the walls of the flasks, these crystals would most likely not be entirely transferred to the dishes. This would result in loss of solids that should have ended up in the dishes. Missing solids would result in weights that were lower than the actual solid weights.

113. D Look carefully at the answer choices. Think about the role that water is playing in each step of method 2. Because the water in the dish is distilled water (before the removal of the glass cover), spilling some of it would have no effect on the results at all. This supports choice D. Choices A, B, and C are more likely to have an effect on the accuracy of the results because any spill or addition to the amount of sample water used would change the results.

114. B   To solve this question, refer to the experimental data. Compare runs 1 and 2. When the concentration of X doubles and Y stays the same, note that the rate of product formation quadruples. This implies that the rate with respect to X is squared. Now compare runs 1 and 3. When the concentration of X is constant and Y doubles, the rate doubles. This implies that the rate with respect to Y is to the first power. Thus, the overall reaction order is likely $2 + 1 = 3$.

115. A   To calculate the heat of formation, combine the given equations to show how the basic elements combine to form ethanol. Remember to change the sign of ΔH if you have to reverse the equation. Follow these steps:

1.   Reverse the first equation:

$$2CO_2 + 3H_2O \rightarrow C_2H_5OH + 3O_2 \qquad \Delta H = +327.0$$

2.   Multiply the second equation by three and reverse:

$$3H_2 + 3/2O_2 \rightarrow 3H_2O \qquad \Delta H = 3(-68.3)$$

3.   Multiply the third equation by two:

$$2C + 2O_2 \rightarrow 2CO_2 \qquad \Delta H = 2(-94.1)$$

Sum all the ΔH values and arrive at the heat of formation of ethanol.

$$\Delta H \text{ total} = 327 + (-204.9) + (-188.2) = -66.1 \text{ kcal/mol.}$$

116. C   The best way to solve this problem is to make up some simple numbers to plug-in. This is a very useful strategy on the MCAT. Suppose the object fell from rest at a height of 10 m. Use the kinematic equations to solve. Its final velocity would be:

$v_f^2 = v_o^2 - 2ay$
$v_f^2 = 0 \text{ m/s} - 2(10 \text{ m/s}^2)(-10 \text{ m})$
$v_f = \text{about } 14 \text{ m/s}$

If the object fell from rest only 5 m, its final velocity would be:

$v_f^2 = v_o^2 - 2ay$
$v_f^2 = 0 \text{ m/s} - 2(10 \text{ m/s}^2)(5 \text{ m})$
$v_f = \text{about } 10 \text{ m/s}$

The ratio of $10/14 = 0.71$.

117. B   The elements at the bottom of the periodic table have low ionization energies because they are shielded from the positive charge of the nucleus, and these elements have large atomic radii. The farther the electrons are from the nucleus, the easier it is for the outer electrons to be lost.

118. B   When a solute is added to a pure solvent, the boiling point of the solvent is elevated. The boiling point elevation equation is: $\Delta T_b = ik_bm$, where i is the number of particles into which the solute dissociates when dissolved in solvent, k_b is a constant, and m is molality. The i value for NaCl is two because this salt dissociates completely. The molality of NaCl is moles per kilogram of water. Find the number of moles per kilogram: (2 g/100 g water)(59 g/mol)(1000 g/kg) = 0.34 mol/kg. Thus, $\Delta T_b = (2)(0.52)(0.34) = 0.36°C$. The boiling point is then $100°C + 0.36°C = 100.36°C$.

89

This is a challenging information presentation passage (physics). The passage introduces a device known as a galvanometer. The device is described and presented in a way so as to test your understanding of electromagnetism. A diagram and equation are presented. Half the questions are calculation-based and the other half are conceptual in nature.

119. D Start by thinking about how to find torque. Recall that torque equals force times lever arm. The force on one side of the loop is given by F = B I L. In this case, you have F = (0.3 T)(0.001 A)(40)(0.015 m). Next, you should consider that there are two forces (one from either side of the loop). Also note that the lever arm is 0.01 m. Thus, T = (0.3 T)(0.001 A)(40)(0.015 m)(2)(0.01 m) = 3.6×10^{-6} N m.

120. B You are being asked to find the resistance associated with a given voltage and current. Remember Ohm's law? V = IR. You want a current of 1 mA to coincide with 1 V, so R = V/I = 1000 Ω.

121. A This conceptual question requires that you understand the passage description of how a galvanometer works. Use the process of elimination to evaluate each possible answer choice. A bent pointer could give readings too high or too low, so choice B can be eliminated. Choices C and D may be eliminated because the formula given in the passage supports that a decreased current or magnetic field will give reduced restoring forces a low reading. Choice A is the remaining choice, and the best answer to this question. An overstretched coil spring will not have the restoring force of a healthy spring, so the pointer should deflect too much.

122. B Recall that a higher spring constant means a stiffer spring. Using a high spring constant would make it more difficult, i.e., take more force and more current, to give a full-scale deflection. Choices A, C, and D describe ways to make a more sensitive galvanometer; more turns, a higher B field, or longer loops are all ways to make a more sensitive galvanometer.

123. C Use the equation given in the passage:

F = BIL. In this case, we have
F = (0.3 T)(0.00025 A)(40)(0.015 m) = 0.000045 N

124. B In question 120, a description of a shunt resistor is given. A shunt resistor can be used to determine the voltage range, and can be switched externally. The question asks you which option would be the easiest way to change the voltage range. It makes sense that an external switching from a shunt resistor would be an easier way to change the voltage range than having to manipulate the internal components of the galvanometer. Note that the other answers (pointer, magnetic field, number of coil turns) are all structures deep inside the galvanometer itself.

This is a problem-solving passage (general chemistry) that covers the topic of salts and precipitation reactions. A table is presented that shows various cation groups, reagents, and precipitation products. Most of the questions are answered easily by looking at trends and products shown on the table. Several basic conceptual questions are also asked.

125. B This question only requires that you refer to the table and interpret the meanings of the data presented. Notice that Cd^{2+} is a group 2 cation. Look at the reagent given for Cd^{2+} (H_2S). Also note the insoluble compound produced (CdS). Thus, Cd^{2+} is precipitated with H_2S to form CdS.

126. A In an acid solution, the concentration of sulfide would be very low. The only sulfides that would precipitate under these conditions are very insoluble and have very low K_{sp} values. This means that the group 2 sulfides are less soluble than the sulfides of groups 3 through 5.

127. D Changes in concentrations do not affect the value of equilibrium constants, so choices A and B can be ruled out on this basis. The hydronium ions from the hydrogen sulfide appear on the right side of the equation determined in question 125. Any reagent reacting with a product will pull the equilibrium forming that product to the right. This is an example of Le Chatelier's principle at work.

128. **C** Because the concentrations of the sulfide and hydroxide are unknown, the best answer is to conclude that the hydroxide must be less soluble (and have a lower K_{sp}). It is possible to precipitate a compound with a higher K_{sp} if the concentrations of the ions involved are high enough, but generally, the least soluble compounds are the ones that precipitate.

129. **A** The wording of the choices gives you clues here. Notice that choice A uses the word "generally." This is supported by the table. The table shows that only three of the chloride cations precipitate as the chloride salts. Many other chloride salts are soluble. Thus, choice A is a true statement. Now look at the other choices. Choice B is emphatic and not supported by data in the passage. Choice C is not supported by data in the table. Choice D is an incorrect statement.

130. **B** Because the identification of ions present is not quantitative, the group 1 ions could be correctly identified without precipitating 100% of the group 1 ions present. Any group 1 ions remaining in solution would precipitate on addition of hydrogen sulfide. This would lead to false-positive results in the group 2 cations. None of the group 1 cations would remain when the group 3 cations precipitate, so all the errors would be in the identification of the group 2 cations.

PASSAGE XI

This is a problem-solving passage (physics). In this passage set, four different containers are shown and the density values for several different fluids are presented. As with other problem-solving–type passages, the questions tend to focus on basic conceptual principles and simple calculations.

131. **D** This question tests your understanding of fluid statics. The greater the vertical distance below the surface, the greater the pressure. Container D shows point X at a greater vertical distance from the surface of the fluid than the other containers. In addition, Pascal's principle implies that the pressure at two locations on the same horizontal level below the surface of a fluid is the same in a fluid at rest. Thus, the pressure at point X in containers A, B, and C is the same.

132. **A** The upward force a submerged object experiences is equal to the weight of the fluid that the object displaces. This is known as Archimedes' principle. The buoyant force associated with this upward force = the weight of the water displaced by the object = (fluid density)(g)(volume fluid displaced).

133. **C** The pressure exerted on the sphere will be the sum of the atmospheric pressure acting on the surface of the fluid and the pressure acting on the object at a depth h below the surface. Thus, $P_B = P_{atm} + \rho gh = (10^5 \text{ Pa}) + (1000 \text{ kg/m}^2)(10 \text{ m/s}^2)(5 \text{ m}) = 1.5 \times 10^5$ Pa.

134. **C** Surface tension is defined as the force per unit length exerted on the surface layer. Cohesion, or attraction of like molecules, occurs on the surface of a liquid to create a film that minimizes surface area and potential energy. Adhesion refers to attraction of like molecules (water) to another type of molecule (glass).

135. **D** The best way to solve this problem is to think about it conceptually. The object is buoyed-up because the buoyant force trying to bring the object to the surface is greater than the object's weight. Thus, the tension can be found by subtracting the weight from the buoyant force: $T = V\rho g - mg = (10 \text{ cm}^3)(0.2 \text{ kg/cm}^3)(10 \text{ m/s}^2) - (1 \text{ kg})(10 \text{ m/s}^2) = 10$ N.

136. **C** Maximizing exposure means minimizing the fraction of the object submerged. Because the fraction submerged equals the ratio of the density of the object to that of the medium, a large medium density would tend to minimize the ratio. Glycerin has the greatest density.

137. **D** Lewis bases are electron donors. Ammonia has an unbonded pair of electrons that is attached to nitrogen. These electrons can be donated to form bonds to other compounds. Ammonia can also act as a proton acceptor. A good example is the addition of water to ammonia, which produces ammonium ion and hydroxide:

INDEPENDENT QUESTIONS

$$NH_3 + H_2O \rightarrow NH_4^+ + OH^-$$

138. D Choice A is a statement that is not true. The satellite moving at constant speed will not have a constant velocity. Remember that velocity is a vector quantity. The direction of the velocity vector is constantly changing in circular orbits. Choice B is a true statement. The satellite has a centripetal acceleration holding it in a circular orbit. This acceleration is always acting as long as the satellite orbits. Choice C is not true. If a centripetal acceleration acts on a mass, a centripetal force is produced. Thus, two of the statements are not true, making the best answer choice D.

139. D Look for an explanation that could explain why the boiling point of water is much higher than hydrogen sulfide. First, realize that oxygen is more electronegative than sulfur. This would lead to a more partial negative charge on oxygen and more partial positive charges on hydrogen in the H_2O molecule compared to the H_2S molecule. This, in turn, would lead to strong hydrogen bonds for H_2O. Choice A is not as good a choice because the molecular geometry of H_2O and H_2S is similar. Choices B and C are also incorrect choices. Van der Waals forces and London forces are temporary dipoles which affect all molecules.

140. D If an electron is captured by a nucleus, the atomic number does not increase but the atomic mass decreases by one. Recall that the atomic number of an electron is 0, while the atomic mass of the electron is given the value -1. Thus, $4 + 0 = 4$. $7 + (-1) = 6$.

141. B This question can be solved conceptually or with a calculation. Start by thinking about what is going on. By the end of the first second, the cyclist reaches a velocity of 5 m/s. If the cyclist continues to accelerate at 5 m/s per second, then by the end of the second second, the velocity will be 10 m/s. The average velocity over the 2 seconds will be (0 m/s + 10 m/s) = 5 m/s. Thus, 2 seconds are required at an average velocity of 5 m/s. If you found this confusing, feel free to calculate the answer. Use the kinematic equation relating distance, time, and acceleration to answer this question: $x = v_0 t + \frac{1}{2}^2$. Plugging in values from the question:

$$10\,m = (0\,m/s)(t) + \frac{1}{2}(5m/s^2)(t^2)$$
$$t = 2\,sec$$

142. D Bond dissociation energies can be used to find the energy change associated with a reaction. Recall that ΔH rxn = Σ bond energy broken bonds $-$ Σ bond energy formed bonds = $[2(490) + 4(420)] - [2(720) + 4(460)] = -620$ kJ/mole. This corresponds to choice D. The negative sign suggests that the reaction is exothermic.

Biological Sciences

PASSAGE I

This passage (biology) describes the basics of the drug-receptor theory. Many students find this passage challenging. You are not expected to know anything specific about this topic, but you do need to understand receptor–ligand binding and the terminology explained in the passage. The questions determine if you can apply several terms (potency, efficacy) correctly to answer questions. You must also understand the plot that accompanies the passage. Many of the questions can be answered by applying information from the passage to the questions.

143. D If you skimmed the question stems before reading the passage, the answer to this question will "pop out" at you when you read the first paragraph. The answer is stated directly in the last sentence of the first paragraph. Choices B and C were placed by the author to mislead you. They are not supported by the passage. Because of the uncertainty regarding the membrane hypothesis described in the passage, choice A is not totally unreasonable, and is an attractive choice. However, choice D is the best choice based on the wording in the last sentence of the first paragraph.

144. B This question requires some knowledge not found in the passage. This is why you have to review biology in your MCAT preparation. Transcription creates RNA which is translated into proteins. The question stem states that steroids bind to intracellular protein receptors. Inhibiting this process will eliminate the receptor for steroids and therefore decrease the effects of steroids. Choice D is incorrect because if there is less intracellular receptor for steroids, there is no mechanism for a transitory increase in steroid drug effect.

145. C Use the process of elimination to solve this problem. In the passage it is stated that drug-receptor theory draws on enzyme kinetics. Choice B describes one way of forming the drug–receptor complex. Therefore, this is identity, not analogy. Choice D is incorrect because V_{max} is analogous to efficacy, not drug–receptor complex formation. The hard part is choosing between choices C and A. Choosing C over A requires remembering that in order for an enzyme to have a biological effect, the substrate must bind to the active site. Similarly, a drug binds in order to exert a biological effect.

146. B The graph shows a different maximal response for drugs A and B. The height of the curves—synonymous with maximal response—reflects efficacy, which clearly differs between drugs A and B. Potency is best expressed by the EC_{50}. Drugs A and B achieve 50% of their maximal response at almost an identical point on the x-axis; therefore, they have the same potency.

147. B The passage states in the last sentence of the final paragraph that the EC_{50} is a concentration. Looking at the curve given with the passage, notice that concentration is plotted on the x-axis of the CE curve. This supports choice B. Choice A is incorrect. Although it is necessary to use the y-axis to find the EC_{50}, it does not define the EC_{50}. Choice D is incorrect because the height of the curve is based on the y-axis. Choice C is incorrect because the slope is dependent on both the x-axis and the y-axis.

148. D This is an evaluation-type question. Although these are not as common as some of the other question types, it is important to have experience evaluating arguments. Look at each statement and decide whether or not it is true. If you can find the three true statements, you will know which must be false. Choices A and B follow directly from the definitions of potency and efficacy. Choice C is a safe deduction based on what is stated in the passage. Choice D is a false statement and the answer to this question because nowhere in the passage is a statement made relating potency and efficacy to one another; they are defined independently.

149. D This question requires that you relate definitions given in the passage to findings on the drug curves. Use the process of elimination to evaluate the merit of each choice. When drugs have different efficacies (different heights of the CE curves), the less efficacious drugs (lower maximum response) are partial agonists. This was defined in the passage. Choices A through C are incorrect. Drug D is more potent (lower EC_{50}) than drug C despite C's greater efficacy. Drug A elicits a greater maximal response than drug D, which makes drug A more efficacious than D. Drugs A and C yield the same maximum, and are therefore equally efficacious.

PASSAGE II

This is a problem-solving passage (organic chemistry) that tests your understanding of electrophilic aromatic substitutions. The passage gives you some important clues because it shows the reaction mechanism of a Friedel-Crafts reaction; this is an example of electrophilic aromatic substitution. An important trend for these reactions is described in the second paragraph, and the results of various Friedel-Crafts reactions are shown in the table. Most of the questions require that you understand the mechanism shown and can make inferences from the data table. In addition, you are expected to know the basics of organic chemistry.

150. A Much information can be drawn from the table. Examination of the table should help you predict that methylbenzene will produce a paradisubstituted product. This alone allows you to eliminate choices B, C, and D, which show either meta-substituted or orthosubstituted products. The exact solution to this question may be surprising unless you examined the mechanism carefully while reading the passage. The mechanism involves a carbocation intermediate, and carbocation in-

93

termediates can rearrange if a more stable carbocation is possible. The re-arrangement that occurs when propyl chloride is the source of the carbocation is:

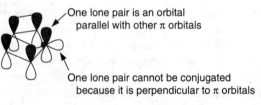

This explains the isopropyl structure in choice A.

151. C   In the first paragraph, the passage states that aromatic systems tend to undergo reactions that regenerate aromaticity. Also remember that aromatic substrates tend to be stable. Aromatic systems still react with electrophiles (by electrophilic aromatic substitution rather than electrophilic addition). Thus, choice A is incorrect. Choice B is incorrect because aromatic substrates are not more reactive toward nucleophiles than nonaromatic substrates. Choice D can be eliminated because aromatic substrates are not generally unstable.

152. C   Structure C best shows that one resonance form representing the intermediate of electrophilic attack on nitrobenzene at the para position places two positively charged atoms immediately adjacent to each other. Because like charges repel, this makes the intermediate extremely unstable and disfavored.

153. B   This question requires that you integrate information presented in the passage with data provided in the table. The passage describes a deactivated aromatic system as one that reacts slower than benzene. The second entry in the table has a smaller rate than benzene (the first entry in the table), so it is therefore a deactivated substrate.

154. A   All the choices are disubstituted products. Look carefully at the choices and think about which group would be present on the ring before the Friedel-Crafts reaction occurs. This group will direct the incoming group to a specific position. For the MCAT, make sure that you know which groups are activating, deactivating, and the type of directors they are (ortho, meta, para). To create paranitromethylbenzene using a Friedel-Crafts reaction (choice A), the starting material would be nitrobenzene. The nitro group would direct incoming substituents to the meta, rather than the para position. The product shown in A would not be produced in this manner. Choices B, C, and D are all possible products of the Friedel-Crafts reaction.

155. A   The passage states that aromatic systems undergo electrophilic aromatic substitution. You are looking for the compound which is aromatic. In addition, you must recall how to determine whether a compound is aromatic. To choose which substrate is aromatic, just ask the following questions:

1. Is it cyclic? (They all are.)
2. Is it planar? (They all can be.)
3. Is it conjugated? (C and D are not because they have sp^3 carbons in the ring.)
4. Does it have $4n + 2$ pi electrons?

The structure in choice B has only two double bonds and no lone pairs; thus it has 4 pi electrons. There is no integer value for n that can make $4n + 2 = 4$. The structure in choice A has two double bonds. The oxygen has two lone pairs, only one of which can be counted because the other is not conjugated with the pi system. The conjugated p-orbitals are perpendicular to the ring system, but only one lone pair can be in this space. Thus, there are 6 pi electrons. $4(1) + 2 = 6$ so the system is aromatic.

One lone pair is an orbital parallel with other π orbitals

One lone pair cannot be conjugated because it is perpendicular to π orbitals

This is an information presentation passage (biology) that covers several topics in physiology and contains a data plot. The passage is very descriptive, and reviews hepatic blood flow and liver disease. In addition, you are given information about the circulation of bilirubin and the bilirubin levels of some patients. The MCAT does expect you to know about basic liver structure and function, yet not the detail described in this passage. This is why the passage explains so much. . . . it is providing you some of the information you need to answer questions.

156. C As mentioned in the passage, blood from the gastrointestinal system goes to the liver before going to the rest of the body. This setup allows the liver to inactivate the majority of orally administered propranolol before the rest of the body "sees" it. This concept, known as first pass effect, explains why choices A and B are incorrect. Choice B, although not technically an oral administration, is essentially the second stage of oral administration. Once in the portal vein, the drug would be directly inactivated by the liver. Choice C would give higher levels because an arm vein is part of systemic circulation and therefore does not go directly to the liver. Choice D is incorrect because choice C would give a higher systemic blood level than choice A or B.

157. D This question is straight recall from the second sentence of the second paragraph, and will help you to assess how effectively you are identifying or retaining definitions and names. Choice B is incorrect because bilirubin is mentioned in the passage as a heme catabolite. Choice C is a nonsense term and is not described in the passage. Choice A is the attractive choice. Although the passage describes that ligandins are proteins found in liver cells, the passage never uses the term hepatic proteins. This is a very vague, descriptive term.

158. A This question depends on your recall of vascular pathways and the ability to infer from the passage. Blood leaving the liver, as stated in the passage, enters the systemic circulation via the vena cava. Blood in the vena cava enters the right side of the heart, followed by the pulmonary system. From the lungs, blood enters the left side of the heart, finally traveling out the aorta to the rest of the body. When liver function is the concern, the site of increased resistance that is closest to the liver will have the more immediate effect. Therefore, right-sided heart failure can easily impair flow through the liver.

159. C You are asked to compare the four patients. The only place where data are given for the patients is in the graph. Go right to the graph and look for a way to compare the patients. The graph plots bilirubin concentration for each patient. Ask yourself what the link is between destruction of red blood cells (RBCs) and bilirubin. Remember that RBCs contain hemoglobin which breaks down into bilirubin when metabolized. Thus, you would expect that the patient who has the highest bilirubin concentration would have the most problem with RBC destruction.

160. A Nutrient-laden blood enters fetal circulation through the umbilical vein. Because these nutrients do not need detoxifying, this blood can bypass the liver. The ductus venosus—a connection between the umbilical vein and the vena cava—accomplishes this for the fetus. The ductus arteriosus connects the pulmonary artery to the aorta, allowing blood to bypass the lungs. Choice C, the foramen magnum, is a distractor; it is a large opening in the base of the skull through which the brain stem protrudes. The foramen ovale connects the right and left atria, allowing blood to bypass the right heart and therefore lungs of the fetus.

Air samples are collected in an apparatus and subjected to gas chromatography. You are then given a chromatogram and standard curves for two compounds. The questions that follow the passage ask you to interpret both experimental techniques and results. In addition, you are expected to be able to work with the graphs conceptually and mathematically.

161. D The pump pulling less air than expected would result in less styrene from the air collecting in the tube. The amount analyzed would be less than the amount actually present and the actual amount would be underestimated. The addition of more styrene than measured to the standards would result in a larger peak, so by comparison, the peaks in the unknown samples would be smaller than needed to get an accurate concentration. This would also result in underestimation of the amount of styrene present. This reasoning best supports choice D.

162. B Use the process of elimination to arrive at the best answer. The passage mentioned that this chromatogram was from an air sample from a polystyrene plant. It is certainly possible, and likely, that other compounds were present in the air. If the air sample contained only two pure substances, you would expect two peaks. Choices A and C are possible explanations, but there is no information in the passage to suggest that these compounds are unstable. Also note that choices A and C would each pose a plausible explanation for the finding and it would be difficult to know which was better between these choices. If you see this type of situation on the MCAT, chances are that both choices are incorrect responses. Choice D is unlikely because the passage does not discuss reactivity. In addition, if reaction occurred for both styrene and butadiene, it would be likely that more than three different products would be formed.

163. A A shorter retention time in the column would suggest that attractive forces holding the compound of interest in the column are minimized. Without even knowing the structures of butadiene and styrene, the most reasonable answer to choose would take into account that the faster moving compound has fewer attractions to the column coating. The first three choices (A, B, and C), indicate this type of interaction. Thus, eliminate choice D. How do you determine which is best among choices A, B, and C? Notice that choices B and C require that you know about the polarity of the column. Columns can be polar or nonpolar. Without knowing whether the column was polar or not (and the passage would have given this information if it were important), you have no way to discriminate between B and C. Choice A is independent of column polarity, and is supported by the last sentence of the passage, which indicates that butadiene is smaller than styrene.

164. B This is a simple data interpretation question. The standard curve on the left belongs to butadiene and a retention time of 3.2 minutes is given. A response of 7 corresponds to a concentration of 1.5 mol/L. The standard curve on the right belongs to styrene and a retention time of 6.1 minutes is given. A response of 8 corresponds to a concentration of 2.5 mol/L.

165. D Choice A is incorrect because extraction does not require air volume measurements. Analysis by gas chromatography does not require that air volumes be known, so eliminate choice B. The standard curves plot concentration versus response, and can be generated without knowing an air volume. However, the volume of air is needed so the amount determined in the tube can be converted to an air concentration (units on concentration are amount/volume).

INDEPENDENT QUESTIONS

166. C Alcohols form strong hydrogen bonds (H-bonds) with one another. To boil a liquid, the vapor pressure must be increased to atmospheric pressure. To accomplish this increase, the liquid must be volatilized; i.e., the hydrogen bonds must be broken. Although H-bonds are generally considered relatively weak, a large amount of them connect alcohol molecules, and together, they represent an attractive force that results in higher boiling points.

167. A This question tests your understanding of dihybrid crosses. The gametes produced by two dihybrid parents will occur in a classic phenotypic dihybrid ratio of $9:3:3:1$. This means that 9/16 of the offspring will have both genes in the dominant form phenotypically, 3/16 of the offspring will have the first gene dominant and the second gene recessive, 3/16 of the offspring will have the second gene dominant and the first gene recessive, and 1/16 of the offspring will have both genes recessive. If the horned form is dominant and short hair is dominant, 9/16 of the gametes (offspring) should have horns and short hair, 3/16 horns and long hair, 3/16 hornless and short hair, and 1/16 hornless and long hair. Look at each of the answer choices. Based on the discussion given above, only choice A gives the correct ratio.

168. **D**   The double bond tends to be electron-rich and attract electrophiles (electron-seeking molecules and ions). Because of their electron-rich character and ability to spread out charge, double bonds can stabilize carbonium ions or free radicals on adjacent carbons. This stabilization occurs via resonance in which the p-orbital of the carbonium or free radical is lined up with the π-bond of the double bond. Choices A, B, and C all accurately describe carbon–carbon double bonds.

169. **B**   The blockage of bile flow will interfere with bile release into the intestinal tract. Bile is released into the duodenum of the small intestine. Bile acts to emulsify fats and aid in their absorption. In addition, bile helps with the absorption of fat-soluble vitamins. Protein absorption does not depend on bile. Proteins are absorbed after enzymatic degradation. The key enzymes involved in protein degradation include trypsin, chymotrypsin, and pepsin. Carbohydrates are also enzymatically broken down. Key carbohydrate degradation enzymes include salivary amylase and pancreatic amylase.

This is a research study passage (biology). The passage starts by giving you an overview of the physiological effects of cardiovascular exercise. Next, you are given the details of a research study. A table is presented showing the effect of exercise on sedentary versus exercising men for a number of variables. Two questions test your knowledge of muscle and nerve tissue. Two additional questions ask you to interpret the results of the study. A final question asks you to manipulate data found in the table.

170. **D**   The passage states that the resting metabolic rate was greater in exercising men than in sedentary men. If muscle samples were evaluated at the microscopic level, you should expect that the muscle samples from exercising men have more mitochondria. As you recall, mitochondria are the organelles of aerobic respiration. The other choices are easy to eliminate. Choice A, or Golgi apparatus, is an intracellular organelle involved with packaging and glycosylating proteins. Lysosomes are involved in enzymatic degradation of intracellular waste and foreign matter. The smooth endoplasmic reticulum plays a role in hydroxylation, detoxification, and steroid synthesis.

171. **B**   Choice A is a false statement. The table displays a reduction in maximal heart rate of about 5 beats per minute for exercising men. Thus, it appears that the exercise schedule used was effective in decreasing the maximum heart rate. Do not become confused and compare maximal heart rates of exercising men to those of sedentary men. This is not what the answer choice is asking you to evaluate. Choice C is false. The maximum oxygen consumption increased: $(2.60 - 2.36) =$ 0.24 L/min or 14.4 L/hr. Choice D cannot be confirmed by the passage. There is no information given about heart rates in general, or heart volumes. Choice B is true. Cholesterol levels increased in both exercising and sedentary men.

172. **C**   This question is asking you to make a generalization about the implications of the study. You must decide whether or not the study has a link to longevity. Is there a positive or negative correlation to longevity shown? No. There is no mention of longevity for either the exercising or sedentary men. The only mention of age in the passage is that of the age of the volunteers at the beginning of the study (range, 60 to 65 years). Thus, the results of the study neither support nor refute the contention that exercise programs may prolong longevity.

173. **D**   This is a knowledge-based question that does not appear directly linked to information given in the passage. The SA node acts to slow the heart rate through its release of acetylcholine. Remember that the parasympathetic nervous system uses acetylcholine as both its preganglionic and postganglionic (target tissue) neurotransmitter. The sympathetic nervous system uses acetylcholine in its ganglionic synapse, and norepinephrine at its postganglionic synapse (at the target tissue). Epinephrine is a hormone released by the adrenal medulla in times of acute stress. Dopamine is an important neurotransmitter in the brain.

174. D   The passage states that exercising men had an increase in metabolic rate. As you recall, the metabolic rate is increased primarily by increased levels of thyroid hormone. If the level of thyroid hormone increases, by a negative feedback mechanism at the hypothalamic–pituitary level, the thyroid hormone decreases the release of thyroid-stimulating hormone (TSH). The remaining choices have little relationship to any data given in the passage. Cortisol is a steroid hormone produced by the adrenal cortex, which mediates long-term stress. It also increases blood sugar levels. Epinephrine is a hormone produced by the adrenal medulla, which helps mediate acute stress. It increases blood sugar levels and heart rate. The growth hormone is mainly responsible for growth during childhood and adolescence.

175. C   Maximum oxygen consumption for exercising men at baseline: 2.36 L/min. Maximum oxygen consumption for exercising men after exercise: 2.60 L/min. % increase = (final value − original value)/(original value) = (2.60 − 2.36)/(2.36) = 0.10 = 10%.

PASSAGE VI

176. B S_N2 stands for substitution nucleophilic bimolecular. The reaction shown is a substitution reaction (the DNA chain substitutes for the diphosphate leaving group). The reaction is also nucleophilic (the electrons on the oxygen of the OH attack the phosphorus atom). Finally, the reaction is also bimolecular (two molecules involved) as described in the passage.

177. D   Think about the chemistry behind the action of azidothymidine (AZT). AZT has an azido group rather than an OH group in the position which acts as a nucleophile. The nitrogens of an azido group are not nucleophilic. Once AZT is incorporated into the DNA chain, no other nucleotides can be added. This results in premature termination of the transcription.

178. D   Look carefully at the mechanism shown in the passage. The mechanism shows one phosphate under attack by the nucleophile, and the other two phosphates coming off of the substrate. In other words, the two phosphates act as a leaving group.

179. B   Carbohydrates in cyclic structures are described as either furanoses (five-membered rings) or pyranoses (six-membered rings). The position of the anomeric substituent (usually drawn at the position to the right of the oxygen in the ring) must also be described. Alpha is used to describe when this substituent is drawn down, and beta is used when this substituent is drawn up. Notice that in the carbohydrate ring, the anomeric carbon (the carbon to the right of the oxygen on the ring) has its substituent drawn in the up position. Thus, this is a beta furanose.

180. B   The passage states that reverse transcriptase is found in retroviruses. From your studies of biology, you should be aware that humans do not have a reverse transcriptase. This is an enzyme that allows the virus to create DNA from RNA. This fact makes the enzyme an attractive target for therapy. This makes choice B a reasonable choice. Now evaluate the other choices. Choice A is not supported by the passage. Also note that it is an emphatic statement, and these are rarely correct in the biological sciences. This is because emphatic statements require only one exception in order to contradict them. Choice C is also not supported by data in the passage. There is no information given on AZT synthesis. Choice D is the attractive (tricky, but not the best) choice. This is a true statement, but it does not answer the question being asked very well. The question asks why inhibitors of reverse transcriptase are useful in treatment. The question does not ask why reverse transcriptase is important to retroviruses.

PASSAGE VII

This passage is an information presentation passage (biology). The passage presents information on Parkinson's disease (PD), and describes the disease process at a level that you should understand based on your biology knowledge. Neurons, neurotransmitters, enzymes, and mental diseases are described. The passage contains primarily information recall and application-type questions. A conceptual question in genetics is also given. Previewing the question stems is very helpful in a passage like this. You will be able to find the answers to questions quickly if you have an idea what the questions will test you on.

181. B   This is an information recall question which is best solved by eliminating choices that are described in the passage to be related to basal ganglia dysfunction. Epilepsy is the only choice not mentioned in the passage as being associated with basal ganglia dysfunction. This supports choice B. Epilepsy is generally thought of as a cerebral cortex abnormality. Huntington's disease, schizophrenia, and PD all share some form of basal ganglia dysfunction.

182. C   As mentioned in the passage, levodopa (L-dopa), the precursor to dopamine, is converted, in both the central nervous system (CNS) and periphery, to dopamine. Peripheral dopamine formation is thought to be responsible for adverse effects of L-dopa such as nausea, vomiting, hypotension, and arrhythmia. This information is given in the second paragraph. Choice A is incorrect because this is how the nausea problem can be avoided, not caused. Choice B is incorrect because excess peripheral dopamine is at fault. Choice D is a finding of PD, not a treatment artifact.

183. C   This answer requires understanding the new information presented in the question—dopamine blocks prolactin release—as well as remembering a fact from the passage—antipsychotics are dopamine blockers. Treatment with dopamine blockers disinhibits prolactin release, bringing about an increase in milk production. This best supports choice C. With this reasoning, it is easy to eliminate choices A, B, and D.

184. C   Carbidopa's mechanism of action, blockade of peripheral dopa decarboxylase, is defined in the passage. Dopa decarboxylase converts L-dopa to dopamine. If L-dopa is given alone, the majority is converted to dopamine in the periphery rather than the CNS. When carbidopa is given simultaneously, peripheral conversion of L-dopa is blocked, allowing for most of the L-dopa to reach the CNS where it is converted to dopamine. Choice A is the incorrect site for carbidopa. Choice B describes the problem that carbidopa solves. Choice D defines L-dopa.

185. D   The passage states that the goal of PD drug therapy is to restore dopamine levels in the brain. Choice D is the only drug that does not increase dopamine neurotransmission. Choices A through C are all used in PD. Choice D is a routinely used antipsychotic medication.

186. C   The best way to solve a simple genetic cross-type question is to draw a 2×2 Punnett square. If P is the gene for this form of PD, and p is the normal gene, then each parent is Pp. A cross between two Pp genotypes yields ¼ PP, ½ Pp, ¼ pp. Both the PP and Pp genotypes will be likely to develop the disease. Adding the PP and Pp fractions together gives ¾. The Punnett square showing the parental gametes (in bold) and the net results of the crosses is shown below:

	P	**p**
P	PP	Pp
p	Pp	pp

This is an information-presentation passage (organic chemistry) that describes a specific type of catalyst. The questions that follow the passage require that you understand the structure and function of this catalyst, and types of reactions in which this catalyst is involved. Most of the questions are problem-solving and conceptual questions that do require a small amount of information from the passage itself.

PASSAGE VIII

187. C   Answering this question correctly requires that you read the passage carefully. Also, use the process of elimination to arrive at the best answer. You are not expected to predict reaction products of the answer choices. The passage discusses

99

the difficulty in performing reactions between inorganic salts and organic compounds. The answer choices test whether you can recognize which compounds listed are inorganic salts and organic compounds. Those choices that do not contain the correct combination of reactants will not best show a reaction which would require a phase-transfer catalyst. Choices A and D are incorrect because ethyl magnesium bromide and sodium ethoxide are both organic salts. Choice B is incorrect because it does not involve any salts at all. Choice C is the best answer by the process of elimination. Note that choice C provides an inorganic salt (potassium permanganate) and an organic compound (ethylene).

188. **A**   This is a conceptual question testing your understanding of solubility and complex formation. A phase-transfer catalyst analogous to 18-crown-6 would have to complex a cation in the cavity of the compound. To hold the anion in place, the atoms lining the opening in the compound should be able to donate electrons (like oxygen) and should be electronegative enough to carry a partial negative charge. Choice B is incorrect because this compound does not have the capacity to complex with a cationic molecule. Choices A, C, and D differ from one another based on the identity of the atom lining the opening of the compound. Of the different atoms in the possible answers, nitrogen is the most electronegative. The most electronegative atom would most strongly complex a cation in the cavity of the compound.

189. **D**   This is a conceptual question testing your understanding of bond types. A coordinate covalent bond is a covalent bond in which both electrons come from the same atom (rather than normal covalent bonds which consist of one electron from each atom). The oxygen atoms of 18-crown-6 donate electron pairs into the cation, thus forming coordinate covalent bonds. Ionic bonds are not formed here. For ionic bonding to be occurring, electrons would be transferred from one atom to another, with a positive ion and a negative ion formed. There would be electrostatic attraction between the ions.

190. **B**   Evaluate the choices using the process of elimination. Eliminate choices that do not make sense based on your knowledge of organic chemistry, or that are not supported by the passage. Choices C and D do not make sense. You have no way to predict whether or not a compound will precipitate. Choice A may or may not be true depending on whether the organic compound is polar or nonpolar. Choice B is the most reasonable choice. Ions in aqueous solutions are surrounded by water molecules. This makes a solvent "cage" which shields the anion from surrounding molecules. This will make such reactions in water occur very slowly because the reacting species cannot easily get close to each other.

191. **C**   If you answered question number 187 correctly, you should have little difficulty with this question. To hold cations, the phase transfer catalyst needs a strong electronegative atom. Conversely, for the catalyst to hold onto an anion, the atoms lining the center of the phase transfer catalyst must be electropositive (bearing a partial positive charge). To bear a partial positive charge, the atom lining the opening must be less electronegative than carbon. Because boron is to the left of carbon in the periodic table, it is less electronegative. Choice B has no atoms to complex with the anion. Choices A and D have atoms (nitrogen, sulfur), and are more electronegative than boron.

INDEPENDENT QUESTIONS

192. **B**   It is important to know which tissue layer gives rise to which important organ or structure. Ectoderm gives rise to the nervous system, epidermis of the skin, hair, cornea and lens of the eye, adrenal medulla, and other structures. Mesoderm forms cartilage and bone, muscle, dermis and connective tissue, blood cells, heart and blood vessels, adrenal cortex, spleen, gonads, and kidneys. Endoderm forms linings of internal organs (lungs, intestines), liver, thyroid gland, pancreas, parathyroid glands, and other structures. In this question, the researcher wants to interfere with the formation of the heart. This is best accomplished during or after gastrulation, such that the mesodermal germ layer is affected. Specifically

blocking mesodermal differentiation will best interfere with formation of the heart. This is supported by the action of drug B.

193. B Acidity is enhanced when the conjugate base is further stabilized. By placing an electron-withdrawing group on the ring, the phenoxide is further stabilized when the charge spreads over more atoms (greater delocalization). The methoxy group is electron-inducing and destabilizes the phenoxide.

194. C Osteoblasts are bone forming cells. As osteoblasts secrete bone matrix, they become trapped in the bone substance. Once trapped in bone matrix, osteoblasts are known as osteocytes. The role of osteocytes is to maintain the bone matrix. Osteoclasts are bone-resorbing cells. Bone is not converted into cartilage. However, in early formation of the skeleton, cartilage may serve as a skeletal framework and can be resorbed and replaced with bone matrix. This process is known as endochondral bone formation.

195. D Glycolysis occurs in the cytoplasm of eukaryotic cells. Oxidative phosphorylation, the Krebs cycle, and electron transport all occur in the mitochondria of eukaryotic cells. Specifically, the Krebs cycle occurs in the mitochondrial matrix. Oxidative phosphorylation and electron transport occur on the inner mitochondrial membrane.

196. D The numbering of the substituents on the benzene ring is done to produce the smallest total. Therefore, number from the ethyl group toward the nitro group. List the substituents in alphabetic order.

This passage covers topics in evolution and behavior. You are given extensive introductory information about different types of mimicry. Whenever the MCAT gives you such a detailed description of related terms (in this passage, different types of mimicry), you can bet that a series of questions will follow the passage, testing your ability to discriminate among the terms. The passage also presents an experiment in which a species of moth was studied. A data table provides an overview of the experimental results. The questions require that you recall and use the terminology described, as well as interpret the results of the experiment.

197. C This is a very straightforward information recall question. The answer is directly stated in the first paragraph. The passage states that aposematic mimicry refers to a situation in which a toxic organism advertises its poisonousness. None of the other choices describe the type of mimicry given in the question stem as well as choice C.

198. A Batesian mimicry is defined in the passage as protective mimicry that is aposematic. The day-moth that is painted to resemble a toxic swallowtail is an appropriate example. Choice B is a broad concept that may be applicable in this case if it were not a manmade contrivance. Choice C is not described in the passage. Recall that commensalism occurs when there is a relationship between two species in which one species benefits and the other neither benefits nor is adversely effected. Choice D is incorrect because aggressive mimicry requires some malicious act on the part of the mimic. This is not the case here, as the mimic's "act" is merely to prolong its survival.

199. D Refer to the section of the passage that describes the behavior of this species. Note that the passage describes that *Aspidontus* mimics, then bites and feeds from *Labroides*. Use the process of elimination to choose the best description of this relationship. Based on the descriptions given in the first paragraph, aggressive mimicry (choice D) best describes the relationship between these two species.

200. A This is a data interpretation question. These questions are common in research study passages. Start by evaluating the data table. Note that the group of moths painted to resemble *B. philenor* was recaptured in higher numbers than those resembling the tiger swallowtail. This implies greater survival for *B. philenor* versus the tiger swallowtail. This supports choice A. Eliminate choices C and D. Statistical significance by day 1 is not pertinent to the question. Aggressive mimicry is not an appropriate description of this experiment; protective mimicry is exemplified by the release–recapture experiment.

201. A   This question requires some careful thought. Ask yourself, "What is the difference between choices A and B?" Note that choice A describes a permutation caused by the researchers. Choice B may describe a result of the differences between the moth groups. Any conclusions regarding survival based on the release–recapture experiment are not valid if experimental methods rather than natural forces influence the organism's behavior. If one group's ability to fly was diminished by painting, then the number recaptured would have been adversely affected by the experiment and may not necessarily represent the number that survived. This may prevent any conclusion regarding survival. Choice B is not correct because such an influence is precisely what the experiment is looking to discover.

202. B   Fitness refers to the inherited—not acquired—traits that make an organism more or less well-suited to its environment. A profound environmental factor for these mice is the presence of the cat. Resemblance to a cat is an ideal way to increase fitness for such a mouse. Speciation (choice A) is the formation of a new species from a previously existing species. Different species, by definition, cannot produce fertile offspring. Only if this cat–mouse were unable to breed with other mice would speciation have occurred. Choice C is nonsensical. Choice D is incorrect because this is protective mimicry.

203. C   To solve this question, refer back to the first paragraph. Müllerian mimicry occurs when the model and mimic are both distasteful to predators. This is consistent with the question stem posed. Now, look at the other choices. Choice B is incorrect because the question stem does not say that the mimic benefits at the expense of the model. Protective mimicry occurs when an edible organism mimics a distasteful one. This is contradictory to the question which says that both species of butterflies are distasteful to birds. Choice A is also incorrect because protective mimicry does not occur and the question does not suggest that there is an aposematic mimic. Both of these must be present for batesian mimicry to occur.

PASSAGE X

This passage presents an overview of a microbiological disease (syphilis). You are told about the organism responsible for the disease as well as the natural history of the disease. Various tests are also discussed and a data table is presented. These question types emphasize information recall, data interpretation, and conceptual question types.

204. C   The passage states that the organism responsible for syphilis is a spirochete. From your review of biology, you should know that a spirochete has a corkscrew shape. Round or spherical bacteria are cocci. Rod-shaped bacteria are just known as rods. There are no common bacteria which are cylindrically shaped.

205. C   Only light that hits the object makes it to the eye. This configuration afforded by the special substage condenser results in a light object and a dark background. Light microscopy presents the opposite situation (choice A). Choice B is meant to confuse you because it does not follow from anything discussed in the passage, though it is not necessarily an impossibility. Choice D is a false assumption based on the converse, which is true: *T. pallidum* is not visible through light microscopy but it is visible through darkfield microscopy.

206. D   This is an application question in which you have to apply information given in the passage to a specific situation. Solve this question by eliminating conditions that are possible for the situation described. This man has no symptoms of syphilis. He could be latent or a false positive, so eliminate choices A and B. A *T. pallidum* hemagglutination assay (TPHA) test could differentiate between the two (choices A and B). Lyme disease is listed as one of the many causes of positive nontreponemal tests, so eliminate choice C. Tertiary syphilis has characteristic CNS and cardiovascular symptoms, so choice D is an incorrect statement and the answer to this question.

207. B   Solve this question by evaluating each choice based on its own merit. Choice A is backwards—a positive Venereal Disease Research Laboratory test (VDRL) and a negative TPHA is the common false-positive due to lack of specificity of nontreponemal tests. Cardiolipin is not a treponemal antigen, as stated by the passage. From your biology knowledge, you must know that antigens are proteins frequently found on the surface of bacteria. Choice D is wrong because the table shows TPHA giving a positive result in only 65% of 1° syphilis patients. This is lower than the other two. Choice B is the most reasonable choice. Forty percent of cases progress to tertiary syphilis; therefore 60% do not progress beyond primary or secondary syphilis.

208. **D** Look carefully at the data table. There is a precipitous decrease in percentage of positive test results for the nontreponemal tests as a patient progresses from 2° to 3° syphilis. These tests measure anticardiolipin antibodies. Choices A through C are all incorrect statements. 2° syphilis gives almost 100% positive results for all tests; TPHA goes from 65% to 100% positive (1° to 2°), suggesting an increase in treponemal antibodies.

This is a problem-solving passage (organic chemistry). Although you are given some information about Grignard's reactions in the passage, you are already expected to know some things about them. A data table showing the effect of substrate selection on yield is given along with a diagram showing Grignard's reaction. Most of the questions require that you use the process of elimination carefully to arrive at the best answers. Two questions may be answered easily from information given in the passage. The other questions are based on an understanding of the mechanism responsible for Grignard's reaction.

209. **A** The answer to this question is provided in the passage. The passage specifically mentions that alcohols are obtained from aldehydes, ketones, and esters by hydrolysis (addition of water) of the salts produced after addition of Grignard's reaction.

210. **C** This question is not difficult if you carefully evaluate each choice, rather than trying to come up with the answer on your own. Look at the choices. Choice A is false. The carboxylic acid group has an electrophilic carbon. Choice B is incorrect as well. The same Grignard's reaction is used in all the reactions shown in the table. To choose between C and D, think a little about the chemistry involved. The passage states that the major drawback of reagents with nucleophilic carbon atoms is that the carbon atoms are strongly basic. Thus, any substrate with an acidic hydrogen will participate in an acid–base reaction rather than a carbon–carbon bond-forming reaction. The net result is that an acidic group like a carboxylic acid (CO_2H) will donate a proton to the basic carbon of Grignard's reaction (CH_3CH_2MgBr), resulting in a hydrocarbon (CH_3CH_3) and a salt (CO_2MgBr), but not a salt that leads to an alcohol after hydrolysis. Thus, choice C is better than choice D.

211. **A** This difficult conceptual question tests whether you understand the mechanism of the Grignard's reaction. From your review of organic chemistry, you may recall that Grignard's reagents can react with carbon dioxide to prepare carboxylic acids. Grignard's reagent allows addition of an alkyl group to the carbon-oxygen double bond of carbon dioxide. However, in this question, you are given a compound with no carbonyl group. You must decide the most likely place where Grignard's reaction will attack first. Some choices you will be able to eliminate because they do not make sense. Other choices will be either contradicted or supported based on information given in the passage. Look carefully at the possible choices. First, recall that Grignard's reagents do not attack halides, so eliminate choice B. The passage states that Grignard's reactions attack electropositive atoms. Choice D isolates oxygen, an electronegative atom. Eliminate this choice. The difficult part of this question is choosing between choices A and C. The passage states that Grignard's reagents will attack any electropositive atom. Determine which atom is more electropositive between choices A and C. The carbon outlined in choice A has its electrons "pulled" by the strongly electronegative chlorine. In addition, oxygen pulls on its electrons as well. The carbon in choice A is likely to be more electropositive than the hydrogen in choice C. The passage does indicate that Grignard's reactions do not occur to a significant extent in protic solvents. Protic

solvents include water, alcohols, and amines. Do not consider this a major issue because both choices A and C are alcohols.

212. B Choice A is a part of the mechanism for Grignard's reaction, but does nothing to explain why two Grignard's reaction molecules react. Choice C can be eliminated because it is not a correct part of the mechanism (nucleophilic attack on carbonyls results in a tetrahedral intermediate). Choice D is incorrect because it has arrows drawn in the wrong direction. Choice B is best. It shows that the OR group of the ester can be expelled. This regenerates the carbonyl, which can be attacked by a second Grignard's reaction molecule.

213. D The passage helps you out a great deal in this question. At the end of the first paragraph, the passage states that, "This explains why Grignard's reagents only produce significant yields in aprotic solvents." Remember that aprotic solvents include nonpolar solvents like chloroform and ether. Choices A, B, and C would be considered polar and protic. In addition, out of the solvents listed, only the diethyl ether has no acidic proton (the protons attached to single- and double-bonded carbon atoms are not acidic). The other choices, (A, B, and C), would all react with Grignard's reagent so quickly that the substrate would have no Grignard's reagent left to react with.

214. C Choices A, B, and D will all produce alcohols on addition of Grignard's reagent and subsequent hydrolysis. Choice C looks different from the other choices. This should indicate the possibility that this compound will behave differently than the others. This compound has an acidic hydrogen because H_2SO_3 is an acid, and so is HSO_3R, so an acid–base reaction would occur, rather than the normal Grignard's reaction attack on the carbonyl atom.

INDEPENDENT QUESTIONS

215. D Name these sugars based on the number of carbon atoms and the type of functional group each sugar contains. Glucose has six carbons and an aldehyde group in the straight-chain form. Therefore, it is considered an aldohexose. Fructose has six carbons and a ketone group, and is considered a ketohexose.

216. C The dorsal lip of the blastopore leads to the differentiation of a neural groove. Transplantation of the dorsal lip early in development will give rise to induction of an extra neural groove if the dorsal lip is placed beneath undifferentiated ectoderm. This is a classic example of tissue induction!

217. D The genetic code is considered degenerate because several different codons may code for a single amino acid. Choice A is incorrect because it transposes the relationship between codons and amino acids. Choices B and C are true statements but do not answer the question being asked.

218. A This is the E1 reaction. E1 is a two-step, unimolecular reaction. The first step involves the dissociation of the leaving group from the substrate, resulting in a carbocation intermediate. The second step involves removal of a proton by a base and the formation of a double bond. For alcohols, the E1 reaction is an acid-catalyzed dehydration reaction which proceeds through a carbocation intermediate. The alcohol is first protonated and then acts as a leaving group. Before protonation, the hydroxy group is a poor leaving group.

219. B When hydrostatic pressure increases, fluid is forced out of the capillary and into the tissue (interstitial) space. You should expect that intravascular volume will decrease and interstitial volume will increase. This best corresponds with choice B.

Verbal Reasoning

Time: 85 minutes
Questions: 1–65

Directions: There are nine reading passages in the Verbal Reasoning Test. Each passage is followed by several questions. After reading a passage, select one best answer to each question. If you are not certain of an answer, eliminate the alternatives that you know to be incorrect and then select an answer from the remaining alternatives.

Passage I (Questions 1–7)

If we consider our own country in its natural prospect, without any of the benefits and advantages of commerce, what a barren, uncomfortable place it would be. Historians of nature tell us that no fruit grew originally among us except for hips and haws, acorns and pignuts, and other delicacies of the like. Furthermore, our climate itself, without the assistance of art, can make no further advances toward a plum than to a sloe. Our melons, our peaches, our figs, our apricots, and cherries, are strangers among us, imported in different ages, and naturalized in our English gardens; and that they would all degenerate and fall away into the trash of our own country, if they were wholly neglected by the planter, and left to the mercy of our sun and soil. Nor has commerce more enriched our vegetable world, than it has improved the whole face of nature. Our ships are laden with the harvest of every climate: our tables are stored with spices, oils, and wines; our rooms are filled with Chinese ornamental treasures, and adorned with the workmanship of Japan. Our morning's draught comes to us from the remotest corners of the earth; we repair our bodies by the drugs of America, and repose ourselves under Indian canopies.

My friend Sir Andrew calls the vineyards of France our gardens; the Spice Islands our hotbeds; the Persians our silk weavers, and the Chinese our potters. Nature indeed furnishes us with the bare necessities of life, but barter and exchange give us a great variety of what is useful, and at the same time supplies us with everything that is convenient and ornamental. While we enjoy the remotest products of the North and South, we are free from those extremities of weather that give them birth; that our eyes are refreshed with the green fields of Britain, at the same time that our palates are feasted with fruits that rise between the tropics.

For these reasons, there are not more useful members in a commonwealth than merchants. They knit mankind together in a mutual web of good offices, distribute the gifts of nature, find work for the poor, distribute wealth to the rich, and give magnificence to the great. Our English merchant converts the tin of his own country into gold, and exchanges his wool for rubies. The people of India are clothed in our British manufacture, and the inhabitants of the frozen zone warmed with the fleeces of our sheep.

When I have been upon the Change, I have often fancied one of our old kings standing in person, where he is represented in effigy, and looking down upon the wealthy concourse of people with which place is everyday filled. In this case, how would he be surprised to hear all the languages of Europe spoken in this little spot of his former dominions, and to see so many private men, who in his time would have been the vassals of some powerful baron, negotiating like princes for greater sums of money than were formerly to be met with in the royal treasury!

Trade, without enlarging the British territories, has given us a kind of additional empire: it has multiplied the number of the rich, made our landed estates infinitely more valuable than they were formerly, and added to them an accession of other estates as valuable as the lands themselves.

From John Licktenstein, *Enrichment of Our World Through Barter and Exchange.* © 1997 By New World Press.

1. According to the passage, which of the following is true?

    A. Great Britain's former fertility is no longer.
    B. Trade has more than compensated for Great Britain's lack of natural resources.
    C. France is the garden of Great Britain.
    D. Great Britain acquires luxuries and conveniences from other countries in exchange for wool.

GO ON TO THE NEXT PAGE.

2. The Change could also be called:

   A. the stock exchange.
   B. the court.
   C. the New Way.
   D. the commodities exchange.

3. How would you describe the changing attitude of the author within the passage toward what he calls the barren, uncomfortable spot of earth [that] falls to our share?

   A. Dismayed to optimistic
   B. Joyful to degrading
   C. Bemused to cheerful
   D. Piteous to uplifted

4. According to the passage, which of the following statements could be made about the produce in Great Britain?

   A. It is indigenous to Great Britain.
   B. It was forced to adapt to British soil.
   C. It includes melons, peaches, figs, apricots, and cherries.
   D. It will be neglected, will degenerate, and will be left to the mercy of the soil.

5. The author of the passage might see merchants as:

   A. necessary evils.
   B. the fabric that holds economic society together.
   C. former vassals of powerful barons.
   D. of some use to the commonwealth.

6. This passage would most likely be found in which type of book?

   A. An urban planning text
   B. A sociology text
   C. A history text
   D. An accounting text

7. According to the passage, the advantages of trade do NOT include:

   I. Not having to deal with the extremities of weather
   II. The improved variety of harvest
   III. The diminished inequities between the rich and the poor
   IV. Not needing to expand the British empire

   A. I, II, and III only
   B. II, III, and IV only
   C. III and IV only
   D. I and II only

Passage II (Questions 8–12)

Innovations in music have followed technical advances, perhaps for all of history. First was the transition from primitive instruments to modern instruments such as the piano, the violin, the flute, and so on. Then came a transition to amplified instruments like electric guitars. Advances in studio techniques also changed the way music was conveyed to the listener. The English pop bands were among the first to push the boundaries of stereo recording. Naturally, transitions at every stage have produced controversy. Some fans have never forgiven some former acoustic artists for "going electric."

Things are no different with the latest innovation in musical technology—digital sampling. However, sampling has given rise to not only aesthetic but also legal controversy. Machines now enable musicians to record sound from other sources and to use a keyboard to play them back. Artists can use selections of any length from the original source, change the pitch and speed, play the music backwards, repeat it any number of times, and layer it over other sounds. Artists frequently use samples from previous musical recordings, and herein lies the legal controversy, because to sample music, someone else must have made the original. This is a fair argument against musicians who substantially build their songs around recognizable pieces of prior recordings, because the original artist can still be associated with the sampled material in the public's consciousness.

Sampling has a range of uses in popular music today. In its most blatant form, it involves stealing the bass line, riff, chorus, or entire instrumental track from a previous popular song. Some musicians use sampling in a more moderate way, inserting various shorter riffs and vocal passages as embellishments to their songs. At the other extreme are artists who sample from a wide range of original sources, including movies, obscure old records, and the sounds of nature and urban environments. The artists distort these sounds until they are unrecognizable, and then layer them up in remarkable ways to form rich, sonic textures, which results in something like an aural collage. Some rap groups have mastered this technique. Numerous British dance bands combine this collage effect with more traditional rock-and-roll technology—lead guitar, bass, and drums. These are the true artists of sampling. Unlike those who lazily borrow their songs wholesale and simply rap new lyrics over them, these artists transform their medium into something original and provocative. The transformation of a medium to produce something new and unexpected is the true mark of artistic genius.

Adapted from R. Wilson, *Digital Sampling: A Great Musical Advance.* © 1995 By R. Wilson and *Rolling Stone Magazine.*

The main aim of the introductory paragraph is to:

A. contrast sampling with other technological innovations in music.
B. reduce the controversy over sampling by placing it in historical perspective
C. demonstrate the author's objections to sampling.
D. compare the British pop bands to primitive musicians.

9. What other word(s) could the author have used for "stealing" in the third paragraph, without changing the overall argument in the paragraph?

 I. Pilfering
 II. Adapting
 III. Hijacking

 A. I and III only
 B. I and II only
 C. II and III only
 D. I, II, and III

10. Which of the following is implied by the passage?

 A. The author advocates legal warning labels on sampling machines.
 B. The English pop musicians were more innovative artists than American musicians.
 C. The acoustic artists "going electric" is analogous to the use of digital sampling.
 D. None of the above

11. Which of the following is NOT part of the analogy the author draws between sampling and electric guitars?

 I. Both caused controversy when they were introduced.
 II. Musicians used both to advance musical form.
 III. Both are marks of musical genius.

 A. I and III only
 B. I only
 C. III only
 D. II and III only

12. What word best describes the author's tone?

 A. Cautionary
 B. Dubious
 C. Cynical
 D. Enthusiastic

Passage III (Questions 13–19)

Medieval philosophers were concerned with formulating a logically sound proof of God's existence. At that time in Europe, Christianity and classical scholarship met up with each other. Medieval Christian thinkers admired the Greek philosophers' dedication to pure reason, and so tried to reconcile Christian doctrine with philosophical methodology. However, the results were distinctly unsuccessful. One famous problem that beset each argument for God's existence was an equally powerful argument that He did not exist, which is known today as the "Problem of Evil."

The problem of evil can be stated very simply, once one has an outline of the characteristics of the god for which medieval philosophers sought proof. His characteristics are summarized as four important statements. First, God is omnipotent. Second, God is omniscient. Third, God is perfectly benevolent. Say, we were to grant that all three of these statements were true. Now, consider a fourth proposition: Evil exists.

These four propositions cannot all be true at the same time. One proposition has to be eliminated if we are to preserve logical consistency. The medieval philosophers fought this result, but it is inescapable. Why? Because if God is omnipotent, He can do anything, including making a world in which evil does not exist. If He could not make such a world, then He would not be omnipotent, that is, there would be something He could not do. This means that proposition number 1 mentioned previously would be false. If God is omnipotent, then either he doesn't know about evil, in which case proposition number 2 previously mentioned is false, or He doesn't care, in which case proposition number 3 is certainly false. What benevolent creator would let its creations suffer, if it was in His power to stop that suffering?

The faithful, unwilling to give up any of the three characteristics of their god, will look to proposition number 4, to try to throw it out or revise it so that it no longer contradicts the other three statements. Maybe, they argue, what seems like evil and suffering to us is really part of an overall greater good, the logic of which only God understands. Maybe evil really doesn't exist; we just think it does, because of our limited point of view. But this argument is beyond the pale. Our world is full of death, illness, famine, pollution, war, ad infinitum. Innocent children starve to death, or are caught in passing gunfire, or die slow deaths trapped in the rubble of earthquakes. Who could stare these facts in the face and still maintain that the victims' suffering is not really suffering? That it is all for the best in the end? To deny proposition number 4 is to callously deny the very real suffering of human beings in our world.

Things look bad for the god of medieval Christianity. The medieval philosophers did not give up trying to find an argument that proved his existence, but they also never solved the problem of evil. It is a problem that bothers Christian philosophers to this day.

From Larry M. Christiansen, *A View of God in Medieval Times.* © 1993 by L.M. Christiansen.

13. Which of the following conclusions are supported by the arguments in this passage?

    I. God's existence can never be proved using logic.
    II. Rational people shouldn't believe in the god of medieval Christianity.
    III. God cannot violate the rules of logic.

    A. I and II only
    B. II and III only
    C. I, II, and III
    D. None of the above

14. If one were to believe that both God and Satan exist, Satan being responsible for the evil in the world, which proposition would one be denying?

    A. 1
    B. 2
    C. 3
    D. 4

15. What is the author's argument against the faithful in the fourth paragraph?

    A. A benevolent God wouldn't allow children to suffer.
    B. It is unjustified to deny the fourth proposition.
    C. The doctrine of faith is logically inconsistent.
    D. Those who deny the fourth proposition must not have experienced suffering themselves.

16. Someone might argue that God must make his creations suffer pain in the same way that a parent must make his or her child suffer the pain of going to the dentist—for the child's own future good. What would be a disanalogy between God and the parent?

    A. The parent is bound by laws of physics and biology.
    B. God could make teeth that don't decay.
    C. God could make dentistry painless.
    D. All of the above

17. What does the author mean by "beyond the pale" in the fourth paragraph?

    A. Unilluminating
    B. Unacceptable
    C. Confused
    D. Disingenuous

18. What does the author mean by "perfectly benevolent" in proposition 3?

    I. All-loving
    II. All-good
    III. All-knowing

    A. I and II only
    B. I and III only
    C. II and III only
    D. I, II, and III

19. Which of the following conditions would eradicate the problem of evil?

    I. If evil had never existed and would never exist.
    II. If we were to believe that God is not omniscient.
    III. If we were to abandon logical methodology.

    A. I and III only
    B. II only
    C. I, II, and III
    D. None of the above

In animals, rabies has been classified into two forms: dumb rabies or furious rabies. In dumb rabies, the animal (e.g., the dog), after an incubation period of 2 to 8 weeks, exhibits a change of character and habits, becoming morose, and dies of paralysis within a few days of the onset of symptoms. In furious rabies, the change of character and habits is more dangerous, because the animal tends to be aggressive. If the animal bites during this period (starting approximately 5 days before the onset of symptoms, and lasting throughout the illness) when the saliva contains virus, there is obvious risk to the person or animal who is bitten. But only 35% to 43% of people bitten by rabid dogs are thought to be infected; the proportion of people who become infected after being bitten by rabid wolves is said to be around 61%. If the bite is through clothing, the cloth may reduce the infection risk by wiping off the saliva. Some rabid animals are not secreting virus all the time.

In man, the incubation period varies from 2 weeks to 2 years, but is usually 1 to 3 months. The shorter periods occur when the bite is severe or is on the hands or face, and the amount of virus introduced is important in this respect.

The two main rabies types may not easily be recognized. In the excited (furious) type, the patient shows an early rise of temperature and early psychological change, becoming anxious, melancholy, irritable, and subject to strange presentiments that may be hysterical in origin. Insomnia is a prominent feature of this prodromal phase. Reflexes are increased, and the pupils may dilate. The wound becomes engorged and tender. Headache and other aches and pains (which may be shooting) occur, and paresthesia of the trunk, face, and limbs may be marked. The patient is fully alert and orientated, but restless. Voluntary movements may be exaggerated, and there may be periods of excitement during which the patient may destroy objects near at hand, but he/she seldom injures other persons. Sexual excitement, with priapism, is common. The face may lack expression, squint may develop, and the patient is unable to close the eyes or mouth. The voice becomes hoarse, and mucus collects in the mouth, which the patient is unable to expel.

Other significant symptoms are associated with rabies. Extremely painful spasms of the throat and larynx occur, causing fear of food and especially drink, which may be so great that the patient cries out in terror when offered a drink. Even draughts of air or bright lights can bring on convulsive seizures, and repeated spasms of respiratory muscles lead to difficulty in breathing and cyanosis. The convulsive seizures become more and more pronounced until the patient dies, usually during a spasm, but sometimes in coma. Death is usually 5 to 10 days after the onset of symptoms.

When rabies is associated with paralysis, the symptoms tend to be less marked, and the diagnosis may be missed. The patient is depressed and apathetic, with fever and malaise, followed by weakness, ataxia, and paralysis. Pain and paralysis may occur first in the legs and then progress to other body regions. Ultimately, death may not take place for a month. Batborne rabies is of this kind, and resembles the paralytic rabies that affects cattle of Central and South America.

Diagnosis is obviously difficult, especially in countries where rabies is not indigenous but occurs in immigrants who, perhaps because of a long incubation period, may have forgotten bites of dogs, cats, or other animals in their own countries before their arrival to the new country. It is therefore very important for medical personnel in non-endemic countries to ask if the patient has been abroad, or has been bitten by an animal, or exposed to bats.

Adapted from Thomas Cartwright, *Infectious Diseases, Etiology, and Diagnosis.* © 1996 By Waverly Press.

20. What makes one type of rabies more dangerous than the other?

    A. The speed with which the venomous saliva reaches the bloodstream
    B. The velocity of the onset of symptoms
    C. The degree to which it is spread to other animals and humans
    D. The brevity of the incubation period

21. Which of the following, according to the information provided in the passage, is true?

    A. More people are bitten by rabid wolves.
    B. All rabid animals carry a deathly virus.
    C. In dumb rabies, animals become less rational and less responsive.
    D. One of rabies' symptoms is inhibited motor skills.

22. According to the passage, which of the following could NOT be determined to be false?

    I. Furious rabies is appropriately named.
    II. Human beings rarely are bitten by dogs with dumb rabies.
    III. The location of the bite on human beings is crucial.
    IV. If you are going to be bitten by a dog, a limb would be preferable to the face.

    A. I and IV only
    B. I only
    C. I and II only
    D. II, III, and IV only

GO ON TO THE NEXT PAGE.

23. The psychological changes that occur in man and animal when affected by rabies include:

A. paralysis.
B. moodiness.
C. headaches.
D. excessive saliva or mucus.

24. From this article, we may conclude that the worst-case scenario would be for a person to have:

A. been bitten by a rabid wolf.
B. been bitten by a dog with furious rabies.
C. convulsive seizures.
D. painful spasms that lead to cyanosis.

25. The following would be an appropriate title for this passage:

A. *Rabies: Source and Solution*
B. *Rabies: Dumb and Furious*
C. *The Fury of Rabies*
D. *Once Bitten, Twice Shy*

26. Complete the following sentence according to information provided in the passage. "Dumb rabies in humans. . . ."

  I. can be caused by bats and cattle from South and Central America.
  II. results in convulsive seizures and repeated spasms of respiratory muscles.
 III. can be hard to identify because its symptoms are less overt.
 IV. rarely occurs in countries where rabies is not rampant.

A. I and IV only
B. II and III only
C. II only
D. III only

Passage V (Questions 27–34)

The word "corporation" derives from the Latin corpus, meaning "body," and corporare, meaning "to make into a body." According to the dictionary definition, a corporation is a body formed under the law as a single individual, and endowed with the rights and responsibilities of an individual, even though it can be composed of more than one person. Corporations conduct their business as single entities, in the eyes of the law, but how far does the analogy go? Do corporations have moral and social responsibilities in the same sense that individual persons do?

Milton Friedman, for one, clearly believes that corporations do not have these responsibilities. He gives his argument in an article tellingly entitled, "The Social Responsibility of Business is to Increase Its Profits." Friedman objects to the very semantics of the claim that "business" has social responsibilities; he argues that only human beings can have them, and so the real question relates to the nature of the social responsibilities of the individual human beings who work in corporations.

When a human being is part of a corporate body, that human being loses his or her human individuality and becomes a cell in a larger body. The person acts as an agent for the owners or stockholders of the corporation, and he or she must abide by their wishes and decisions. This is the nature of the free market: stockholders express their approval of a business's products and practices by purchasing stock; the marketplace expresses its approval by purchasing the company's products. Both stockholders and consumers are and should be free to take their business elsewhere. The corporation itself, in the midst of these market forces, has the responsibility only to increase its profits by selling more of the product, raising its prices, increasing efficiency of production, lowering wages, or whatever else the market will bear.

Friedman argues that if an agent of the company decides to make a business decision based not on the desire to maximize profits but on his own notions of social responsibility, without consulting the stockholders or his superiors, he is imposing taxation on unwilling subjects. The individual might decide to keep prices low because he feels a responsibility to help reduce inflation. This effectively taxes the stockholders or owners. The individual might decide to raise prices to increase the standard of living of the employees. This effectively taxes the consumer. Friedman argues that when a corporate agent acts with company funds and profits in accordance with his own moral and social agenda, he threatens the very fabric of our society. Not only does he go against the principles of free market competition, but he also destroys the foundation of freedom of choice and the guarantee of "No taxation without representation," on which our country was founded. In a capitalist system, we determine as a political body where resources are to be allocated for social goods. When allocations are determined by corporate means rather than by

GO ON TO THE NEXT PAGE.

...al means, we have a socialist system rather than a capitalist one.

rom Sheldon Miller, *The Corporation: Analysis and Arguments.* © 1995 By Sheldon Miller and *University Law Review.*

27. To whom does the word "they" refer to in the first sentence of the second paragraph?

   A. Corporations
   B. Individual persons
   C. Moral and social responsibilities
   D. Opponents of Friedman

28. How does Friedman define taxation?

   A. Assessment of funds for social programs
   B. Contribution of funds for political ends
   C. The additional amount added to the market price of a product
   D. Artificial inflation of prices for personal ends

29. Why do employees lose their individuality in corporations?

   A. Employees must have the same personal political beliefs as their employers.
   B. Employees are not to act on individual beliefs, desires, or opinions.
   C. The automatic nature of corporate work causes employees to lose their personality.
   D. Employees' legal rights are subsumed under the corporate entity.

30. How could taxes ever be justified, according to Friedman?

   A. If greater social good resulted from them
   B. If moral responsibilities were converted to social responsibilities
   C. If the majority of those persons taxed expressed support for the social programs supplied by the tax
   D. Taxes could never be justified

31. How would the author of the passage define socialism?

   A. A system in which corporations are owned by employees, not stockholders
   B. A system in which corporations do have social responsibilities
   C. A system that uses a market economy for political ends
   D. A system in which workers pay taxes by means of lower wages

32. What influence do consumers have?

   I. They can support businesses whose social policies they approve.
   II. They can help reduce inflation by paying higher prices.
   III. They can effectively assess taxes on stockholders.

   A. I only
   B. II only
   C. I and II only
   D. I and III only

33. Which of the following are implied by the first paragraph?

   A. Corporations, like human bodies, can contract diseases from outside sources.
   B. Corporations, like human beings, require at least two "parents" to initially constitute them.
   C. Corporations, like individuals, can be legally tried in courts of law.
   D. None of the above

34. What would be the best title for this passage?

   A. *The Semantics of Taxation*
   B. *Friedman and American Socialism*
   C. *Employees With a Conscience: A Cancer in the Corporate Body*
   D. *The Social Responsibilities of Business: Employees With a Conscience, or Taxation Without Representation?*

GO ON TO THE NEXT PAGE.

Passage VI (Questions 35–42)

American fiction expresses the American myth of the frontier. The heroes of this fiction are unbounded by any of the strictures of society, in any of its manifestations. They refuse to be tied by norms, rules, family ties, conventional life-styles, or place. Their highest aim is to explore, define, and create themselves as individuals. Moreover, they aim to define themselves as individuals completely from scratch.

This drama of the construction of an independent self gets played out in the setting of the American frontier. The unbounded, empty space represents the blank palette on which men write their identities. Examples abound in literature and film. Consider Shane, a man who had to keep moving on, even though he had found a family to take him in and a piece of land on which to settle. Or Marlon Brando in *The Wild One,* lured by the romance of the road, as is Jack Kerouac in *On the Road.* These are 20th-century versions of frontier westerns. These men can't be tied to home and hearth; they have to keep moving so they won't succumb to ordinary patterns of living. In looking for themselves on the open road, they are living the American myth.

All of the protagonists of American frontier narratives are men. Even though young women readers identify with the main characters of these narratives, the role of the female in the stories is antithetical to ideals of individuality and freedom. Female images appear first in the form of the land. The terrain of the American West is portrayed as fertile, soft, and pliant; ready to do the will of the men who settle her; ready to create new life and to be transformed under men's hands. Female characters also appear as the forces of society. They are portrayed either as oppressive ties that try to hold the hero back and down, chaining him to a conventional life (i.e., the nagging wife); or as temptresses (i.e., the gold digger) who try to seduce the hero away from his primary, solitary goal.

If a woman tried to strike out on her own as the male heroes of frontier narratives do, to leave home and family and the conventions of society behind, she would not be praised for living the American myth. She would instead be criticized for abandoning her children and the people who need her. She would be accused of betraying the duties of her sex. The women in narratives that most closely resemble frontier narratives are all still traditionally bound to their children and conventional relations with men. Alice, in the movie *Alice Doesn't Live Here Anymore,* makes a break from her former life to find herself, but she is a widow and has her child with her. In the novel *Anywhere But Here,* a woman also strikes out on the road, headed for the West Coast, but she also has her child with her, and the American dream she pursues involves catching a wealthy man as a husband, and helping her daughter to become a child star.

The literature of the American frontier is perhaps the final frontier of women's quest for equality with men. Someday, women will be able to break from the chains of convention and society, and forge their identities as free individuals, just as men have done in American fiction for generations.

Adapted from Stephen Davidson, *The Role of Women in American Frontier Literary Works.* © 1994 By Stephen Davidson.

35. According to the author, which of the following are elements of the American myth?

    I. Owning land or a home of one's own
    II. Traveling on the open road in the American West
    III. Breaking away from tradition

    A. I and III only
    B. I and II only
    C. II and III only
    D. I, II, and III

36. According to the author, which of the following is associated with masculinity in frontier narratives?

    A. Artistic creativity
    B. Independence
    C. Social norms
    D. Violent temper

37. Which of the following would fit the traditional representation of women in frontier narratives?

    A. A woman who actively divorces her husband and seeks financial support
    B. A woman who makes her husband stay home and take care of the kids.
    C. A woman who operates a successful business
    D. None of the aforementioned

38. Which of the following would not fit the pattern of the traditional hero of the frontier narrative?

    A. A police officer
    B. The President of the United States
    C. An IRS agent
    D. All of the above

GO ON TO THE NEXT PAGE.

Which of the following represent similarities between the nagging wife and the gold digger in the fourth paragraph?

   I. Both represent the difficulties of child rearing
  II. Both sidetrack the hero from his quest for individuality
 III. Both impede the hero's mobility

  A.   I only
  B.   III only
  C.   I and II only
  D.   II and III only

40. According to the fifth paragraph, which is the female version of the American dream, as it is portrayed by the lead character in *Anywhere But Here*?

  A.   To become the widow of an established man
  B.   To live in a well-kept home
  C.   To benefit from the success of one's husband and children
  D.   To hit the road and keep moving

41. What statement best summarizes the change the author hopes will come to American fiction?

  A.   Novels should embrace traditional family values more than they currently do.
  B.   Women characters should be allowed to express their individuality.
  C.   The terrain of the American West should be portrayed as a child rather than a woman.
  D.   Male characters should be shown as taking their responsibilities to their families more seriously.

42. What does the road symbolize in recent American fiction, according to the author?

   I. Restlessness
  II. Freedom
 III. A lust to wander

  A.   I and II only
  B.   II only
  C.   III only
  D.   I, II, and III

Passage VII (Questions 43–49)

When we consider the situation of the human mind in nature, its limited plasticity and few channels of communication with the outer world, we need not wonder that we grope for light, or that we find incoherence and instability in human systems of ideas. The wonder rather is that we have done so well, that in the chaos of sensations and passions that fills the mind, we have found any leisure for self-concentration and reflection, and have succeeded in gathering even a light harvest of experience from our distracted labors.

The resources of the mind are not commensurate with its ambition. Of the five senses, three are of little use in the formation of permanent notions; a fourth, sight, is indeed vivid and luminous, but furnishes transcripts of things so highly colored and deeply modified by the medium of sense, that a long labor of analysis of correction is needed before satisfactory conceptions can be extracted from it. For this labor, however, we are endowed with the requisite instrument. We have memory, and we have certain powers of synthesis, abstraction, reproduction, invention—in a word, we have understanding. But this faculty of understanding has hardly begun its work of deciphering the hieroglyphics of sense and of framing an idea of reality, when it is crossed by another faculty—the imagination. Perceptions do not remain in the mind (as would be suggested by the trite simile of the seal and the wax), passive and changeless, until time wears off their sharp edges and makes them fade. No, perceptions fall into the brain rather as seeds into a furrowed field or even as sparks into a keg of powder. Each image breeds a hundred more, sometimes slowly and subterraneously, sometimes (when a passionate train is started) with a sudden burst of fancy. The mind, exercised by its own fertility and flooded by its inner lights, has infinite trouble in keeping a true reckoning of its outward perceptions. It turns from the frigid problems of observation to its own visions; it forgets to watch the courses of what should be its "pilot stars." Indeed, were it not for the power of convention in which, by a sort of mutual cancellation of errors, the more practical and normal conceptions are enshrined, the imagination would carry men wholly away—the best men first and the vulgar after them. Even as it is, individuals and ages of fervid imagination usually waste themselves in dreams, and must disappear before the race, saddened and dazed, perhaps by the memory of those visions, can return to its plodding thoughts.

Five senses, then, to gather a small part of the infinite influences that vibrate in nature, a moderate power of understanding to interpret those senses, and an irregular, passionate fancy to overlay that interpretation—such is the endowment of the human mind. And what is its ambition? Nothing less than to construct a picture of all reality, to comprehend its own origin and that of the universe, to discover the laws of both the prophesy and its destiny. Is

GO ON TO THE NEXT PAGE.

not the disproportion enormous? Are not confusions and profound contradictions to be looked for in an attempt to build so much out of so little?

From Rae Heftel, *The Mind: It's Wonders and Shortcomings.* © 1993 By Psychology Text Publishing.

43. In paragraph two of the passage, the author uses what he refers to as a "trite simile of the seal and the wax." Which of the following best describes how this simile functions?

    A. The brain is the wax, and the perception is the seal impressed upon the wax.

    B. The seal stamped into wax closes off the brain from new perceptions.

    C. Wax is a substance that may be molded and remolded, like perceptions that constantly change.

    D. The brain is the seal that represents the imprint of perceptions. The wax is raw material.

44. Why might you infer by the author calling the simile "trite"?

    A. Because it is too complex.

    B. Because it is too basic.

    C. Because it is a cliché.

    D. Because people generally do not use seals or wax to close their letters anymore, thereby rendering the simile out-of-touch and useless.

45. According to the passage, what is flawed about sight?

    A. It is not commensurate with ambition.

    B. It is of limited use in the development of notions that have some staying power.

    C. It is vivid and luminous.

    D. It often needs to be corrected and modified because so many people have eye problems that require glasses and contact lenses.

46. The human mind:

    A. is inflexible and nonplastic.

    B. eschews and embraces imagination.

    C. is overrated and underappreciated.

    D. is not equal to its capacity for ambition.

47. The author's use of the "field" and "powder" metaphors for perceptions and the brain implies which of the following assertions?

    I. Perceptions must be nurtured and tended to like important crops.

    II. If perceptions are not handled with care, they can end up exploding into wasted imagination.

    III. The brain is fertile ground in which the seeds of perception can grow and multiply.

    IV. The slow and subterranean growth of perceptions is preferable to sudden bursts of fancy.

    A. I and III only

    B. II and IV only

    C. III only

    D. IV only

48. According to the passage, how does imagination function?

    A. As a product of understanding

    B. As a flood of inner lights

    C. As a catalyst for understanding

    D. As a framing desire for reality

49. How does the author seem to view imagination?

    A. Cautiously

    B. Wistfully

    C. Childishly

    D. Spontaneously

GO ON TO THE NEXT PAGE.

During the 1980s, there was a large population shift the western states. This was especially true in California. Despite high housing costs, traffic problems, and air pollution, people moved to California in large numbers. Thousands of acres of land were converted into suburban housing developments and shopping malls every year in order to compensate for the population growth. Water was drained out of delicate wetlands, and forests were cut at ever-increasing rates. Drawn to the state for its beautiful natural diversity, newcomers contributed to the damage of an already strained environment. Californians were on the rise, diminishing California.

The 1990s have shown some reversal of these trends. This, in part, may be attributable to the natural disasters and riots that occurred in California. The 1990s brought earthquakes, floods, fires, and riots. Business failures and a growing job market outside of California have in part contributed to an exodus from the state. It is interesting to note that the fastest growth in population is now occurring in the South. Once a region of near static growth, homogeneity, and little immigration, the southern states are now boasting new business opportunities and an expanding economy, inexpensive real estate, and a growing multiethnic population. In the 1960s and 1970s, the same trends that are now seen in the South were occurring in California. In the business world, population growth translates into new businesses—new entrepreneurs, new investors, and new consumers. New residents are certainly good for the state's economy. However, some environmentalists claim that even business-minded people will soon be fighting for the environment, as investors seek out new places to put their money where they won't have to battle housing costs, traffic, and pollution. Although environmentalists would love to have big business on their side, many are wary of this political alliance. They claim that if large corporations begin to fight for environmental protection, it will only be in the interest of encouraging more business investment and market expansion within the state, and will lead to increased population and a greater strain on natural resources.

California is the state with the longest list of endangered, threatened, and rare species, a fact that could be interpreted either as a sign of conscientious preservation or as a sign of environmental devastation. Unfortunately, the latter appears to be the case. According to a recent study, 90% of the ancient redwood forests in California have already been cut, 1246 tons of noxious gases are pumped into the air each day in Los Angeles alone, two thirds of California desert lands have been damaged by human use, and 90% of the state's wetlands have been destroyed. The beautiful California coastline has inspired people to fight for preservation, and the California Coastal Act of 1976 was designed to protect the coastline from development. However, even this environmental protection plan is at least partially driven by economic concerns. The state makes billions of dollars every year on tourists who flock to the scenic beaches and coastal cliffs. The California coast is clearly "worth" preserving on several different levels.

The environment has got to start coming before economic concerns. In Los Angeles, businesses are required to meet emission-reduction levels, an important step in reducing pollution in the city with the dirtiest air in the country. However, bills are already being proposed that would allow corporations to sell "emission credits" to companies who fail to meet the standards. If such bills are passed, it is clear that money will once again overpower environmental protection.

From William Howard, *California: Now or Never.* © 1996 By Columbia Press.

50. One can imagine that the author of this passage:

   A. moved to California from a southwestern state.
   B. will move from California to a northwestern state.
   C. owns a business in California.
   D. considers himself/herself a "California native."

51. The underlying logic of this passage could lead the author to support:

   I. tax deductions for environmentally sound businesses.
   II. population quotas.
   III. boycotts of businesses who fail to meet environmental standards.
   IV. very strict environmental standards.

   A. I and II
   B. I, II, III, and IV
   C. III and IV
   D. II, III, and IV

52. According to this passage, the relationship of the population to big business is:

   A. arbitrary.
   B. directly proportional.
   C. inversely proportional.
   D. irrelevant.

53. The passage implies that California deserts have not been aggressively preserved because:

   A. the desert is considered unattractive.
   B. the desert is relatively unpopulated.
   C. there is no water in the desert.
   D. there is little wildlife in the desert.

GO ON TO THE NEXT PAGE.

54. According to the author of the passage, pollution is created by:

A. money.
B. loggers.
C. economics.
D. people.

55. The argument this passage makes is:

A. realistic.
B. controversial.
self-evident.
D. compelling.

56. If a large business corporation proposed an environmental protection plan, the author of this passage would be:

A. elated.
B. cautious.
C. angry.
D. enthusiastic.

57. If the population of California were to suddenly decrease in the year 2001, the author of this passage might attribute the decrease to which of the following?

I. Increased pollution
II. Increased business opportunities
III. Decreased business opportunities
IV. Decreased pollution

A. II and IV only
B. I and II only
C. I and III only
D. I only

Passage IX (Questions 58–65)

The United States public school system is in crisis. As middle-class families continue to move out of the city into the suburbs, the gap between the education of the rich and the poor continues to grow wider. Wealthy families have always had more options available to them than poor families. While a lack of financial resources leaves children of poor families trapped in inner city schools, money has allowed the children of wealthy families to enroll in private schools, or to live in expensive houses in "good" public school districts.

"What is to be done" about the current state of the public school system has been a topic of debate for over 50 years. Recently, failure to compete in international technological markets and an upcoming presidential election have heightened the intensity of this debate. Conservatives have proposed a new plan called "Options" that would operate on the model of the free market.

As the system now stands, the number of students per public school, largely determined by city districts, dictates the allocation of government funds in public schools. Options would turn the United States school system into a mix of public, private, and parochial schools competing with one another for students and government funding. By supplementing student tuition at private institutions, Options would open private schools to more students. Advocates claim that private schools could then begin to compete with public schools for students. In turn, this competition would force public schools to increase their academic excellence, in order to attract students with several schooling options open to them.

Proponents of Options claim that competition for students, "customers," and government funding would ensure excellence in schools. Families would be given vouchers to spend at the school, private or public, of their choice. Those in favor of Options argue that the voucher system would allow families with meager funds to send their children to first-rate private institutions. They also claim that the program would give parents more options in selecting public schools for their children. In most states today, parents must send their children to the public school designated by their housing district. Under the proposed plan, parents would be free to choose the school they would like their children to attend.

Critics of Options claim that the plan is mostly political rhetoric. Because private schools today are almost entirely full, the Options plan would necessitate rapid and extensive building, something the government is not offering to fund. More radical critics of the plan claim that Options would only make the education of the rich better, and the education of the poor worse. They claim that the government will not be able to provide the enormous funds necessary to make private education a real option for all families. Further, with government money tied up in vouchers that will be inadequate for most, funds will not

117

GO ON TO THE NEXT PAGE.

le to help inner city schools rebuild their pro-
a free-market educational system, inner city
will never be competitive.

Before a truly "free" market can be opened, public
nool systems need to be restructured and refinanced. Before spending money on voucher experiments, the government needs to spend money on restructuring public
schools.

Adapted From Maxine Johnson, *The Options Plan: An
Analysis of Educational Change.* © 1995 By Maxine
Johnson.

58. The author of the passage:

    A.   promotes Options.
    B.   is undecided about Options.
    C.   is indifferent about Options.
    D.   rejects Options.

59. Based on information implied by the passage, which
of the following is the real problem behind the current educational crisis?

    A.   Government apathy
    B.   Economic disparity
    C.   Political rhetoric
    D.   Enrollment

60. According to proponents of the Options plan, what
would raise the educational standards of public
schools?

    A.   Money
    B.   Freedom
    C.   Competition
    D.   Scholarships

61. It can be inferred from the passage that the author:

    A.   is a parent.
    B.   teaches at a public school.
    C.   is a politician.
    D.   lives in the suburbs.

62. According to the author of the passage, the Options
plan would widen the gap between the rich and the
poor because:

    A.   vouchers would not be large enough.
    B.   private schools are all in the suburbs.
    C.   the poor live in the inner city.
    D.   public schools are all in the inner city.

63. It can be inferred from the passage that the author
would support:

    I.   increased government funding of public
schools.
   II.   increased school building.
  III.   decreased private school enrollment.

    A.   I and III only
    B.   II and III only
    C.   I and II only
    D.   I only

64. If the Options plan were instituted, schools would
probably begin to hire which of the following?

    A.   College professors
    B.   Political lobbyists
    C.   Lawyers
    D.   Advertisers

65. The Options plan implies that:

    A.   there are too many public schools.
    B.   there are not enough parochial schools.
    C.   private schools offer better quality than public
schools.
    D.   the rich are smarter than the poor.

STOP. IF YOU FINISH BEFORE TIME IS
CALLED, CHECK YOUR WORK. YOU MAY
GO BACK TO ANY QUESTION IN THIS
TEST BOOKLET.

STOP.

Physical Sciences

Time: 100 minutes
Questions: 66–142

Directions: Most questions in the Physical Sciences test are organized into groups, each preceded by a descriptive passage. After studying the passage, select the one best answer to each question. Some questions are not based on a descriptive passage and are also independent of each other. You should also select the one best answer to these independent questions. A periodic table is provided for your use. You may consult it whenever you wish.

PERIODIC TABLE OF THE ELEMENTS

IA																	VIIIA
1 H 1.0	IIA											IIIA	IVA	VA	VIA	VII A	2 He 4.0
3 Li 6.9	4 Be 9.0											5 B 10.8	6 C 12.0	7 N 14.0	8 O 16.0	9 F 19.0	10 Ne 20.2
11 Na 23.0	12 Mg 24.3											13 Al 27.0	14 Si 28.1	15 P 31.0	16 S 32.1	17 Cl 35.5	18 Ar 39.9
19 K 39.1	20 Ca 40.1	21 Sc 45.0	22 Ti 47.9	23 V 50.9	24 Cr 52.0	25 Mn 54.9	26 Fe 55.8	27 Co 58.9	28 Ni 58.7	29 Cu 63.5	30 Zn 65.4	31 Ga 69.7	32 Ge 72.6	33 As 74.9	34 Se 79.0	35 Br 79.9	36 Kr 83.8
37 Rb 85.5	38 Sr 87.6	39 Y 88.9	40 Zr 91.2	41 Nb 92.9	42 Mo 95.9	43 Tc 98.0	44 Ru 101	45 Rh 102	46 Pd 106	47 Ag 108	48 Cd 112	49 In 115	50 Sn 119	51 Sb 122	52 Te 128	53 I 127	54 Xe 131
55 Cs 133	56 Ba 137	57 La 139	72 Hf 179	73 Ta 181	74 W 184	75 Re 186	76 Os 190	77 Ir 192	78 Pt 195	79 Au 197	80 Hg 201	81 Tl 204	82 Pb 207	83 Bi 208	84 Po 209	85 At 210	86 Rn 222
87 Fr 223	88 Ra 226	89 Ac 227															

58 Ce 140	59 Pr 141	60 Nd 144	61 Pm 145	62 Sm 150	63 Eu 152	64 Gd 157	65 Tb 159	66 Dy 163	67 Ho 165	68 Er 167	69 Tm 169	70 Yb 173	71 Lu 175
90 Th 232	91 Pa 231	92 U 238	93 Np 237	94 Pu 244	95 Am 243	96 Cm 247	97 Bk 247	98 Cf 251	99 Es 252	100 Fm 257	101 Md 258	102 No 259	103 Lr 260

120

GO ON TO THE NEXT PAGE.

Passage I (Questions 66–70)

The expression for the escape speed of a particle near a planet's surface applies generally to the surface of any planet or moon. The escape speed is the minimum velocity that a particle must have to free itself of the gravitation of a planet. If R is the radius of the planet and g is the acceleration due to gravity at the surface of the planet (or moon), the escape speed (v_e) is given by:

$$v_e = \sqrt{2gR}$$

In addition to having a velocity exceeding v_e in a direction away from the planet, a particle must not collide with other particles on its outward journey. The chance of a molecule colliding with another molecule depends on the density of the atmosphere, which decreases rapidly with increasing height above the surface of a planet. The term escape level is used to describe the altitude at which a molecule has virtually zero chance of colliding with another molecule. For the earth, the escape level averages about 500 km above the ground, with considerable seasonal and diurnal variation because of temperature change. The escape level is temperature dependent. Data for various planets are given in Table 1.

Table 1. Acceleration of Gravity (g) and Radius and Various Planets

Planet	g in m/s^2	Radius in km
Mercury	3.76	2,439
Venus	8.88	6,049
Earth	9.81	6,371
Moon	1.62	1,738
Mars	3.73	3,390
Jupiter	26.2	69,500
Saturn	11.2	58,100
Uranus	9.75	24,500
Neptune	11.34	24,600

At a molecular level, the speed of a particle depends strongly on its mass and the temperature, according to the following relationship:

$$v_o = \sqrt{\frac{2kT}{m}}$$

where k is Boltzmann's constant $= 1.38 \times 10^{-23}$ J/K.

Some atomic particles have known probable speeds. Table 2 gives probable speeds for several atomic species at two different Kelvin temperatures:

Table 2. Probable Speeds (km/sec) of Several Atomic Species at Two different Temperatures

Atom	Atomic Mass	Speed at 300K	Speed at 600K
H	1	2.24	3.16
He	4	1.12	1.58
O	16	0.56	0.79

66. If the escape speed of Uranus is 22 km/sec, the escape speed of Saturn is approximately:

   A. 24 km/sec.
   B. 30 km/sec.
   C. 36 km/sec.
   D. 42 km/sec.

67. A particle escaping from the surface of a planet strikes another particle in a completely inelastic collision. Which statement best describes this collision?

   A. Kinetic energy is conserved, momentum is conserved.
   B. Kinetic energy is not conserved, momentum is conserved.
   C. Kinetic energy is conserved, momentum is not conserved.
   D. Kinetic energy is not conserved, momentum is not conserved.

68. The escape speed on different planets can be used to explain why some planets have atmospheres and others do not. The order of escape velocities for any given gas for the following three planets at their ambient surface temperatures, in increasing order is:

   A. Jupiter, earth, moon.
   B. moon, earth, Jupiter.
   C. Jupiter, moon, earth.
   D. Earth, moon, Jupiter.

69. The most probable speed of H_2 at 300K is 1.58 km/sec. The most probable speed of O_2 is:

   A. 0.79 km/sec.
   B. 0.39 km/sec.
   C. 0.20 km/sec.
   D. 0.10 km/sec.

GO ON TO THE NEXT PAGE.

scape level of Venus is 200 km. This difference ...pared to the earth is most likely directly related ...o the difference in the two planets':

A. radii.
B. gravitational accelerations.
C. masses.
D. distances from the sun.

Passage II (Questions 71–75)

The atmosphere contains a mixture of gases. These gases contribute to the atmospheric pressure, as the force of gravity on a mass of air exerts a pressure at the earth's surface. This pressure varies with altitude, and slightly with the weather, but is approximately 760 mm Hg or 1 atm. Gas mixtures in the atmosphere are also involved in numerous chemical reactions. Equilibrium reactions are among the most common reactions occurring in the atmosphere. Gas molecules are in a constant state of flux, converting from reactant to product and vice versa.

An atmospheric chemist studied four reactions which are known to be important in atmospheric chemistry. Some of these chemical species are found in abundance in the atmosphere, while others are found in small quantities. Equilibrium expressions for these four reactions were determined. The equilibrium constants were evaluated to help make predictions about the reactions. For purposes of analysis, consider the following equilibria:

Equilibrium 1

$$2\ O_3(g) \rightleftarrows 3\ O_2(g) \qquad K_{eq}\ (2300°C) = 2.54 \times 10^{12}$$

Equilibrium 2

$$2NO(g) + O_2(g) \rightleftarrows 2NO_2(g) \qquad K_{eq}(230°C) = 6.44 \times 10^{-5}$$

Equilibrium 3

$$N_2O_4(g) \rightleftarrows 2NO_2(g) \qquad K_{eq}(230°C) = 4.63 \times 10^{-3}$$

Equilibrium 4

$$CO(g) + H_2O(g) \rightleftarrows H_2(g) + CO_2(g) \qquad K_{eq}(830°C) = 5.1$$

71. At 230°C, which is (are) the major species present in the equilibrium represented by equilibrium 2 if 8 mol of $NO_2(g)$ are allowed to come to equilibrium?

A. $NO(g)$
B. $O_2(g)$
C. $2NO_2$
D. $NO(g)$ and $O_2(g)$

72. What would be the equilibrium constant for equilibrium 1?

A. $[O_3(g)]^3/[O_2(g)]^2$
B. $[O_2(g)]^3/[O_3(g)]^2$
C. $[O_3(g)]^2/[O_2(g)]^3$
D. $[O_2(g)]^2/[O_3(g)]^3$

GO ON TO THE NEXT PAGE.

73. A reaction is found to have K = 1. Which statement about the standard change in Gibb's free energy for this reaction is true?

    A. It must be zero.
    B. It must be greater than one.
    C. It must be positive.
    D. It must be less than one.

74. Based on the information given in the passage, what can be determined about the ΔS for equilibrium 2?

    A. It is negative.
    B. It is positive.
    C. It is zero.
    D. It cannot be determined without ΔG and ΔH.

75. What is the value of the equilibrium constant for the following equilibrium?

$$2NO(g) + O_2(g) \rightleftarrows N_2O_4(g)$$

    A. (6.44×10^{-5})
    B. $(4.63 \times 10^{-3})/(6.44 \times 10^{-5})$
    C. $(6.44 \times 10^{-5})/(4.63 \times 10^{-3})$
    D. 0

Passage III (Questions 76–81)

Waves carry energy, momentum, and information across space without the bulk transfer of matter. For waves to carry information, a change or modulation in one of the fundamental properties of the wave, such as its frequency or amplitude, usually occurs. Without modulation, no information could be sent. The three basic forms of modulation are amplitude, frequency, and pulse modulation. In amplitude modulation, the amplitude of the wave is varied with some regular frequency, and it is this frequency that contains the information. A frequency modulated signal changes its fundamental frequency slightly, about some equilibrium value, and this, again, carries information. Pulse modulation is similar to a digital signal—the wave is either there or it is not. In all three cases, there is one basic frequency, called the carrier frequency. There may be additional frequency components in the wave as well, and those components carry the information.

Waves typically add in superposition. This means that the sum of two waves at the same point in space at the same time is the algebraic sum of each wave separately. When waves of different frequencies are added, a complex waveform results, with periodic points where the wave equals zero. The zero points are called beats and have a frequency equal to the difference in frequency of the component waveforms.

Another interesting property that makes use of superposition is the combination of pure sinusoids. The correct combination of sinusoids of different frequencies allows any desired waveform to be made. For example, a square wave is composed of an infinite number of odd harmonics, as shown in Figure 1. For sharp variations, such as the instantaneous drop of a square wave, very high frequency sinusoids are necessary.

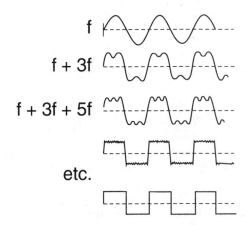

Figure 1. The formation of a square wave by the addition of an infinite number of odd harmonics.

GO ON TO THE NEXT PAGE.

...ch of the following waves could NOT carry infor-...ation?

A.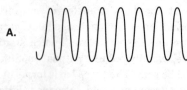

B.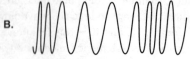

C.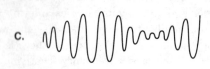

D.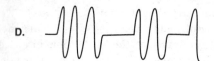

77. Two different tuning forks are struck at the same time. The resulting sound is used as the input to an oscilloscope screen and the result is shown on the upper waveform diagram below. Then a different pair of tuning forks is sounded, resulting in the oscilloscope output shown in the following lower waveform diagram. From just the oscilloscope outputs, we know that the notes in top display are:

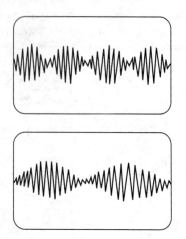

A. closer in frequency.
B. further apart in frequency.
C. equally close in frequency to those in the second display.
D. indeterminable from the oscilloscope output alone.

78. An instrument may be tuned by sounding a standard tuning fork for a certain note at the same time that note is sounded on the instrument. The resultant beats indicate the difference in the two frequencies, and thus how far out of tune the instrument is. How long will it take to perfectly tune an instrument?

A. Several seconds
B. Several minutes
C. Several hours
D. An infinite amount of time

79. A square wave with period of 2 milliseconds is to be constructed from odd harmonics. The lowest frequency needed is:

A. 250 Hz.
B. 500 Hz.
C. 2,000 Hz.
D. an infinite frequency.

80. A square wave is fed into a speaker which cannot faithfully reproduce very high frequencies. The resulting waveform would most likely resemble which of the following:

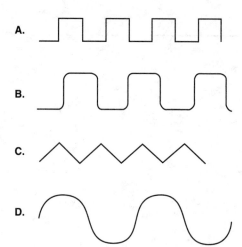

81. A student tunes a radio receiver to a specific carrier frequency. Only the carrier frequency is received, and other frequency components are excluded. Which of the following best describes the reception obtained?

A. Excellent reception is likely.
B. Moderate reception is likely.
C. Distorted reception is likely.
D. No reception is likely.

124

GO ON TO THE NEXT PAGE.

Passage IV (Questions 82–87)

Solubility is important in chemistry, allowing the preparation of some inorganic materials, removal of ions from aqueous solutions, and qualitative analysis. At the molecular level, a solid crystalline material may dissolve into its ionic components by leaving the surface of the crystal and entering the solution. The ions move about in a random fashion. At times, the ions may collide with one another and stick, returning to the crystalline state. Eventually, a dynamic equilibrium is reached, where the rate at which ions leave the crystal state equals the rate at which ions return to the crystals.

The solubility product is a valuable equilibrium constant for compounds that dissociate in solution. Table 1 lists solubilities in water at 25°C for several compounds. Answer the following questions based on the dissociation of compounds in solution and their solubility product values. Assume that ionic compounds that are not listed in Table 1 are more soluble than those that are.

Table 1. Compound Solubility in Water at 25°C

Compound	Solubility Product
Iron(II) hydroxide	1.1×10^{-36}
Lead(II) iodide	1.4×10^{-8}
Lead(II) carbonate	3.3×10^{-14}
Lead(II) chloride	2.4×10^{-4}
Lead(II) sulfide	3.4×10^{-28}
Copper(I) iodide	5.1×10^{-12}
Copper(II) hydroxide	2.2×10^{-20}
Copper(II) sulfide	6.0×10^{-37}
Aluminum hydroxide	1.8×10^{-33}
Silver iodide	8.3×10^{-17}
Silver bromide	7.7×10^{-13}
Silver carbonate	8.1×10^{-12}
Silver chloride	1.6×10^{-10}
Silver sulfide	6.0×10^{-51}
Cobalt sulfide	4.0×10^{-21}

82. The solubility product constant for lead(II) hydroxide is represented by which equation?

A. $K_{sp} = [Pb^{+2}]^2[OH^-]$
B. $K_{sp} = [Pb^{+2}][OH^-]^2$
C. $K_{sp} = [Pb^{+2}][OH^-]/[H_2O]$
D. $K_{sp} = [Pb^{+2}][OH^-]^2/[Pb(OH)_2]$

83. Given a saturated solution of silver carbonate, silver could be removed from solution by:

A. addition of more silver carbonate.
B. addition of sodium chloride.
C. addition of sodium sulfide.
D. addition of sodium hydroxide.

84. The addition of 10 ml of 0.5 M sodium chloride to 10 ml of a 1×10^{-5} M silver nitrate solution would:

A. have no effect as sodium chloride is water soluble.
B. result in the precipitation of sodium chloride.
C. result in the precipitation of silver chloride.
D. result in the coprecipitation of silver and sodium chlorides.

85. A solution containing equal concentrations of lead (II) nitrate and silver nitrate (both completely dissolved) could be separated best by which of the following procedures?

A. Addition of sodium carbonate until precipitation is complete
B. Addition of sodium sulfide until precipitation is complete
C. Addition of sodium chloride until precipitation is complete
D. Centrifuging the solution until the heavier lead salt is pulled to the bottom

86. As silver is generally an expensive metal, how could the silver best be removed from a solution containing equal low concentrations of lead (II) nitrate, silver nitrate, copper (II) nitrate, aluminum nitrate, and cobalt (II) nitrate?

A. Precipitation of aluminum, copper and lead as hydroxides, followed by precipitation of silver as the sulfide
B. Precipitation of aluminum, copper, lead and cobalt as sulfides, leaving silver in solution
C. Precipitation of silver as the sulfide, leaving all other ions in solution
D. The K_{sp} values for the salts of these ions are not different enough to allow good separations

GO ON TO THE NEXT PAGE.

...emistry student is performing a qualitative anal-
...sis scheme, and accidentally precipitates aluminum
hydroxide by adding too much base to the test tube.
Which of the following procedures would allow the
aluminum to dissolve?

A. The addition of iron (II) chloride, because iron (II) hydroxide has a lower K_{sp} than aluminum hydroxide, so iron hydroxide will precipitate, allowing the aluminum to dissolve.

B. The addition of hydrochloric acid, which will remove hydroxide from solution, allowing the aluminum to dissolve.

C. The addition of ammonia, which should chelate the aluminum and dissolve it.

D. More than one of the above are equally suitable.

Questions 88 through 91 are NOT based on a descriptive passage.

88. Potassium has an atomic number of 19. Which electron configuration depicts an excited state of potassium?

A. $1s^2, 2s^2, 2p^6, 3s^2, 3p^6, 4s^1$
B. $1s^2, 2s^2, 2p^6, 3s^2, 3p^7$
C. $1s^2, 2s^2, 2p^6, 3s^2, 3p^5, 4s^1$
D. $1s^2, 2s^2, 2p^6, 3s^2, 3p^5, 4s^2$

89. Masses A and B rest on the massless and frictionless pulley as shown in the diagram below. The mass of A is greater than the mass of B. What is the acceleration of the system?

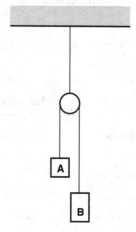

A. g
B. $\{(A - B)/AB\}(g)$
C. $\{(A - B)/(A + B)\}(g)$
D. $\{(A + B)/(A - B)\}(g)$

90. Planet X has a mass one-half the mass of the earth. Planet X has a radius one quarter the radius of the earth. What fraction of the earth's acceleration due to gravity (g_{earth}) is g_X?

A. One quarter of that on earth
B. One eighth of that on earth
C. Eight times that on earth
D. Four times that on earth

GO ON TO THE NEXT PAGE.

91. Paramagnetism, the ability to be pulled into a magnetic field, is demonstrated by:

A. transition elements which have unpaired d orbital electrons.
B. transition elements which have paired d orbital electrons.
C. non-metal elements which have unpaired p orbital electrons.
D. non-metal elements which have paired p orbital electrons.

Passage V (Questions 92–97)

A chemistry student performs an experiment evaluating a current-producing cell. The student sets up a voltaic cell. He mixes ferrous sulfate and ferric sulfate in contact with a platinum electrode in beaker A and cupric sulfate in contact with a copper electrode in beaker B. The two beakers are connected to a voltmeter and the circuit is completed with an ammonium chloride salt-bridge. All metals are pure and all ions are at 1.0 mol/L unless otherwise specified. The system is at 25°C. Figure 1 shows the student's cell:

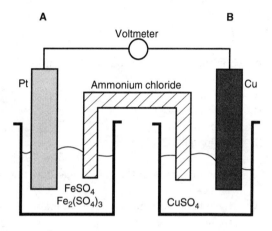

Standard reduction potentials ($E°$), or half-cell potentials, at 25°C:

$$Fe^{+3} + e^- \rightarrow Fe^{+2} \qquad E° = 800 \text{ mV}$$
$$Cu^{+2} + 2e^- \rightarrow Cu \qquad E° = 300 \text{ mV}$$

The student performs the reactions predicted by the diagramed voltaic cell. For reference, the Nernst equation at 25°C can be written as follows:

$$E_{cell} = E°_{cell} - (60/n)(\log Q)$$
E_{cell} = The cell potential in mV
$E°_{cell}$ = The standard cell potential in mV
n = Number of electrons transferred
Q = The reaction quotient

92. In which beaker does oxidation occur?

A. Beaker A
B. Beaker B
C. Both beaker A and beaker B
D. Neither beaker A nor beaker B

...ich reaction below is the spontaneous whole-cell ...action under standard conditions?

A. $Fe^{+3} + Cu \rightarrow Fe^{+2} + Cu^{+2}$
B. $Fe^{+2} + Cu^{+2} \rightarrow Fe^{+3} + Cu$
C. $2\,Fe^{+3} + Cu \rightarrow 2\,Fe^{+2} + Cu^{+2}$
D. $2\,Fe^{+2} + Cu^{+2} \rightarrow 2\,Fe^{+3} + Cu$

94. Which of the following compounds is oxidized in this cell?

A. Fe^{+3}
B. Fe^{+2}
C. Cu^{+2}
D. Cu

95. Which is the best estimation of E°_{cell} in millivolts?

A. 500 mV
B. 800 mV
C. 1,100 mV
D. 1,300 mV

96. The ammonium ions in the salt-bridge flow toward:

A. the site of reduction which contains the Pt electrode.
B. the site of oxidation which contains the Pt electrode.
C. the site of reduction which contains the Cu electrode.
D. the site of oxidation which contains the Cu electrode.

97. The volume of solution at the cathode is doubled by the addition of the appropriate amount of water. All other parameters are held constant. Which of the following statements is true?

I. The E°_{cell} will be unchanged.
II. The E_{cell} will be unchanged.
III. E_{cell} will be greater than E°_{cell}.

A. I only
B. II only
C. III only
D. I and II only

Passage VI (Questions 98–103)

Dams contribute significant amounts of energy to many regions worldwide. Dams harness the energy of flowing water by converting it into electrical energy. In a typical design, the water is allowed to flow down pipes, causing turbines to spin. The spinning turbines can be used to rotate a coil inside a magnetic field, thus creating electricity.

The energetics of fluid dynamics is best explained by Bernoulli's equation. Bernoulli's equation describes the flow of water down a pipe. Each element in the equation describes a pressure or energy state. A common form of Bernoulli's equation is:

$$P_a + \rho g y_a + 0.5\rho v_a^2 = P_b + \rho g y_b + 0.5\rho v_b^2$$

Figure 1 shows a schematic dam system. Assume that the water going through the dam for the generation of electricity enters at the top of the water level on the right side of the dam, and exits at the top of the water level on the left side of the dam. The water levels are indicated by the dashed lines. Assume the density of water is 1,000 kg/m³, and g is 10 m/s², or 10 N/kg.

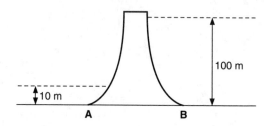

Figure 1.   A schematic dam system.

98. The sequence of energy transformations is best described as:

A. translational kinetic energy, potential energy, rotational kinetic energy, electrical energy.
B. potential energy, rotational kinetic energy, translational kinetic energy, electrical energy.
C. translational kinetic energy, rotational kinetic energy, potential energy, electrical energy.
D. potential energy, translational kinetic energy, rotational kinetic energy, electrical energy.

99. If 1,000 kg/min of water flow through the dam, the maximum power that could be created would be:

A. 9 megawatts.
B. 15 megawatts.
C. 17 megawatts.
D. 900 megawatts.

GO ON TO THE NEXT PAGE.

100. The pressure differential between points A and B at the base of the dam would be:

   A.   90 kPa.
   B.   100 kPa.
   C.   900 kPa.
   D.   1,000 kPa.

101. Which values are required to calculate the velocity of the water flowing out of the dam on the left side?

   g = acceleration of gravity
   h = height difference between right and left sides of dam
   πr^2 = cross-sectional area of pipe used for draining the dam
   d = depth of dam

   A.   d, g
   B.   g, h
   C.   d, g, h
   D.   d, g, h, πr^2

102. A plot of the pressure along the side of the dam, with respect to depth would look like:

A.

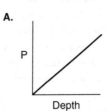

B.

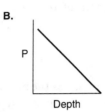

C.

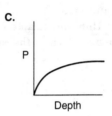

D.

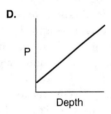

103. If the water on both sides of the dam was replaced with oil and the same amount of oil flows through the dam over a given period, the amount of energy produced by the dam would:

   A.   increase.
   B.   decrease.
   C.   remain the same.
   D.   cannot be determined.

The electrical conduction of an axon can be under-
~~ood by modeling it as an electrical cable covered with
defective insulation that allows the cable to leak current
into the surroundings. Specifically, the current in an axon
can either travel down the nerve's axoplasm or leak out of
the membrane. In this model, we consider several quantities. The first is the resistance of the axon, R, to a current
down its length. This is given to us using the equation for
R in terms of resistivity of the axoplasm, ρ the length of
the nerve, l; and cross-sectional area of the nerve, here
πr^2 where r is the nerve radius.

$$R = \rho l/A$$

The resistance to the leakage current across the membrane
is labeled R_m and the charge per unit area across the membrane divided by the potential difference which exists gives
the membrane's capacitance per unit area, C_m.

The membrane of an axon is thin, so we can approximate it as a flat, parallel plate capacitor. Thus, the capacitance of a length of axon, l long, is:

$$C = C_m(2\pi r l).$$

One adaptation of nerves is the presence of myelin. Supporting cells wrap tightly around an axon, forming a
sheath of myelin. The resulting membrane capacitance is
orders of magnitude smaller for the same length. Thus, the
time it takes to send a signal along the axon ("discharge
the capacitor") is much shorter along a myelinated portion
of nerve compared with an unmyelinated portion. The signal will travel farther and faster in a myelinated axon. The
myelin also increases the membrane's resistance to the
leakage current. Table 1 compares various properties of
myelinated and unmyelinated axons.

Table 1. Comparison Between Myelinated and
Unmyelinated Axons

Property	Myelinated Axon	Unmyelinated Axon
Axoplasm resistivity	2 Ωm	2 Ωm
Capacitance per unit area of membrane	5×10^{-5} Fm^{-2}	10^{-2} Fm^{-2}
Resistance of unit area of membrane	40 Ωm^2	0.2 Ωm^2
Radius, r	5×10^{-6} m	5×10^{-6} m

Another factor to consider is how far a signal can travel
without being amplified. This distance is given by λ, the
space parameter. It is defined as:

$$\lambda = \sqrt{\frac{R_m r}{2}}$$

After this distance, most of the axon's current will have
leaked out of the membrane in the form of leakage current.

104. The resistance of a 1-cm length of a typical axon is:

    A. 25 MΩ
    B. 32 MΩ
    C. 255 MΩ
    D. 312 MΩ

105. A nerve impulse will travel furthest without amplification down a:

    A. large myelinated nerve.
    B. large unmyelinated nerve.
    C. small myelinated nerve.
    D. small unmyelinated nerve.

106. The formation of an action potential is similar to the
discharge of a capacitor across the membrane. This
discharge takes a relatively long period compared
with the discharge of an actual electrical capacitor
because of the:

    A. high axoplasm resistivity.
    B. narrow nerve radius.
    C. slow redistribution of charge across the mem-
brane.
    D. high membrane capacitance.

107. How many ions must travel across a 1-mm stretch of
unmyelinated axon to change the membrane potential from -90 mV to 60 mV?

    A. 2.0×10^{-10} C
    B. 4.7×10^{-10} C
    C. 4.7×10^{-11} C
    D. 2.0×10^{-12} C

GO ON TO THE NEXT PAGE.

108. Assume the typical human Schwann cell which myelinates an axon is 1 mm long and about 1×10^{-6} m wide. It wraps repeatedly (lengthwise) around the membrane of the axon. This results in a membrane capacitance of 5×10^{-5} Fm^{-2}, as in Table 1. If an axon is found with 10-mm long Schwann cells myelinating it, the membrane capacitance would:

A. increase because of the increased separation of charge.

B. increase because of the decreased dielectric between the axoplasm and surroundings.

C. decrease because of the increased separation of charge.

D. decrease because of the decreased dielectric between the axoplasm and surroundings.

Passage VIII (Questions 109–113)

An understanding of molecular structure is critical to the study of chemistry. One of the main theories used to predict molecular shape is the valence-shell electron-pair repulsion (VSEPR) theory. This theory is based on studies showing that the number of valence shell electrons, electron pairing, and electron repulsion contribute to the number of molecules. Table 1 lists a method for determining molecular shape based on VSEPR theory.

Table 1. Method for Determining a Shape Using Valence-Shell Electron-Pair Repulsion (VSEPR) Theory

1. Determine the total number of valence electron pairs in the molecule.
2. Determine the number of electron pairs needed to bond the atoms together. (Take the number of atoms minus 1.)
3. Determine the number of electron pairs that surround the central atom. (Total number of pairs − [3 × number of terminal atoms, excluding H])
4. Determine the number of lone pairs around the central bonding atom. (Take the number of central pairs minus the number of bond pairs.)
5. Put the molecule together and determine the appropriate shape, excluding lone pairs.

Additional data are helpful to make measurements and predictions about molecular shape. Tables 2 and 3 show single bond covalent radii and dipole moments.

Table 2. Single Bond Covalent Radii in Angstroms (Å)

C	0.77	O	0.66
Si	1.17	S	1.04
N	0.70	F	0.64
P	1.10	Cl	0.99
Sb	1.41	I	1.33
H	0.37		

GO ON TO THE NEXT PAGE.

Molecule	Calculated Dipole Moment (M_c)	Experimental Dipole Moment (M_e)
H_2	3.6	0.00
F_2	6.82	0.00
HF	4.4	1.82
HCl	6.10	1.03
FCl	7.82	0.88
KF	10.4	8.60

Finally, the percent ionic character is defined by the following relation:

$$\% \text{ Ionic character} = M_e/M_c \times 100\%$$

109. Estimate the length of the carbon-carbon bond in H_2CCH_2 using the data given in the passage.

- **A.** 1.54 Å
- **B.** 1.29 Å
- **C.** 1.00 Å
- **D.** 0.77 Å

110. The actual length of the carbon-carbon bond is measured to be 1.33 Å by reasonably accurate experiments. Which of the following is the best explanation for the difference found in calculated versus experimentally determined dipole moments for H_2CCH_2?

- **A.** Covalent radii cannot be used because of the dipole moment in this molecule.
- **B.** Use of the covalent radii assumes single bond formation.
- **C.** The lone pairs on the carbon atoms distort the structure of the molecule such that the application of covalent radii is inappropriate.
- **D.** The "pull" of the hydrogen atoms in this molecule is directed away from the central structure such that they reduce the length of the carbon-carbon bond in this molecule.

111. Which molecule below is most ionic in character?

- **A.** F_2
- **B.** HF
- **C.** HCl
- **D.** KF

112. Using your knowledge of chemical structure and data given in the passage, which of the molecule(s) below is(are) polar or nonpolar as indicated?

- **I.** SO_2 is polar.
- **II.** XeF_4 is nonpolar.
- **III.** BeF_2 is polar.
- **IV.** NO is nonpolar.

- **A.** I only
- **B.** I and II only
- **C.** I, II, and IV only
- **D.** II, III, and IV only

113. Phosgene is a dangerous gas with the formula $COCl_2$. Using your knowledge of chemical structure and the VSEPR theory, predict the number of lone pairs surrounding the central bonding atom.

- **A.** 0
- **B.** 1
- **C.** 2
- **D.** 3

GO ON TO THE NEXT PAGE.

114. A projectile is fired in the following trajectory. At the highest point vertically in the path, which of the following statements are true?

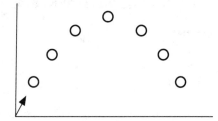

  A. Velocity is zero.
  B. Acceleration is zero.
  C. Velocity and acceleration are perpendicular.
  D. Velocity and acceleration are parallel and both equal.

115. Three capacitors are connected in parallel. Which best describes the equivalent capacitance?

  A. It is less than if the capacitors were connected in series.
  B. It is equal to the average capacitance of the three capacitors.
  C. It is greater than the capacitance of any of the three single capacitors.
  D. It is equal to the equivalent capacitance of the capacitors in series.

116. What volume of 10-M sulfuric acid is needed to prepare 600 ml of 0.5-M sulfuric acid?

  A. 3 ml
  B. 30 ml
  C. 6 ml
  D. 60 ml

117. Consider the following data for a chemical reaction occurring at a temperature of R Kelvin. Which of the following is a true statement?

$\Delta H = X$
$\Delta S = Y$
$\Delta G = X - RY$

  A. The reaction is spontaneous.
  B. The reaction is not spontaneous.
  C. The reaction is at equilibrium.
  D. There is not enough information to determine the type of reaction.

118. Consider a point on the circumference of a rotating wheel. Which of the following would increase the tangential acceleration of the point on the wheel?

  A. If the point was closer to the center of the wheel
  B. If the point was farther from the center of the wheel
  C. If the point had greater mass
  D. None of the above (The acceleration of the point is independent of the location of the point on the wheel.)

he widespread use of radiation in medicine for diag- and therapy has necessitated attention to limiting lic exposure in areas where radiation is being used. limiting exposure is based on three principles: distance, time, and shielding. The flux (particles per unit area) for all types of radiation decreases by a factor of d^{-2} where d is the distance from the point source of radiation. It is best to maximize one's distance from a source. Exposure is also usually proportional to the length of time exposed, so this is best minimized.

Shielding is more complex, and the material used depends on the type of radiation involved. Alpha particles at diagnostic and therapeutic energies are generally stopped by short distances of air, so shielding is not a necessary consideration. Beta particles are also stopped easily by using most common construction materials, such as steel, lead, or concrete. However, caution must be taken to properly shield the brehmstrallung (German for "braking radiation") gamma ray's emitted when a beta particle is slowed in the electric field of a nucleus. The intensity of brehmstrallung released will be proportional to the atomic number, Z, of the medium the beta particle is traveling through.

Gamma rays and neutrons, in contrast, do not have finite ranges, but instead are exponentially attenuated. This attenuation is usually expressed in term of half-value layers. The half-value layer of a material is the thickness of material necessary to attenuate the flux of gamma rays (or neutrons) by a factor of one-half. (This does not include the effect from the $1/d^2$ dependence mentioned above.)

The gamma ray attenuation properties of a material are generally related to the electron density of the material, given by N_aZ/A, where N_a is Avogadro's number, Z is the atomic number of the material, and A is the atomic mass of the material. Thus, the higher the electron density, the greater the attenuation for a given length, and the shorter the half-value layer. For these reasons, dense materials such as lead make excellent gamma ray attenuators. Neutrons are slowed by collisions with nuclei in which momentum is transferred from the neutron to the nucleus. Neutrons colliding with large nuclei lose little momentum in the collision, recoiling at almost the same speed. Therefore, materials for stopping neutrons are similar in mass to a neutron, and absorb much of the neutrons momentum in the collision.

119. The substance with the highest electron density is:

A. $_1^1H$
B. $_2^4He$
C. $_8^{16}O$
D. $_{82}^{207}Pb$

120. Which of the following materials would be best for stopping neutrons?

A. Polyethylene
B. Steel
C. Lead
D. Diamond

121. The best shielding to minimize brehmstrallung production by high-energy beta particles would be:

A. plastic.
B. iron.
C. lead.
D. tungsten.

122. Which of the following is the most important aspect of alpha particle shielding?

A. Time
B. Distance
C. Shielding
D. Ventilation

123. The radiation emitted by a point source is measured using two spherical detectors that surround the source. If one detector has a radius of 1m and the other has a radius of 3m, then the ratio of total particles detected, neglecting attenuation in air, between the 1- and 3-m detectors would be:

A. $\frac{1}{9}$.
B. $\frac{1}{6}$.
C. $\frac{1}{3}$.
D. 1.

124. The half-value layer for a certain energy of gamma ray is 2 cm in steel. A 10-cm wide barrier is placed 10 cm from a gamma ray source. If a flux of N_0 gamma rays per meter squared is measured on the near side of the barrier, what intensity will be measured on the other side of the barrier?

A. $N_0/16$
B. $N_0/32$
C. $N_0/64$
D. $N_0/128$

134

Passage X (Questions 125–130)

The use of indicators is very important in acid/base chemistry. Indicators are acid-base pairs that are added to titration mixtures in small molar amounts to monitor pH. The acidic and basic forms of the indicator are different colors. Indicators tend to react with excess acid or base in titrations to form a colored product, which you can see. Indicators are commonly selected based on their K_a values. Indicators tend to have color changes at particular pH values. A chemist can choose an indicator with a color change in the pH range of interest. Consider Table 1.

Table 1. Common Indicators with their Corresponding K_a Values and Characteristic Colors

Indicator	K_a	Colors (acid–base)
Bromcresol green	2.1×10^{-5}	yellow–green
Bromthymol blue	7.9×10^{-8}	yellow–blue
2,4-Dinitrophenol	1.3×10^{-4}	colorless–yellow
Chlorophenol red	1.0×10^{-6}	yellow–red
Thymolphthalein	1.0×10^{-10}	colorless–blue

125. What is the color of 2,4-dinitrophenol when placed in 0.100 M HCl?

- **A.** Yellow
- **B.** Blue
- **C.** Green
- **D.** Colorless

126. What is the color of thymolphthalein in 1.0 M NaOH?

- **A.** Yellow
- **B.** Blue
- **C.** Green
- **D.** Red

127. Why is only a "drop of indicator" used in titrations and not several milliliters?

- **A.** Because they are soluble salts
- **B.** Because they have acid/base properties themselves
- **C.** Because they are strong acids
- **D.** Because the color change would be too intense

128. Which of these indicators is the strongest acid?

- **A.** Bromphenol blue
- **B.** Bromcresol green
- **C.** Thymolphthalein
- **D.** 2,4-Dinitrophenol

129. Which of these indicators is least ionized or dissociated in aqueous solution?

- **A.** Bromphenol blue
- **B.** Bromcresol green
- **C.** Thymolphthalein
- **D.** 2,4-Dinitrophenol

130. What percentage of thymolphthalein is deprotonated in aqueous solution at pH 10?

- **A.** 25%
- **B.** 50%
- **C.** 75%
- **D.** 100%

or environmental and health reasons, it is important to consider the spread of potentially harmful particulates. Particulates vary in size and are affected by classical Newtonian forces. As a particulate falls, it is attracted to the center of the earth by gravitational force. A retarding force, or air resistance, acts in the opposite direction of particle movement. The forces acting on a fine particle falling in air can be summarized in the following free body diagram (Figure 1).

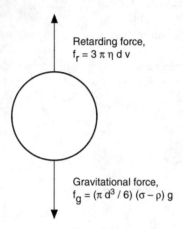

Retarding force,
$f_r = 3\pi\eta dv$

Gravitational force,
$f_g = (\pi d^3 / 6)(\sigma - \rho)g$

Figure 1.   Forces acting on a particle falling in air.

The retarding force is determined by η the viscosity of air (equal to 185×10^{-6} g/cm-sec at room temperature); d, the particle diameter in cm; and v, the velocity at which the particle is falling at centimeters per second.

The gravitational force is determined by d, the particle diameter in cm; g, the acceleration due to gravity; σ, the density of the particle in g/cm³; and ρ, the density of air in g/cm³.

131. The expression $(\pi d^3/6)\sigma$ is equivalent to which of the following?

   A.   The force of gravity on the particle
   B.   The acceleration of the particle
   C.   The mass of the particle
   D.   The weight of the particle

132. When the retarding force equals the gravitational force, there are no net forces acting to accelerate the falling particle. It then reaches its terminal velocity, v_t. An expression for v_t is:

   A. $\dfrac{d*d(\sigma-\rho)g}{18\eta v}$

   B. $\dfrac{d*d(\rho-\sigma)g}{18\eta v}$

   C. $\dfrac{d*d(\rho-\sigma)g}{18\eta}$

   D. $\dfrac{d*d(\sigma-\rho)g}{18\eta}$

133. Which of the following is correct?

   A. $(\pi d^3/6)\rho g$ is a buoyant force; $3\pi\eta dv$ is a friction force
   B. $(\pi d^3/6)\rho g$ is a friction force; $3\pi\eta dv$ is a buoyant force
   C. $(\pi d^3/6)\sigma g$ is a friction force; $3\pi\eta dv$ is a friction force
   D. $(\pi d^3/6)\sigma g$ is a friction force; $3\pi\eta dv$ is a buoyant force

134. Increasing the diameter of a 1μm particle by 2μm will:

   A.   increase the terminal velocity by a factor of 9.
   B.   increase the terminal velocity by a factor of 4.
   C.   decrease the terminal velocity by a factor of 1/4.
   D.   decrease the terminal velocity by a factor of 1/9.

135. A particle of U_3O_8 released from a reactor at a height of 30 m falls at a constant velocity of 1 cm/sec. If a cross-wind carries the particle horizontally at 13 cm/sec, how far can the U_3O_8 be carried from the reactor? Assume $g = 10$ m/s².

   A.   300 m
   B.   390 m
   C.   3,000 m
   D.   3,900 m

GO ON TO THE NEXT PAGE.

136. A researcher is investigating inhalational toxins. It is found that toxicity results when particulate toxins are inhaled into the lungs. To avoid exposing the population to these inhalational toxins, which is the best recommendation this researcher can make?

A. Keep the population beyond the range of the smallest particles which can lodge in the lungs.
B. Keep the population beyond the range of the largest particles which can lodge in the lungs.
C. Keep the population beyond the range of the smallest particles released by the toxic source.
D. Keep the population beyond the range of the largest particles released by the toxic source.

Questions 137 through 142 are NOT based on a descriptive passage.

137. Which of the following reaction types results in the net production of free radicals?

A. Termination
B. Propogation
C. Initiation
D. Initiation and propogation

138. Five moles oxygen gas and 5 mol of hydrogen gas are placed in a large vessel, such that the gases and vessel are at the same temperature. The ratio of the diffusion rate of oxygen molecules to hydrogen molecules is:

A. $1:16$.
B. $16:1$.
C. $4:1$.
D. $1:4$.

139. Two capacitors are charged as a series combination by a 100-V battery. The capacitors have capacitance values of 3 μF and 6 μF, respectively. What is the magnitude of the charge for either capacitor?

A. 100 μC
B. 200 μC
C. 400 μC
D. 600 μC

140. Consider the following chemical reaction. If 64 g of oxygen gas reacted in the forward reaction, how many moles of water are produced?

$$Sn^{+2} + O_2 + H^+ \rightarrow Sn^{+4} + H_2O$$

A. 2
B. 3
C. 4
D. 5

GO ON TO THE NEXT PAGE.

charged particles are projected into a region where a pre-existing magnetic field is present. The magnetic field is perpendicular to the direction of travel of the two particles. If the charged particles are deflected in opposite directions from one another, what can be said of the sign of the charges?

A. The charges are both negative.
B. The charges are both positive.
C. The charges are either both negative or both positive.
D. The charges are of opposite sign.

142. Approximately what percent of $AgNO_3$ is oxygen by weight?

A. 10%
B. 18%
C. 28%
D. 40%

STOP. IF YOU FINISH BEFORE TIME IS CALLED, CHECK YOUR WORK. YOU MAY GO BACK TO ANY QUESTION IN THIS TEST BOOKLET.

STOP.

Writing Sample

Time: 60 minutes total;
30 minutes per essay, each separately timed.

WRITING SAMPLE

Directions: You will be given 30 minutes to complete Essay Topic 1. Once time is called, you MUST stop working on this essay. Please draw a line below the last sentence in your essay to mark your stopping point. You will then have 30 minutes to complete Essay Topic 2. You may NOT work on Essay Topic 1 during the second 30-minute period allotted for Essay Topic 2. Use black ink and do NOT skip lines between sentences. Illegible essays will not be scored.

ESSAY TOPIC 1

Consider this statement:
The object of education should be to teach values, not skills.
Write a unified essay in which you perform the following tasks. Explain what you think the aforementioned statement means. Describe a specific situation in which the object of education might be to teach skills rather than values. Discuss what you think determines when the object of education is to teach values and when it is to teach skills.

ESSAY TOPIC 2

Consider this statement:

Leadership is the ability to direct the public will rather than following it.
Write a unified essay in which you perform the following tasks. Explain what you think the aforementioned statement means. Describe a specific situation in which leadership is demonstrated when following the public will. Discuss what you think determines whether a leader should direct or follow the public will.

Biological Sciences

Time: 100 minutes
Questions: 143–219

BIOLOGICAL SCIENCES

Directions: Most questions in the Biological Sciences test are organized into groups, each preceded by a descriptive passage. After studying the passage, select the one best answer to each question. Some questions are not based on a descriptive passage and are also independent of each other. You should also select the one best answer to these independent questions. A periodic table is provided for your use. You may consult it whenever you wish.

PERIODIC TABLE OF THE ELEMENTS

IA																	VIIIA
1 H 1.0	IIA											IIIA	IVA	VA	VIA	VII A	2 He 4.0
3 Li 6.9	4 Be 9.0											5 B 10.8	6 C 12.0	7 N 14.0	8 O 16.0	9 F 19.0	10 Ne 20.2
11 Na 23.0	12 Mg 24.3											13 Al 27.0	14 Si 28.1	15 P 31.0	16 S 32.1	17 Cl 35.5	18 Ar 39.9
19 K 39.1	20 Ca 40.1	21 Sc 45.0	22 Ti 47.9	23 V 50.9	24 Cr 52.0	25 Mn 54.9	26 Fe 55.8	27 Co 58.9	28 Ni 58.7	29 Cu 63.5	30 Zn 65.4	31 Ga 69.7	32 Ge 72.6	33 As 74.9	34 Se 79.0	35 Br 79.9	36 Kr 83.8
37 Rb 85.5	38 Sr 87.6	39 Y 88.9	40 Zr 91.2	41 Nb 92.9	42 Mo 95.9	43 Tc 98.0	44 Ru 101	45 Rh 102	46 Pd 106	47 Ag 108	48 Cd 112	49 In 115	50 Sn 119	51 Sb 122	52 Te 128	53 I 127	54 Xe 131
55 Cs 133	56 Ba 137	57 La 139	72 Hf 179	73 Ta 181	74 W 184	75 Re 186	76 Os 190	77 Ir 192	78 Pt 195	79 Au 197	80 Hg 201	81 Tl 204	82 Pb 207	83 Bi 208	84 Po 209	85 At 210	86 Rn 222
87 Fr 223	88 Ra 226	89 Ac 227															

58 Ce 140	59 Pr 141	60 Nd 144	61 Pm 145	62 Sm 150	63 Eu 152	64 Gd 157	65 Tb 159	66 Dy 163	67 Ho 165	68 Er 167	69 Tm 169	70 Yb 173	71 Lu 175
90 Th 232	91 Pa 231	92 U 238	93 Np 237	94 Pu 244	95 Am 243	96 Cm 247	97 Bk 247	98 Cf 251	99 Es 252	100 Fm 257	101 Md 258	102 No 259	103 Lr 260

GO ON TO THE NEXT PAGE.

PASSAGE I (Questions 143–149)

Chronic obstructive pulmonary disease is a group of respiratory disorders characterized by airflow obstruction. Bronchial asthma is a common example. Airflow obstruction in asthma is caused by inflammation of the bronchial wall, contraction of the bronchiolar smooth muscle, and increased mucous secretion. Symptoms include shortness of breath, coughing, and wheezing on expiration. Because resistance in an airway is inversely related to the fourth power of its radius, it is easy to understand how asthma can seriously interfere with the flow of air.

Two general categories of asthma exist: extrinsic and intrinsic. Extrinsic asthma begins in childhood, usually in patients with a family history of allergy. First exposure to the allergen causes production of specific immunoglobulin E (IgE) antibodies, which attach to mast cells in lung tissue. Subsequent exposure results in allergen binding to the IgE molecules and triggering degranulation of the mast cells. This allergen-induced degranulation is known as a type I hypersensitivity response. Mast cell granules release histamine, leukotrienes, and prostaglandins that promote airflow obstruction. Intrinsic asthma, on the other hand, begins in adulthood and is not associated with allergy. The mechanism of bronchial hyperactivity responsible for intrinsic asthma is unknown.

Many drugs are available to treat symptoms of asthma, but none offers a cure. Cromolyn is an effective prophylactic agent that stabilizes mast cells, decreasing their ability to degranulate. Not all patients respond to cromolyn, but those who do show improvement that is approximately equal to that obtained from other mainstay drug treatments of asthma.

The forced expiratory volume (FEV_1) is the volume of air that can be expired in 1 second after maximal inspiration. In normal individuals, the FEV_1 is 80% of the forced vital capacity (FVC), which is the total volume of air that can be expired after maximal inspiration. In asthmatics, the FEV_1 usually decreases more than FVC. Therefore, the ratio FEV_1/FVC can be used to monitor the success of therapeutic intervention. The histogram shown in Figure 1 summarizes data from a clinical trial, in which four patients were tested with a new asthma drug.

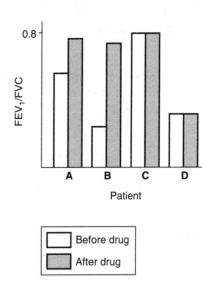

Figure 1. FEV_1/FVC for four patients given a new asthma drug.

143. What effect will a two-fold decrease in the diameter of an airway have on its resistance?

   A. A 16-fold decrease in resistance
   B. A 16-fold increase in resistance
   C. An eight-fold decrease in resistance
   D. An eight-fold increase in resistance

144. Clinical studies sometimes include controls as a means of verifying that a drug has no adverse affects on a healthy individual. Which patient in Figure 1 most likely represents a control?

   A. Patient A
   B. Patient B
   C. Patient C
   D. Patient D

145. If it is revealed that patients A and B have extrinsic asthma and patients C and D do not, then what assumption might one make regarding the experimental drug?

   A. It will treat intrinsic asthma successfully.
   B. Its mechanism is similar to that of cromolyn.
   C. It does not reach the lungs.
   D. It will be used only in children.

146. What might be assumed regarding patient A's response to the drug?

   A. Mean airway radius has increased.
   B. His/her airway resistance has increased.
   C. His/her FEV_1/FVC has decreased.
   D. A, B, and C are correct.

145

GO ON TO THE NEXT PAGE.

147. Which of the following does not occur during inspiration?

    A. There is increased intrapleural pressure.
    B. There is increased thoracic volume.
    C. There is diaphragmatic contraction.
    D. Energy is consumed.

148. Suppose that all four patients in Figure 1 have the same FVC. Before drug treatment, which patient would one expect to blow out a candle slowest?

    A. Patient A
    B. Patient B
    C. Patient C
    D. Patient D

149. Which of the following anatomic regions in the lungs contains the greatest surface area for gas exchange?

    A. Bronchioles
    B. Bronchi
    C. Alveolar ducts
    D. Alveolar sacs

PASSAGE II (Questions 150–154)

Many biologically important compounds contain rings of various sizes. The stability of the various sizes of rings is an important factor to consider when attempting to synthesize such compounds and their analogues. The following arguments present three hypotheses about the factors controlling the stability of rings.

Chemist 1

In cycloalkanes, the stability of a particular size is related to the rings' ability to have bond angles approaching 109°. Rings such as cyclopropane must have angles much smaller than this value (an equilateral triangle has 60° angles) and will have a great deal of angle strain. Extremely large rings must have angles much larger than 109° and also have a great deal of ring strain. Thus, the stability of a ring of size n can be determined by comparing the angles in a regular polygon of size n to 109°. The greater the difference between these angles, the less stable the ring, and the harder that ring will be to synthesize.

Chemist 2

Cycloalkanes, unlike straight-chain alkanes, have a large number of eclipsed, or nearly eclipsed bonds. The stability of a ring is directly related to its ability to assume a conformation with a minimal amount of eclipsing interactions between different atoms. The greater the number of eclipsing interactions, the less stable the molecule will be, with a corresponding increase in the difficulty of its synthesis.

Chemist 3

The stability of cycloalkanes is dependent on the nonbonded contacts between atoms. Steric repulsion between atoms increases as the distance between the atoms decreases. Some rings force atoms to approach too closely, these ring sizes will be unstable and difficult to synthesize.

GO ON TO THE NEXT PAGE.

150. Chemist 3 might have which of the following to say about double bonds in the *trans* configuration in medium rings?

    A. The *trans* configuration would introduce a great deal of angle strain in the ring, resulting in an unstable ring.

    B. The *trans* configuration would relieve a great deal of angle strain in the ring, resulting in a stable ring.

    C. The *trans* configuration would result in a large amount of steric crowding in the ring, resulting in an unstable ring.

    D. The *trans* configuration would relieve a large amount of steric crowding in the ring, resulting in a stable ring.

151. Which chemists' arguments are most seriously challenged by the observation that rings larger that 11 are stable?

    A. Chemist 1, because the angles in an 11-membered polygon would be considerably smaller than 109°

    B. Chemist 1, because the angles in an 11-membered polygon would be considerably larger than 109°

    C. Chemist 3, because the steric crowding in large rings would be large

    D. Chemist 3, because the steric crowding in large rings would be small

152. Whose argument represents the largest factor contributing to the instability of cyclopropane?

    A. Chemist 1, because the bond angles in cyclopropane are distorted very far from 109°

    B. Chemist 2, because the bond angles in cyclopropane are distorted very far from 109°

    C. Chemist 2, because the eclipsing interactions in cyclopropane are very large

    D. Chemist 3, because several atoms in cyclopropane are sterically crowded

153. Which chemist would be most surprised by the observation that cyclopropane opens readily to an open-chain compound?

    A. Chemist 1, because the bond angles of cyclopropane are close to 109°

    B. Chemist 2, because the eclipsing interactions in cyclopropane are very small

    C. Chemist 2, because the eclipsing interactions in cyclopropane are very large

    D. Chemist 3, because there are no sterically crowded atoms in cyclopropane

154. How would chemist 2 explain the experimental observation that 6- and 14-membered rings have the same amount of strain?

    A. Both 6- and 14-membered rings have the same bond angles, and the same strain.

    B. Both 6- and 14-membered rings are able to avoid nonbonded contacts, and thus have the same strain.

    C. Both 6- and 14-membered rings have the same eclipsing interactions, and thus the same strain.

    D. Both 6- and 14-membered rings have similar angle strain, although in opposite directions, and thus the same strain.

Virus particles, or virions, are relatively simple in overall structure. Virions are composed of either RNA or DNA, encased in a protein coat called a capsid. Some viral particles are surrounded by a lipoprotein envelope, whereas others are not. The viral genome may be single-stranded or double-stranded, linear or circular, and segmented or nonsegmented. The viral capsid is composed of structural units called capsomeres, which are aggregates of viral-specific polypeptides. The capsid maintains a three-dimensional symmetry which is classified as either helical, icosahedral, or complex.

Virions can only replicate in living cells. Viruses take over some cellular organelles and may use host cell enzymes. The replication process generally involves attachment of the virus to the cell membrane. Attachment is followed by penetration, and uncoating of the viral genome. The first proteins synthesized are generally early proteins involved in genome replication. Synthesis of the late proteins, structural proteins of the virion, comes later. In the final stages of replication, assembly of virions occurs, followed by release. Cell death may or may not occur.

There are two main strategies by which viruses interact with the host. Some viruses penetrate host cells, at which time they incorporate their genetic material into the host genome. This allows the virus a period of "rest," or latency. This strategy is demonstrated by the human immunodeficiency virus (HIV), which may sit in human T cells for many years before becoming active. Other viruses rapidly commandeer cellular function, produce many progeny, and rupture the cell membrane as they are released. A prime example of this strategy of viral survival is shown by the hepatitis virus. Once a host is infected, within 2 weeks, viral replication is complete, and infected liver cells rupture as progeny escape. This results in the death of many liver cells and liver dysfunction. Liver dysfunction is shown by the jaundice that patients with active hepatitis demonstrate. In addition to acquired immune deficiency syndrome (AIDS) and hepatitis, viruses are responsible for a vast array of illnesses in humans and other mammals. Human illnesses caused by viruses include mumps, measles, herpes, polio, shingles, influenza, and some forms of leukemia.

155. What cellular organelle is most likely used by viruses to synthesize capsomeres?

   A. Nucleus
   B. Nucleolus
   C. Smooth endoplasmic reticulum
   D. Ribosomes

156. What is the most likely origin of the viral envelope?

   A. Synthesis in the smooth endoplasmic reticulum
   B. Synthesis of a membrane by viral enzymes
   C. Synthesis by viral capsomeres
   D. The host cell membrane

157. Which life cycle does HIV described in the passage demonstrate?

   A. The latent cycle
   B. The lysogenic cycle
   C. The lytic cycle
   D. The replication cycle

158. Which of the following is not true about viruses?

   I. A virus with an RNA genome may use viral enzymes to replicate it and transcribe mRNA.
   II. A virus with an RNA genome may use viral enzymes to replicate complimentary DNA.
   III. Some viruses may reproduce by binary fission.

   A. I only
   B. III only
   C. I and II
   D. I and III

159. Which of the following are the least likely hosts for viral infection?

   A. Bacterial cells
   B. Mammalian cells
   C. Fungal cells
   D. None of the above. All three types are equally likely hosts for viral infection.

PASSAGE IV (Questions 160–164)

The therapeutic value of a drug does not only depend on its ability to inhibit an enzyme, or negatively impact bacterial processes. A compound that is to be used as a drug must make its way to the site where it is needed. The ability of a drug to get to the site where it must act is its bioavailability. Some drugs, such as painkillers, must get to the brain, others must stay in the bloodstream, and still others are needed in all the cells of the body.

For a drug to get from one part of the body to another, it must diffuse across lipid membranes which act as strongly hydrophobic barriers. Drugs must be hydrophobic enough to diffuse into the lipid membranes without being so hydrophobic as to get stuck. For many types of drugs, this property is pH dependent. The ability of drugs with ionizable groups to diffuse across membranes is strongly affected by their ionization state. Carboxylic acid groups have a pK_a of about 3. Greater than this pH level, they are charged and can no longer diffuse across membranes. An acidic drug taken orally will first reach the stomach, where the pH is around 2. It will then diffuse across the gastric mucosa to the bloodstream, where the pH is 7.2 and become trapped. Table 1 shows the typical pH in select body tissues and fluids.

Table 1. pH Values in Select Body Compartments

Body Compartment	pH
Stomach	1.0–3.0
Intestinal lumen	5.0–6.6
Plasma	7.2–7.4
Kidney	5.0–6.6
Cerebrospinal fluid	7.2–7.4

Table 2 shows some ionizable groups commonly found in drugs in both their acidic and basic forms.

Table 2. Acidic and Basic Forms of Ionizable Groups and Their pK_a's

Group	Acidic Form	Basic Form	pK_a
−COOH	−COOH	−COO⁻	3.0
−NH₂	−NH₃⁺	−NH₂	9.2
1,3-Diketone	1,3-Diketone	Enolate	9.0

160. What factor other than a drug's ability to affect a biological process determines the effectiveness of the drug?

   A. The ability of the drug to interrupt bacterial growth
   B. The ability of the drug to reach its site of action
   C. The ability of the drug to diffuse freely into lipid bilayers
   D. The ability of the drug to ionize at the site of action

161. What would happen to an amine ($-NH_2$) taken orally?

   A. It would diffuse from the stomach to the bloodstream before becoming trapped in its ionizable form.
   B. It will move from the stomach to the intestinal lumen before becoming able to diffuse into the bloodstream.
   C. It will not be absorbed into the bloodstream at all.
   D. It will be hydrolyzed in the stomach.

162. Which of the following would be most likely to pass into a lipid membrane and remain there?

   A.
   B.
   C.
   D.

163. If appropriate substituents could be chosen for an amine to lower its pK_a to 6.8, which of the following sites would the amine ultimately be found?

    A. It will transfer from the bloodstream to the kidneys before becoming ionized, thus being trapped in the kidneys.
    B. It will freely diffuse between both sites.
    C. It will transfer from the bloodstream to the kidneys before becoming neutral, thus being trapped in the kidneys.
    D. It will be ionized in the bloodstream and will not diffuse to the kidneys.

164. What would happen to a carboxylic acid $(-CO_2H)$ injected into the bloodstream?

    A. It will transfer from the bloodstream to the kidneys before becoming ionized, thus being trapped in the kidneys.
    B. It will not become ionized and can diffuse to all compartments of the body.
    C. It will transfer from the bloodstream to the cerebrospinal fluid (CSF) before becoming ionized, thus being trapped in the CSF.
    D. It will be ionized in the bloodstream and will not diffuse to other parts of the body.

Questions 165 through 168 are NOT based on a descriptive passage.

165. A researcher performs experiments attempting to characterize the action potentials generated by neurons. Based on the basic properties of action potentials, which of the following findings would be least likely from these experiments?

    A. Action potentials would be found to have a fixed strength.
    B. Action potentials would be found to be generated at a certain maximal rate in nerves.
    C. Action potentials would be found to only propagate unidirectionally in nerves.
    D. Action potentials would be found to cause neurotransmitter release in nerve terminals.

166. Which resonance structure for 1,3,5-hexatriene is the most stable?

    A. $^+CH_2CH-CH=CH-CH=CH^-$
    B. $CH_2-CH=CH-CH=CH-CH_2$
    C. $^-CH_2=CH-CH=CH-CH=CH_2^+$
    D. All have equal stability

167. *Escherichia coli* is a common intestinal bacterium. One would expect a typical *E. coli* cell to be about the size of which of the following?

    A. A human liver cell
    B. A polyribosome
    C. An amoeba
    D. A mitochondria

168. In the reaction of ethene and HCl, H^+ ion acts as the:

    A. nucleophile.
    B. electrophile.
    C. carbanion.
    D. carbonium ion.

PASSAGE V (Questions 169–174)

Intracerebral microdialysis is a technique used to measure extracellular levels of neurotransmitters. A very thin probe is inserted into a brain region of interest. At the tip of the probe is a semipermeable membrane that allows most ions and neurotransmitters to pass through. Dialysate, fluid that is similar in electrolyte composition to the brain's extracellular fluid, is pumped down to the tip of the probe, where it can pick up molecules of neurotransmitter. This fluid is pumped out of the probe, collected, and analyzed for transmitter content.

The goal of microdialysis experiments is to attempt to visualize synaptic transmission events. A simple experiment might show that the presence of a drug increases the level of a neurotransmitter in the dialysate. Conditions can then be manipulated to establish whether the drug-induced release of neurotransmitter is neuronally mediated or direct. In the case of neuronally mediated release, the drug binds far from the synapse then elicits an action potential, which arrives at the synapse and causes vesicular release of neurotransmitter. Direct release of neurotransmitter, on the other hand, is accomplished by drugs that bind directly at the synapse and no nerve impulse is required for neurotransmitter release.

The data in Table 1 was collected during microdialysis experiments. The effect of drugs A, B, C, and D on neurotransmitter levels was evaluated. These drugs were tested with and without tetrodotoxin (TTX), a drug which blocks sodium channels in neurons.

Table 1. Results of Microdialysis Experiments Performed in Brain Region with High Myelin Content

Condition	Change in Neurotransmitter Level
Drug A	Increase
Drug A + TTX	Increase
Drug B	Increase
Drug B + TTX	No change (baseline)
Drug C	Decrease
Drug C + TTX	Decrease
Drug D	Decrease
Drug D + TTX	No change (baseline)

169. Which drug (see Table 1) would you choose to enhance transmitter levels in a patient suffering from multiple sclerosis, a demyelinating disorder?

  A. Drug A
  B. Drug B
  C. Drug C
  D. Drug D

170. Which of the following statements is not true about depolarization?

  A. Depolarization occurs when the resting potential of a nerve cell becomes less negative.
  B. Depolarization increases the chances that a nerve impulse will be triggered from a nerve cell.
  C. Depolarization occurs when the inside of a nerve cell becomes more negative in relation to the outside of the cell.
  D. Depolarization is a graded potential.

171. Why is the dialysate ionically similar to brain extracellular fluid?

  A. It is similar to prevent disruption of neuronal function.
  B. Ionic makeup of dialysate allows smooth flow.
  C. It is similar to maintain positive resting potential of neurons.
  D. It is similar to provide nutrients to neurons.

172. What effect is found when a calcium chelator is included in the dialysate?

  A. It inhibits neuronally mediated transmitter release.
  B. It inhibits direct, vesicular transmitter release.
  C. Both A and B are correct.
  D. Neither A nor B is correct.

173. Which part of the neuron transmits signals towards the cell body under normal circumstances?

  A. Dendrite
  B. Axon
  C. End plate
  D. Perikaryon

174. A terminal autoreceptor is a synaptic receptor that mediates a direct decrease in the amount of neurotransmitter released. Which drug shown in Table 1 might be acting at a terminal autoreceptor?

  A. Drug A
  B. Drug B
  C. Drug C
  D. Drug D

PASSAGE VI (Questions 175–179)

Ethers are important organic solvents for many different types of reactions. Ether molecules are polar because of the geometry at the oxygen atom but they can dissolve organic compounds because of the hydrocarbon components. They are also aprotic. The range of substances that will dissolve in ethers is dependent on the different R groups used.

The synthesis of ethers is commonly performed using the Williamson ether synthesis. This reaction involves the use of an alkoxide as a nucleophile and an alkyl halide as the electrophile in an S_N2 reaction (Figure 1).

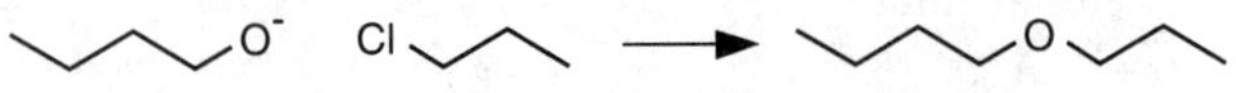

Figure 1.   Williamson ether synthesis.

Symmetrical ethers allow only one choice of alkoxide and alkyl halide, by asymmetric ethers can be divided on either side of the oxygen atom when determining starting materials. The basicity of alkoxides promotes elimination as a side reaction so correct choice of alkyl halide and alkoxide is a crucial factor in obtaining good yield of ether. Figure 2 shows various yields obtained from the use of different alkoxide and alkyl halide combinations.

Desired ether	Alkyl halide	Alkoxide	Yield
			78%
			81%
			75%
			42%

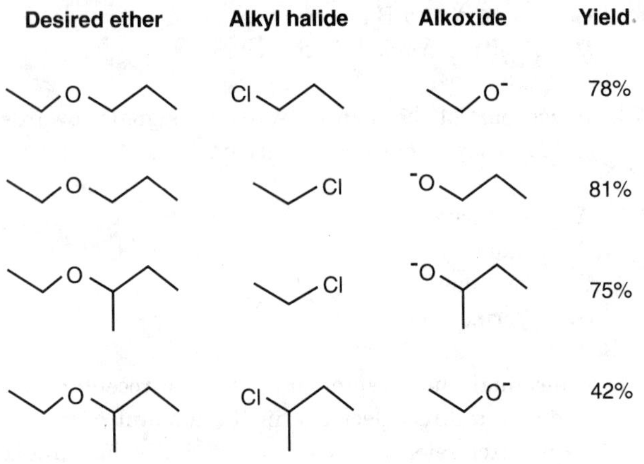

Figure 2.   Yields obtained from different alkoxide and alkyl halide combinations.

175. What side product would be expected for the third entry in Figure 2?

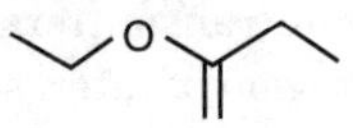

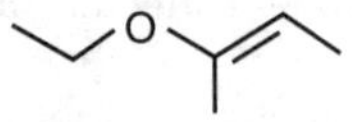

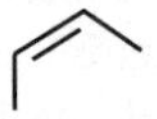

176. Which of the following mechanisms applies to the Williamson synthesis?

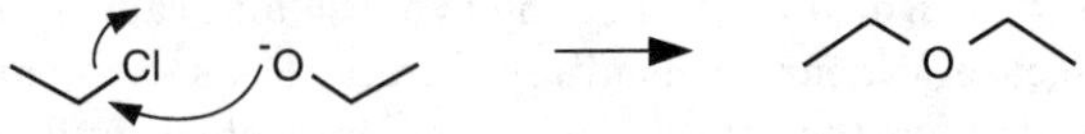

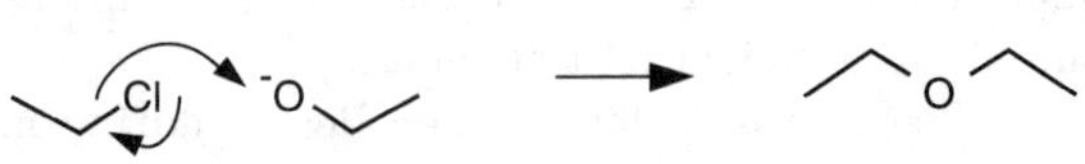

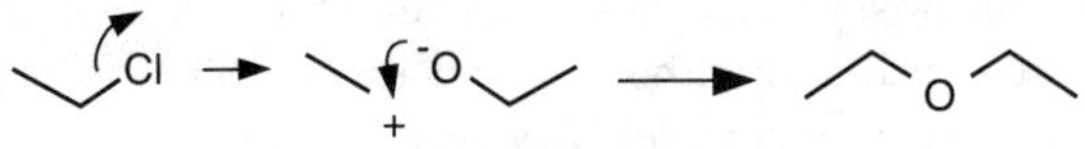

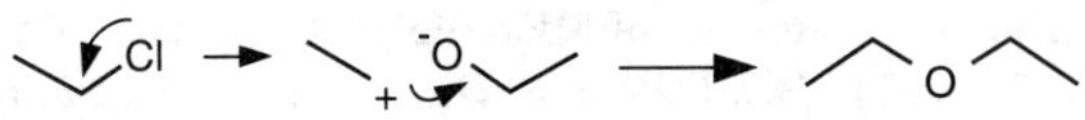

177. Why are ethers useful solvents?

   A.   Ethers are useful solvents because they are easily synthesized.
   B.   Ethers are useful solvents because they can dissolve both polar and nonpolar solvents.
   C.   Ethers are useful solvents because they can hydrogen bond to unstable products making the reaction more favorable.
   D.   Ethers are useful solvents because they tightly solvate ions, stabilizing them.

152

GO ON TO THE NEXT PAGE.

178. Which of the following is the best combination of starting materials for the preparation of methyl isopropyl ether?

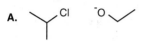

A.

B.

C.

D.

179. Why does the fourth entry in Figure 2 have such a poor yield?

A. The alkoxide is not nucleophilic enough to displace the halide.

B. The alkyl halide is not nucleophilic enough to displace the oxide.

C. The alkoxide is too sterically crowded to attack the electrophilic carbon.

D. The alkyl halide is too sterically crowded to attack the electrophilic carbon.

PASSAGE VII (Questions 180–185)

The cardiac cycle is a complex sequence of events in which the electrical and mechanical action of the heart results in the generation of pressure within the cardiovascular system. The cardiac cycle begins with atrial contraction, which increases the volume of blood in the ventricles. The phase in which blood fills the relaxed ventricle is known as diastole. The pressure of the blood in the ventricles at the end of atrial contraction is known as ventricular end-diastolic pressure, or VEDP.

Once blood has filled the ventricles, ventricular contraction, or systole occurs. The volume of blood in the ventricle just before the onset of ventricular contraction is known as ventricular end-diastolic pressure or VEDV. Blood is pumped from the ventricles to either the pulmonary artery or aorta. A small volume of blood is left in the ventricles after systole. The ventricular end-systolic volume or VESV is the volume of blood remaining in the ventricle at the end of ejection.

Several other terms are important in the study of the cardiac cycle. Stroke volume is the volume of blood ejected with each beat. The ejection fraction equals the stroke volume divided by the VEDV. The ejection fraction is a percentage which indicates the volume of blood ejected with a heartbeat divided by the blood volume present in the ventricle at the end of diastole.

To best understand of the cardiac cycle, pressure-volume loops can be drawn. In these loops, it is possible to record changes in ventricular pressure and volume during a cardiac cycle. These loops are useful because they provide information as to the function of the ventricles. Figure 1 shows a normal pressure-volume curve from a human heart. Point 1 represents VEDV. Point 2 marks the onset of systole. Point 3 is the beginning of isovolumetric relaxation, whereas point 4 is the onset of VESV.

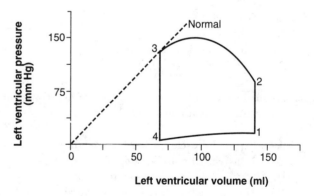

Figure 1. A normal pressure-volume curve for the heart.

(Reprinted with permission from Bullock J, Boyle J, Wang MB: *NMS Physiology*, 3e. Baltimore, Williams & Wilkins, 1995, 164.)

153

GO ON TO THE NEXT PAGE.

180. Which best describes the state of ventricles during ventricular diastole?

    A. Contracting and isovolumetric
    B. Relaxing and isovolumetric
    C. Contracting and not isovolumetric
    D. Relaxing and not isovolumetric

181. Which point on Figure 1 represents the beginning of isovolumetric relaxation of the ventricle?

    A. Point 1
    B. Point 2
    C. Point 3
    D. Point 4

182. Based on information given in the passage, which of the following best represents stroke volume?

    A. VEDV—VESV
    B. VEDP—VEDV
    C. VESV—VEDV
    D. VEDV—VEDP

183. If the atria or veins deliver more blood to the ventricles during diastole, which of the following will increase the most?

    A. VESV
    B. VESP
    C. VEDV
    D. None of the above (VESV, VESP, and VEDV all increase an equal amount.)

184. Which of the following processes occur between points 4 and 1 in Figure 1?

    A. Diastole
    B. Systole
    C. Isovolumetric relaxation
    D. Isovolumetric contraction

185. Microscopic examination of a biopsy of heart muscle would show which appearance?

    A. Striated muscle, no intercalated disks
    B. Nonstriated muscle, intercalated disks
    C. Striated muscle, intercalated disks
    D. Nonstriated muscle, no intercalated disks

PASSAGE VIII (Questions 186–190)

α, β-Unsaturated carbonyl compounds contain two electrophilic sites that can be attacked by nucleophiles. Nucleophilic attack at the carbonyl group is called 1,2-addition. Nucleophilic attack at the alkene is called 1,4-, or conjugate, addition. One frequently used nucleophile in conjugate additions is the enolate. Enolates are formed by the addition of a strong base to a carbonyl compound. The hydrogens on carbons adjacent to carbonyl groups are considerably more acidic than the other hydrogens. Enolates predominantly perform conjugate addition with α, β-unsaturated carbonyl compounds. A useful application of this reactivity is the Robinson annulation, and is shown in Figure 1.

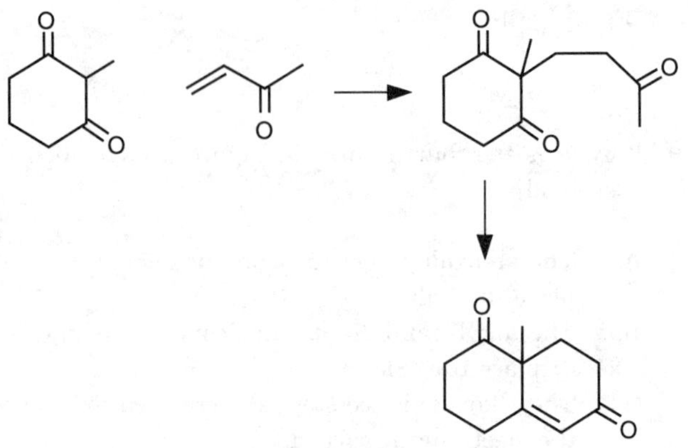

Figure 1.   An example of the Robinson annulation reaction.

The Robinson annulation is an extremely useful method for making fused ring systems. It actually consists of one conjugate addition, followed by a 1,2-addition. The alcohol formed in the 1,2-addition step eliminates very easily even in a basic solution to form a new α, β-unsaturated carbonyl system.

186. Why are hydrogens on carbons adjacent to carbonyl groups more acidic than hydrogens farther away?

    A. The resulting cation is stabilized by resonance.
    B. That position bears a partial positive charge, attracting basic reagents.
    C. The resulting anion is stabilized by resonance.
    D. That position bears a partial negative charge, attracting basic reagents.

GO ON TO THE NEXT PAGE.

187. Based in part on information provided in the passage, where would the enolate most likely form in 1,3-cyclohexanedione?

A.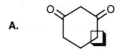

B.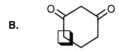

C.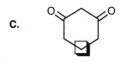

D.

188. Why does the intermediate alcohol formed in a Robinson annulation eliminate easily?

    A.   Because it is so unstable
    B.   Because it is so stable
    C.   Because the product formed is so unstable
    D.   Because the product formed is so stable

189. According to the passage, what is the benefit of the Robinson annulation?

    A.   It produces fused rings.
    B.   It produces carbonyl compounds.
    C.   It produces α, β-unsaturated carbonyl compounds.
    D.   It produces alcohols.

190. Which of the following structures shows why one site of conjugate addition in an α, β-unsaturated carbonyl compound is electrophilic?

A.

B.

C.

D.

191. Which of the following is the correct sequence of post-absorption events?

   A.   Absorption, liver, hepatic vein, hepatic portal vein, inferior vena cava, right atrium
   B.   Absorption, hepatic vein, liver, hepatic portal vein, inferior vena cava, right atrium
   C.   Absorption, hepatic portal vein, liver, hepatic vein, inferior vena cava, right atrium
   D.   None of the above

192. The organ most responsible for the rapid equilibrium of acid-base balance in the body is the:

   A.   lung.
   B.   kidney.
   C.   liver.
   D.   spleen.

193. In a given muscle, the best explanation for stronger muscle contraction is:

   A.   increased strength of action potentials.
   B.   more action potentials with variable motor unit thresholds.
   C.   alternate activity of flexor-extensor muscle antagonists.
   D.   increased motor neuron activation of motor units.

194. Consider the titration curve given for an unknown amino acid. The side chain of this amino acid is most likely:

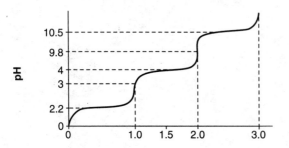

Moles of NaOH added

   A.   neutral, nonpolar.
   B.   acidic.
   C.   basic.
   D.   neutral, polar.

195. In humans, albinism is determined by a recessive gene (a). Syndactyly, a condition in which two or more fingers or toes are joined by a web of muscle and skin, is determined by a dominant gene (B). If a couple knows their genotypes are BbAa and bbAa, what is the probability that their offspring will both be albino and have joined fingers or toes?

   A.   ⅛
   B.   ¼
   C.   ½
   D.   ⅙

156

GO ON TO THE NEXT PAGE.

Diabetes mellitus (DM) is characterized by high blood sugar (hyperglycemia) caused by the inadequate action of insulin on body tissues. The action of insulin is inadequate because of reduced circulating levels of insulin or resistance of target tissues to its actions. The reduced action of insulin leads to numerous diseases, including microvascular disease, blindness, kidney failure, hardening of the arteries, and disease of the peripheral nerves.

DM may be classified into two categories: type I, or insulin-dependent, diabetes and type II, or adult-onset, diabetes. Type I diabetes is also known as juvenile diabetes because many patients are first affected by the disease in childhood or adolescence. Type I diabetic patients show an almost complete lack of insulin, whereas type II diabetics tend to have a partial lack of insulin and resistance to the action of insulin. Type I diabetes may be linked to abnormal immune system function, where antibodies against normal body tissues are produced. It is also believed that an infectious cause and a genetic predisposition play roles in the development of the disease. Obesity and a family history correlate strongly with type II diabetes.

Insulin binds to specific receptors on cells, and aids in the transport of glucose into cells. This process is potassium dependent, such that under the influence of insulin, potassium ions move into cells with glucose. In normal patients, an increased blood sugar level stimulates the pancreas to release insulin. Insulin is secreted into the circulation by cells in the islets of Langerhans. Once in the circulation, insulin allows glucose to enter cells for metabolism and energy storage. This acts to decrease the blood sugar level. In the absence of insulin, or in cases of insulin resistance, blood sugar levels increase to abnormally high levels.

Cells are unable to take up glucose without the presence of insulin. Thus, these cells are unable to use glucose as an energy source. This stimulates the cells to use an alternate form of energy. Most cells begin to breakdown fat stores. Fatty degradation leads to the release of ketones and acid into the blood (ketoacidosis). Laboratory tests of blood samples for patients with poorly controlled diabetes frequently show hyperglycemia, excess ketones, acidosis, and increased potassium levels.

196. Which of the following hormones is most opposed to the function of insulin?

    A.   Somatostatin
    B.   Aldosterone
    C.   Oxytocin
    D.   Glucagon

197. A sample of blood from a patient with diabetes is found to contain antibodies against the receptors on cells that normally bind glucose. Which type of diabetes does the patient most likely have?

    A.   Type I
    B.   Type II
    C.   Either type I or II with an equal likelihood
    D.   Both type I and type II

198. Which cells produce insulin in the pancreatic islets of Langerhans?

    A.   Alpha cells
    B.   Beta cells
    C.   Delta cells
    D.   Gamma cells

199. Consider a patient with abnormally high blood potassium levels and normal glucose levels. Which treatment would be best for decreasing blood potassium levels in this patient?

    A.   Giving intravenous (IV) insulin and potassium together
    B.   Giving IV glucose and potassium together
    C.   Giving IV insulin and glucose together
    D.   Giving IV glucose alone

200. Which hormone does not increase blood sugar?

    A.   Thyroid hormone
    B.   Cortisol
    C.   Epinephrine
    D.   Angiotensin

201. A sample of glucose is radioactively labeled with carbon 14. A sample of this glucose and normal insulin is given via IV to a patient. What is the ultimate fate of the radioactivity?

    A.   The radioactive glucose will circulate indefinitely.
    B.   The radioactive glucose will be metabolized and the radioactivity will be found in amino acids.
    C.   The radioactive glucose will be metabolized and form radioactive pyruvic acid.
    D.   The radioactive glucose will be metabolized and form radioactive carbon dioxide.

202. In the presence of insulin, glucose is taken into cells by facilitated diffusion. Which statement best describes this process?

A. The process requires a specific carrier and requires energy.
B. The process requires a concentration gradient and requires energy.
C. The process requires a specific carrier and does not require energy.
D. The process does not require a concentration gradient and requires a specific carrier.

PASSAGE X (Questions 203–207)

In the open, animals appear to find safety in numbers. Single individuals with no place to hide seem to be at greater risk for predation than those in groups. Following these ideas, a noted ecologist presented a model of the "geometry of the selfish herd" based on the idea that predators attack the nearest prey individual. Therefore, animals will be motivated by self-interest to assemble in groups as each attempts to reduce its "domain of danger," the area around it in which a predator might appear closer to it than to some other individual.

Although this behavior may be the evolutionary source of many animal's social behavior, it may work to the disadvantage of the group as a whole. If a predator begins to recognize milling or schooling behavior of prey as a easy targets, then the solitary animal might be favored to survive. Thus, an equilibrium might exist between forces compelling herding behavior and those compelling a solitary lifestyle. Seasonal predation patterns may lend a temporal variation to the direction favored in this equilibrium.

Experimental evidence is difficult to come by in this domain. One study found that small birds fly in a loose formation when flying above a bird of prey, but cluster tightly when below the bird of prey. The interpretation given is that because a bird of prey usually attacks talons first, as it plunges into a flock it is more likely to injure itself than attack an individual small bird.

One experiment filmed the "flight" of a hawk model, in a stereotyped manner, over doves attracted to a bait. The flock size was varied between 2 and 21 doves. It was hypothesized that larger groups would react faster.

The relationship between flock size and reaction time is shown in Figure 1. Increasing flock size is on the x axis; reaction time is presented on the y axis in terms of increasing number of motion picture frames filmed between the flight of the first dove and the time the model passed directly over the feeding point.

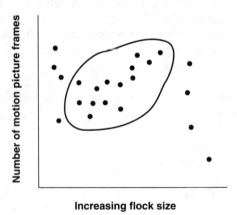

GO ON TO THE NEXT PAGE.

203. When a predator approaches, a faster, stronger animal forces its way into the center of the group while a weaker animal is on the periphery. If the first animal leaves more offspring than the second, what principle has been illustrated?

A. Natural selection
B. Differential reproduction
C. Speciation
D. Genetic drift

204. Which implication from the "selfish herd" model is correct?

A. Prey at the center of the herd are safer than those at the periphery.
B. Predators that travel alone are unsafe.
C. Herds are safer than individuals.
D. Animals' goal is to increase "domain of danger."

205. Which of the following would not explain why grouping increases average safety of group members?

A. Sensory apparatus of the entire group is available to detect predators.
B. Predators may be confused by a tightly packed group.
C. The group is larger and more easily detected by predators.
D. The group may be able to defend against or discourage a predator when a single individual cannot

206. What is the best implication of the hawk experiment's hypothesis?

A. There is earlier warning of predator approach for all members of the flock.
B. There is increased safety of individuals in flock.
C. There is increased safety of the group as a whole.
D. Hawk flight can be modeled.

207. No significant relationship was found between flock size and reaction time in the hawk/dove study. However, if the data is analyzed for flock sizes between four and fifteen doves (circled data points only) there is an almost linear relationship. Which does not contribute to this finding?

A. Flocks of two or three were nervous and experienced many false alarms.
B. Flocks larger than 15 were preoccupied by competition for bait and did not react.
C. The analysis of this subset of data is in accord with the hypothesis.
D. Flocks of 14 reacted more slowly than flocks of seven.

PASSAGE XI (Questions 208–213)

The transformation of n-butyl alcohol to 2-methylhexane involves five separate reactions. The consequence of separate reactions is that each reaction may proceed with an independent mechanism. In addition, because each reaction is associated with an independent yield of product, the multiple step pathway to product formation holds consequences for final product yield. Because the synthesis of n-butyl alcohol to 2-methylhexane involves five steps, even relatively high yields for each reaction involve a great deal of loss before the end of the synthesis. For example, if 1 mole of n-butyl bromide were used at the beginning, and each reaction produce an 88% yield of product, the overall yield for the series would be 52%.

The five reactions associated with the synthesis of 2-methylhexane from n-butyl alcohol are shown as equations 1 through 5.

Equation 1

$$CH_3(CH_2)_3OH + HBr \rightarrow CH_3(CH_2)_3Br + H_2O$$

Equation 2

$$CH_3(CH_2)_3Br + Mg \rightarrow CH_3(CH_2)_3MgBr$$

Equation 3

$$CH_3(CH_2)_3MgBr + (CH_3)_2C=O \rightarrow CH_3(CH_2)_3C(CH_3)_2OMgBr$$

Equation 4

$$CH_3(CH_2)_3C(CH_3)_2OMgBr + HBr \rightarrow \text{alkene mixture}$$

Equation 5

$$\text{Alkene mixture} + H_2 + Pd/C \rightarrow CH_3(CH_2)_3CH(CH_3)_2$$

208. Which of the following best describes the mechanism of equation 1?

A. S_N1
B. S_N2
C. E1
D. E2

209. Which of the following is one of the alkenes obtained by the reaction shown in equation 4?

A.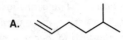

B.

C.

D.

210. Why does the mixture of starting materials used for the reaction shown in equation 5 produce only one product?

A. The alkenes are conformational isomers and the resulting alkane is achiral.
B. The alkenes are regioisomers and the resulting alkane is achiral.
C. The alkenes are stereoisomers and the resulting alkane is achiral.
D. The alkane is achiral so any alkene could produce it.

211. Equation 4 describes the result of what two reactions?

A. Hydrolysis and addition
B. Hydrolysis and elimination
C. Hydrolysis and substitution
D. Hydrolysis and reduction

212. If the reaction shown in equation 1 had been performed with the hydroxyl group at a highly substituted chiral center, what type of product would have been expected?

A. The product would not have been chiral.
B. The product would have been optically pure.
C. The product would have been partially racemic.
D. The product would have been racemic.

213. What is the stereochemistry of the reaction shown in equation 5?

A. The stereochemistry follows Markonikov's rule.
B. The stereochemistry follows Zaitsev's rule.
C. The stereochemistry is anti.
D. The stereochemistry is syn.

Questions 214 through 219 are NOT based on a descriptive passage.

214. Rank the following molecules in order of decreasing boiling point.

$CH_3CH_2CH_3$ $CH_3CH_2CH_2OH$ CH_3CH_2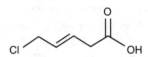

1   2   3

A. 3,2,1
B. 2,1,3
C. 1,3,2
D. 2,3,1

215. What is the proper order of the phases of mitosis?

A. Interphase, prophase, metaphase, anaphase, telophase
B. Interphase, telophase, metaphase, prophase, anaphase
C. Interphase, prophase, anaphase, telophase, metaphase
D. Prophase, metaphase, anaphase, interphase, telophase

216. The correct IUPAC name for the following compound is:

A. 1-chloro-2-pentanoic acid.
B. 5-chloro-3-pentanoic acid.
C. 1-chloro-pent-2-eneoic acid.
D. 5-chloro-2-butenoic acid.

GO ON TO THE NEXT PAGE.

217. In humans, the major blood type differences are determined by multiple alleles designated I^A, I^B, and i. I^A and I^B are codominants and I is recessive. Gene combinations $I^A I^A$ and $I^A i$ produce type A blood. $I^A I^B$ produces type AB blood; $I^B I^B$ and $I^B i$ produce type B blood; and ii produces type O blood. If one parent has type A blood, the other has type B blood, and they have a child with type O blood, what is the probability that their next child will have type AB blood?

    A.   0%
    B.   25%
    C.   50%
    D.   100%

218. The following orbital framework best depicts which hydrocarbon listed below?

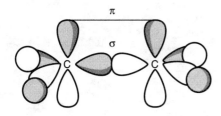

    A.   Ethane
    B.   Ethene
    C.   Ethyne
    D.   Ethanal

219. Which of the following are not characteristics of fungi?

    A.   They are eukaryotes.
    B.   They may be either haploid or diploid.
    C.   They may reproduce sexually or asexually.
    D.   Because they have no mitochondria, they are capable only of glycolysis.

STOP. IF YOU FINISH BEFORE TIME IS CALLED, CHECK YOUR WORK. YOU MAY GO BACK TO ANY QUESTION IN THIS TEST BOOKLET.

ANSWERS AND EXPLANATIONS

Verbal Reasoning

1. B The beginning of paragraph one makes it clear that Britain lacks natural resources. That trade compensates for this lack is emphasized throughout paragraph one, but particularly beginning with the sentence, "Traffic gives us a great variety of what is useful, and at the same time supplies us with everything that is convenient and ornamental. . ." and continuing through the rest of the paragraph. Wrong choices: Choice A rings false because the passage indicates in paragraph one that Great Britain was not fertile in the first place. Choice C is invalid because while "Sir Andrew calls the vineyards of France our gardens" in paragraph one, this is a rather whimsical opinion, and certainly not a fact. And while the English merchant may sometimes trade in wool (paragraph two), to say that "Great Britain. . . in exchange for wool" is far too large a statement after referring to the "English merchant."

2. D The materials being traded and exchanged are "commodities." They are not stock "shares" or "certificates," which eliminates choice A. And although the author mentions "old kings" in paragraph three, this passage has nothing to do with the court (choice B). Choice C is too vague to have any significance.

3. C Choice C is the best choice. The author begins the passage by telling us about the inadequacies of Great Britain, but does so with the assistance of amusing details: "can make no further advances toward a plum than to a sloe, and carries an apple to no greater a perfection than a crab." Halfway into the first paragraph he starts to laud the wonders of trade. It is safe to say that he is "upbeat" throughout this passage, which would leave us only one option: "bemused to cheerful." While bemused means "bewildered" or "lost in thought," it is not necessarily negative; and the author does seem to be wandering through his thoughts, to some degree. Wrong choices: While we might want to say that the author starts out "joyful" (choice B), in no way can we call the latter part of the passage "degrading." And while he ends up quite optimistic (choice A) or uplifted (choice D), he certainly does not start out dismayed or piteous.

4. B Paragraph one states that "our melons are strangers among us, imported in different ages, and naturalized in our English gardens," which supports this choice. The fact that these fruits were imported makes Choice A invalid (indigenous meaning native). Choice C might be tempting because the passage mentions these fruits in particular, but it would seem clear that these fruits are examples of Great Britain's produce, and not the sum total. Choice D also comes directly from the first half of paragraph one, but would only be true "if they were wholly neglected by the planter. . .," which is a big "if."

5. B The first two sentences of paragraph two support this: ". . . there are not more useful members in a commonwealth than merchants. They knit mankind together. . . ." Clearly, the author sees merchants having much more than "some use" (D) and being far from evil (A). He refers to "vassals of some power baron" in paragraph three (C) as what merchants of other lands might have been in

163

another day and age, but this is not to be taken literally, because the merchants being discussed had not been vassals.

6. C This question does not provide the most obvious answer—an economics text—so you must look for the next best option. Although markets probably exist largely within cities, this passage has nothing to do with how to plan a city, which eliminates choice A. It does not discuss the social or societal impact of trade thoroughly, which eliminates choice B. An accounting text would not provide information in such a highly rhetorical and anecdotal way, thus eliminating choice C (in other words, an accounting text would be much more "dry"). We could, however, find this information in a history text, were we studying Great Britain.

7. C The key to this question is recognizing the negative phrase "advantages do not include." We know that from paragraph one, the advantages of trading do include "not having to deal with the extremities of weather" (I) and "improved variety of harvest" (II). Therefore, these statements contradict the question, leaving III and IV, or C. Wrong choices: while in the end of paragraph three, the author writes, "Trade, without enlarging the British territories, has given us a kind of additional empire," he does not tell us that without trade, we would need to expand the British empire, which makes IV appropriately false (which answers the question). And nowhere does he mention "diminished inequities between rich and poor"; therefore, III also answers the question, which points again to choice C.

PASSAGE II

8. B In the introductory paragraph, the author compares (not contrasts) sampling to other technological advances in music history. Choice A is incorrect because the introductory paragraph does not offer contrast. The author mentions objections to other innovations but raises none against sampling, which makes choice C incorrect. Eliminate choice D, because British pop bands are not compared to primitive musicians in the first paragraph.

9. A "Pilfering" is another word for "stealing." "Hijacking" is also a form of stealing, that is, abducting a person unfairly. "Adapting" does not carry the negative meaning the author conveys in the rest of the paragraph.

10. C The first paragraph introduces the issue of acoustic artists going electric. The first sentence of the second paragraph ties the changes in music to the innovation of digital sampling. The early part of the passage supports choice C. Eliminate choice A, because the author mentions legal problems associated with sampling but never places legal responsibility on any party. Choice B is incorrect. The author praises English pop bands for pushing the boundaries of recording and being innovative, yet does not compare them to American musicians. Choice D can be eliminated because choice C is supported by the passage.

11. C The author uses the analogy of comparing electric guitars and sampling for the purpose of pointing out controversy and advances. The author mentions only the genius of artists who use sampling (paragraph five), but nowhere indicates that sampling and electric guitars are marks of genius. Thus, statements I and II are true, and statement III is false. This makes C the best choice.

12. D The author is not cautionary because, although legal controversies are mentioned, the passage does not include any warnings to anyone. The author is not dubious because no doubts are expressed. The author is not cynical about sampling, but praises it as a new art form in the final paragraph.

PASSAGE III

13. A This passage offers a historical overview of religious medieval reasoning and analysis. Logic and reason win their confrontation with Christianity in this passage. The passage supports the assertion that God's existence can never be proved using logic (statement I). The final paragraph of the passage indicates that the medieval philosophers did not give up trying to find an argument that proved God's existence. The passage demonstrates that a tremendous amount of energy went into logical reasoning of God's existence. The passage also supports statement II; the final paragraph suggests that the god of medieval Christianity is not very believable. Statement III does not answer the question being asked, because the author never says whether God could defy logic.

14. **A** Based on information in the passage, proposition 1 would be violated. Proposition 1 states that God is omnipotent (all-powerful) and can make a world in which evil does not exist. If proposition 1 is denied, then God would then share His power with Satan.

15. **B** The argument here concerns the fourth proposition, not the third. The author is not calling the faithful illogical or ignorant. The author claims that they look evil and suffering in the face and call it something else.

16. **D** This is a tricky question. This question is asking you to note the difference between God and humans as suggested by the passage and apply this difference in answering a question. You are specifically asked for a disanalogy (comparative difference) between God and the parent. The passage states that God is all-powerful, according to proposition 1. The parents would not be all-powerful, and would be bound to the limitations of humans. This means that God could accomplish choices B and C. The parent would be bound by the limitations of humans described in choice A. This makes choice D correct.

17. **B** Quickly reread the fourth paragraph. Note that the phrase carries a negative meaning. From the context of the passage, the phrase likely means either "incorrect" or "intolerable." It is clear that the author does not accept the argument. This best supports choice B. Choices A and C do not follow the logic of the argument. Choice D, or "disingenuous" means "insincere" and also does not follow the logic of the argument.

18. **A** This question is easy to answer by the process of elimination. Perfectly benevolent suggests kindness and generosity. "Omniscient" means all-knowing. Eliminate statement III. This allows you to eliminate choices B, C, and D. The best answer must be choice A.

19. **C** All of the conditions listed would eradicate the problem of evil as described in the passage. Statements I and II remove one of the propositions described in the passage, and therefore circumvent the contradiction. Statement III would also eradicate the problem of evil, because if one abandons logic, one won't worry about a contradiction.

20. **C** Paragraph one asserts that "in furious rabies the change of character and habits is more dangerous as the animal tends to be aggressive." This aggressiveness impacts on the animal's tendency to lash out at other animals and humans. Although choices A, B, and D certainly are part of the deadly disease's course, the passage does not directly connect them to the difference between the two types of rabies as overtly as the information in choice C.

PASSAGE IV

21. **D** The words "inhibited motor skills" are not used directly in the passage, but many equivalents are cited: "paralysis" in paragraph one, "paresthesia" in paragraph four, and many of the symptoms mentioned in paragraph seven. Choice A, on first glance, may look correct, but the passage does not state that more people are bitten by rabid wolves (see paragraph one). It says, "the proportion [of people thought to be infected] bitten by rabid wolves is around 61% ." In other words, the rabid wolves are more deadly, but it is not necessarily true that more people are bitten by rabid wolves. In paragraph one we learn that not all rabid animals carry the deadly virus (only a certain percentage of them), thus eliminating choice B. And though choice C may sound sensible, paragraph 1 (or any other paragraph) supports this assertion.

22. **A** The key to this passage is to be aware of the double negatives: "could not be determined to be false." In your mind, change this to: "could be determined to be true" or even "could be true." And remember, your response is "according to the passage," so don't let your own knowledge or even common sense get the best of you. According to the passage, furious rabies is a lethal and even violent virus. While we have been told that furious rabies is more dangerous because the animal is more aggressive, we do not know that people are rarely bitten by dogs with

dumb rabies. The passage chose to exclude this information. Therefore, statement II would not be true. Statement III, on first reading, sounds true, but ask yourself, "Crucial to what"? Simply saying that something is "crucial" does not provide us with enough information. Therefore, we cannot determine that statement III is true. Statement IV is supported with information in paragraph two. Therefore, statements I and IV are true.

23. **B** The key word in this question is "psychological." While man or animal may exhibit any or all of these symptoms, only one of them is psychological: moodiness. The other symptoms are physical.

24. **A** Paragraph one asserts that the proportion of people who become infected after being bitten by rabid wolves is 61%; this is a considerably worse percentage than the 35% to 43% bitten by rabid dogs with furious or dumb rabies, thus invalidating choice B. And although choices C and D are terrible options, this article discusses the larger issue of rabies and its effects rather than the relative or comparable horror of specific symptoms.

25. **B** We can readily eliminate choices C and D. The first is too limited; the article discusses dumb as well as furious rabies. The latter is too lighthearted for such a serious subject. The real decision is between choices A and B. Although choice A may sound better, the article provides no solutions to rabies, only a few ideas of which scenarios are better and worse, and possible avenues to diagnosis. The most straightforward title, in this case, is the most appropriate.

26. **D** There are several tricks in this question. Statement I mixes up the information provided in paragraph seven, but the most obvious giveaway is that the question asks about "dumb rabies in humans," not animals. Paragraph seven refers to rabies of cattle in South and Central America. Thus, statement I is false. Statement II is false because the symptoms described occur as the result of furious rabies (see paragraph five). We do not know if they occur with dumb rabies. Statement III is true, and directly supported by the topic sentence of paragraph seven. The key is to realize that "dumb rabies" is being referred to as "paralytic." This goes back to the beginning of paragraph one. Statement IV has no support in the text. Therefore, statement III (D) is correct.

PASSAGE V

27. **A** The last sentence of the first paragraph poses a question about corporations. The first sentence of the second paragraph answers that question as it pertains to what Friedman believes. The content of the second paragraph indicates that Friedman believes corporations do not have moral and social responsibilities in the same way that individual persons do.

28. **A** Answer this question by using the process of elimination. Taxation is discussed in the final paragraph. Choices C and D are incorrect because employees can effectively tax shareholders by keeping prices down. Choice B is incorrect because taxation is the assessment, not the payment of funds. Choice A is the best choice.

29. **B** The passage only says employees can't act on different political beliefs in their capacity as employees, if those actions violate the directives of the stockholders. Choices A and D are incorrect because employees can still have individual beliefs and rights in their private lives. Choice C is not mentioned or supported in the passage.

30. **C** The passage asserts that Friedman's objection is to taxation without representation, that is, without one's opinion being considered. Carefully evaluate the choices. Choices A and B do not suggest that those being taxed have any say in where tax funds go. Friedman does not voice any objection to the concept of taxation as a principle, only that taxation and representation should go hand in hand. Choice C is the most reasonable. This choice suggests that tax funds should go to programs benefiting those who were taxed.

31. **C** This is a difficult question because the author never quite defines socialism in this passage. Thus, it is important to use the process of elimination to answer this question. The final sentences of the passage discuss Friedman's opinion of capitalistic systems versus socialistic systems. He indicates that when allocations

are determined by corporate means, we have a socialist system. Choice A is incorrect because corporation ownership is not related to the definition of socialism by the passage. Socialism is not discussed in terms of corporative social responsibilities, which thus eliminates choice B. Choice D is not supported by the theoretical discussions in the passage. Although the passage indicates that a socialist system involves allocation by corporate means rather than political means, the passage also indicates that corporate actions may threaten the fabric of society and violate the principles of free market competition. Choice C is the best choice because it links the author's discussion of market economy and politics to socialism.

32. A   Higher prices increase inflation (see paragraph four). Eliminate statement II as a true statement. The passage describes how a company agent can assess "taxes" on stockholders. Consumers don't charge stockholders, so eliminate statement III. Statement I is true, which makes A the best choice.

33. C   Corporations are considered to be individuals under the law. The author doesn't make an analogy to outside infection, so eliminate choice A. Choice B can be eliminated because the author never says that a corporation must be composed of more than one person.

34. D   The introductory paragraph of this passage raises several questions relating to the responsibilities of corporations. The passage then discusses moral and social responsibilities of corporations and Friedman's opinions. The citation at the end of the passage "The Corporation: Analysis and Arguments" suggests that the passage is about corporative issues rather than just taxation, socialism, or Friedman's opinions. Choices A and B are too limited in scope to be acceptable titles for this passage. Choice C focuses on employees rather than on the responsibilities of the corporation. Choice D is the best title because it combines the key concepts expressed in the passage: responsibilities, business, taxation, and representation.

---

35. C   Traveling is mentioned in paragraphs two and four, which supports statement II. The introductory paragraph discusses the importance of breaking from tradition, which supports statement III. The frontier myth is to leave one's land or home behind. Statement I is not supported by the passage. Thus, choice C is best.

36. B   Male heroes of frontier narratives strive to be independent of social norms. This correlates best with choice B. Choice C is opposite of the author's description of masculinity. Choices A and D are incorrect because the author never mentions creativity or temper.

37. B   Frontier woman are discussed in the fourth paragraph. The passage indicates that frontier women in narratives appear as forces of society, with oppressive objectives. This represents a version of the nagging wife—a woman who ties her husband to home and family and won't let him strike out on his own. Choices A and C describe women who, by the standards of the time, are not seeking a conventional frontier life.

38. D   The traditional heroes of frontier narratives are generally men who cannot be tied to traditional home life: they are rebels. The heroes of frontier narratives do not fit the description of any of the answer choices. Note that answer choices A, B, and C all describe characters who uphold the norms and laws of society as part of their job.

39. D   The nagging wife and the gold diggers in the fourth paragraph both represent general ties of social expectations. The nagging wife and temptress both try to sidetrack the hero from his quest for individuality. Both impede the hero's freedom and mobility. Statement I is incorrect because neither the nagging wife or temptress represent the difficulties of child rearing.

40. C   Choice A is incorrect because there is no indication in the passage that the woman wants to become a widow. Choice B is not supported or implied by the passage. Although the American dream may include an element of home stability and aesthetics, this is not discussed or implied. Choice D better describes the frontier male hero. Choice C is best because it describes the purposeful seeking out of a wealthy man and the potential benefit of her child's success.

41. B   The passage implies that the author wants fiction in which women characters are portrayed as male characters have been portrayed (see paragraph six). This is best described by choice B.

42. D   Note that all three of these words or phrases carry a related, similar meaning; all are tied to movement and the desire to be free. All three of these words accurately describe the use of the word "road" in American fiction. The characters have a lust to wander, and a restlessness to keep moving. The characters also seek the freedom to define themselves. The use of "road" adds imagery to the fictional narratives.

PASSAGE VII

43. A   This is a challenging question. The "seal and the wax" are directly compared to "perceptions and the brain." Therefore, the brain is the wax, and perceptions are the seal impressed into the wax, that is, the "trite simile" that the author wants to convey, in order to refute it. Wrong choices: we might make the easy mistake of thinking of the seal as "sealing in" perceptions (choice B), but keep in mind that of the seal and the wax, one has to be the brain, and one has to be perception. Choice C excludes the seal from the equation, and therefore cannot be correct. Choice D says that the seal is both brain and perception, and the wax is something else altogether.

44. B   The author spends much of this passage discussing the complexity of how the brain functions, citing, among other clues, "chaos" (paragraph one) and "fertility" of perception (paragraph two). Therefore, to say that this simile is too complex would not make sense. Also, something that is trite would tend to be the opposite of complex, which totally eliminates choice A. Choice C is the real temptation. The image of the "seal and the wax" certainly is cliché, but the author is not complaining because this phrase is overused (which is the main problem of the cliché). He is complaining because it is too basic, or reductive. Finally, choice D is too overstated to be correct. And at the time the author was writing, seal and wax may well have been in common use.

45. B   The second sentence of paragraph two asserts that the "formation of permanent notions" is our goal, and that three senses are of little use. The author begins to praise sight as being useful in this way, but then says, "but. . . . ," which implies that this sense has some (although limited) use in the development of these notions. Choice A is invalid because it does not refer to sight; it refers to the "resources of the mind" (sentence one, paragraph two). Choice C can be eliminated because the fact that sight is "vivid and luminous" is not a flaw. Choice D makes no sense because this passage is not about ophthalmology.

46. D   This is stated, or paraphrased, in the first sentence of paragraph two. Although the first paragraph asserts that the human mind has "limited plasticity," that does not make it "inflexible and implastic" (choice A). Common sense may tell us that the human mind cannot eschew (shun) and embrace imagination. The passage may, indeed, imply that we must do so, but it is too long a leap of inference, thus eliminating choice B. Choice C expresses opinions that are not supported in this passage.

47. C   The key to this question is not letting your imagination run too wild with inference. You may decide that statement I sounds true because perceptions are referred to as "seeds in a furrowed field." Stick to the passage, though. The author does not say anything about these seeds needing to be nurtured. Instead, he says that the mind exercises "its own fertility." Therefore, statement I is not true, which eliminates choice A. Statement II is not supported in the text, although toward the end of paragraph two, the author does refer to men of "fervid imagination. . ." wasting themselves in dream. Still, there is no direct correlation between these perceptions and this waste. Therefore, choice B can be eliminated, which also invalidates statement IV, taking choice D from the running. And although statement IV might seem to fit with the author's tone, he does not express a preference for one type of perceptual growth over another; he only expresses caution.

48. B Don't make this question more difficult than it is. The author refers to the mind being "flooded by its inner lights" in paragraph two. He may not be directly referring to imagination, but we can infer as much. This choice is better than the others. At no time in the passage does imagination become "a product of" (choice A) understanding or "a catalyst for" (choice C) understanding. And although paragraph three refers to constructing "a picture of all reality," imagination is only one part of the "endowment of the human mind."

49. A The end of paragraph two is a not-so-veiled warning of being carried away by imagination. And yet the writer acknowledges that the "passionate fancy" (paragraph three) of imagination is part of the human mind. The author does not view imagination "wistfully," (i.e., with yearning). Nor is the tone of this piece "childish"; instead, it seems to be more critical of "sudden bursts of fancy." And although the writer may think that imagination is spontaneous, that is, that it occurs suddenly, without provocation, there is nothing "sudden" about his opinion of imagination.

PASSAGE VIII

50. D Only someone who considers themselves a native Californian could make this argument with any credibility. The passage does not support the immigration or emigration of the author, which thus eliminates choices A and B. Choice C is a poor choice because the author also seems to be very anti-business.

51. D See paragraph four. The author is very concerned with population growth, businesses and persons who pollute the environment, and poor environmental protection. The attitude of the author supports statements II, III, and IV. The author clearly does not want to give breaks to businesses, so eliminate statement I.

52. B See paragraph two. The passage implies that business activity is related to population growth. Although the passage does not state that this relationship is directly proportional, it is clear that there is a positive correlation and that there is not an inverse relationship.

53. A See paragraph three. The author implies that the coast was preserved because tourists are attracted to its beauty. Inverting this assumption, it can be inferred that because the desert is not being preserved, tourists must not be going there, and therefore it must not be considered as attractive. Choice B is an attractive choice. Although it appears logical based on its content, it does not follow from the logic and content discussed in the passage. Choices C and D are irrelevant statements that do not follow from the topics discussed.

54. D The answer to this question is discussed in the first paragraph. The second to last sentence in this paragraph implies that newcomers to California (people) contribute to the damage of the environment. Although some people might claim that economics is the primary cause, the author always relates business to population growth.

55. B This is a pretty extreme argument. The author uses some facts in presenting his argument, yet most of the discussion is based on his interpretation of the issue. The author is very opinionated, and it is imaginable that a member of the business community would strongly disagree with this author's opinions. Some may feel that the author's argument is compelling, yet some would disagree with the argument and not feel compelled at all.

56. B Refer to paragraph two. The author says that other environmentalists are wary of businesses that seem to be pro-environment. This indicates that the author would most likely be cautious. Based on the arguments given in the passage, it would be hard to imagine that the author would be elated or enthusiastic about a corporative environmental plan proposal. It is also unlikely that the author would be angry that a business entity proposed a plan to protect the environment.

57. C This is an easy question because the passage suggests that population growth is inversely linked to pollution and directly linked to increased business opportunities. In paragraph two, the author claims that business and population mutually augment one another. Thus, decreased population would be connected to decreased business opportunities (statement III). In paragraph two the author also claims that pollution, among other things, might lead businesses and people to invest their money elsewhere (statement I).

---

58. D Notice that the thesis of this passage is in the last paragraph. Allow yourself to be flexible when it comes to finding the thesis in a passage: in general, you can find the thesis at the beginning, but not always. Also notice that in this particular argument, the author includes viewpoints from both sides of the debate, not just one. However, the argument is not simply reporting on both sides and then leaving it up to the reader to decide how she/he will judge the debate; this passage definitely contains an opinion about voucher experiments in schooling, even after reporting on both sides of the argument. In paragraph six, the author finally makes her own claims, and they are clearly most closely aligned with the critiques of "Options" posed by others in paragraph five.

59. B Paragraph one points out that the gap between the education of the rich and the poor is growing wider. Paragraph five also deals with the economic differences between various bodies of students. The passage clearly points out that the real problem behind the current educational crisis is fiscal and economic disparity between groups of students.

60. C The opinions of proponents of the Options program are discussed in paragraphs three and four. As a matter of fact, the answer to this question (competition) is given directly in the first sentence of the fourth paragraph.

61. B Look for evidence of some bias on the author's part. Note that the author appears to write the passage as an insider—a person who has been directly exposed to the disparity between groups of students. In addition, note that the author supports public schools quite fervently, especially in paragraph six. This analysis leads one to believe that the author is likely a teacher or administrator who is involved in the public schools.

62. A Paragraph five suggests that vouchers will be inadequate for poor students to attend private school. The interrelationship of public and private schools does not provide an explanation for why the gap would be widened between the rich and poor.

63. C The author never argues for a decrease in private schooling, thus eliminating statement III. However, the author does argue for increased government funding of public schools (statement I) in paragraph six, and implies that more schools need to be built (statement II) in paragraph five. This best supports choice C (I and II).

64. D Use inference to answer this question. Because the Options plan would institute a competitive market system, it can be inferred that schools would need advertisers to attract clients. Based on the content and tone of the passage, there is not good reason to assume that college professors or lawyers need be hired. Political lobbyists would likely be more valuable during the debate of whether or not to institute the Options plan, not after the plan was instituted.

65. C Use the process of elimination to select the best choice. Clearly, choices A, B, and D are either false statements or gross overgeneralizations. The Options plan seeks to make it easier for more students to attend private institutions instead of public institutions. The passage implies that private schools may offer a better education than inner city, financially strapped public schools.

Physical Sciences

This is an information-presentation passage in which the escape speed of particles near the surface of various planets is discussed. Two different data tables are provided in an attempt to overwhelm you with data. Only Table 1 is actually necessary to answer the questions. The questions require you to evaluate the two given equations and pull information from Table 1.

66. C This question asks you estimate the escape speed of a planet given the escape speed of another planet. Based on Table 1, the major difference between Saturn and Uranus is the radius of each planet. Because escape velocity is proportional to the square root of the planet's radius, Saturn, approximately two times the radius should have approximately 1.4 times the escape velocity, or $22 \times 1.4 \sim 36$ km/sec. Do not be fooled by the answer of 30 km/sec, because that value is too low. After all, this rough approximation is ignoring the increase in g that is also present, and the fact that Saturn's radius actually increases by more than two-fold.

67. B This is a conceptual question not directly related to the passage. You are being asked if you know which quantities are conserved in an inelastic collision. Remember that in an inelastic collision, momentum is conserved and kinetic energy is not conserved. In elastic collisions, both momentum and kinetic energy are conserved.

68. B Use inference to solve this question. Quick inspection of the table shows that the values for g and R increase as you go from the moon to earth to Jupiter. The same will happen with the values for the escape velocities.

69. B To solve this question, look for a relationship that allows you to calculate speed. The second equation given in the passage relates speed and mass. This equation says that the most probable speed is inversely proportional to the square root of the mass. Diatomic hydrogen has a mass of 2 amu, while diatomic oxygen has a mass of 32 amu. This is a 16-fold difference, or a 1/16 ratio. The square root is 1/4, so you expect the most probable speed to be 1/4 that of diatomic hydrogen, or 0.39 km/sec.

70. D This is an information recall question. The passage gives you all the information you need to answer this question. Note that the passage gives the escape level of the earth as 500 km. This compares to an escape level of 200 km for Venus. As stated in the passage, the escape level is temperature dependent. This explains the difference in escape levels noted for Venus and earth. Venus will have a higher surface temperature because of its proximity to the sun. Choices A and B can be eliminated because the table reveals that the radius and acceleration due to gravity do not differ much. Choice C is not directly supported by the passage.

This is a problem-solving passage (general chemistry). In the passage, four equilibrium reactions important in atmospheric chemistry are presented. As with all problem solving passages, the questions that follow are pretty straightforward. Generally, problem-solving passages stress conceptual questions and simple calculation questions. The questions in this passage are primarily basic conceptual questions about equilibrium expressions.

71. D This is a basic conceptual question testing your understanding of equilibria. Before going further, understand these basic points about equilibrium constants:

1. K is a constant for any given reaction as long as the temperature does not change.
2. K determines which is in greater concentration at equilibrium; the products or the reactants.
3. Because K is determined by reactant and final product concentration, it is independent of the number of intermediate steps in the reaction mechanism.
4. If K is greater than 1, there are more products than reactants at equilibrium, and the reaction "lies to the right." If K is less than 1, there are more reactants than products at equilibrium, and the reaction "lies to the left."

The question asks you to specifically evaluate equilibrium 2. The question also asks about the species present at 230 degrees. The equilibrium constant is provided at that temperature. The equilibrium constant is less than 1 so more of the left-hand species will be present at equilibrium.

171

72. B The expression for the equilibrium constant is products over reactants raised to their stoichiometric coefficients. Also keep in mind that if you are given a reaction on the MCAT that contains pure substances (pure liquids and pure solids), these do not appear in equilibrium expressions.

73. A This is an important conceptual question. It tests your understanding of the relationship between the change in Gibb's free energy (ΔG) and K. When a system is at equilibrium with K = 1, equal amounts of products and reactants are formed. Neither side of the equilibrium is energetically favored. Thus, $\Delta G°$ is zero. For your reference, these are the other two important relationships between $\Delta G°$ and K which have been tested on the MCAT:

1. When $\Delta G° < 0$, K > 1
2. When $\Delta G° > 0$, K < 1

74. A Entropy is a measure of disorder. The best way to think about this question is to see how many moles of particles are on each side of the equilibrium. When looking at equilibrium 2, note that you exchange 3 mol of gaseous starting material for 2 mol of gaseous product. This means that you have become more ordered (lost disorder) and ΔS is negative.

75. C The given equation is formed by combining equilibria 2 and 3. When adding equations together, the equilibrium constants must be multiplied. When reversing a reaction before adding it to another, the reciprocal must first be taken. In this question, equilibrium 2 was added to the reversed form of equilibrium 3. Thus, K for equilibrium 2 was multiplied by the reciprocal of equilibrium 3. This corresponds with choice C.

PASSAGE III

This is an interesting example of an information-presentation passage (physics). A good deal of information about the transfer of information in the form of waves is presented. Many of the questions that follow this passage are information-recall questions, which may be answered from information presented directly in the passage. In addition, the concepts of beats and beat frequency are tested. Finally, you are asked to interpret the meaning of several waveforms. The interpretation questions in the passage can be answered by applying principles described in the passage.

76. A This question tests your ability to apply the wave descriptions given in the passage to diagrams of waves. As stated in the passage, a wave with a single, continuous frequency cannot carry information. Note that choice A shows no variation. Choice B could carry information, and is an example of frequency modulation. The other choices could carry information; choice C shows an example of amplitude modulation, and choice D shows pulse modulation.

77. B To answer this question, you must understand the concept of beats and beat frequency. Remember that the beat frequency equals the absolute value of the difference in frequencies of two sounds ($f_{beat} = |f_1 - f_2|$). In other words, if two tuning forks of different frequencies are sounded, beats will be heard. The beat frequency equals the difference in frequencies of the tuning forks. If tuning forks with the same frequency are sounded, no beats will be heard. In this question, looking at the oscilloscope outputs shows you the beat pattern produced. The top wave has more beats, thus a higher beat frequency. This means that the two original notes were further apart in frequency.

78. D Use logic and your understanding of beats to answer this question. When tuning the instrument, one waits to hear the beats. As the frequency gets smaller and smaller, the waiting time to hear a beat (the period between beats) gets longer and longer. One would have to wait forever to be sure that a beat was never coming.

79. B Period = 1/f. A square wave of period 2 msec will have a fundamental frequency of (1)/(0.002 sec) = 500 Hz. As mentioned in the passage, all other waves will be odd multiples of the fundamental frequency.

80. **B** Use the process of elimination to answer this question. Note that the passage mentions that high frequencies are what give waves sharp changes. Without these high frequencies, you might expect to see the edges rounded as they are in choice B. This is the most reasonable choice. Choice A is incorrect because it shows unaffected square waves. Choices C and D are unlikely because they show waves that are very divergent in shape from the given square waves.

81. **D** Look back to the passage to find information on carrier frequencies. The passage implies that the carrier frequency carries no information. The additional frequency components in the wave carry the information. If a student only tunes to a carrier frequency and the other frequency components are excluded, no audible reception is likely. If the other frequency components are not excluded, reception will occur. It is not possible to determine the quality of reception without more information.

This is a problem-solving MCAT passage (general chemistry). The topics tested in this passage include solubility products, saturated solutions, and precipitation reactions. Most of the questions are conceptual and test your understanding of basic solubility concepts. Solubility questions are a favorite MCAT chemistry topic.

82. **B** The best way to write out a K_{sp} equation is to first write out the balanced reaction. For lead (II) hydroxide, this would be: $Pb^{+2} + 2OH^- \rightarrow Pb(OH)_2$. Recall that K_{sp} is the product of all ions formed by dissociation of the compound, raised to the power of their coefficients. Two hydroxide ions are formed by the complete dissociation of the compound, resulting in a squared term. The K_{sp} would then be: $K_{sp} = [Pb^{+2}][OH^-]^2$.

83. **C** This conceptual question tests your understanding of solubility and precipitation. Recall that any ion product that is greater than K_{sp} means that precipitation will occur. In this question, you are looking for a way to get silver to precipitate out of solution. Adding more silver carbonate to a saturated solution of silver carbonate would not cause precipitation of silver. As a matter of fact, the additional silver carbonate would not even dissolve in solution because the solution is already saturated with this compound. Thus, eliminate choice A. The best way to get silver to precipitate is to add a compound to the silver carbonate solution which will allow silver to combine with a different anion and form a compound which has a lower K_{sp} than silver carbonate. Look at the remaining answer choices. If sodium sulfide were added, the sodium and sulfide ions would dissociate and silver sulfide could form. Silver sulfide is much less soluble than silver carbonate so adding sodium sulfide to a saturated silver carbonate solution would result in precipitation of silver sulfide. Choices B and D are not as good as choice C because their associated solubility products are greater than silver sulfide.

84. **C** The K_{sp} for silver chloride has been exceeded and some silver chloride will precipitate. Here is how to predict this:

$[Cl^-] = (10 \text{ ml})(0.5 \text{ mol/L})/(20 \text{ ml}) = 0.25 \text{ mol/L}$
$[Ag^+] = (10 \text{ ml})(1 \times 10^{-5})/(20 \text{ ml}) = 5 \times 10^{-6}$
$[Ag^+][Cl^-] = 1.25 \times 10^{-6}$, which is greater than the K_{sp}

85. **B** The best way to separate silver and lead is to add sulfide (S^{2-}) until all of the Ag^+ precipitates as Ag_2S. Because the K_{sp} of Ag_2S is smallest, it will precipitate first. Then, you can centrifuge and decant the solution which will now contain lead (Pb^{2+}).

86. **C** Carefully work backward by evaluating each answer choice. Choices B and C are better than A. It is only necessary to use one simple step to remove the silver. The K_{sp} value of silver sulfide is very low and simple precipitation as silver sulfide would leave all the other ions unaffected and still in solution. Choice D is not supported by the passage. Choice C is a better choice than B because the best way to remove silver from solution is the simplest, cleanest way. Choice B requires an additional (unnecessary) step over choice C.

87. B   Aluminum would redissolve if the concentration of hydroxide in solution was significantly decreased. The addition of acid, such as HCl, would react with and hydroxide ion and form water as a byproduct. This technique is far superior to the technique described in choice A. The addition of iron will probably result in the precipitation of iron without re-dissolution of the aluminum (depending on the amount of excess base added. Choice C is incorrect because chelation does not necessarily lead to dissolution. Choice D is incorrect because only one choice is true.

INDEPENDENT QUESTIONS

88. D   Atoms in excited states have electrons in lower energy orbitals promoted to higher energy orbitals. Choice A shows the ground state or lowest energy state for potassium. Choice B has 7 electrons in a p orbital that can hold only 6 electrons. Choice C has only 18 electrons, not the 19 electrons of potassium. Choice D has one of the 3p electrons promoted to the higher energy orbital, the 4s.

89. C   This is a challenging Newtonian physics problem. The best way to approach this problem is to realize that equivalent tensions act on both A and B and is transmitted across the pulley. Each of these tensions acts to oppose the weight of each pulley. Call the tension opposing the weight of A to be T_1, whereas the tension opposing the weight of B to be T_2. In the next step, write $F = ma$ for each block. Based on the relative magnitude of the masses, the prediction would be that $Bg > T_2$ (because block B is falling towards the ground) and $T_1 > Ag$ (because block A is moving upwards).

$$F = ma$$
$$T_1 - Ag = Aa$$
$$Bg - T_2 = Ba$$

Because $T_1 = T_2$, add the equations and cancel T_1 and T_2:

$$Bg - Ag = Aa + Ba$$
$$(A - B)g = (A + B)a$$
$$a = \{(A - B)/(A + B)\}(g)$$

90. C   The force of attraction between two bodies is $F = Gm_1m_2/r^2$, where G is the universal gravitation constant, m_1 and m_2 are the masses of the two bodies, and r is the distance separating them. The g value of a body (acceleration due to gravity) $= Gm_{body}/r^2$, where $m =$ mass of body and $r =$ the body's radius. Compared with the earth, planet X has a mass 1/2 and a radius 1/4 of earth's values. Plug these ratios into the formula for g: $g_{planet\ X} = G(1/2)/(1/4)^2 = G(1/2)/(1/16) = 8\ G$. This implies that g for planet X would be eight times that of g on earth.

91. A   Paramagnetic elements are substances that tend to move into a magnetic field. They also tend to have one or more unpaired electrons. Most transition metals and their compounds in oxidation states involving incomplete inner electron subshells are paramagnetic.

PASSAGE V

This is a problem-solving passage (general chemistry). The passage tests your understanding of electrochemistry. Electrochemistry is a commonly tested topic on the MCAT. This passage specifically tests concepts from galvanic (voltaic) cells. In the past, MCAT examinations have also tested electrolytic cells and concentration cells.

92. B   Because this is a voltaic cell, the overall E^o must be positive. Cu is oxidized. The spontaneous cell reaction is: $2Fe^{+3} + Cu \rightarrow 2Fe^{+2} + Cu^{+2}$. The copper loses 2 electrons and is said to be oxidized. Thus, oxidation occurs at the anode which is beaker B.

93. C The balanced whole reaction is given in question 92. Recall that the overall balanced reaction does not contain electrons. Arrive at the balanced reaction by manipulating the two given half-reactions as follows:

1. $Fe^{+3} + e^- \rightarrow Fe^{+2}$
2. $Cu^{+2} + 2e^- \rightarrow Cu$

Step 1: Multiply equation 1 by two: $2Fe^{+3} + 2e^- \rightarrow 2Fe^{+2}$
Step 2: Reverse the second equation and combine equations: $2Fe^{+3} + 2e^- + Cu \rightarrow 2Fe^{+2} + Cu^{+2} + 2e^-$
Step 3: Cancel electrons: $2Fe^{+3} + Cu \rightarrow 2Fe^{+2} + Cu^{+2}$

Another important point: Remember that in electrochemistry, you do not multiply the electrical potential values of half-reactions by coefficients used to balance the reactions.

94. D The compound being oxidized loses electrons (*L*oss of *E*lectrons = *O*xidation, *G*ain of *E*lectrons = *R*eduction. A useful mnemonic to remember this is: *LEO* the lion goes *GER*.

Other common terms used on the MCAT include oxidant and oxidizing agent. The oxidant is the substance that gets reduced. The oxidant is also called the oxidizing agent. Note that the reductant or reducing agent is the substance that gets oxidized.

95. A Because the reaction with cupric ion has a half-cell potential of only 300 mV, cupric ion has less potential to be reduced than the ferric ion. You know this because the passage gives the potentials as reduction potentials, and cupric ion has a smaller reduction potential than ferric ion. This leads you to know that the copper metal would be oxidized in the overall reaction. This implies that you have to reverse the given equation for cupric ion and write it as an oxidation: $Cu \rightarrow Cu^{+2} + 2e^-$. This would make copper's potential to be oxidized -300 mV. The overall standard cell potential would be $800 + (-300) = 500$ mV.

96. A A salt bridge usually contains a solution such as KCl. The salt bridge completes the circuit of an electrochemical cell by allowing ions to flow such that charges are balanced. It is also important to know that electrons flow from the anode to the cathode in any electrochemical cell. In the cell described in the passage, electrons flow from the anode to the cathode. This results in the cathode solution becoming negative. The cations in the salt bridge (ammonium ions) therefore flow towards the cathode (where reduction occurs) and the anions in the salt bridge flow towards the anode (where oxidation occurs).

97. D This is a conceptual problem. To solve this problem you need to look at the Nerst equation and see what effect a change in ion concentration will have on E_{cell}. When the volume at the cathode is doubled, the concentrations of ions at the cathode are halved, becoming 0.50 mol/L. The concentration of cupric ion is still 1.0 mol/L at the anode. Plugging this in for ferrous and ferric ions in this case will not change the cell voltage (both are squared and the log of 1 equals zero). Hence, the standard cell potential equals the whole cell potential and both are unchanged. The Nerst equation for this reaction is $E_{cell} = 500$ mV $-(60/2)(\log[Fe^{+2}]^2[Cu^{+2}]/[Fe^{+3}]^2)$.

---

98. D Questions relating to energy transformations are very common on the MCAT. In this question, the water has potential energy at the top of the dam. This potential energy is converted to translational kinetic energy as the water falls, to rotational kinetic energy as the water turns the turbine, and lastly to electrical energy.

99. B It is important to know the basic definition of power: Power = work/time. To find power, start by finding the work done. You can find work by realizing that the work done equals potential energy lost. And the PE = mgΔh. Thus, power = mgΔh/t. So, (1000 kg/min)(10 N/kg)(100 m − 10 m)/(60 sec/min) equals 15 megawatts. Remember that 1 W = 1 J/s = 1 Nm/s.

100. C   The pressure difference between two points in water is equal to the weight of a column of water between the two levels. Point A has 10 m of water above it, point B 100 m. The difference is $(90\ m)(1{,}000\ kg/m^3)\ (10\ N/kg) = 900$ kPa.

101. B   There are two methods that can be used to answer this question, an easy one and a more difficult one. Let's start with the easy way: Torricelli's equation is helpful to know for the MCAT: $v = (2gh)^{1/2}$. This equation allows you to calculate the velocity of fluid or an object dropped from rest from a height above a reference point. The equation also tells you that velocity is dependent on g and h. The more difficult way: You can answer this question by evaluating Bernoulli's equation, which is given in the passage. To find the velocity of water flow, evaluate each variable in Bernoulli's equation and its necessity in the formula. Take the left side of Bernoulli's equation to be the A side and right side to be the B side. P_a and P_b are not needed to calculate velocity because both are atmospheric and cancel each other out. The level of the water on the B side is not changing appreciably, so the v_b term is ~zero. And if you take 10 m above the ground as your reference point, the y_a term is also ~zero. So you are left with: $0.5\ \rho v_a^2 = \rho g y_b$. Canceling the ρ terms and solving for v_a gives the velocity on the left side. All you needed was g and the height difference between right and left sides of dam.

102. D.   This question tests your conceptual understanding of depth and pressure relationships. The pressure at the surface is atmospheric pressure. You should expect that the pressure will then increase linearly with depth. Eliminate choice B immediately because it shows pressure decreasing with depth. Choice A is incorrect because it shows that there is zero pressure at the surface, rather than a positive atmospheric pressure. Choice C shows a nonlinear relationship. Only choice D has a linear increase not starting at zero pressure.

103. B   Think about this question conceptually. Why did the question ask you to replace the water with oil? What is the difference between oil and water anyway? Answer: Oil is less dense than water (it floats on water). This means that oil will have less mass for the same volume. Because PE = mgh, less mass is associated with less potential energy. This means that less power will be generated.

PASSAGE VII   This is an information-presentation passage (physics) that describes the electrical properties of axons. The resistance and capacitance of axons are described with equations, and a formula is given to calculate the distance a signal can be transmitted without amplification. A data table is also given that contains several constants for both myelinated and unmyelinated axons. The questions test your conceptual understanding of capacitance and your ability to apply the given equations.

104. C   The resistance is given by the expression $R = \rho l/A$. For an axon, ρ from the table is 2 Ωm, λ is 1 cm = 10^{-2} m, and the area is πr^2 where r is 5×10^{-6}m. Thus, $R = (2\ \Omega m)(10^{-2}m)/\{(3.14)(5 \times 10^{-6}m)^2$. Crunching through the calculation gives 255 MΩ.

105. A   As stated in the passage, signals will travel further down myelinated axons. This allows you to eliminate choice B. Also, if you look at the dependence of the space parameter on radius, r, you find it increases with increasing r. Thus, large axons will carry signals longer before dissipating. This allows you to eliminate choices C and D.

106. C   The wording of this question helps lead you to the correct answer. The question emphasizes the long period needed for the discharge of an action potential compared with an electrical capacitor. Look for an answer choice that explains the slow discharge. Only choice C emphasizes a slow phenomenon. In a biological system, the charge is carried by ions such as Na^+ and K^+ traveling through channels and pores in the membrane; this is much slower than the flow of current in electrical conductors, or in the spark discharge of a capacitor.

107. C   The answers are given in coulombs, which is a unit of charge. You are actually being asked the charge associated with a capacitance and a voltage. Using Q = CV, and the equations for C given in the passage, you have: $Q = CV = C_m(2\pi$

rl)(V) = (150 mV)(0.01 Fm^{-2})(2π)(5×10^{-6} m)(1×10^{-3} m), which reduces to 4.7×10^{-11} C.

108. C The passage states that the membrane can be treated as a parallel plate capacitor. For a parallel plate capacitor, the capacitance decreases with increasing charge separation, so wrapping a thicker myelin sheath will separate the charge further and result in decreased capacitance. This supports choice C and contradicts choice A. Choices B and D can be eliminated. Although the question states that the myelin cells are lengthened, the insulating material (dielectric) in between the charges is still myelin, and the dielectric does not change.

This is an information-presentation passage (general chemistry). This passage presents to you information on valence-shell electron-pair repulsion (VSEPR) theory. Three data tables are given. The first data table presents the rules for the theory. Tables 2 and 3 provide data for finding covalent radii and dipole moments, respectively. You must focus on what is being asked and not become overwhelmed with all the data given. The questions primarily ask you to take information and data given in the passage and apply it to answering questions.

109. A Start answering this question by thinking which table will provide you a way of estimating the length of a carbon-carbon bond. The only table that gives you any measurement close to bond length is Table 2. Table 2 gives bond covalent radii. Because the molecule is diatomic and the bond is assumed to be covalent, you can simply add the radii for carbon: 0.77 + 0.77 = 1.54 A. Although Table 2 gives single bond covalent radii and the molecule given (ethene) has a double bond, this is your best estimate based on the information provided.

110. B Answer this question by working backward through the answer choices and see which choice is best. Choice A is incorrect because it does not explain the differences observed. In addition, dipole moment is not linked to the length of covalent radii in the passage. Choice C may be eliminated, as there are no lone electron pairs on the carbon atoms in this molecule. Choice D is incorrect because hydrogen atoms do not pull on the central structure of the molecule to reduce bond length. Choice B is the best choice by the process of elimination. Using the data in the passage, you might expect a bond length of 1.54. If experimental measurements yield a considerably smaller bond length you can assume multiple bonds are involved. Recall that ethene has a double bond.

111. D It is best to approach this question strategically. Whenever you are asked to answer a question on the MCAT that is not a core MCAT science topic, you can assume that the passage will give you information on how to answer the question. This is definitely true in this case. The percent ionic character formula is not something that you are supposed to have memorized for the MCAT. This means that you should refer back to the passage to find a solution. The last sentence of the passage gives you the formula: % ionic character = $M_e/M_c \times 100\%$. Table 3 gives values for M_e and M_c. Plugging in values from Table 3 shows you that choice D has the greatest ionic character.

112. B SO_2 has a bent geometry because it has one lone pair about its central atom (calculate using VSEPR theory). Molecules with dipole moments are generally polar. Xe is a square planar molecule with the F atoms arranged symmetrically around the central Xe atom. Such a molecule has no dipole moment and is considered nonpolar. BeF_2 is linear, has no dipole moment and is therefore nonpolar. NO is polar as it is diatomic with an electronegativity difference between the bonded atoms, therefore has a dipole moment.

113. A The total number of valence electron pairs is (4 + 6 + 7 + 7)/2 = 24/2 = 12. The number of electron pairs needed to bond the atoms together is (4 − 1 = 3). The number of electron pairs that surround the central atom is 12 − (3 × 3) = 3. The number of lone pairs around the central bonding atom is 3 − 3 = 0. This structure corresponds to trigonal planar. Note that the VSEPR theory requires no knowledge of the Lewis structure.

114. C This question is a purely conceptual question testing your understanding of projectile motion and free fall. When an object is projected into the air, the acceleration of gravity (g) acts on it. The magnitude of g is constant all throughout the flight and is directed downward toward the center of the earth. At the highest point vertically in the path shown, the projectile has reached its high point and no longer moves vertically. However, it is critical to remember that the projectile will still move horizontally. This is because the projectile was launched at an angle to the horizontal. Separating the initial velocity into components allows you to think of a separate velocity in the x and y directions. Thus, at the high point, there is no vertical velocity and only horizontal velocity. The g vector is perpendicular to the horizontal velocity vector at this point.

115. C To answer this question, you must understand the relationships for equivalent capacitance:

ΣC in parallel: $C_{total} = C_1 + C_2 + C_3$
ΣC in series: $1/C_1 + 1/C_2 + 1/C_3$

Based on these relationships, only choice C is correct.

116. B The best way to solve this problem is to realize that an equivalent number of moles of sulfuric acid are present before and after the dilution. To find the number of moles, multiply molarity times volume.

$(\text{Molarity})(\text{Volume})_{before} = (\text{Molarity})(\text{Volume})_{after}$
$(10 \text{ mol/L})(x \text{ ml}) = (0.5 \text{ mol/L})(600 \text{ ml})$
Solving for x = 30 ml.

117. D This is a tricky question. Use the relationship: $\Delta G = \Delta H - T\Delta S$ to determine spontaneity. Plug the given values into this equation: $(X - RY) = X - R(Y)$. Notice that both sides of the equation cancel out. This means that the answer cannot be determined. The system is at equilibrium when $\Delta G = 0$, but in this question both sides of the equation cancel.

118. B Recall that $a_t = r\alpha$. As the point gets farther from the center of the flywheel, r increases, and therefore, a_t increases. Thus, choices A and D are incorrect. Mass is not a variable in acceleration equations, making choice C incorrect. Choice B is the best choice.

PASSAGE IX

This is a very wordy information-presentation passage (physics) that discusses radiation use in medicine. This passage almost appears to be as long as a verbal reasoning passage. Occasionally on the MCAT you will find a long passage like this. Most of these long passages will have several information-recall questions that can be answered directly from information given in the passage. In addition to testing science, these long, wordy passages also assess your verbal reasoning ability.

119. A The passage defines electron density as NZ/A, where N is Avogadro's number, Z is the atomic number, and A is the atomic mass. Look carefully at the answer choices and find which choice has the greatest value for electron density. Remember that the electron density definition given in the passage is atomic number over atomic mass. In each case except for hydrogen where $Z/A = 1$, the ratio of Z/A is less than 0.5, and tends to decrease as Z get larger.

120. A According to the passage, neutrons are stopped best by collisions with nuclei of small masses. Polyethylene contains a lot of hydrogen, perfect for stopping neutrons. Steel is mostly iron with some carbon for strength, lead contains large nuclei, and diamond is pure carbon—all poorer choices.

121. A The passage states that the brehmstrallung intensity released is proportional to the atomic number of the medium the beta particle is traveling through. Thus, to minimize brehmstrallung production, you want to select a material with a low atomic number. Look carefully at the choices. Plastic clearly is the least dense and would have the lowest atomic number. Plastic is mostly carbon and hydrogen—much lower Z than iron, lead, or tungsten.

122. B As mentioned by the passage, alpha particles are stopped by short distances of air. Choice B is best supported. Choices A, C, and D are neither supported nor implied by the passage.

123. D The passage states that the flux (particles per unit area) falls by a factor of $1/d^2$. Although the flux in particles per area decreases as $1/d^2$, the area of the detectors is different. The larger detector likely has an area greater than the smaller detector (area varies as r^2). If you consider both the area and the flux, the total number of particles will remain the same. Thus, the 3-m detector sees 1/9 the flux at any given area, but has nine times the total area, so the ratio is 1.

124. D Passing through 10 cm of steel is 5 half-value layers, so the attenuation is a factor of $1/2^5 = 1/32$. However, there is also the $1/d^2$ drop-off. The distance doubled, so the answer is $1/32 * 1/4 = 1/128$.

This is a problem-solving passage. The questions that follow the passage refer extensively to the table and require a conceptual understanding of several topics. The topics tested include acid/base, indicators, and pH.

125. D Start by thinking about what the pH of 0.100 M HCl will be. Recall that pH = $-\log[H^+]$. The pH of [0.1 mol/l] HCl = $-\log[10^{-1}] = 1.0$ Look at the K_a value for 2,4-dinitrophenol given in the table. Notice that its K_a value would correspond to a pH of about 4 ($-\log[10^{-4}] = 4$). The pH of the acid solution is less than the pH at which the indicator would be expected to change colors. Thus, the indicator would likely remain colorless in solution.

126. B The best way to find the color of thymolphthalein is to know what the pH of the solution will be. Do this by first finding the pOH of the solution and knowing that pH + pOH = 14. A 1.0 mol/L NaOH solution has a pOH = $-\log[OH^-]$ = $-\log[1.0 \text{ mol/L}]$ = 0. pH is then $14 - 0 = 14$. At a pH of 14, the table implies that thymolphthalein will be blue.

127. B This is an information-recall question that is supported by information presented in the passage. Answer this question by evaluating each statement based on its own merit. Then use the process of elimination to select the best choice. Most of the information you need to answer this question is given in the passage. Here is a quick overview: Note that the passage states that indicators are a conjugate acid–base pair that is added to titration mixtures in small molar amounts to monitor pH. The acidic and basic forms of the indicator are different colors. Indicators tend to react with excess acid or base in titrations to form a colored product that you can see. Choice B is supported by this passage description. Choice A can be eliminated because the passage does not support that indicators are soluble salts. Choice C is incorrect because indicators are conjugate acid–base pairs, rather than strong acids. Choice D is incorrect because color changes are not based on the volume of indicator added. It generally does not matter how much indicator is present to cause a characteristic color change.

128. D This is actually an easy question that can be answered based on quickly looking at the table. The strongest acid has the largest acid dissociation constant (K_a).

129. C Look at the table given in the passage. The indicator with the smallest acid dissociation (K_a) is the least dissociated in aqueous solution.

130. B Notice that this question gives you a pH which is equivalent to the pK_a of the indicator. Recall that the $pK_a = -\log[K_a]$. Noting that the given pH = pK_a is very useful. When the two quantities are equivalent, you are at a buffer region where 50% of the indicator will be in the protonated form and 50% will be in the deprotonated (anion) form. A good way to think about this question is to picture the Henderson-Hasselbalch equation in your mind: pH = pK_a + log[base/acid]. If the pH and pK_a are equivalent, the [base] = [acid].

This is a problem-solving passage (physics) based on Newtonian physics. The passage presents the forces acting on a falling particle. The forces are described with two different equations. The passage expects that you understand the meaning of each equation and apply each equation appropriately.

131. C   This question is asking you the meaning of a part of one of the formulas. You should know that the gravitational force acting on any object = mg, where m = mass and g = acceleration of gravity. Look carefully at the overall formula: $\{(\pi d^3)/6\}\{(\sigma - \rho)(g)\}$. Note that the g term is there and that the rest of the equation must be equal to mass. The left-hand part of the equation, $\{(\pi d^3)/6\}$, must relate to the particle's volume. From information given in the passage, you can predict that the $(\sigma - \rho)$ term relates to density. Density times volume gives mass. Choice A is incorrect because this is equivalent to the entire formula. Choice B is incorrect because the acceleration of the particle equals g. Choice D is also incorrect. The weight of the particle would equal the force of gravity on the particle or mg.

132. D   This question asks you to solve for a single variable. Before proceeding with the algebra, look carefully at the answer choices. Choices A and B give an expression for terminal velocity with velocity as one of the variables. This allows you to eliminate these choices. To go about solving for v, set the two given equations equal and solve for v: $\{(\pi d^3)/6\}\{(\sigma - \rho)(g)\} = 3\pi \eta dv$; $v = d^2(\sigma - \rho)g/18\eta$

133. A   Your understanding of forces is tested in this conceptual question. Clearly, f_r is a friction force—it is retarding or slowing the particle's movement through the air. Recall that friction forces act in an opposite direction as the direction of motion. Because $3\pi\eta dv$ must relate to air friction, you can eliminate choices B and D. Now look at the $\{(\pi d^3)/6\}(\rho)(g)$ term. The passage tells you that the ρ term is the density of air. Why is the density of air considered in a term that helps determine mass of the falling particle? Perhaps a correction factor to the mass of the particle is being added to account for a buoyant force provided by the air. That buoyant force would decrease the force of gravity on the particle. This correction factor would be proportional to how much air is displaced. This reasoning best supports choice A.

134. A   To solve this question, look for a quantitative relationship that equates diameter and terminal velocity. Remember that you solved for the terminal velocity in question 132. Note that the terminal velocity relates to the square of the diameter: $v = d^2(\sigma - \rho)g/18\eta$. Thus, a 3 μm particle will fall nine times faster than a 1-μm particle.

135. B   This is a cleverly disguised projectile motion problem. Start by calculating how long the particle is in the air. The particle falls 30 m at 1 cm/sec, so it will fall for 3,000 seconds. Now that you know the amount of time in the air, simply multiply the horizontal velocity (13 cm/sec) by the time in the air to find the horizontal displacement. Its horizontal displacement is 13 cm/sec × 3,000 seconds ~390 m.

136. A   This is an application question requiring you to infer from the passage and reason through the answer choices. First, the question implies that toxicity is encountered when particles lodge in the lungs. This is a great clue, because it sets up the tone and direction of the best answer. Choices A and B best repeat this wording. Look at choices C and D. Although it seems reasonable to avoid exposing the population to toxins by range considerations, the question stem clearly emphasizes that toxicity is related to which particles lodge in the lungs. Choices B and D may be eliminated because the smaller particles are likely to lodge deeper in the lungs. In addition, you know that large particles fall quickly, so they will not spread as far horizontally as smaller, slowly falling particles.

INDEPENDENT QUESTIONS

137. C   This conceptual question tests your understanding of free radical reactions. Termination results in a net decrease in the number of radicals. Generally, in termination reactions, two radical species combine to form a nonradical species. In propagation reactions, a radical species transfers its electron to a different compound, propagating the radical electron. Usually, the number of radical species overall does not change. In initiation reactions, a nonradical species is split into two or more radical species. There is a net production of free radicals.

138. D The concept of gaseous diffusion is frequently tested on the MCAT. You should know that the diffusion rate is the inverse root of the molecular weights of the gases. Therefore, the rate of diffusion of $O_2/H_2 = (2/32)^{1/2} = 1/4$.

139. B For series capacitors, $1/C_t = 1/C_1 + 1/C_2$. For this question, $1/C_t = 1/3\ \mu F + 1/6\ \mu F$, $1/C_t = 3/6\ \mu F$, and $C_t = 2\ \mu F$. To find the charge, recall that $Q = CV$. $Q = (2\ \mu F)(100\ V) = 200\ \mu C$.

140. C Always remember to use a balanced reaction to predict the molar products of a reaction. Start by balancing the given reaction. Split the given reaction into two half-reactions. This aids in balancing the reactions:

$$Sn^{+2} \rightarrow Sn^{+4}$$
$$H^+ + O_2 \rightarrow H_2O$$

Now, balance atoms and balance charge for each half-reaction. Add electrons to balance charge as necessary.

$$Sn^{+2} \rightarrow Sn^{+4} + 2e^-$$
$$4e^- + 4H^+ + O_2 \rightarrow 2H_2O$$

Finally, multiply the first half-reaction by two to help balance electrons when the two equations are added. This allows the electrons to cancel when the half-reactions are added to give the final, balanced reaction.

$$2(Sn^{+2} \rightarrow Sn^{+4} + 2e^-)$$
$$4e^- + 4H^+ + O_2 \rightarrow 2H_2O$$
$$2Sn^{+2} + 4H^+ + O_2 \rightarrow 2Sn^{+4} + 2H_2O$$

To answer this question, note that 64 g of oxygen gas (MW = 32 g/mol) represents 2 mol of oxygen gas. Looking at the balanced reaction, the ratio of oxygen gas to water is 1:2. Thus, you should expect 4 mol of water to be produced.

141. D This question tests your understanding of magnetic fields and their effect on charged particles. If a particle is projected into the path of a magnetic field which is oriented perpendicular to the direction of particle travel, it will be either attracted by the field or repelled by the field. If the two charges described in this question behave differently in the presence of the same field, it suggests that the charge of the particles are of the opposite sign.

142. C Use the periodic table provided on the first page of the Physical Sciences test to find the molecular weight of silver nitrate. MW = 108 + 14 + 3(16) = 170 g/mol. The weight of oxygen in this compound is 3(16) = 48 g/mol. The percent of silver nitrate that is oxygen by weight is 48/170 = 0.28 or 28%.

Biological Sciences

PASSAGE I

This is a complex information-presentation passage (biology) that presents the topic of asthma and introduces some new terminology. It is strategic to read the question stems of this passage and then quickly look at the graph before reading the passage. This will allow you to find the important information in the passage that specifically pertains to the questions. The first three paragraphs of the passage introduce the causes of asthma, the different types of asthma, and some drugs that are used to treat this disease. The fourth paragraph gives some new definitions (FVC, FEV_1), which are critical to understand in order to answer the questions that follow the passage. Finally, a table is presented that shows the ratio of FEV_1/FVC for four different patients given a new asthma drug.

143. B This question is easy to answer if you realize that an equation relating airway resistance and radius is given in the last sentence of the first paragraph. Remember to always write out relationships between variables given in a passage. This passage indicates that resistance is inversely related to the fourth power of radius, or ($R = 1/r^4$). A two-fold decrease in radius means $R' = 1/(1/2r)^4$. $R' = 16r$. Thus, the new resistance is 16-fold greater due to a two-fold decrease in radius.

144. C Controls usually represent the most normal patient or situation. The purpose of a control is to give a baseline or normality so that an experimental procedure or substance can be tested. To determine the control in this passage, find the patient who is the most normal. Note that the passage indicated that a normal ratio is about 0.8. Only patient C had a ratio of 0.8. In addition, it is helpful to find a patient who did not appear to respond to the treatment. Patient C had a normal FEV_1 before drug treatment as well as after drug treatment and is clearly the control subject. Patients A and B responded to drug treatment, so they would not represent controls. Choice D is not a control because this patient does not have a normal FEV_1/FVC ratio.

145. B Solve this question by the process of elimination. Look carefully at the table. Patient D was clearly not helped in any way by the drug as indicated by the poor FEV_1 before and after drug administration. However, patients A and B had FEV_1 values that were improved by the drug, suggesting that it has some positive effect on extrinsic asthma. Choice A is not supported because the passage gives no information that patients A or B have intrinsic asthma. If the drug only fails in the patient without this form of asthma, then it is fair to conclude (given the choices) that its mechanism may be similar to that of cromolyn, which would also be ineffective on intrinsic asthma. Choice C is not supported because it makes sense that the drug should reach the lungs to have an effect, and the passage provides no information on how the drug works. Choice D is not as good as choice B. Although the age of onset for extrinsic asthma does correspond to childhood, the passage provides no information to support that the experimental drug will only be used in children.

146. A Patient A's FEV_1 has increased after drug treatment, suggesting decreased airway obstruction. The likely reason for decreased obstruction is decreased resistance, which is accomplished by increasing the airway radius. Look at the other choices. Choice B is incorrect because if the airway resistance has increased, you would expect a lower FEV_1/FVC ratio. Choice C is contradicted by the table. Choice D is incorrect because only choice A is a correct statement.

147. A Inspiration is an active process that requires energy consumption. Thus, choice D is a true statement. You are able to inhale by contracting your diaphragm and intercostal muscles. This acts to push down on the abdominal organs and to expand the chest upward and outward. The net result of inhalation is an increase of thoracic volume. By the process of elimination, choice A must be the correct response. What is the reasoning behind a decreased intrapleural pressure during inspiration? Remember the gas equation $PV = nRT$. When taking a breath, your chest expands, leading to an increase in V. Because n, R, and T are essentially constant, this increase in V must be accompanied by a decrease in P. Another way of looking at it is that increased thoracic volume leads to a decreased intrapleural pressure relative to atmospheric pressure, which causes air to follow the pressure gradient into your lungs.

148. B Given the assumption of identical FVC, the patient with the lowest ratio before drug treatment would be the one able to exhale the least amount of air in 1 second. This makes sense because FEV_1 is defined in the passage as the amount of air that can be exhaled in 1 second. The less air exhaled per unit time, the more difficult it is to blow out a candle. Patient B had the lowest ratio before drug treatment.

149. D This is a knowledge-based question. By far, the greatest surface area for gas exchange occurs in the alveoli, also known as alveolar sacs. Choice A is incorrect because the bronchioles are smooth muscle lined bronchial tubes which help control air flow to the alveoli. Bronchi are large, cartilage-containing airways. Alveolar ducts are very small ducts which branch into alveoli.

This is a persuasive-argument–type passage (organic chemistry). Persuasive-argument passages present you with viewpoints on a particular topic. The passage usually expresses opposing viewpoints. The questions that accompany the passage usually test your understanding of the arguments and require that you evaluate the validity of the arguments. Although these are the least-common type of passage on the MCAT, it is important that you understand how to approach this type of passage. In this passage, three chemists give arguments presenting three different hypotheses about the factors controlling the stability of cycloalkane rings. Evaluate the validity of each hypothesis based on your understanding of conceptual organic chemistry. Make notations in the margin beside each hypothesis outlining the point of each chemist. Then, answer the questions based on your understanding of each hypothesis and its accuracy regarding the chemistry described. It is very important that you understand the position that each chemist takes on the subject. The questions focus on the differences between the arguments of each chemist.

150. C   Chemist 3 argued from the standpoint of nonbonded contacts, or steric crowding. This is best "echoed" by choices C and D. A trans-double bond in a ring results in a hydrogen aimed toward the carbon atoms across the ring. This results in steric crowding, and an unstable structure. Thus, choice D is incorrect and choice C is the best answer.

151. B   An 11-sided polygon would have very obtuse angles (greater than 109°) and by chemist 1's argument, this should indicate an unstable ring. The observation that such large rings are stable contradicts the major point in chemist 1's arguments.

152. A   The bond angles in cyclopropane are 60°. This is 49° away from the ideal angle. This introduces a large amount of angle strain. It is true that the bonds in cyclopropane are eclipsed, but the effect is not nearly as large as the angle strain.

153. D   Cyclopropane actually manages to keep its hydrogen atoms farther from each other than in normal eclipsed conformations because of the small internal bond angle. This results in very small steric interactions. Thus, chemist 3 would call cyclopropane stable and its ability to open would be surprising.

154. C   Chemist 2 argued from the perspective that eclipsing interactions influence the stability of rings. Two rings with the same stability must therefore, have the same eclipsing interactions.

This is an information-presentation passage (biology) that reviews viruses. This passage should be easy to understand and comprehend because much of the information you should already be familiar with. Basic viral structure, replication, and life-cycle alternatives are topics that the MCAT will expect you to know. More advanced topics such as capsid structure and specific viral details, (e.g., human immunodeficiency virus [HIV] virus), are provided in the passage so that you can be asked about them based on the information provided. Most of the questions that follow this passage require a good conceptual understanding of cell structure and simple microbiology.

155. D   The best way to answer this question is to refer back to the passage. The first paragraph indicates that capsomeres are aggregates of viral-specific polypeptides. Thus, the host cellular organelle used by viruses to synthesize capsomeres would be the organelle associated with protein synthesis or translation. Only choice D, ribosomes, are actively involved in translation. The nucleus is a region in the cell, surrounded by a nuclear membrane, which contains the DNA. Transcription occurs in the nucleus. The nucleolus is a nuclear organelle associated with the synthesis or ribosomal RNA (rRNA). Smooth endoplasmic reticulum is involved in the glycosylation of proteins and steroid/lipid metabolism. Do not confuse the rough endoplasmic reticulum with the smooth endoplasmic reticulum. The rough endoplasmic reticulum is associated with ribosomes and is involved in protein synthesis; however, this is not a choice in this question.

156. D This is a knowledge-based question. Viruses do not generally have the ability to synthesize a lipid envelope. Thus, choices A and B are incorrect. Choice C is incorrect because it misuses terminology and makes no sense. Those viruses which require a lipid envelope "steal" a section of the host cell membrane. This is strategic because the virus will then contain host intrinsic and extrinsic plasma membrane proteins which confer host antigenicity. This may be protective to the virus. It is important that you know that not all viruses contain a lipid membrane. Some viruses contain only a protein structure on their outermost surface.

157. B This questions that you understand the two major forms of viral life cycle. The lytic cycle is associated with viral penetration of the host, followed by rapid commandeering of host cellular function, replication of viral progeny, and host cell rupture. The lytic cycle leads to host cell death. The lysogenic cycle is very different from the lytic cycle. Once the viral penetration occurs, the viral genetic material integrates into the host's DNA. The viral genes are usually kept inactive by a viral repressor protein. The viral DNA usually replicates with the host chromosome and is transmitted to progeny cells during cell division. Eventually, the viral genes become activated, and induction of the lytic cycle may occur. This leads to viral gene transcription, viral protein translation, viral assembly, and ultimately, viral release. The passage describes the HIV life cycle. The life cycle as described is most like the lysogenic cycle. Choice C is incorrect because HIV incorporates into the host genome and has a period of latency. Choice A is incorrect, although it is an attractive choice. Although latency does occur, there is no such accepted terminology as a "latent cycle." The use of the word "latent" is only descriptive. Choice D is also incorrect because "replication cycle" is not an accepted terminology to describe a viral life cycle.

158. B This is a multiple-multiple choice question. Look at each statement and evaluate it based on its own merit. Then, use the process of elimination to arrive at the best answer. Statements I and II are more difficult to evaluate than statement III. Recall that bacteria reproduce by binary fission. Viruses do not reproduce by this mechanism. Thus, statement III is false. Now look at the answer choices. If you know statement III is a false statement, choices A and C must be incorrect. Either choice B or D is the correct response. To determine which is best, evaluate statement I. From your review of biology, you should remember that viruses can have either RNA or DNA as their genetic material. If a virus has RNA as its genetic material, it must be able to transcribe it into viral mRNA. Thus, statement I is reasonable. This makes choice B the best choice. For your information, statement II is a correct statement. Some viruses, like HIV, contain only viral RNA. To incorporate into the host chromosome, the virus synthesizes complementary DNA to its own RNA to allow incorporation into the host DNA. The virus does this with a viral enzyme known as reverse transcriptase.

159. C Fungal cells are the least likely hosts for viral infection. Bacterial cells are infected by a well-known group of viruses known as bacteriophages. Mammalian cells are infected by hundreds of different types of viruses. Common mammalian viruses include the cold viruses, hepatitis virus, HIV, polio virus, measles virus, etc.

PASSAGE IV

This is a problem-solving passage (organic chemistry). Although this passage presents some theory on how drugs move from one part of the body to another, the passage itself requires that you apply problem-solving skills and apply information in the passage to answering questions. Two data tables are provided. The first data table gives the pH range of different body compartments. You can predict that this table will be used in answering questions that pertain to specific body compartments. The second table provides a list of the acidic and basic forms of various groups and their associated pK_a values. This table can be useful in predicting the ionic form of a compound containing these groups.

160. B This is an information recall question. The first and second sentence of the first paragraph emphasizes that a drug must not only be able to inhibit an enzyme or process, but it must also reach the site where it is needed. Choice A does not support the focus of the first paragraph. Choices C and D are not supported by any specific information given in the passage.

161. C Recall that at the pK_a of a species, one-half of the species will have a specific proton and one-half will not have a specific proton (one-half of the species will be in the acidic form, and one-half will be in the basic form). At pH values below the pK_a, the acidic form predominates. At pH values above the pK_a, the basic form predominates. An amine has a pK_a of 9.2. This implies that below a pH of 9.2, an amine will be in its acidic, or charged form ($-NH_3+$). Because the acidic form of an amine is charged, it will not be able to diffuse through lipid bilayers.

162. D The most hydrocarbon-like structure will be most likely to diffuse into the lipid bilayer and remain there. The answer given in choice D has the greatest number of carbon atoms and the fewest number of oxygen atoms.

163. A If an amine could be made with a pK_a of 6.8, it would not be ionized in the bloodstream and would be able to diffuse across membranes. Once it reaches the kidneys, the concentration of protons is high enough (because of the pH being less than the pK_a) to protonate the amine and the drug would be trapped in the kidneys.

164. D The passage indicates that the pK_a of a carboxylic acid is given as 3.0. Thus, at any pH greater than 3.0, the carboxylic acid will donate its proton to water and be in its basic form. In its basic form, a carboxylic acid will carry a negative charge ($-COO^-$) which is charged. Thus, an injected carboxylic acid would remain in the bloodstream.

---

165. C Choice A is a true statement. Action potentials have a fixed strength based on the concentration of intracellular and extracellular sodium and potassium. You can alter the peak of an action potential by changing the concentration of sodium and potassium ions in and around a neuron. Choice B is also a true statement. Nerves generate action potentials at a maximum rate. The rate is dependent on the specific type of nerve. Choice D is a correct statement. Action potentials stimulate the release of calcium stores in nerve terminals. This leads to neurotransmitter release from vesicles in the nerve terminal. Choice C is an incorrect statement and the answer to this question. Nerves have the potential to propagate bidirectionally. However, practically speaking, action potential transmission often occurs unidirectionally because one region of nerve is often in refractory period and cannot transmit action potentials.

166. B This question asks for you to determine which structure is the most stable resonance structure. Notice that all the structures shown are true resonance structures for this compound. Structures A and C are very similar and are charged species. Choice B is an uncharged species. Choices A and C are resonance structures that contribute to the overall resonance hybrid (or average of all resonance forms). However, these forms are charged and therefore less stable than their uncharged counterpart, shown in choice B.

167. D This question has been asked in one form or another several times on the MCAT. A common theory for the origin of mitochondria suggests that mitochondria may have evolved from bacterial cells. There are many similarities in internal structure between mitochondria and some bacterial cells. One of the similarities is size. Choice A is incorrect because a liver cell is many times greater in size than a typical bacterial cell. A polyribosome is smaller than a bacterial cell (bacteria contain ribosomes). An amoeba is much larger than a typical *Escherichia coli* cell.

168. B   The following mechanism shows that the electron rich C—C attacks the electron deficient proton (H⁺) and forms a carbocation intermediate. Because the H⁺ seeks to gain an electron to neutralize the charge, it acts as an electrophile.

This is a research-study passage that contains elements of an information presentation passage (biology). The passage presents details of a biological research technique known a microdialysis. In addition, results of microdialysis experiments performed with four different drugs with or without tetrodotoxin (TTX) are provided in a table. Some of the questions that follow this passage test to see if you can comprehend and draw conclusions from the data presented. Several conceptual questions and knowledge-based questions are also included.

169. A   This is a challenging question. Use the process of elimination to arrive at the best answer. The question asks you to select a drug that would enhance transmitter levels. Only drugs A and B resulted in an increase in transmitter levels, so choices C and D can be eliminated. Choosing A over B is based on the insensitivity to TTX shown by drug A. Sensitivity to TTX, as with drug B, suggests that the drug requires an action potential in order to enhance transmission. Myelin is crucial for adequate conduction velocity. If myelin is dysfunctional or absent, then a drug that will work effectively must not depend on proper conduction of action potentials. Therefore drug A, a direct releaser of neurotransmitter, will be the appropriate choice in this situation.

170. C   This question tests your conceptual understanding of depolarization and action potentials. Graded potentials are local changes in voltage induced by a stimulus. Depolarization is a graded potential. Depolarization occurs when the resting potential becomes less negative, for example, from -70 to -50 mV, and the inside of the cell becomes more positive. Depolarization increases the chances that a nerve impulse will be triggered.

171. A   In research study passages, it is common to find questions testing your understanding of experimental components and apparatus. This question asks you why the fluid used in the probe, dialysate, is ionically similar to brain extracellular fluid. The best way to answer this question is to think about where the dialysate fluid is located in relation to other fluids. Note that the passage indicates that a semipermeable membrane is found at the tip of the probe. The semipermeable membrane allows ions to pass. Any differences in ionic composition between brain extracellular fluid and the dialysate would rapidly come to equilibrium. This could disrupt neuronal resting potential, which is dependent on the difference between intracellular and extracellular ionic gradients. Neuronal function, of course, depends on proper resting potential. Now look at the choices. Choices B and D are nonsensical. Choice C is an incorrect statement because the resting potential is negative. Choice A is the best choice by the process of elimination. Also note that choice A is a very reasonable, general statement. Choices B, C, and D are much more restrictive and exacting. Noticing the wording and specificity of answer choices can provide you a clue if you are having difficulty answering a specific question by other means.

172. C   Start by asking yourself why a calcium chelator was introduced in this question. Obviously, calcium must play a role in nerve conduction. Brainstorm and think about the role of calcium in the synapse. Recall that action potentials depolarize the presynaptic membrane of a synapse. This causes calcium ions to rush into the cell through voltage-sensitive calcium ion channels. This stimulates synaptic vesicles to fuse with the presynaptic membrane. Neurotransmitter is released by exocytosis into the synaptic cleft, where it diffuses to the postsynaptic membrane. Now apply your recall of the role of calcium to answer this question. Vesicular release of transmitter, be it direct or neuronally mediated, requires increased cytoplasmic calcium. A calcium chelator in the dialysate would remove extracellular calcium. This would be expected to prevent vesicular release. Thus, statements A and B are true, and the best answer is choice C.

173. **A**   This question tests your understanding of the different regions of a neuron. The dendrite, by definition, transmits signals towards the cell body; the axon away from the cell body. The end plate is often used to describe the termination of a motor neuron onto muscle fibers. Perikaryon is another word for cell body.

174. **C**   The key words in the question are *direct* and *decrease*. Evaluate the table carefully. Only drugs C and D lead to a decrease in transmitter levels. Thus, eliminate choices A and B. Drug C, unlike drug D, is not sensitive to TTX, suggesting that no nerve impulse is required. Therefore, drug C demonstrates the only direct decrease of transmitter levels.

This is a problem-solving passage (organic chemistry) which provides an overview of common reactions involving ethers. This passage does give some information about ethers, but does not provide answers to questions in the passage text. You are expected to understand basic reactions mechanisms, and ether geometry and solubility. In addition, a data table is provided with the reactants, desired products, and yield of Williamson ether synthesis reactions. You are expected to be able to predict reasons for the observed experimental yields.

175. **B**   The passage states that the basicity of the alkoxide promotes elimination as a side reaction. Use this clue to help predict the side product. Elimination is the loss of hydrogen and a leaving group from adjacent atoms to form an alkene. Determine whether the alkyl halide or the alkoxide will undergo elimination. Chloride is a leaving group, but the oxygen shown in the alkoxide column is not a leaving group. Thus, it is more likely that the alkyl halide will undergo elimination. When chloride and hydrogen are lost from the alkyl halide shown in the third entry of Figure 2, ethene is formed. Based on the clue provided in the passage, this is the major side product formed.

176. **A**   The passage states that the Williamson ether synthesis is an S_N2 reaction. S_N2 stands for substitution, nucleophilic, bimolecular. Substitution indicates that the alkoxide will substitute itself for the chloride. Nucleophilic means that the reactions involve attack of electrons an electropositive site. Bimolecular means that two molecules are involved in the slow step of the reaction. You should remember that S_N2 and E2 are concerted (single-step) reactions, whereas S_N1 and E1 are not concerted.

177. **B**   This is an information recall question. The answer is taken directly from the first two sentences of the first paragraph of the passage.

178. **D**   Look at Figure 2 and see if you can speculate why the yield falls off so dramatically for the fourth entry. Notice that the alkyl halide in the fourth entry is not a primary alkyl halide. The trend that should be observed is that the yield is fairly constant unless the alkyl halide is not primary. For this reason, choice A will definitely not produce a good yield (although any ether produced would be the desired one). Choices B and C would not produce the correct ether, they would produce methyl propyl ether, not methyl isopropyl ether. Choice D would produce the correct product in good yield.

179. **D**   This question asks you to provide a mechanism for the low yield observed in the fourth table entry. From the last question, note that the alkyl halide is not a primary alkyl halide (it is secondary). S_N2 reactions are very sensitive to steric crowding at the site of nucleophilic attack (the carbon attached to the leaving group). This is because of the need for the nucleophile to approach this site from the side opposite the leaving group. If the nucleophile cannot approach, no substitution will occur. This is the case for the fourth entry in Figure 2.

187

This is a problem-solving passage (biology) that tests your ability to understand terminology and interpret graphical data to solve problems. Two of the questions that follow the passage are straightforward conceptual or knowledge-based questions. The remaining questions require that you apply terminology given in the passage and your understanding of the curve to answer questions. It is very strategic to make notes to yourself in the margins of the passage summarizing the meaning of the terms described. In addition, make notes on the curve, indicating the meaning of each limb of the curve. This will help both your comprehension and ability to answer questions quickly and efficiently.

180. D   In the first paragraph of the passage, the passage states that blood fills the relaxed ventricle during diastole. Thus, choices A and C are incorrect. Now look at choices B and D. The difference between these choices is the use of the word *isovolumetric*. This word means "same volume." During diastole, blood fills the ventricle and the volume of the ventricle increases. Thus, diastole is not isovolumetric. This best supports choice D.

181. C   To answer this question, and some of the questions that follow, an understanding of the curve is critical. It is also important to think about how the heart fills with blood, contracts, and ejects blood. Start at point 1 on the curve. Note that as you move toward point 2, the ventricular volume stays the same yet the pressure increases. This is isovolumetric contraction of the ventricle. As you move from point 2 to point 3, the volume decreases and the pressure increases. This must represent contraction of the ventricle and ejection of blood. From point 3 to point 4, the ventricular volume is unchanged yet the ventricular pressure decreases. This represents relaxation of the ventricular muscle. Finally, from point 4 to point 1, the ventricular volume increases with little change in pressure. This must represent ventricular filling. Now that you understand the curve, let's answer the question being asked. Based on the discussion given above, the beginning of isovolumetric relaxation would be found at point 3.

182. A   This is a confusing question because the answer choices are filled with new terminology. Start by identifying any choices that are easy to eliminate. Two of the choices do not make sense. The passage defines VEDP as ventricular end-diastolic pressure. This term refers to the pressure in the ventricle at the end of diastole. This will not provide any information about volume. Because the question asks for how to find stroke volume, (the volume of blood ejected with a heartbeat), eliminate any choices which contain VEDP. This leaves choices A and C. Notice that these choices are simply rearrangements of one another. It makes sense that the blood ejected with a heartbeat would be equal to the volume of blood in the heart just after filling (VEDV) less the volume of blood in the heart just after ejection or systole (VESV). Thus, choice A is the best choice.

183. C   This question tests to see if you understand the described terminology. If more blood is delivered to the ventricles during diastole, the ventricular volume will increase. Of the terms listed in the choices, the VEDV will increase the most. The increased filling of the ventricle during diastole will have a direct effect on increasing VEDV. VESV and VESP are not changed much by increasing the ventricular filling during diastole. VESV and VESP are the volume and pressure found at the end of systole. At the end of systole, ventricular blood has been already been ejected.

184. A   Answer this question by the process of elimination. Between points 4 and 1, the volume of the ventricle is increasing with little effect on pressure. Choices C and D are incorrect because these choices include the word "isovolumetric." The filling of the ventricle is not an isovolumetric process. Because the heart does not appear to be contracting between points 4 and 1, (pressure is not changing much), this region of the curve is best considered diastole.

185. C   This is a knowledge-based question that tests your understanding of the structure of cardiac muscle. Cardiac muscle is striated muscle. Skeletal muscle is also striated, but smooth muscle is nonstriated. The unique feature of cardiac muscle is the presence of intercalated disks. These structures are special gap junctions that electrically couple all the muscle cells in the heart. This allows the action potentials generated in one cell to spread to all other cells, causing the entire heart to contract.

This is an information-presentation–type passage (organic chemistry). You are provided an overview of enolates and the Robinson annulation reaction. The passage describes the steps of the annulation reaction as well as the importance of enolates. The questions asked are based on both information presented in the passage and a conceptual understanding of the basic chemistry. Several questions ask that you apply your understanding of the principles to predict reaction products.

186. C This is a conceptual question testing your understanding of hydrogen ions and their effect on the acidity of organic compounds. When a proton is given off from a neutral compound, the remaining organic compound must be negatively charged. When that negative charge is formed adjacent to a carbonyl group, there is another resonance structure that can be drawn to represent the actual structure:

The second resonance form shown above has a negative charge on oxygen, rather than carbon. Because oxygen is farther to the right on the periodic table than carbon, this is more favorable than having the negative on the carbon. Hydrogens farther away from the carbonyl group do not have any stabilizing contributions from resonance structures.

187. D Because the enolate is stabilized by spreading the negative charge onto the oxygen of the carbonyl (see figure in answer to question 186), having two adjacent carbonyl groups would certainly be better than one. Look carefully at the choices. Choice D shows a carbon which would have two carbonyl groups directly adjacent to it. This would be a favored position for the enolate to form because of the resonance stabilization which can occur. This is a better choice than C, which shows a carbon two positions away from the carbonyl groups. Choices A and B are not stabilized nearly as well as choice D.

188. D The last paragraph of the passage indicates that the alcohol formed in the 1,2-addition step eliminates very easily. It does not state whether or not the alcohol is unstable or not. Generally speaking, alcohols are stable compounds. There is no information to believe that the intermediate alcohol is particularly unstable. Some students miss this question because they assume that all intermediates are unstable compounds. This is not true. Intermediates may be stable, reactive compounds. However, in this question, one can assume that the final product, an α,β-unsaturated carbonyl compound, is more stable than the intermediate. The alcohol intermediate eliminates easily because the α,β-unsaturated carbonyl compound is very stable, (due to delocalization), and is easily formed.

189. A This is an information recall question. This answer came directly from the last paragraph of the passage.

190. B Electrophilic means that a site is electron-loving. In other words, it attracts electrons. Because electrons are negatively charged, a site that is positively charged or partially positively charged will be electrophilic. Choice A is incorrect because it has no positive charge. Choices C and D have partial positive charges and partial negative charges close to one another. This in effect tends to cancel the electrophilic sites of these molecules. Choice B is the correct choice because the partial positive charge is far enough away from the negative charge to act as an electrophilic site.

191. C This question tests your understanding of the circulation of the digestive system. After foodstuffs are digested in the stomach and duodenum, nutrients are absorbed by capillaries in the wall of the small intestine. From the small intestine, blood travels through the portal vein to the liver. In the liver, blood passes through a second capillary bed where waste products are removed, and metabolic activities occur. After passing through the liver, blood travels through the hepatic veins to the inferior vena cava. Vena cava blood empties into the right atrium. The postabsorption bloodflow is a classic portal system. By definition, a portal system is a pattern of bloodflow in which blood passes through two capillary beds connected by venous vessels. A portal system follows this pattern: artery → capillary → vein → capillary → vein.

192. A The lungs are responsible for the minute-to-minute regulation of acid-base balance. When the blood pH decreases and the blood becomes acidic, the lungs aid in "blowing-off" more carbon dioxide. When the pH increases and the blood becomes more basic, the respiratory rate decreases and less carbon dioxide is lost. Recall that carbon dioxide relates to blood acidity because it is formed when carbonic acid is broken down by carbonic anhydrase in the lungs. The overall equation is: $H^+ + HCO_3 \rightarrow H_2CO_3 \rightarrow H_2O + CO_2$. The kidney is responsible for the long-term control of blood pH. the kidney is able to secrete hydrogen ions and reabsorb bicarbonate ions. These processes are slow and require a matter of days to have a significant effect on blood pH. The liver and spleen do not play a role in blood pH regulation.

193. D The way to increase the strength of contraction is the increase the activation of motor units. This increased activation recruits more sarcomeres and therefore increases contraction strength. Stronger muscle contractions come about when more muscle fibers are stimulated to contract. Choice A is incorrect because action potentials are all-or-none phenomena, and do not generally vary in strength. Although it is possible to affect the peak of an action potential (by altering the concentration of sodium and potassium ions in solution), this change does not result in a stronger muscle contraction. Choice B is incorrect because the dorsal root ganglion is a sensory ganglion. Choice C is incorrect because alternate activity of flexor and extensor muscles leads to movements that cancel out one another. The alternate activity of flexors and extensors do not lead to stronger muscle contractions.

194. B Notice that this curve has three plateau regions, suggesting three pK_a values. The pK_a for the carboxyl group of an amino acid is about 2.3. This corresponds to the midportion of the first plateau on the graph. The pK_a for the amino group is about 9.7. On this graph, the midplateau region of the third plateau is at 10.5. Although this is a bit off from what you normally find, this is likely the amino group of the amino acid. The second plateau, with a pK_a at 4.0 must be the side chain of this amino acid. This sidechain has an acidic, (it is much lower than 7.0), and is likely an acidic amino acid.

195. A The chance of a child being albino equals the chance of a child inheriting the (aa) genotype. From each parent comes a ½ chance of inheriting an albino allele. Therefore, the chance of inheriting the (aa) genotype = ½ × ½ = ¼. The chance of inheriting syndactyly equals the chance of inheriting a single B allele (the allele is dominant; only one allele is needed). Only one parent has a B allele, and the chance of inheriting it is ½. To inherit both syndactyly and albinism: ¼ × ½ = ⅛.

PASSAGE IX This is an information-presentation passage (biology) that discusses diabetes, insulin, and glucose metabolism. Some of the information will be new to you. However, from your knowledge of biology, you are expected to understand the information presented. The questions that follow the passage are one of two question types. You are asked several conceptual questions based on your knowledge and understanding of basic physiology. In addition, several application-type questions are asked that require that you take a principle presented in the passage and apply it to solve a particular problem.

196. D   Glucagon increases the breakdown of glucagon (storage form of glucose) in the liver. This increases blood glucose. On the other hand, insulin increases the conversion of glucose to glucagon. This decreases blood glucose. Insulin also is required to help cells uptake glucose. In the absence of insulin, cells are unable to transport glucose. This can lead to cell starvation and cell death. Choice A is incorrect because somatostatin is a hormone produced by the pancreas which decreases digestive activity. Choice B is incorrect because aldosterone acts to increase sodium reabsorption and potassium secretion in the distal convoluted tubule of the kidney. Aldosterone also plays an important role in the regulation of blood pressure. Choice C is incorrect because oxytocin is a posterior pituitary hormone which is involved in stimulating contraction of the smooth muscle in the breast (lactation) and uterus (labor).

197. B   This is a difficult question because the passage contains information that may mislead you. Refer back to the passage to look for key information to help you answer this question. In the second paragraph, the passage states that patients with type II diabetes have a resistance to the action of insulin. Type I patients have almost a complete absence of insulin. Although the passage mentioned that type I diabetes may be linked to immune system problems, do not be misled by this information. The question states that antibodies are found against the receptors on cells which bind glucose. The antibodies are not directed against insulin. This is an important distinction. If the antibodies were directed against insulin, you would expect little or no insulin to be found in the blood. This would support type I diabetes. If the antibodies are directed against receptors which bind glucose on cells, the level of insulin in the blood could be normal. However, because insulin helps bring glucose into cells, the cells without functional glucose receptors would be resistant to the action of insulin. This most supports type II diabetes. The best answer to this question is choice B.

198. B   Pancreatic tissue contains thousands of cell collections known as islets of Langerhans. These islets contain three cell types: alpha cells, beta cells, and delta cells. Glucagon is made in the alpha cells. Insulin is made by beta cells. Somatostatin is made in the delta cells. There are no gamma cells in the Islets of Langerhans.

199. C   This is an information-presentation question. The answer to this question is found in the first two sentences of paragraph three. The passage indicates that, under the influence of insulin, potassium ions move into cells with glucose. An effective way to decrease abnormally high levels of potassium in the blood is to give glucose with potassium. Glucose must be given, so that the patient with normal glucose levels does not become hypoglycemic (low blood sugar). This would occur if insulin was given alone.

200. D   Thyroid hormone increases the metabolic rate and blood glucose. Cortisol, produced by the adrenal cortex, is a steroid hormone which helps the body deal with long-term stress. It also increases blood glucose. Epinephrine is produced by the adrenal medulla. It is effective in helping the body deal with acute stress. Epinephrine increases the heart rate, and increases both the blood pressure and blood glucose. Angiotensin is a hormone that increases blood pressure but has no effect on blood glucose. Angiotensin is produced as follows: angiotensinogen is produced in the liver, and is converted to angiotensin I by the enzyme renin, which is produced by the kidney. Angiotensin I is converted to angiotensin II by an enzyme in the lung. Angiotensin II is the strongest vasoconstrictor substance produced by the body.

201. D   It is very important to read the question very carefully. It asks what is the ultimate fate of the radioactively labeled glucose. Based on information given in the passage, you should expect that the labeled glucose should be taken up into cells. From your knowledge of biology, you know that glucose is the energy source that cells use to make adenosine triphosphate (ATP). Glucose is metabolized by glycolysis with the formation of pyruvate. Pyruvate is converted to acetyl CoA, which then enters the Krebs cycle. Carbon dioxide is a waste product of the Krebs cycle. Finally, oxidative phosphorylation and electron transport occurs, producing water as a waste product. To answer this question, think about what happens to the radioactively labeled carbon atoms. Carbon atoms are lost in the Krebs cycle as carbon dioxide. It is likely that the radioactive carbon atoms will ultimately be found in the carbon dioxide produced by metabolism. Choice C is not as good a choice, because pyruvic acid is an intermediate in the full metabolic breakdown of glucose. Although some trace radioactivity may be found in amino acids, (amino acids can be synthesized using sugars), this is not the main place radioactivity will be found. Eliminate choice B. Choice A is incorrect because the glucose will be taken up into cells and will not circulate indefinitely.

202. C This is a knowledge-based question, otherwise independent of the passage. Facilitated diffusion is a type of passive transport in which solute molecules are moved down a concentration gradient by a carrier protein. No input of energy is required. Active transport requires both a specific carrier and energy input.

PASSAGE X

This is a research-study passage (biology) that covers topics in evolution and behavior. A model of predation is presented and some key concepts in animal behavior are discussed. Two experiments are described in this passage. The first experiment is described, but no data is presented. The second experiment involving the "flight" of a hawk model is described and data is presented. The questions focus on conceptual principles discussed in the passage and interpretation of the meaning of the experiments.

203. B Use the process of elimination to arrive at the best choice. This strategy is especially important in this question because two of the choices are close to one another. Start with the choices that are easy to eliminate. Speciation (choice C) is the formation of a new species due to the development of breeding incompatibility within a species. Genetic drift (choice D) is a change in the gene pool of a population due to chance. Neither of these choices are described by this question. Choices A and B are both correct terms which describe the overall process described. However, you must choose between these two choices. Differential reproduction is the production of more offspring by more fit individuals in a given species. Natural selection is the broad term to describe the mechanism for evolution. Natural selection includes the following three concepts: (1) more individuals are produced than can be supported by the environment, (2) survival of the fittest, and (3) individuals who are better suited to their environment are likely to leave more offspring than less fit individuals (differential reproduction). This question illustrates differential reproduction more than it illustrates all the concepts of evolution. Thus, choice B is the best choice.

204. A The selfish herd model is discussed in the first paragraph of the passage. The only tenet of the selfish herd model is that animals are motivated by self interest (i.e., selfish) to hide themselves from prey even if it means using peers as a shield. This implies that an individual's domain of danger, or how exposed to prey it is, reaches nadir values at the center of a group. The model does not compare group travel to solitary travel (choices B and C). Choice D is incorrect because the domain of danger is decreased as a result of this selfish behavior.

205. C This question requires that you consider the merits of ideas not discussed in the passage on the basis of whether they can explain the observation given. Evaluate each choice to see if the statement being made is reasonable. Choices A, B, and D, if they are true, all offer support for the notion that groups are safer than individuals. Choice C, if it is true, would decrease average safety levels of group members. Thus, choice C would not explain why grouping increases average safety for members.

206. A The passage states the hypothesis of the hawk experiment. The hypothesis is that faster reaction times will be found in bigger flocks. The question asks you what the implication of this hypothesis is. The question does not ask you to evaluate the data derived from the experiment. Choice A does follow the hypothesis. If bigger flocks have faster reaction times, this can provide earlier warning of predator approach for members of the flock. Choices B and C are not as good as choice A. No implication about safety can be made without making too many assumptions. Choice D is not an implication derived from the hypothesis.

207. **D**   Look carefully at the graph. Note that only the circled data points show a strong correlation between reaction time and flock size. Both extremes of the x-axis deviate from this linear relationship. Choices A and B explain why the smaller and larger size groups respectively did not fit. Imperative to analyzing choices C and D is an understanding of the potentially ambiguous description of how reaction time is measured. The number of film frames counted from the instant the first bird reacted to the hawk model until it passed over the feeding site means that trials where the group reacted quickly will show a large number of frames. The higher up on the y-axis the flock's score, the faster their alarm was sounded. Indeed, within the circled data points the hypothesized result occurred: larger flocks reacted faster. Flocks of 14 doves reacted more quickly than those of seven, making choice D incorrect.

This is a problem-solving passage (organic chemistry) that presents a step-synthesis of an alcohol from an alkane. Five reactions are shown, outlining the synthesis of the desired alcohol. A problem associated with multiple-step–synthesis reactions (poor yield) is described, and an example is given. The questions expect that you understand various reaction types, and can predict the geometry of the products produced.

208. **B**   Identifying the type of reaction mechanism is one of the most common organic questions asked on the MCAT. Equation one shows a substitution reaction. There are no double bonds formed, so that elimination does not occur. Because the hydroxyl group is at a primary carbon atom, the substitution must go by S_N2. Recall that S_N2 prefers less substituted electrophiles (primary or secondary carbons), although S_N1 prefers more substituted electrophiles (tertiary > secondary > primary) S_N2 reactions go by a single step with a transition state. In this question, note that the hydroxyl is not a good leaving group and must be protonated first. The mechanism is shown below:

209. **D**   To produce an alkene mixture, an elimination reaction must occur. The elimination reaction can only produce double bonds adjacent to where the oxygen atom originally was. The only exception to this would be in cases of carbocation rearrangement. However, in this question, the reactant has a tertiary carbocation and will not rearrange. The only alkene shown that has a double bond adjacent to the carbon which had the oxygen attached is choice D.

210. **B**   The best way to answer this question is to draw the structures of the two alkenes. The two alkenes produced are:

These are not stereoisomers because they differ by more than just the spatial orientation of the atoms. Eliminate choice C. These are not conformational isomers because they differ by more than rotation around single bonds. Eliminate choice A. Choice D is incorrect because it transposes the terms alkane and alkene. The alkenes produced are regioisomers.

211. B The first reaction that occurs is the hydrolysis of the salt (RO^- + ^+MgBr). This results in an alcohol (ROH) and a magnesium halide salt ($MgBr_2$). Because the reagent used for the hydrolysis is an acid, acid-catalyzed dehydration of alcohols can occur (an elimination reaction) to produce alkenes.

212. D Because reaction 1 is a nucleophilic substitution reaction, its mechanism will depend on the substitution of the carbon attached to the hydroxyl group. With a highly substituted carbon, the mechanism will be S_N1, which results in racemic product. The intermediate carbocation is flat, and is equally prone to attack by the Br^- nucleophile from either side. This results in a racemic mixture.

213. D This question tests your understanding of hydrogenation reactions in the presence of metal catalysts. Hydrogenation occurs at the surface of the metal catalyst used. The alkene adsorbs to the surface of the metal and picks up two hydrogen atoms from the metal. This occurs much faster than internal rotation, so the addition is syn. Markovnikov's rule states that electrophilic addition to a carbon-carbon bond involves the intermediate formation of the more stable carbocation. This rule helps predict the stereochemistry of hydrogen halide addition and halogenation reactions, but is not useful in hydrogenation reactions.

INDEPENDENT QUESTIONS

214. D Aldehydes and ketones can H-bond with water molecules because they contain the polar carbonyl group. However, because they do not contain a hydrogen directly attached to the polar atom (oxygen), they do not form H-bonds to themselves. Alcohols have the ability to H-bond to themselves; therefore they have higher boiling points than aldehydes or ketones of similar molecular weight. Both aldehydes and ketones are more polar than alkanes and can H-bond to water; for this reason, they have higher boiling points than hydrocarbons of similar molecular weight.

215. A The correct order of mitosis is interphase, prophase, metaphase, anaphase, telophase/cytokinesis. During interphase, cells grow and DNA synthesis (replication) occurs. In prophase, DNA condenses to form visible chromosomes. The nucleolus disappears and the mitotic spindle forms. In metaphase, the chromosomes align along the equator of the cell with each chromosome oriented perpendicular to the spindle. In anaphase, sister chromatids separate as microtubules shorten. At the end of anaphase, each pole has the same set of chromosomes. In telophase, daughter nuclei are reformed and division of the cytoplasm (cytokinesis) occurs.

216. B Number the carbons starting from the carbonyl carbon of the acid. The acid takes priority over the double bond. The double bond starts at carbon 3 and the Cl is at carbon 5. The base name is pentene. Because the carboxylic acid is always the terminal group, it is not necessary to split up the name as in choice C.

217. B The fact that the child is type O (the ii genotype) means that the parents must be I^Ai and I^Bi. Considering the genotypes of the parents, the chance of getting a I^AI^B child is 1/4, or 25%.

218. B Notice that each carbon has three sp^2 hybridized orbitals. Recall that double bonds are formed when the sp^2 orbitals form a sigma bond by direct end-to-end overlap of atomic orbitals. The p-orbital can form a pi bond with a properly aligned p-orbital. These relationships lead to the formation of a double bond. The compound shown must be a double-bond-containing compound, namely ethene. Recall that the bond geometry of sp^2 hybridized orbitals is trigonal planar.

219. D Fungi are eukaryotic organisms which have very diverse lifestyles. Many fungi are multicellular, although some are unicellular. All fungi have mitochondria. Some species of fungi are haploid, while others are diploid. They may reproduce sexually or asexually and produce spores. They reproduce by a process known as budding.

Verbal Reasoning

Time: 85 minutes

Questions: 1–65

Passage I (Questions 1–7)

William Whewell classified the British geological community of the 1830s as belonging to two different groups—the "catastrophists" and the "uniformitarians." The French comparative anatomist and naturalist Georges Cuvier, considered by many to be the father of catastrophism, proposed that the past history of the earth was comprised of long periods of geological "tranquility" separated by sudden, great geological disturbances, or catastrophes. He believed that these catastrophic disturbances were short-term in nature and of a kind and magnitude not experienced today. Furthermore, some proponents of catastrophism suggested that there was some direction to the earth's history and that God, or some other supernatural force, probably played some role in controlling the direction and nature of geological change. The British geologist Charles Lyell, however, gave a drastically different picture of past geological phenomena. In his book, *Principles of Geology,* Lyell set forth the principles of uniformitarianism, actualism, and the steady-state theory. It was to these principles that the uniformitarians subscribed. Lyell proposed that present geological processes were of the same kind and intensity as those of the past and that they showed no sign of any direction or progression. Thus, uniformitarians suggested that geological change was gradual and continuous, rather than sudden and catastrophic. Moreover, they minimized God's role in controlling geological change.

Both catastrophists and uniformitarians provided what they felt was good evidence to support their own points of view. Much of the catastrophists' evidence was based on what they believed was the result of the most recent catastrophic event—the great flood described in Genesis. Cuvier and others pointed to the existence of distinct layers of freshwater and marine organisms in the Paris Basin and bones of extinct animals at the bottom of a Yorkshire cave as evidence of the sudden great flood. Cu-

vier also argued that the discovery of perfectly preserved frozen mammoths in Russia proved that other types of catastrophic events, such as sudden great freezes, had occurred in the past. Lyell, however, provided evidence that he felt would support the notion of slow, gradual, and steady geological change. For example, he pointed to the known slow, yet constant elevating effects of volcanoes, such as Vesuvius and Etna, and provided an explanation for the unusual erosion pattern seen on the columns of the ancient Temple of Serapis at Pozzuoli that was compatible with uniformitarian views. During the 1830s, the British naturalist Charles Darwin provided further evidence for Lyell's notions of slow geological change. Darwin's theory of coral reef formation (due to subsidence) and notes on earthquake activity in certain regions of South America (due to gradual uplifting of the earth) strongly supported Lyell's three principles of actualism, uniformitarianism, and the steady-state theory.

The ideas of the catastrophists were much closer in line with the teachings of the Christian church than were those of the uniformitarians. Catastrophists, for the most part, believed that the earth was relatively young, that catastrophic events shaped the world, and that God played some role in directing the earth's history and/or governing the physical laws that mediated geological phenomena. These ideas either totally supported or closely paralleled those of the church. Additionally, the catastrophists attempted to explain the timing of the earth's development in a manner that would be somewhat compatible with the time-frame explanation given in the Bible. Uniformitarians, on the other hand, supported notions that did not totally agree with, or support, those of the Bible. For example, Lyell and other uniformitarians argued that the earth's surface was not exclusively shaped by such catastrophic events as Noah's flood. They also rejected the notion that geological processes show direction and progression. Moreover, the uniformitarian's time line for age of the earth greatly exceeded that suggested in the Bible.

GO ON TO THE NEXT PAGE.

1. According to the passage, which of the following are supported?

    I. Lyell was British and a religious zealot.
    II. Sudden freezes and uplifting of the earth due to earthquake activity supported Cuvier's postulates.
    III. The effects of volcanoes do not support the actualists' tenets.

    A. I and II only
    B. II and III only
    C. III only
    D. None of the above

2. Based on information presented in the passage, one can conclude that Darwin's ideas parallel those of which of the following?

    A. Lyell
    B. Cuvier
    C. Nineteenth-century theologians
    D. None of the above

3. Which was the most recent geological evidence used to support the catastrophists' position?

    A. London Basin
    B. Great flood
    C. Ancient temple erosion
    D. Coral reef formation

4. Cuvier proposed that geological disturbances were:

    A. subject to change.
    B. gradual and continuous.
    C. noncatastrophic in nature.
    D. short-term in nature.

5. Evidence supporting the uniformitarian position:

    A. was supported by the Paris Basin findings.
    B. was antithetical to that of the steady-state position.
    C. was postulated by Lyell in his book *Principles of Geology*.
    D. paralleled 19th century Judeo-Christian ideology.

6. Gradual and continuous upheavals of an earthquake fault lines would:

    A. parallel Darwin's theory of coral reef formation.
    B. align with the tenets of Lyell.
    C. align with the tenets of Cuvier.
    D. not apply to either theory discussed in this passage.

7. Based on the passage, the author holds that:

    A. the catastrophist viewpoint is correct.
    B. the uniformitarian viewpoint is probably correct.
    C. one viewpoint is much better supported than the other.
    D. there is some validity and support for each viewpoint.

A certain gorilla at the Central Park Zoo in New York sometimes takes a standing leap to her broad trapeze. She sits there, swinging violently for a time, and then suddenly drops without a jar—indeed, descends as lightly as a feather might float to the ground. Walking through the monkey house at the Bronx Zoo, we stop before the cage of an orangutan as he jumps to his lead-pipe trapeze with half an orange in one hand and a handful of straw in the other. He tucks the wisp of hay under his neck and, lying on his back as contentedly as if at rest in a hammock, sucks at the orange from time to time—an exhibition of equilibrium that is difficult to account for.

The gorilla's master feat—the standing leap to a swing the height of her head—is matched by the pigeon when it flies at full speed, stops short, pauses, and without a detour flies back in the direction from which it came. At dusk, four or five impalas will timidly emerge from their shelter, then bound through the air, in a succession of 20-foot leaps, to the end of their runway. Perhaps Clement Moore had seen or heard of impalas and was thinking of them when, in *A Visit from St. Nicholas,* he wrote of Santa Claus' reindeer skimming the housetops.

The swimmer has a valuable lesson in muscular control as he watches a sea lion round the curve of its pool, corkscrewing in a spiral as its changes from the usual position to swim upside down. Hardening-up exercises in military training, with obstacles to surmount and ditches to clear, involve skills that are neatly mastered by animals. In the wilds, bands of gibbons swing from tree to tree just like army trainees swing by ropes or work along the bars of a jungle gym.

Animals are "propelled by muscles that move their bones as levers, up and down or from side to side." The ways in which the movements of their muscles vary provide an ever-fascinating sight. The motions of animals are so rapid that we really need the aid of an expert such as James Gray to analyze them for us. In his book *The Motions of Animals,* Mr. Gray says that the bear—a browser, not a runner—rests on the entire foot when walking. The horse and the deer—built for speed—rest on tiptoe (the hoof); the hock never touches the ground.

An essential rule of safe living is well illustrated by animals: work when you work, play when you play, and rest when you rest. Watch two young bears wrestling, rolling, pushing, and attacking. One tires, climbs to a broad rock, and stretches out full length on its paws. The other stands up, leans forward till it can reach with its mouth the ear of the bear on the rock, and keeps tugging at the ear as though dragging a hassock forward by the ear. The rester gets up, comes down, and once more both are tumbling, capsized and capsizing.

There is nothing more concentrated than the perseverance with which a duck preens its feathers or a cat washes its fur. The duck spreads oil on its feathers with its beak from a small sac above the tail. The feathers then lie smooth and waterproof, reminding us that we too must take time to care for our bodies and equipment. For as much as 15 minutes at a time, a leopard will, without switching to another area of its body, wash a small patch of fur that is not sleek enough to satisfy the animal. It may then leap to its shelf, a board suspended by rods from the ceiling of the cage. Dangling a foreleg and a hindleg on either side of the shelf, its tail hanging motionless, the leopard will close its eyes and rest.

Patience on the part of animals is self-evident. In studying, photographing, or rearing young animals, human beings also need patience. We have in Helen Martini a thrilling example of what may be done for young animals by a human being. Mrs. Martini has reared two sets of tiger cubs, a lion cub, and various other baby animals for the Bronx Zoo.

The zoo shows us that privacy is a fundamental need of all animals. For considerable periods, animals in the zoo will remain out of sight in the quiet of their dens or houses. Glass, recently installed in certain parts of the snake house at the Bronx Zoo, makes it possible to see in from the outside, but not out from the inside.

We are the guests of science when we enter a zoo; and, in accepting privileges, we incur obligations. Animals are masters of earth, air, and water, brought from their natural surroundings to benefit us. It is shortsighted, as well as ungrateful, to frighten them or to feed them if we are told that feeding will harm them. If we stop to think, we will always respect chains, gates, wires, or barriers of any kind that are installed to protect the animals and to keep the zoo as a museum of living marvels for our pleasure and instruction.

8. The author of this passage, as well as being an essayist, is a poet. In her poems, she often describes animals in order to access human emotions and situations. Using the information in the passage, which of the following analogies might NOT be appropriate?

   I. Gorilla as acrobat
  II. Impala as shy person
 III. Orangutan as aerialist

  A. I and III only
  B. II and III only
  C. II only
  D. I only

9. The swimmer referred to in paragraph three is which of the following?

  A. Author
  B. Reader
  C. Sea lion's trainer
  D. Anyone who swims

10. Which of the following implications can be drawn from the information in paragraph two?

   A. Reindeer had not been mentioned in literature previous to Clement Moore's *A Visit from St. Nicholas.*
   B. The author finds some kinship between impalas and reindeer.
   C Reindeer do not exist, but are creations of literature.
   D. The word "runway" implies that impalas are being compared to airplanes.

11. The author covers a great deal of territory in her article about the zoo. Her discussion of bears is particularly evocative. From the information in paragraph five, we could make which of the following inferences?

   I.   Bears do one thing at a time, and thoroughly.
   II. Never move too quickly around a bear.
   III. Bears are subtly allied with boats.

   A. I and II only
   B. I and III only
   C. III only
   D. II and III only

12. The author's attitude toward animals might be described as which of the following?

   A. Tolerant
   B. Carefree
   C. Admiring
   D. Adoring

13. Were we to assess the central point of this passage, we might declare which of the following as an apt summary?

   A. We can learn a great deal about animals if we carefully observe them in zoos, which mimic their natural habitats.
   B. Animals have habits and predilections that transcend their environments; in the zoo, in particular, animals need a great deal of privacy.
   C. We can learn a great deal about ourselves by carefully observing animals.
   D. Animals are masters of earth, air, and water, brought from their natural surroundings to benefit us.

14. In paragraph six, the author discusses the self-cleansing habits of the duck and leopard. We may infer which of the following from the information dispensed?

   A. The author thinks that human beings do not spend sufficient time on personal hygiene.
   B. The author finds certain animals to be painstaking creatures.
   C. The author believes that human beings would benefit from a waterproofing mechanism.
   D. The author asserts that leopards are obsessed with a sleek coat.

"Carrier" has become one of the most controversial words in United States AIDS discourse. Although casually used to describe those who have acquired the HIV virus, the word carrier has always been a "loaded" term. In discussions of AIDS, carrier implies not only "having" or "holding," but also "transmission." Carriers are perceived to be "passers" as well. Thus, the term *carrier* subtly marks those with the AIDS disease, or the HIV virus, as potentially dangerous to noncarriers. Perceived danger leads to real fear, and it is out of this fear that reactionary conservatives have made horrific suggestions for quarantining those with the HIV virus or AIDS.

Although some people would claim that vocabulary is not of central importance in fighting AIDS, especially when immediate health care, medical research, and national education are desperately needed, the language we will use to discuss these problems and negotiate these plans will have a fundamental effect on how we deal with the crisis at hand. The words we choose will include implications, connotations, and points of view. These words will take their meanings from specific cultural contexts.

Have you ever heard persons with AIDS describe themselves as carriers? The word is always used by those who think they do not have AIDS, to describe those who they think have AIDS. The word is generally used by white, middle-class heterosexuals, and has been applied variously to foreigners, IV drug users, and gay men. Although heterosexual teenagers are the fastest growing group of people with AIDS, the term has yet to be applied to this group. AIDS is spreading among young heterosexuals, but no one is calling them "carriers." White middle-class heterosexuals only use the word carrier, along with its negative connotations, to describe groups it already discriminates against. I propose that the term HIV-positive is more appropriate and accurately describes the status of a person without the highly negative label. A number of years ago, a new face was brought to center stage in media coverage of AIDS. When a prominent basketball star announced that he had tested positive for the HIV virus, he became a public representative for the male heterosexual population who were HIV-positive. This individual has been called "brave"; he has yet to be called a carrier. The finger of blame has moved magically over this male basketball player to point at the latest arrivals on the list of carriers: heterosexual women. Somehow, this athlete's sexual promiscuity has been overlooked, whereas that of his sexual partners, the heterosexual women who passed the virus to him, has been explicitly highlighted. Why did this occur? Why wasn't this athlete held accountable for his high-risk behavior? Why did the public feel sorry for him when it appears that he brought on this problem himself? Did the public wonder or ask if this person transmitted the virus to unsuspecting partners? The answer to these questions must lie in societal value systems, sexual prefer-

ence partiality, gender biases, and public admonition for star athletes. Although heterosexual men continue to be praised for sexual promiscuity, heterosexual women have long been criticized for this same behavior. Given the history of cultural discrimination, it isn't really any surprise that women, and not this particular male athlete, were marked as the carriers in this transmission.

Recently, a small AIDS activist group turned the tables on carrier connotations. They staged a creative protest, which was overwhelmingly not publicized by the mass media. In this protest, a prominent conservative senator was singled out and sent a public message. This senator was a well-known leader in the opposition to AIDS education, and a known anti-AIDS crusader. A large banner was created by the activist group. Inscribed on the banner was the following phrase: STOP THE SPREAD OF DANGEROUS POLITICS. The banner was marched in front of this senator's home and office. By attempting to mark this senator as a dangerous carrier, the activist group also redefined what is truly "dangerous" (and spreading) in the current AIDS debate: homophobia, racism, and sexism. As long as terms with negative connotations continue to be used to describe people with AIDS, political policies will be built around the prejudices of those in power.

15. It can be inferred that the author would prefer to substitute which of the following words for the word carrier?

   A. Passer
   B. Contaminated person
   C. Infected person
   D. HIV-positive

16. According to the author, in addition to meanings, words also signify which of the following?

   I. Points of view
   II. Prejudices
   III. Programs

   A. I only
   B. I and II only
   C. I and III only
   D. I, II, and III

17. If the author of the passage were to put together an educational panel on AIDS, the panel would consist mostly of which of the following?

   A. Doctors
   B. Literature professors
   C. Politicians
   D. HIV-positive people or people with AIDS

200

18. What is the tone of this passage?

    A. Confidential
    B. Flippant
    C. Ardent
    D. Persuasive

19. According to the author, what causes discrimination?

    A. Sexual preference
    B. Power
    C. Ignorance
    D. Fear

20. According to the author of the passage, language:

    A. is not as important as political activism.
    B. is not as important as medical research.
    C. is always full of prejudices.
    D. affects thoughts and beliefs.

21. The author implies which of the following?

    A. The basketball star should call himself a carrier.
    B. Heterosexuals should be called carriers.
    C. The basketball star's sexual partners should not be called carriers.
    D. Everyone should be called a potential carrier.

22. Based on implications of the passage, which group has the most cultural power in the United States?

    A. Heterosexual men
    B. Senators
    C. Famous athletes
    D. White men and women

Passage IV (Questions 23–30)

Biblical scholars have long debated the meaning behind the seemingly contradictory depictions of the relationship between God and Abraham in Genesis 18 and Genesis 22. Although a tension may exist between the Abraham of Genesis 18:22 to 23 and the Abraham of Genesis 22, the two are certainly not irreconcilable. The Abraham of Genesis 18 does not challenge the faithfulness of the Abraham of Genesis 22, because the two chapters present Abraham relating to the Lord in two very different situations. The first scene is a lesson in justice, whereas the second is a test of faith. Taken together, the two scenes present a relationship between man and God in which man may question God concerning the nature of justice, provided he does not deny the Lord's ultimate power to judge, but he must never question the Lord in matters concerning faith. Both interactions point to a hierarchical relationship between Abraham and the Lord, one in which Abraham pleases the Lord as long as he acknowledges and respects the Lord's ultimate, overriding power.

In Genesis 18, Abraham successfully questions the Lord without angering him. Abraham does not arouse the wrath of God because his manner in addressing the Lord remains humble at all times. Abraham begins most of his questions with "Oh let not the Lord be angry. . ."; and states repeatedly, "Behold, I have taken upon myself to speak to the Lord, I who am but dust and ashes." One can see that although Abraham may question the Lord, he also reaffirms the Lord's greater power as well as his own mortal inferiority.

The Lord does not ask Abraham to perform any task in Genesis 18. In this interaction the Lord merely tells Abraham of his plan to destroy Sodom and Gomorrah, and almost invites questions by telling Abraham: "Shall I hide from Abraham what I am about to do, seeing that Abraham shall become a great and mighty nation, and all the nations of the earth shall bless themselves by him? No, for I have chosen him, that he may charge his children and his household after him to keep the way of the Lord by doing righteousness and justice. . ." (Genesis 18:17). Thus, Abraham's questions to the Lord do not arise out of insolence, but out of a desire to understand the nature of the Lord's justice, which Abraham and his descendants have been commanded to uphold.

In Genesis 22, the interaction between the Lord and Abraham takes place on quite different terms from those of Genesis 18. In this later chapter, the Lord directly asks Abraham to perform a task for him. He tests Abraham's faith, telling him to sacrifice his innocent son, a command most would find cruelly unjust. However, because he has been directly called upon to act by the Lord, Abraham cannot protest this injustice. Any misgivings or qualms on Abraham's part would signify great insolence and a lack of respect for the power of the Lord. Thus, in order to demonstrate his understanding of the hierarchical nature of the

GO ON TO THE NEXT PAGE.

relationship between himself and the Lord, Abraham obeys the Lord without hesitation.

Taken together, Genesis 18 and 22 describe a clearly unequal relationship between Abraham and the Lord, one in which Abraham must at all times respect the superior position of the Lord. Abraham is permitted to question the Lord in matters concerning the nature of justice, but only when his own action is not involved. When Abraham himself is called upon to act by the Lord, he must obey without hesitation. Questioning a command from the Lord would undermine the hierarchy of their relationship. Thus, because he understands the nature of his relationship to the Lord, Abraham remains a faithful servant to him at all times, questioning the essence of God's justice only when appropriate according to the terms of their relationship.

23. In Genesis 22, Abraham follows Gods commands:

    A. in order to please God.
    B. in order to prove his worth to God.
    C. because he respects God.
    D. because he is inferior to God.

24. The one thing Abraham can never do is:

    A. question God.
    B. anger God.
    C. disobey God.
    D. displease God.

25. The author of the passage believes that:

    A. the Bible is confusing.
    B. the Bible is intriguing.
    C. the Bible is compelling.
    D. the Bible is consistent.

26. In Genesis 22, God tests Abraham:

    A. to make sure Abraham understands his role.
    B. because God doesn't trust Abraham.
    C. because God is angry with Abraham.
    D. to further illustrate God's systems of justice.

27. From the preceding passage, the reader can infer that God is which of the following?

    A. Amiable
    B. Wrathful
    C. Indecisive
    D. Rational

28. Based on inferences from the passage, one would expect that Abraham can question God:

    A. when he doesn't understand God's actions.
    B. when he doesn't understand God's instructions.
    C. when God wants him to ask questions.
    D. when he doesn't like God's actions.

29. The relationship of God to Abraham is most like that of:

    A. doctor to patient.
    B. manager to employee.
    C. husband to wife.
    D. pope to king.

30. From the passage, it is clear that Abraham:

    A. fears God.
    B. trusts God.
    C. loves God.
    D. likes God.

GO ON TO THE NEXT PAGE.

In a very real sense, rock music was implicit in the music of the first Africans brought to North America. This transplanted African music wasn't exactly boogie-woogie or jazz, but it did have several characteristics that survive in American music today. It was participatory; often a song leader would be pitted against an answering chorus, or a solo instrument against an ensemble, in a call-and-response fashion. It sometimes attained remarkable polyrhythmic complexity, and always had a kind of percussive directionality or rhythmic drive. Vocal quality tended to be hoarse or grainy by European standards, although there was also considerable use of falsetto. Melodies fell within a relatively narrow range and often incorporated flexible pitch treatment around certain "blue notes." There was some improvisation, but always within the limits of more or less traditional structures.

All of these characteristics are evident in quite a few rock and roll records. For example, in "What'd I Say," the lead singer calls out a lead melody while a chorus responds, and riffing horns answer his piano figures. The singer's band rhythm section drives relentlessly, and superimposes fancy accent patterns over the basic beat. The singer's voice has a hoarse, straining quality, with occasional leaps into falsetto. His melody is narrow in range and blues-like, and the improvisations that occur never threaten the continuity of the song's gospel-derived metric and harmonic structure.

One shouldn't conclude from these similarities that pure African music was somehow transformed into rock and roll. Music in Africa was always flexible, ready to accommodate new influences from the next village or from foreign cultures; and in America, plantation owners and preachers tried to stamp it out entirely. Accordingly, African music adapted. The traits that survived without much alteration tended to be of two kinds. Some were musical imponderables like vocal quality or rhythmic drive, aspects of style so basic to the culture they were rarely considered consciously and were therefore immune to conscious change. Other traits—blues scales, call-and-response forms—were close enough to some varieties of European folk music to be assimilated and perpetuated by whites.

The acculturation of black Americans to mainstream musical values proceeded more and more rapidly as the 20th century gathered momentum, but pockets of tradition remained. In 1940, when Charlie Christian and T-Bone Walker were already playing modern jazz and blues on electric guitars, a team of interviewers in the Georgia Sea islands found elderly residents who still knew songs in African languages and how to make African drums. Elsewhere, the bedrock African culture persevered most tenaciously in the black church, just as in Africa itself religion, magic, and music had been closely linked in a kind of composite cultural focus. This is why the most African-sounding rock and roll has always come from the church, from gospel-inspired blues shouters or from former gospel singers, whose "Shout" was an old-fashioned ring shout done up with band accompaniment.

The music brought to America by European settlers determined most of the forms in which both old and new song materials would be set. Song stanzas of four and eight bars were a heritage of European epic poetry and narrative ballads; there are examples of such things in some traditional African music, but only as one formal scheme among many. The narrative ballad itself, with its objective performer who comments on but does not become involved in the action, was a European product very foreign to the mainstream of black tradition. A ballad vogue among blacks during the late 19th century did produce memorable songs such as "Stagger Lee" and "Frankie and Johnny," several of which were revived by early rockers.

In isolated rural areas, particularly Appalachia and the Ozarks, traditional English, Scotch, and Irish dance music survived, along with folk fiddling. But even there the African banjo became as popular as the fiddle. The guitar, which had been derived by the Spanish and Portuguese from the African Moors, came later. During the late 19th and early 20th centuries, white country musicians developed a tradition of virtuosity on all of these instruments. Their repertoires retained many old-time folk ballads, dance tunes, and hymns, but black-influenced minstrel tunes, blues-like ballads, and camp meet songs were also popular.

31. Which of the following can be inferred from the passage?

   A. Charlie Christian and T-Bone Walker were influenced by traditional African music.
   B. Rock and roll derives directly from African music.
   C. "Stagger Lee" and "Frankie and Johnnie" were logical outgrowths of the transplant of African music to America.
   D. "Shout" contains several characteristics of traditional African music.

32. Traditional African music contains which of the following characteristics?

   I. A high "head voice" at times from the male vocalist
   II. A more hoarse or grainy vocal quality from vocalists
   III. Participation from both audience and performer

   A. I and II only
   B. II and III only
   C. III only
   D. I, II, and III

33. A thesis statement for this passage might read as which of the following?

   A. The influence of African transplanted music and culture on the 20th century American music scene is too vast to be discussed.
   B. What we call "American" music is really an amalgam of transplanted African and European musical traditions that have adapted to and learned from each other.
   C. What we call American music, although a combination of many traditions, has been greatly influenced by transplanted African music and culture.
   D. Pure African music was not just transformed into rock and roll.

34. Why would the singer, described in the second paragraph, NOT be called "an objective performer"?

   A. His band's rhythm section drives relentlessly, and he superimposes fancy accent patterns over the basic beat.
   B. His voice has a hoarse, straining quality, with occasional leaps into falsetto.
   C. His melody is narrow in range and blues-like, and the improvisations never threaten the continuity of the song's gospel-derived metric and harmonic structure.
   D. He calls out a leading melody while a chorus responds, and riffing horns answer his piano figures.

35. Which of the following would NOT contribute to why we cannot conclude that pure African traditional music was directly transformed into rock and roll?

   A. Teams of interviewers in the Georgia Sea islands found elderly residents who still knew songs in African languages.
   B. European settlers brought song stanzas of four and eight bars to America, which determined how many American songs would be written.
   C. Music in Africa was always changing according to the needs of the people and new influences, even before this music was transplanted to America.
   D. Imponderables such as vocal quality or rhythmic drive, aspects of style so basic to the culture, were rarely considered consciously, and therefore could not consciously change.

36. According to the passage, what role did the church play in the preservation and adaptation of African traditional music?

   A. The church helped black Americans acculturate to mainstream 20th-century values.
   B. The church inspired blues shouters.
   C. Religion and music were closely related in Africa, and that connection was maintained in America.
   D. African church music calls for a great deal of call-and-response as well as ring shouts.

37. According to the information in the passage, which of the following would not be true of white country musicians?

   A. Their repertoires were not influenced by the African musical tradition.
   B. They developed a mastery of a variety of stringed instruments.
   C. Their repertoires were influenced by the European musical tradition.
   D. They lived primarily in rural isolation.

GO ON TO THE NEXT PAGE.

Nature has made reasonably adequate provision for regulating the amount of light entering the eye—eyelashes to screen the light from above or reflect from below, the orbicularis to "screw up" the eye, the active pupil, and the uveoretinal pigment. The Eskimos make use of slotted strips of bone or wood to cut out snow-reflected light, but many races and individuals survive, without adventitious aid, the fiercest rays of the sun. Spectacles are, however, worn to indicate that the wearer is "literate," for why should they be worn if he is unable to read? The wearing of sunglasses has become a social custom for some people, as much as a practical necessity. Many people wear dark glasses to see without being seen, or to add a fictitious glamour or mystery to an otherwise unconvincing physiognomy. Neither the softly shaded lighting of a restaurant or hotel lounge or the light outdoors on dull days menaces even the most photophobic eyes, yet no other optical product is manufactured, distributed in such enormous quantities, and worn so indiscriminately and capriciously.

A High Court judge, Mr. Justice Philamore, in giving judgment against a driver, recently said: "I do not suppose her ability to keep a proper lookout was enhanced by wearing dark glasses. It seems an extraordinary thing to do when driving a car by night."

Sunglasses were probably worn before spectacles were invented to correct errors of refraction. The emerald through which Nero watched the flames was in the nature of a sunglass, and tourmaline lenses with their polarizing quality were used by the Chinese. The ophthalmic surgeon is often asked for advice by those living or contemplating living in countries where the sun is more evident than in northern climes. A brief review of the physiological principles involved may help to explain the conditions under which the use of tinted lenses is expedient.

Visible light consists of electromagnetic vibrations of wavelengths between the values of 4000 and 7600 angstroms. Below 4000 A, ultraviolet radiation, and above 7600 A, infrared radiation replace the visible spectrum. Prolonged exposure to infrared rays may produce lens changes, as in glassblower's cataract, and exposure to excessive ultraviolet radiation may produce a variety of effects, such as solar photophthalmia or snow blindness, in which photophobia, lacrimation, ciliary neuralgia, blepharospasm, edema of the eyelids, and even corneal ulceration may occur. Industrial photophthalmia occurs in people engaged in occupations where sources of light rich in short waves are used, such as in arc welding and oxyacetylene burning, or where short circuiting of high-tension currents is likely to occur. Exposure to these wavelengths may cause edema of the macula, followed by pigment proliferation and a central scotoma. Similar changes follow sun gazing or watching an eclipse.

There are many indications for wearing smoked or tinted glasses. Many surgeons advise the wearing of smoked or tinted glasses after cataract extraction, because the retina cannot immediately tolerate the increased intensity of light following the removal of the opaque cataract. In some myopic persons in whom the pupil is habitually dilated, in blond people who lack uveal pigment, and especially in albinos, the wearing of dark glasses is justifiable. In the military, smoked or tinted glasses are worn frequently, even in dark conditions. Night fighters and night pilots, who may depend on visual control rather than on instrument control, night drivers, and darkroom workers such as radiographers can achieve maximum dark adaptation before starting on their duty by wearing dark glasses for a period; the minimum period is about 15 minutes, which varies with the individual and his age.

38. "The Eskimos make use of slotted strips of bone or wood to cut out snow-reflected light, but many races and individuals survive, without adventitious aid, the fiercest rays of the sun." The second part of this sentence (starting with "but") has what relationship to the first part of the sentence?

    A. Part II proves Part I.
    B. Part II ridicules Part I.
    C. Part II negates Part I.
    D. Part II contradicts Part I.

39. The quotation in paragraph two of the passage might be an example of which of the following?

    A. Amusement
    B. Parody
    C. Sarcasm
    D. Censoriousness

40. Based on the tone of the passage, which of the following actions might the author endorse?

    A. Wearing sunglasses at night
    B. Sunglasses being worn by the literate
    C. Wearing sunglasses to correct errors of refraction
    D. Wearing sunglasses to approximate glamour

41. According to the passage, the first sunglasses were:

    A. made of precious stones.
    B. untinted.
    C. used by Greeks and Chinese.
    D. awkward and handheld.

205

GO ON TO THE NEXT PAGE.

42. Which of the following statements may NOT be false?

    I. Those living in southern climes may suffer from greater sun damage to their eyes.

    II. Electromagnetic vibrations of wavelengths above 7600 angstroms cause excessively bright light.

    III. Glassblowers need to be especially wary of prolonged exposure to infrared rays.

    A. II only
    B. II and III only
    C. I only
    D. I and II only

43. If the author of this passage were to provide one piece of advice, it might be which of the following?

    A. When in doubt, shade.
    B. Do as the ancient Romans did.
    C. Accessorize!
    D. The sun knows no master.

44. Ophthalmic surgeons provide a variety of advice concerning the sun, particularly concerning which of the following people?

    I. People who have had cataracts removed and are therefore insensitive to low-intensity light

    II. People who depend on being able to see their instrumentation

    III. Nearsighted people with large pupils

    A. II only
    B. I and II only
    C. II and III only
    D. III only

Passage VII (Questions 45–51)

Spontaneous generation, the formation of living organisms from nonliving matter, became a subject of considerable interest to Pasteur and his colleagues during the early 1860s. Pasteur's initial interest in the origin of microscopic life probably stemmed from observations he made in the 1850s while studying the process of fermentation. During that time, Pasteur had demonstrated that microorganisms could be observed whenever fermentation occurred. Although it was concluded that microorganisms were responsible for the fermentative process, Pasteur felt that one fundamental question had to be addressed: that was, where did the microorganisms causing fermentation come from? There was much debate on this question. Did the microorganisms originate from "parent" microorganisms, as had been previously suggested by Redi and Spallanzani, or did they arise spontaneously from inanimate matter, as had been suggested by proponents of spontaneous generation such as Van Helmon, Needham, and Pouchet. Being the inquisitive person he was, Pasteur felt compelled to investigate the issue of the origin of microbial life. As Pasteur was aware of at the time, any "germ theory" of fermentation, putrefaction, and/or disease could not be firmly established as long as the belief in spontaneous generation persisted. Thus, as far as Pasteur was concerned, the 1860s were the right time for the origin of microbial life controversy to be solved once and for all.

Pouchet's 1858 presentation to the Paris Academy of Sciences stimulated renewed interest in the issue of the origin of microbial life. During his speech, Pouchet reported that he was successfully able to generate microbial life de novo. The fact that Pouchet and the theory of spontaneous generation supported a materialistic notion greatly disturbed French conservatives like Pasteur. Conservatives could not accept the idea that life was continually being created or that organisms could be generated de novo. These notions were anti-God and anti-Bible in nature. Thus, Pasteur's own religious convictions probably also motivated him to conduct experiments that would attempt to disprove Pouchet, materialistic beliefs, and the theory of spontaneous generation.

Finally, it should be pointed out that early 19th-century advances in microscope technology gave researchers like Pasteur the interest and ability to focus greater attention on the origin and role of microscopic organisms. The creation of new and improved lenses and better overall microscope design allowed greater magnification and image clarity. This, in turn, allowed scientists to study life at finer levels.

Pasteur possessed numerous personal traits and innate abilities that contributed to the success of his experiments dealing with the issue of spontaneous generation. Three of these characteristics—his devotion to his work, need to work independently, and gift for creative and con-

GO ON TO THE NEXT PAGE.

vincing public demonstrations and debates—were especially significant and are worthy of special mention.

From an early age, Pasteur believed in a solid work ethic. He devoted himself to each and every project he became involved in, and his work on spontaneous generation was no exception. He remained in the laboratory for most of the day and often spent his evening reviewing observations and/or results of the experiments that had been carried out during the day. In addition to Pasteur's concern with the quantity of work performed, much attention was given to the quality of work performed. For example, when an experiment called for obtaining air samples from different locales, Pasteur thought that it would be best to go on an expedition. He traveled from Paris to the French countryside, then on to Mont Poupet, and finally to the peak of Mont Blanc. Moreover, he braved 2 days of subfreezing temperatures in order to collect air samples from the peak. Pasteur was obviously dedicated to his work.

Several other features contributed to Pasteur's success. Pasteur's need to work independently also contributed to overall scientific productivity. By working alone, he was free to do whatever experiments he wanted and could express his experimental creativity. He also had an innate gift for scientific discussion and debate. One of his first and most successful public lectures centered on the controversy surrounding the issue of spontaneous generation. As was true of all his lectures, Pasteur's superior oratorical skills, elegant and dramatic demonstrations, and strong experimental data left the audience nearly, if not totally, convinced of his own beliefs.

Pasteur's contributions to the biological sciences include the introduction of the "germ theory," the field of bacteriology, and new biological technology. Pasteur's work on the issue of spontaneous generation provided the basis for the germ theory—that is, the understanding that fermentation, decomposition, putrefaction, and disease are all caused by microorganisms. Because of Pasteur, later scientists such as Koch and Lister began focusing their attention on the role of microorganisms in nature and other "microscopic phenomena," such as the study of immunology.

45. The passage suggests that the underlying conflict between Pouchet and Pasteur:

A. was related to specific political beliefs.
B. was based on scientific experiments.
C. had a religious footing.
D. focused on the evidence supporting spontaneous generation.

46. According to the passage, Pasteur believed that any alternative theory to spontaneous generation required:

A. evidence supporting the germ theory.
B. convincing proponents of spontaneous generation that alternative theories were supported by data.
C. persuasion and time.
D. losing the belief in spontaneous generation.

47. Which of the following statements is best supported by the passage regarding Pasteur's work?

A. His work devotion contributed to his phenomenal scientific productivity.
B. His strong conservative values were the most important influence on his work.
C. Pasteur made very important contributions to science in the field of "bacteriology," expanding on the work of predecessors such as Koch and Lister.
D. Pasteur's work was better supported by the church and was less "anti-God" in nature than the work of proponents of spontaneous generation.

48. The Mont Blanc excursion supports the fact that Pasteur's underlying personality may well be described as which of the following?

A. Adventurous
B. Opinionated
C. Labile
D. Compulsive

49. Which of the following statements are true?

I. Pasteur was concerned with enlightening and convincing others of his beliefs.
II. Pasteur most likely did not collaborate extensively with other investigators.
III. Pasteur played an important role in moving biological science from a theoretical to a data-supported science.

A. I and II only
B. II and III only
C. I and III only
D. I, II, and III

GO ON TO THE NEXT PAGE.

50. A fellow scientist and personal friend of Pasteur would likely have made which of the following statements?

    A. Pasteur was as eager to enlighten and convince the world as he was to discover the truth.

    B. Pasteur contributed much to the field of bacteriology and immunology.

    C. Pasteur really did benefit from his early associations with Lister and the use of improved microscopes.

    D. Pasteur was a great scientist, but he did have poor skills in public lecturing and personal association.

51. Based on the information presented in the passage, a ranking of events or persons in chronological order from oldest to most recent would be which of the following?

    I. Immunology
    II. Germ theory
   III. Spontaneous generation

    A. I, II, III
    B. III, II, I
    C. III, I, II
    D. I, III, II

Passage VIII (Questions 52–59)

The issue of advertising by health care professionals has been quite a controversial topic over the last 10 years. Much of this controversy began in 1977 when the Federal Trade Commission (FTC) filed an antitrust lawsuit against the American Medical Association (AMA) and several smaller state medical associations. The FTC charged that these medical organizations were interfering with "fair trade" because their code of ethics prohibited members from advertising. The commission argued that prohibiting advertising prevents the consumer from learning about the type and cost of available services which, in turn, tends to reduce competition and fix prices. A recent article by Dyer states that the position of the FTC was that the reason medical costs were as high as they were was because "doctors have a monopoly on health care delivery and can thus maintain artificially high costs for their own profit." If doctors were not prohibited from advertising, it is argued, prices would come down, because patients could shop for the best "deals."

Although the AMA refuted the charges made by the FTC, several other professional organizations, including the American Bar Association and the American Dental Association, removed restrictions on advertising by their members. A 1982 United States Supreme Court ruling finally removed this issue by barring the AMA from making any reference to restriction of advertising and the solicitation of patients in any of its publications.

It is worth mentioning that many physicians are still trying to change several rules and regulations that interfere with their right to advertise as they wish. Recently, the Nebraska AMA delegation requested the AMA Council on Ethical and Judicial Affairs to revise its official opinion on the use of patient testimonials in professional advertisements. The delegation asked that the AMA change its constitution and bylaws so as to allow physicians to advertise patients' testimonials regarding the quality of services rendered, the physician's skill, and so on; the AMA denied this most recent request.

The issue of physician advertising is as controversial today as it was in the 1970s. However, recent fiscal changes in the field of medicine have encouraged some doctors to aggressively advertise. As physicians discover that managed care medicine is associated with less independence and autonomy, some physicians have been pursuing elective fields in medicine. A good example of a popular field of elective medicine is the aesthetic or cosmetic surgery field. Aesthetic surgery has greatly expanded in recent years due to public demand for cosmetic procedures and physician desire to perform elective, direct reimbursement procedures. The rapid growth of the burgeoning cosmetic surgery field is a good example of the complex issues that relate to physician advertising.

The issues of ethical and fair advertising also arise in the cosmetic surgery field. First of all, most states do not

GO ON TO THE NEXT PAGE.

restrict what surgical procedures a physician can perform. Thus, any licensed physician can perform any procedure he/she wants to do. Most hospitals restrict the use of their operating rooms to board-eligible or -certified surgeons, but private surgical centers outside of hospitals and in-office operating suites do not have these restrictions. Thus, some unqualified surgeons are doing cosmetic procedures in private surgical facilities without any legal restriction. These unqualified physicians advertise themselves as "cosmetic surgeons" or "laser surgeons." The public does not know that there is no specific training or board certification for "cosmetic surgery" or "laser surgery." Gynecologists, dermatologists, and even emergency room physicians are performing complex cosmetic surgery procedures, including breast surgery, facial surgery, and liposuction. These physicians are not plastic surgeons who are properly trained to perform cosmetic surgery. The only AMA–recognized board to perform full-body cosmetic plastic surgery is the American Society of Plastic and Reconstructive Surgery (ASPRS). It is interesting that the ASPRS quietly discourages its members from advertising. The irony is that unqualified physicians doing cosmetic surgery are advertising aggressively, and confusing the public into believing that they are adequately trained. On the other hand, the properly trained plastic surgeons are being pressured by their professional board to "rise above the unqualified," and to limit their advertising.

52. The Nebraska AMA delegation request is an example that:

   A. many physicians want more freedom in the way they can advertise.
   B. the delegation was in agreement with the AMA.
   C. physicians are concerned that advertising will diminish the professionalism of medicine.
   D. the quality of physician services is best scrutinized in order to assure quality care.

53. Note the following quotation: "One possible way to control the seemingly uncontrollable health sector could be to treat it as a business and make it respond to the same marketplace influences as other American business and industries." This quotation is most consistent with a statement made by which of the following people?

   A. An average private practice physician
   B. A supreme court judge
   C. An official of the AMA
   D. An official of the FTC

54. Based on the information in the passage, which statements are both true and supported?

   I.   Most physicians favor the right to advertise.
   II. Professional advertisements are considered unethical by the AMA and the FTC.

   A. I only
   B. II only
   C. I and II
   D. Neither I nor II

55. The decision made by the Supreme Court regarding the AMA is best described as which of the following?

   A. Confrontational
   B. Encompassing
   C. Divisive
   D. Expansive

56. What is the author's attitude about aesthetic surgery?

   A. The author is supportive of aesthetic surgery.
   B. The author is against aesthetic surgery.
   C. The author appears to have mixed feelings about aesthetic surgery.
   D. The author's attitude is unknown.

57. In the final paragraph of the passage, what does the author suggest is ironic?

   A. It is ironic that physicians are advertising cosmetic surgery services.
   B. It is ironic that the qualified surgeons "feel" some advertising restrictions, whereas the unqualified physicians are advertising heavily.
   C. It is ironic that the ASPRS is restricting physician advertising for those physicians who perform cosmetic surgery.
   D. It is ironic that restrictive advertising still occurs today, well over 20 years after the antitrust litigation with the AMA.

58. Based on information presented in the passage, why are all physicians who want to perform cosmetic surgery allowed to advertise and perform cosmetic procedures?

   A. It is an application of the "fair trade" principle.
   B. It is because of an ASPRS mandate.
   C. It is due to an AMA declaration.
   D. It is because hospitals can restrict only some physicians from performing procedures.

59. What is the most likely reason that the ASPRS discourages advertising of its members?

    A. It feels that advertising conflicts with AMA policy.

    B. It feels that advertising supports FTC policy.

    C. It feels that advertising "cheapens" or deprofessionalizes the field of plastic surgery.

    D. It feels that advertising encourages competition.

Passage IX (Questions 60–65)

These days, so many marriages end in divorce that our most sacred vows no longer ring with truth. "Happily ever after" and "Till death do us part" are expressions that seem on the way to becoming obsolete. Why has it become so hard for couples to stay together? What goes wrong? What has happened to us that close to one half of all marriages are destined for the divorce courts? How could we have created a society in which 42% of our children will grow up in single-parent homes?

Even though each broken marriage is unique, we can still find the common perils, the common causes for marital despair. Each marriage has crisis points, and each marriage tests endurance and the capacity for both intimacy and change. Outside pressures, such as job loss, illness, infertility, trouble with a child, care of aging parents, and all of the other plagues of life, hit marriage the way hurricanes blast our shores. Some marriages survive these storms, and others don't. Concern and tension about money take each partner away from each other. Obligations to demanding parents or still-depended-upon parents create further strain. Couples today must also deal with all of the cultural changes brought on in recent years by the women's movement and the sexual revolution. The altering of roles and the shifting of responsibilities have been extremely trying for many marriages.

The struggle to survive in marriage requires adaptability, flexibility, genuine love and kindness, and empathy strong enough to feel what the other is feeling. Many marriages fall apart because both partners cannot imagine what their mates want or cannot communicate what he/she needs or feels. Anger builds until it erupts into a volcanic burst that buries the marriage in ash.

It is not hard to see, therefore, how essential communication is for a good marriage. A man and a woman must be able to tell each other how they feel and why they feel the way they do; otherwise, they will impose on each other roles and actions that lead to further unhappiness. In some cases, the communication patterns of childhood—of not talking, talking too much, not listening, distrust and anger, withdrawal—spill into the marriage and prevent a healthy exchange of thoughts and feelings. The answer is to set up new patterns of communication and intimacy.

Sometimes people pretend that a new partner will solve the old problems. Most often extramarital relations destroy a marriage because this allows an artificial split between the good and the bad—the good is projected on the new partner, and the bad is dumped on the head of the old partner. Dishonesty, hiding, and cheating create walls between men and women. Infidelity is just a symptom of trouble. It is a symbolic complaint, a weapon of revenge, as well as an unraveler of closeness. Infidelity is often that proverbial last straw that sinks the camel to the ground.

Alright, marriage has always been difficult. Why then are we seeing so many divorces at this time? Yes, our

GO ON TO THE NEXT PAGE.

modern social fabric is thin, and yes, the permissiveness of society has created unrealistic expectations and thrown the family into chaos. But divorce is so common because people today are unwilling to exercise the self-discipline that marriage requires. They expect easy joy, like the entertainment on television and the thrill of a good party.

Marriage takes some kind of sacrifice, not dreadful self-sacrifice of the soul, but some level of compromise. Some of one's fantasies and some of one's legitimate distress have to be given up for the value of the marriage itself. Marriage requires sexual, financial, and emotional discipline. Married men and women cannot follow every impulse and cannot allow themselves to stop growing or changing.

60. The author claims that many marriages fail because:

   I. problems arise about money.
  II. one partner is sexually unfaithful.
 III. partners fail to talk to one another.

  A. I and II only
  B. II and III only
  C. I and III only
  D. I, II, and III

61. Based on the content of this passage, the author would probably suggest that a couple interested in getting married, and staying married, wait until:

  A. issues of possible infertility are rectified.
  B. the elderly, ill parents of the couples have died.
  C. both choices A and B.
  D. neither choice A or B.

62. Based on the information provided in the passage, the author condemns extramarital relations because:

   I. it "steals" sex from the faithful partner.
  II. it allows one partner to wrongly associate all the good things of life with the new partner.
 III. it allows dishonesty to damage open communication.

  A. II and III only
  B. I, II, and III
  C. I and II only
  D. I and III only

63. The author explicitly believes which quality is necessary in marriage?

  A. Unquestioning, unlimited self-sacrifice
  B. Effective communication
  C. An ability to earn a high income
  D. Physical attractiveness

64. The author sees the most apparent cause of an increase in divorce to be:

  A. harder life situations for modern couples.
  B. a falling economy.
  C. the lack of tolerance for difficulty.
  D. the sexual revolution.

65. Based on the passage, the proportion of marriages ending in divorce is:

  A. higher in the West than in the South.
  B. 42%.
  C. lower in the East than in the West.
  D. close to 50%.

STOP. IF YOU FINISH BEFORE TIME IS CALLED, CHECK YOUR WORK. YOU MAY GO BACK TO ANY QUESTION IN THIS TEST BOOKLET.

Physical Sciences

Time: 100 minutes
Questions: 66–142

PHYSICAL SCIENCES

Directions: Most questions in the Physical Sciences test are organized into groups, each preceded by a descriptive passage. After studying the passage, select the one best answer to each question. Some questions are not based on a descriptive passage and are also independent of each other. You should also select the one best answer to these independent questions. A periodic table is provided for your use. You may consult it whenever you wish.

PERIODIC TABLE OF THE ELEMENTS

IA																	VIIIA
1 H 1.0	IIA											IIIA	IVA	VA	VIA	VIIA	2 He 4.0
3 Li 6.9	4 Be 9.0											5 B 10.8	6 C 12.0	7 N 14.0	8 O 16.0	9 F 19.0	10 Ne 20.2
11 Na 23.0	12 Mg 24.3											13 Al 27.0	14 Si 28.1	15 P 31.0	16 S 32.1	17 Cl 35.5	18 Ar 39.9
19 K 39.1	20 Ca 40.1	21 Sc 45.0	22 Ti 47.9	23 V 50.9	24 Cr 52.0	25 Mn 54.9	26 Fe 55.8	27 Co 58.9	28 Ni 58.7	29 Cu 63.5	30 Zn 65.4	31 Ga 69.7	32 Ge 72.6	33 As 74.9	34 Se 79.0	35 Br 79.9	36 Kr 83.8
37 Rb 85.5	38 Sr 87.6	39 Y 88.9	40 Zr 91.2	41 Nb 92.9	42 Mo 95.9	43 Tc 98.0	44 Ru 101	45 Rh 102	46 Pd 106	47 Ag 108	48 Cd 112	49 In 115	50 Sn 119	51 Sb 122	52 Te 128	53 I 127	54 Xe 131
55 Cs 133	56 Ba 137	57 La 139	72 Hf 179	73 Ta 181	74 W 184	75 Re 186	76 Os 190	77 Ir 192	78 Pt 195	79 Au 197	80 Hg 201	81 Tl 204	82 Pb 207	83 Bi 208	84 Po 209	85 At 210	86 Rn 222
87 Fr 223	88 Ra 226	89 Ac 227															

58 Ce 140	59 Pr 141	60 Nd 144	61 Pm 145	62 Sm 150	63 Eu 152	64 Gd 157	65 Tb 159	66 Dy 163	67 Ho 165	68 Er 167	69 Tm 169	70 Yb 173	71 Lu 175
90 Th 232	91 Pa 231	92 U 238	93 Np 237	94 Pu 244	95 Am 243	96 Cm 247	97 Bk 247	98 Cf 251	99 Es 252	100 Fm 257	101 Md 258	102 No 259	103 Lr 260

214

GO ON TO THE NEXT PAGE.

Passage I (Questions 66–70)

Fiberoptic scopes, or endoscopes, are commonly used in medicine to visualize internal structures. They are made of a flexible material which can carry light from a light source at the base of the instrument to internal structures such as the digestive tract.

These scopes are used to visualize the esophagus, stomach, and duodenum by passing the scope via the oral cavity. Because the endoscopes are made of flexible material, they can be guided around turns and twists in body cavities. The nasal passages and throat can be examined using a fiberoptic scope passed through the nose. The colon, cecum, and small bowel/large bowel junction can be visualized by a fiberoptic scope passed via the rectum.

An experiment was conducted by an investigator to test a new experimental fiberoptic scope. It is not known whether or not the scope will function as an endoscope, and an experiment is conducted to test this hypothesis. The experimental scope is shown in Figure 1, and is made of material X (n = 2.00). Light is emitted from the source with $\theta_2 = 65°$.

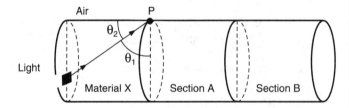

Figure 1. The experimental fiberoptic scope.

66. Does this experimental scope act as an endoscope?

    A. Yes
    B. No
    C. At times, depending on the intensity of the light source
    D. There is not enough information to determine

67. Where is the light in the region of section B of the experimental fiberoptic scope?

    A. In material X
    B. In the material X–air interface
    C. In the air
    D. In a different medium

68. At point P in the diagram above, light would best be described as:

    A. dispersed.
    B. refracted.
    C. totally internally reflected.
    D. directed down the air–material X interface.

69. What would be the sine of the critical angle for light going from glass (n = 1.5) into air?

    A. 0.33
    B. 0.50
    C. 0.67
    D. 1.00

70. A physician is trying to investigate an abnormal growth in a patient's small intestine. It is estimated that the growth is more than 200 cm from the oral cavity. Standard fiberoptic scopes are usually no more than 110 cm in length. Radiographic studies or visualization with fiberoptic scopes passed into the gastrointestinal (GI) tract via the oral cavity are both accepted lines of practice to evaluate such growths. The physician makes the following statement: "I think that x-ray techniques may be better than endoscope techniques to investigate this growth because I would have to use such a long scope to reach the growth that the image intensity would be decreased." Is the physician correct?

    A. Yes
    B. No
    C. Sometimes, depending on the nature of the power source
    D. There is not enough information to determine

215

GO ON TO THE NEXT PAGE.

Passage II (Questions 71–75)

The pH of rainwater is affected by the components of air that can dissolve into the water in the atmosphere and dissociate to form hydronium ions. The pH of rainwater unaffected by pollution is 5.6. However, industrial pollution decreases that value to 4.6 because of the presence of sulfur dioxide. Carbon dioxide occurs naturally in the atmosphere, and affects the pH of water according to the following three equations:

Equation 1: $CO_2 + H_2O \rightleftarrows H_2CO_3(aq)$
Equation 2: $H_2CO_3(aq) \rightleftarrows H^+(aq) + HCO_3^-(aq)$
Equation 3: $HCO_3^-(aq) \rightleftarrows H^+(aq) + CO_3^{2-}(aq)$

Sulfur dioxide is a pollutant that is found in the atmosphere near populated areas. The dissolution and dissociation of sulfur dioxide into water vapor in the atmosphere are governed by the following three equations:

Equation 1: $SO_2 + H_2O \rightleftarrows H_2SO_3(aq)$
Equation 2: $H_2SO_3(aq) \rightleftarrows H^+(aq) + HSO_3^-(aq)$
Equation 3: $HSO_3^-(aq) \rightleftarrows H^+(aq) + SO_3^{2-}(aq)$

These equilibria are governed by some of the equilibrium constants shown in Table 1. K_H is the Henry's law constant for the dissolution reaction. K' and K'' are the dissociation constants for the first and second ionization, respectively. Note that for ammonia this constant is for the reaction of ammonia with water to form ammonium hydroxide.

Table 1. Equilibrium Constants

Compound	$K_{H(mol/L \cdot atm)}$	$K'_{(mol/L)}$	$K''_{(mol/L)}$
CO_2	0.045	3.8×10^{-7}	3.7×10^{-11}
SO_2	5.4	2.7×10^{-2}	10^{-7}
NH_3	90	1.6×10^{-5}	—

71. Which of the following values corresponds to the equilibrium constant for reaction 1?

   A. 3.7×10^{-11} mol/L·atm
   B. 3.8×10^{-7} mol/L
   C. 0.045 mol/L·atm
   D. 3.7×10^{-11} mol²/L²·atm

72. If an air sample were found to contain equal amounts of carbon and sulfur dioxide, what is true about the total aqueous concentration of species containing carbon?

   A. It will be less than the concentration of sulfur-containing species.
   B. It will be greater than the concentration of sulfur-containing species.
   C. It will be equal to the concentration of sulfur-containing species.
   D. There is not enough information to decide.

73. Although the concentration of sulfur dioxide in air is usually much less than the concentration of carbon dioxide, it has a great effect on the pH of rainwater. Which of the following explains this observation?

   A. Sulfur dioxide has a much greater K_H.
   B. Sulfur dioxide has a much greater K'.
   C. Sulfur dioxide has a much greater K''.
   D. Sulfur dioxide has much greater K_H and K' values.

74. Which of the following relationships correctly describes the dissolution reaction of carbon dioxide?

   A. $[HCO_3^-][H^+]/[H_2CO_3]$
   B. $[H_2CO_3]/[CO_2]$
   C. $[CO_3^{2-}][H^+]/[HCO_3^-]$
   D. $[HCO_3^-]/[CO_3^{2-}][H^+]$

75. Water vapor in a gas sample containing equal amounts of ammonia and carbon dioxide would be:

   A. acidic.
   B. basic.
   C. neutral.
   D. not enough information to determine

GO ON TO THE NEXT PAGE.

Passage III (Questions 76–81)

The cyclotron was invented in 1930 by Dr E. O. Lawrence. It was the first machine developed to accelerate charged particles to high velocities by causing them to pass repeatedly through the same accelerating region. A cyclotron, shown in Figure 1, is made of two hollow, metal, semicircular structures called dees. The dees exist in a uniform magnetic field which is perpendicular to their plane. Protons or other positive ions are injected into a space between the two dees. These positively charged particles move in circular orbits encompassing both dees. An electric generator reverses the potential difference between the dees at the orbital frequency of the ions so they are accelerated each time they pass through the gap between the dees. This increases their velocity and consequently their orbital radius, but does not alter their period. The functioning of the cyclotron depends on the fact that the period is independent of the velocity.

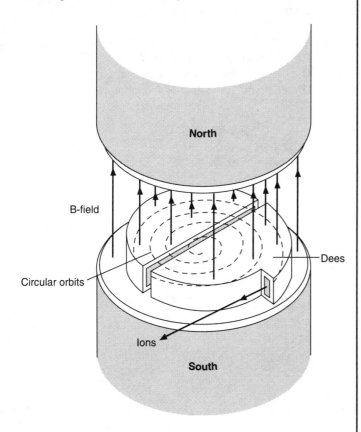

Figure 1. A cyclotron.

The development of the cyclotron was made possible by several observations. First, the period or time required for a charged particle to complete one circular orbit in a uniform magnetic field (B) is independent of the speed of the particle (v). Second, the period (T) for a particle of charge (q) and mass (m) is $vT = 2\pi R$, where R is the radius of the orbit. Finally, the radius of the orbit (R) = mv/qB.

76. Based on the data given in the passage, increasing the velocity of a particle increases which of the following?

    A. The radius of the orbit
    B. The period
    C. The charge of the particle
    D. The mass of the particle

77. A sample of charged particles are subjected to the action of a cyclotron. If the magnitude of the magnetic field increases by a factor of two, what is the most likely effect on the period, assuming stable charge and mass?

    A. The period increases by a factor of two.
    B. The period decreases by a factor of two.
    C. The period increases by a factor of four.
    D. The period decreases by a factor of four.

78. A particle of charge (q) and mass (m) is placed between the dees of a functioning cyclotron. If the period of particle motion is found to progressively increase over time, the orbital frequency would most likely:

    A. remain unchanged.
    B. progressively increase.
    C. progressively decrease.
    D. assume a value of zero.

79. Which of the following would NOT increase the energy of moving charged particles in the cyclotron?

    A. Increasing the mass of the particles
    B. Increasing the velocity of the particles
    C. Increasing the period of the particles
    D. None of the above

80. As the angle between the radius of particle orbit and the magnetic field decreases, the magnetic force F_{mag}:

    A. increases.
    B. decreases.
    C. stays the same.
    D. Not enough information to determine

81. Cyclotrons can be used to bombard nonradioactive materials, causing nuclear reactions and the release of alpha, beta, and gamma particles. These particles may be subjected to a magnetic field. Which particle would be least likely deflected in a magnetic field?

    A. Alpha particles
    B. Beta particles
    C. Gamma particles
    D. All three particles would be equally deflected

Passage IV (Questions 82–87)

People who drive while under the influence of alcohol are responsible for many injuries and deaths each year. The ability to rapidly test a suspected intoxicated driver for blood alcohol content is essential for legal documentation. One of the most commonly used rapid testing devices is known as a breath analyzer. The breath analyzer is an instrument that uses a simple redox system to allow very fast determination of a driver's blood alcohol content. The chemical reaction involved is shown as reaction 1.

Reaction 1:

$$3CH_3CH_2OH + 2K_2Cr_2O_7 + 8H_2SO_4$$
$$\rightarrow 3CH_3COOH + 2Cr_2(SO_4)_3 + 2K_2SO_4 + 11H_2O$$

The ethanol (CH_3CH_2OH) in a person's breath is directed into an acidic solution of potassium dichromate ($K_2Cr_2O_7$). The orange yellow dichromate ion reacts to form the green chromic ion in the chromic sulfate [$Cr_2(SO_4)_3$] produced in the reaction. The instrument then measures the degree of this color change and converts that color change to blood alcohol level.

This breath analyzer is a portable system that very quickly allows police officers to determine if a driver is legally intoxicated. Tests performed with breath analyzers are usually verified with a more reliable blood test. In many states, a person with blood alcohol level of 0.1% by mass or greater is considered intoxicated.

82. Which of the following best describes reaction 1?

  A. An oxidation/reduction reaction
  B. A hydrolysis reaction
  C. A single replacement reaction
  D. A disproportionation reaction

83. In reaction 1, potassium acts as:

  A. an oxidizing agent.
  B. a reducing agent.
  C. a spectator ion.
  D. a preservative.

84. In reaction 1, chromium acts as:

  A. an oxidizing agent.
  B. a reducing agent.
  C. a spectator ion.
  D. a preservative.

85. What is the most important consideration for using potassium dichromate in this reaction rather than another compound with similar reactivity?

  A. It is very specific for reacting with ethanol.
  B. It is very accurate.
  C. It is colored differently from the product of the reaction.
  D. It is yellow.

86. What is the advantage of using a breath analyzer over a blood test?

  A. It is faster.
  B. It is more portable.
  C. It is more accurate.
  D. All of the above.

87. What comparison can be made between the reactivity of ethanol and dichromate?

  A. Dichromate is more reactive.
  B. Dichromate is less reactive.
  C. Ethanol has a lower reduction potential.
  D. Ethanol has a higher reduction potential.

GO ON TO THE NEXT PAGE.

88. A projectile is fired from ground level. It is fired at a velocity of 10 m/sec at an angle of 60 degrees to the horizontal. The projectile lands at ground level at a distance of 50 m from its starting point. How long does the projectile take to reach it highest point in the air?

   A.   5 seconds
   B.   10 seconds
   C.   15 seconds
   D.   20 seconds

89. What volume of 0.15 mol/L H_2SO_4 is needed to neutralize 30 mL of 0.2 mol/L NaOH?

   A.   20 mL
   B.   40 mL
   C.   60 mL
   D.   80 mL

90. A solid block of unknown volume X is suspended from a string attached to an immobile surface. In scenario 1, the block hangs in air. In scenario 2, the block is submerged in fluid Y. The tension in the string measured in scenario 1 is 10 N. When the block is submerged in fluid Y ($\rho = 100$ kgm^{-3}), the string tension is 8 N. What is the density of the block?

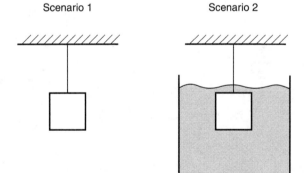

   A.   50 kgm^{-3}
   B.   100 kgm^{-3}
   C.   500 kgm^{-3}
   D.   1000 kgm^{-3}

91. A positive charge is placed in the vicinity of an electric field. The potential energy of the positive charge increases the most when it is moved in what relation to the field?

   A.   Opposite the field
   B.   In the same direction as the field
   C.   Perpendicular to the field
   D.   Removed from the effects of the field

Passage V (Questions 92–97)

Automobile engines operate at high temperatures, which allow nitrogen and oxygen gas to react to form nitric oxide according to reaction 1.

Reaction 1: $N_2(g) + O_2(g) \rightleftarrows 2 NO(g)$

The nitric oxide released into the atmosphere reacts rapidly to form nitrous oxide, an unpleasant-smelling, poisonous brown gas. This process is shown in reaction 2.

Reaction 2: $2 NO(g) + O_2(g) \rightarrow 2 NO_2(g)$

To reduce the emissions of nitric oxide, automobiles are now manufactured with catalytic converters. Catalytic converters actually serve two purposes. They first complete the combustion of carbon monoxide and other incompletely combusted organic compounds. This occurs at a high temperature over a metal catalyst. The second function of catalytic converters is to convert nitric oxide back to nitrogen and oxygen through the use of a different metal catalyst, which must be done at a lower temperature.

92. Based on information given in the passage, reaction 1 is:

    A. exothermic.
    B. endothermic.
    C. neither exothermic nor endothermic.
    D. cannot be determined.

93. Under atmospheric conditions, nitric oxide undergoes reaction 2 rather than the reverse of reaction 1 because:

    A. reaction 2 is more favorable.
    B. reaction 2 is much faster.
    C. reaction 2 is much slower.
    D. reaction 1 is irreversible.

94. The need for a catalyst to promote the reverse of reaction 1 indicates that:

    A. it is exothermic.
    B. it is endothermic.
    C. it has a high activation energy.
    D. it has a low activation energy.

95. The change in entropy for reaction 2 would be:

    A. positive.
    B. negative.
    C. zero.
    D. cannot be determined.

96. Which of the following best describes the purpose of a catalytic converter?

    A. To adsorb pollutants in the exhaust
    B. To catalyze reactions between pollutants in the exhaust
    C. To complete combustion and reduce nitric oxide
    D. To complete combustion and oxidize nitric oxide

97. Reaction 2 involves which of the following?

    A. Oxidation of the nitrogen and reduction of the oxygen gas
    B. Oxidation of the nitrogen and oxidation of the oxygen gas
    C. Reduction of the nitrogen and oxidation of the oxygen gas
    D. Reduction of the nitrogen and reduction of the oxygen gas

GO ON TO THE NEXT PAGE.

Passage VI (Questions 98–103)

Human speech is made possible by the application of basic physics principles to complex anatomic structures in the aerodigestive tract. One of the most involved of the anatomic regions of the aerodigestive tract is the larynx. The larynx contains the vocal cords, and a series of small muscles which act to tighten and move the cords. The vocal cords act to create vibrations in the air. In addition to the vocal cords, the nasal and oral cavities act as resonant structures, and are important in the production of the quality of human speech.

The vibrations of the vocal cords can be understood by applying Bernoulli's equation. As air rapidly moves through the opening between the cords, its velocity is large, and this has an effect on pressure. The pressure effects cause the cords to start to close. During exhalation, pressure builds up below the vocal cords, forcing the cords to open.

The resonant function of the oral and nasal cavities can be understood by applying a simple model. A pipe open at one end and closed at another end simulates the nose and mouth (open pipe end) and closed vocal cords (closed pipe end). For purposes of this model, the distance between the nose/mouth and vocal cords can be measured. For the average adult, the distance between these structures is approximately 0.17 m. Assume that the speed of sound is 344 m/sec.

98. The rapid increase in air velocity moving between the vocal cords causes what effect on vocal cord pressure?

    A. Increased pressure
    B. Decreased pressure
    C. No effect on pressure
    D. An unpredictable effect on pressure

99. Which of the following is the fundamental frequency of the pipe model?

    A. 200 Hz
    B. 300 Hz
    C. 500 Hz
    D. 900 Hz

100. The first overtone of the pipe model would be closest to:

    A. 400 Hz.
    B. 600 Hz.
    C. 900 Hz.
    D. 1,500 Hz.

101. An increase in tension on the vocal cords would have what effect on the period of sound produced by the cords?

    A. The period would increase.
    B. The period would decrease.
    C. The period would remain the same.
    D. There is not enough information to determine.

102. Two subjects are studied. One person has a voice with a fundamental frequency of 250 Hz. The other person has a voice with a fundamental frequency of 300 Hz. If both subjects are stationary, and speak simultaneously, what beat frequency is heard?

    A. 50 Hz
    B. 250 Hz
    C. 350 Hz
    D. 550 Hz

103. If the average human voice has a frequency of 300 Hz, what is the average wavelength of a human voice in air?

    A. 0.6 m
    B. 0.8 m
    C. 1.1 m
    D. 2.0 m

The use of orbiting satellites has revolutionized the world we live in. For example, we can now watch live television broadcasts from the other side of the world. We are able to communicate and transmit messages thousands of miles in just an instant—this is all without the use of wires or cables.

The basic principle here is the use of electromagnetic (EM) waves to transmit information. Television, for example, is transmitted as EM waves with a frequency in the range of 10^8 Hz. These waves are transverse waves composed of electric and magnetic fields oscillating in phase. EM waves cannot travel in curved paths around the objects—they travel only in straight lines. Thus, the strategy in EM wave transmission is to beam waves from one site to another in a straight line. This is where satellites come into play. The function of many satellites is to merely reflect an incoming wave to another site (either on the ground or in the sky), just like a mirror can be used to reflect a light beam from place to place. The following questions pertain to satellites, circular motion, and EM waves. Variables are used when referring to certain distances or lengths.

104. What is the approximate wavelength of television waves?

    A. 0.3 m
    B. 3.0 m
    C. 30.0 m
    D. 300.0 m

105. Consider the Earth a perfect sphere of radius R km. What would be the total distance a television EM wave would have to travel if it were to originate at the North Pole, travel to a satellite orbiting above the equator which is located a distance A km from the earth's center, and then be reflected to a television set located at the South Pole?

    A. $(A + R)^{1/2}$ km
    B. $2(A^2 + R^2)$ km
    C. $A^2 + R^2$ km
    D. $2 (A^2 + R^2)^{1/2}$ km

106. What are the units of G, the universal gravitation constant (Newton's constant)?

    A. N/m kg^2
    B. kg^2/Nm^2
    C. Nm^2/kg^2
    D. None of the above

107. What is gravity at a distance of H km above the surface of the earth given that the gravity (g) at the earth's surface is 10 m/sec^2 and that the radius is R km?

    A. $10 (R + H)/R^2$ m/sec^2
    B. $10 R^2/(R + H)^2$ m/sec^2
    C. $(R + H)^2/10R^2$ m/sec^2
    D. $(R + H)/10 R$ m/sec^2

108. The universal constant (Newton's constant), G, has a magnitude of X on a planet of mass A. What would be the magnitude of the constant on a planet of mass 3A?

    A. ⅓ X
    B. X
    C. 3 X
    D. None of the above

GO ON TO THE NEXT PAGE.

Passage VIII (Questions 109–113)

Many experiments can be performed to determine the molecular weight of a gas. One very simple experiment can be performed as follows: An Erlenmeyer flask is filled with water, which is then poured into a graduated cylinder. The volume of water is recorded; then the Erlenmeyer flask is cleaned, dried, and weighed. 10 mL of a chosen liquid is then poured into the flask. The flask is fitted with a top having a small hole and placed on a hot plate until the last of the liquid vaporizes. The flask is then quickly placed in an ice-water bath for 10 minutes. The flask is then re-weighed to determine the amount of liquid remaining in the flask. The data shown in Table 1 were collected using this procedure.

Table 1.   Determining Molecular Weight

Compound	Volume of Water (ml)	Initial Weight (g)	Final Weight (g)
Butane	125	375	525
Ethanol	125	375	525
Water	125	375	460

109. Which of the following assumptions do NOT need to be made to calculate the molecular weight of the gases?

    A.   The liquids vaporize to form ideal gases.
    B.   The room is at standard conditions.
    C.   The vaporized liquid does not exchange quickly with gases in the atmosphere.
    D.   The ice bath is 0°C.

110. What type of error would be expected if the volume of liquid used were exactly the amount of gas needed to fill the space in the flask?

    A.   The calculated value would be too low due to exchange of desired gas with atmospheric gases.
    B.   The calculated value would be too high due to exchange of desired gas with atmospheric gases.
    C.   The calculated value would be too high due to incomplete vaporization of the sample.
    D.   The calculated value would be too low due to incomplete vaporization of the sample.

111. What error in the calculated molecular weight would be observed if the cooling time were not sufficient to condense all of the gas?

    A.   The calculated value would be too high due to the presence of additional gas in the flask.
    B.   The calculated value would be too low due to the presence of additional gas in the flask.
    C.   The calculated value would be too high due to the absence of liquid in the flask.
    D.   The calculated value would be too low due to the absence of liquid in the flask.

112. Which of the following equations would be used to calculate the molecular weight from the data obtained in this experiment?

    A.   Liquid weight / (22.4 × volume)
    B.   Liquid weight × 22.4 / volume
    C.   Liquid weight × volume / 22.4
    D.   Liquid weight × volume × 22.4

113. Which statement explains why the calculated value of the molecular weight for butane using the data in Table 1 is too low?

    A.   The molecules of butane are large enough that the volume they occupy becomes significant.
    B.   The molecules of butane are small enough that the volume they occupy is insignificant.
    C.   The molecules of butane strongly attract each other.
    D.   The molecules of butane strongly repel each other.

114. How much current passes through the 2-ohm resistor?

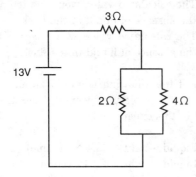

A. 1 A
B. 3 A
C. 2 A
D. 13 A

115. When aluminum metal reacts with ferric oxide (Fe_2O_3), a displacement reaction takes place. Fe(s) and a second product are formed. If 0.1 mol Al is allowed to react with 0.1 mol-Fe_2O_3, how many moles of iron will be produced?

A. 0.05 mol
B. 0.075 mol
C. 0.01 mol
D. 0.15 mol

116. An object rotates in a circular orbit in a counterclockwise direction with ever-increasing speed. Which vector best depicts its net acceleration?

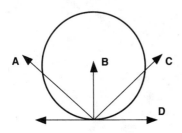

117. An unknown radioactive sample is investigated in a laboratory and determined to have a mass of 192 g. The sample is placed in a containment chamber and inspected 120 days later. It is found to have a mass of 0.75 g. What is the half-life of this sample?

A. 5 days
B. 10 days
C. 15 days
D. 30 days

118. A light source is placed underwater and is used to illuminate the water's surface. Assume that n_{water} = 1.33 and n_{air} = 1.0. Which best illustrates the correct light rays?

A.

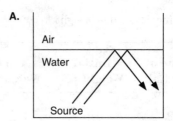

B.

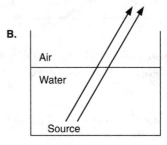

C.

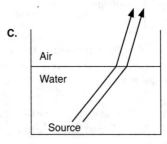

D.

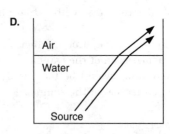

GO ON TO THE NEXT PAGE.

Passage IX (Questions 119–124)

A Plexiglas hollow tank with a side drainage tube is firmly attached to a metal platform with frictionless wheels that rest on the ground surface as shown below. The ground surface is perfectly horizontal and frictionless. A sturdy open–close valve device is located near the end of the drainage tube. The drainage tube extends 50 cm from the bulk of the tank and has a diameter of 5 cm (Figure 1). The dimensions of the tank are given in the diagram below, as well as several alphabetical reference points. A data table summarizing known physical parameters for the three media used in the experiments described below is provided for reference purposes. Three sets of experiments are performed by students enrolled in a first-year level physics laboratory to learn about mechanical properties of fluids and solids. In each experiment, the tank is filled with only one test fluid so that the fluid column is initially 600 cm high. Atmospheric pressure in the laboratory was measured to be 10^5 N/m^2.

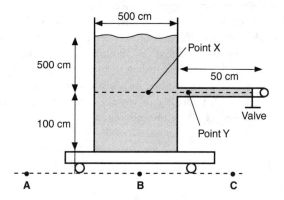

Figure 1

Experiment 1: The students fill the empty tank with pure water. Studies involving hydrostatics (valve in "closed" position) and hydrodynamics (valve in "open" position) are then performed. All water is removed from the tank on completion of the studies.

Table 1.   Physical Parameters

Fluid	Density (kg/m³)	Viscosity (N s/m²)
Water	1,000	1.8×10^{-3}
Ethanol	800	1.2×10^{-3}
Glycerin	1,200	0.6

Experiment 2: The students next fill the empty tank with pure ethanol and repeat all experimental procedures performed in experiment 1. The tank is then drained.

Experiment 3: Finally, the students fill the empty tank with glycerin and repeat all experimental procedures.

119. What is the pressure at point Y when the tank is filled with ethanol?

    A. 1.1×10^5 N/m^2
    B. 1.2×10^5 N/m^2
    C. 1.3×10^5 N/m^2
    D. 1.4×10^5 N/m^2

120. Suppose that the tank was sealed from the atmospheric pressure. What would be the ratio of the pressures at point X when the tank is filled with glycerin versus ethanol?

    A.   2:3
    B.   3:2
    C.   5:6
    D.   6:5

121. Which of the following graphs best depicts the relationship between the velocity of the water as it exits the drainage tube and time?

122. The tank is filled with water, then the drainage tube valve is opened. What is the velocity of the tank–platform system 2 seconds after the valve is opened if the mass of the water exiting the tank during the first 2 seconds is considered a unit mass that is 1/100 of the total mass of the remaining tank–platform system?

- **A.** 0.05 m/sec, toward point A
- **B.** 0.05 m/sec, toward point C
- **C.** 0.10 m/sec, toward point A
- **D.** 0.10 m/sec, toward point C

123. Which of the following vectors correctly depicts the direction of the acceleration of a unit of water just subsequent to exiting the drainage tube?

A.

B.

C.

D.

124. About how far will the initial water droplets travel in the horizontal direction before hitting the ground?

- **A.** 5 m
- **B.** 10 m
- **C.** 15 m
- **D.** 20 m

Passage X (Questions 125–130)

Teeth are covered and protected by a hard enamel layer composed of hydroxyapatite [$Ca_5(PO_4)_3OH$]. The process of building this enamel layer is called mineralization and the reaction involved is shown as reaction 1.

Reaction 1:

$$5Ca^{2+}(aq) + 3PO_4^{3-}(aq) + OH^-(aq) \rightarrow Ca_5(PO_4)_3OH$$

The hydroxyapatite formed by the mineralization process is not water soluble, and provides a strong, decay-resistant coating. A drop in pH will, however, promote the demineralization, as shown in reaction 2.

Reaction 2:

$$Ca_5(PO_4)_3OH \rightarrow 5Ca^{2+}(aq) + 3PO_4^{3-}(aq) + OH^-(aq)$$

Sugar foods generally cause a decrease in pH as they are broken down by bacteria. Certain types of foods also have a low pH without processing by bacteria. All these foods contribute to tooth decay by demineralizing the tooth enamel. Fluoride toothpastes help to prevent tooth decay in two ways: (1) they inhibit the ability of bacteria to break down sugars; (2) fluoride can replace the hydroxide ion in the formation of an enamel-like solid, fluorapatite, as shown in reaction 3.

Reaction 3:

$$5Ca^{2+}(aq) + 3PO_4^{3-}(aq) + F^-(aq) \rightarrow Ca_5(PO_4)_3F$$

125. Which of the following is the best explanation for why a decrease in pH results in demineralization?

- **A.** The increase in hydronium concentration results in the decomposition of the phosphate.
- **B.** The concentration of hydroxide decreases, pulling the equilibrium position of reaction 1 to the left.
- **C.** The decrease in hydronium concentration results in the decomposition of the phosphate.
- **D.** The concentration of hydroxide increases, pulling the equilibrium position of reaction 1 to the right.

126. Which of the following is NOT a reason for the use of fluoride in prevention of tooth decay?

- **A.** Fluoride prevents a decrease in pH.
- **B.** Fluoride helps to prevent demineralization.
- **C.** Fluoride remineralizes with fluorapatite.
- **D.** Fluoride kills bacteria instantly.

GO ON TO THE NEXT PAGE.

127. Which is NOT true about hydroxyapatite?

    A. It is ionic.
    B. It is not soluble in acid.
    C. It is not water soluble.
    D. It is not soluble in base.

128. How can the acid solubility of fluorapatite be compared with that of hydroxyapatite?

    A. It would be more water soluble because fluoride is a stronger base than hydroxide.
    B. It would be less water soluble because fluoride is a stronger base than hydroxide.
    C. It would be more water soluble because fluoride is a weaker base than hydroxide.
    D. It would be less water soluble because fluoride is a weaker base than hydroxide.

129. Which of the following is the best Lewis dot structure for the polyatomic ion produced in the demineralization process?

    A.

$$:\overset{..}{\underset{..}{O}}:$$
$$:\overset{..}{\underset{..}{O}} - \underset{\overset{|}{}}{P} - \overset{..}{\underset{..}{O}}:$$
$$:\overset{..}{\underset{..}{O}}:$$

    B.

$$:\overset{..}{\underset{..}{O}}:$$
$$:\overset{..}{\underset{..}{O}} - P = \overset{..}{O}$$
$$:\overset{..}{\underset{..}{O}}:$$

    C.

$$:\overset{..}{\underset{..}{O}}:$$
$$\overset{..}{O} - P - \overset{..}{O}$$
$$:\overset{..}{\underset{..}{O}}:$$

    D.

$$\overset{..}{O}$$
$$:\overset{..}{\underset{..}{O}} - P = \overset{..}{O}:$$
$$:\overset{..}{\underset{..}{O}}:$$

130. Where would the charges be localized in the phosphate ion?

    A. There would be a $(+1)$ on the phosphorus and (-1) on each oxygen.
    B. There would be (-1) on each oxygen.
    C. There would be (-1) on three of the four oxygens.
    D. There would be a (-3) on the phosphorus.

Passage XI (Questions 131–136)

Newton's laws of motion can be applied to many dynamic systems. One of the most common dynamic systems is the pulley system, in which bodies are attached to one another and to immobile surfaces by strings or ropes. To evaluate dynamic bodies involving pulleys and strings, each body is treated as if it were a particle of definite mass, so that the forces acting on it are assumed to act at a point. Strings or pulleys are generally considered massless.

Pulleys are machines that provide a mechanical advantage in many situations. They are considered massless and frictionless, and they serve to change the direction of tension in the string which runs over the pulley. Pulleys are useful in lifting objects and applying forces in a mechanically advantageous way. Figure 1 shows two basic pulley systems being investigated by physics students. Assume that the weights, W, have equal magnitudes and that a force, F, is applied to keep the systems at rest. In addition, assume that the pulleys and ropes are masses and friction is negligible.

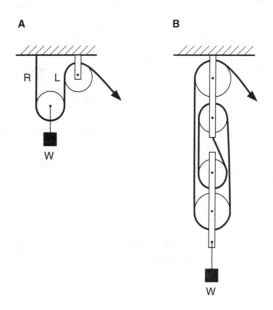

Figure 1. Two basic pulley systems.

Mechanical advantage is defined as the number of parallel ropes supporting a pulley to which a load is attached. It is a useful term in describing and classifying pulley/load systems.

131. In diagram A, how does the equilibrium tension in the left side of the rope compare with that on the right?

    A. Left > right
    B. Right > left
    C. Right = left
    D. Not enough information to determine

132. In example B, the combinations of pulleys shown have what effect, if any?

   A. They reduce the force needed to lift the weight.
   B. They decrease the torque on the system.
   C. They change the direction of force but do not change its magnitude.
   D. The pulleys have no net effect on the system.

133. What applied force is needed to lift the weight at constant speed in example A?

   A. 4 W
   B. 2 W
   C. W
   D. W/2

134. What applied force is needed to lift the weight at constant speed in example B?

   A. 4 W
   B. 2 W
   C. W
   D. W/4

135. Which best describes the lower pulley in example A?

   A. Its position depends wholly on downward forces.
   B. It adjusts its position based on variable tension levels along the string.
   C. It adjusts its position along the string to allow an even distribution of tension.
   D. Its positional changes destabilize tension levels in the string.

136. The mechanical advantage of example B is closest to which of the following?

   A. 1
   B. 2
   C. 3
   D. 4

Questions 137 through 142 are NOT based on a descriptive passage.

137. Which of the following must be known to calculate the power output of an engine?

   A. Amount of work performed and time required to perform work
   B. Mass and amount of work performed
   C. Acceleration and time required to perform work
   D. Force produced and time required to produce force

138. An object is placed 10 m in front of a convex mirror. The image produced is found to be approximately 7 m on the other side of the mirror. Which of the following best describes the image?

   A. Upright and diminished
   B. Inverted and enlarged
   C. Upright and enlarged
   D. Inverted and diminished

139. The diagram below represents the paths of three different particles that are traveling in the plane of the paper. A uniform magnetic field passes perpendicularly through the plane and is directed into the plane of the paper. Which is most likely true?

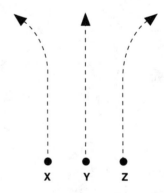

   A. Particles X and Z are both positively charged.
   B. Particles X and Z are both negatively charged.
   C. Particle X is positively charged, whereas particle Z is negatively charged.
   D. Particle X is negatively charged, whereas particle Z is positively charged.

GO ON TO THE NEXT PAGE.

140. A galvanic cell is constructed with the following two elements and their ions. What is the E° for the net reaction of the oxidation of magnesium metal and the reduction of lead metal?

$$Mg(s) \rightarrow Mg^{+2} + 2e^- \qquad E° = 2.37 \text{ V}$$
$$Pg(s) \rightarrow Pb^{+2} + 2e^- \qquad E° = 0.126 \text{ V}$$

- **A.** −2.496 V
- **B.** +2.496 V
- **C.** −2.244 V
- **D.** +2.244 V

141. A bullet is fired into a block of wood hanging from a string as shown in the following diagram. The bullet has mass x, and the block has mass y. The bullet initially has a speed v before impact. After bullet impact, the bullet–block system swings h meters vertically. What is the KE of the bullet–block system at impact?

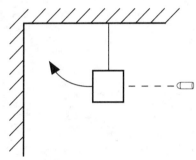

- **A.** ½(x + y)v
- **B.** (x + y)gh
- **C.** ½(x + y)h
- **D.** ½ vg(x + y)

142. The unit of an elastic modulus can be:

- **A.** N/m².
- **B.** kgm/sec³.
- **C.** Ns/m².
- **D.** Nkg/msec².

STOP. IF YOU FINISH BEFORE TIME IS CALLED, CHECK YOUR WORK. YOU MAY GO BACK TO ANY QUESTION IN THIS TEST BOOKLET.

Writing Sample

Time: 60 minutes total;
30 minutes per essay, each separately timed.

WRITING SAMPLE

Directions: You will be given 30 minutes to complete Essay Topic 1. Once time is called, you MUST stop working on this essay. Please draw a line below the last sentence in your essay to mark your stopping point. You will then have 30 minutes to complete Essay Topic 2. You may NOT work on Essay Topic 1 during the second 30-minute period allotted for Essay Topic 2. Use black ink and do NOT skip lines between sentences. Illegible essays will not be scored.

ESSAY TOPIC 1

Consider this statement:

One must be inflexible in matters of ethical principle.

Write a unified essay in which you perform the following tasks. Explain what you think the preceding statement means. Describe a specific situation in which it might be advantageous to be flexible in matters of ethical principle. Discuss what you think determines when inflexibility or flexibility is better in dealing with matters of ethical principle.

ESSAY TOPIC 2

Consider this statement:

In education, the new way is rarely the best way.

Write a unified essay in which you perform the following tasks. Explain what you think the preceding statement means. Describe a specific situation in which a new way may be the best way to educate. Discuss what you think determines whether a new way or an older way is the best way to educate.

Biological Sciences

Time: 100 minutes
Questions: 143–219

BIOLOGICAL SCIENCES

Directions: Most questions in the Biological Sciences test are organized into groups, each preceded by a descriptive passage. After studying the passage, select the one best answer to each question. Some questions are not based on a descriptive passage and are also independent of each other. You should also select the one best answer to these independent questions. A periodic table is provided for your use. You may consult it whenever you wish.

PERIODIC TABLE OF THE ELEMENTS

IA																	VIIIA
1 **H** 1.0	IIA											IIIA	IVA	VA	VIA	VIIA	2 **He** 4.0
3 **Li** 6.9	4 **Be** 9.0											5 **B** 10.8	6 **C** 12.0	7 **N** 14.0	8 **O** 16.0	9 **F** 19.0	10 **Ne** 20.2
11 **Na** 23.0	12 **Mg** 24.3											13 **Al** 27.0	14 **Si** 28.1	15 **P** 31.0	16 **S** 32.1	17 **Cl** 35.5	18 **Ar** 39.9
19 **K** 39.1	20 **Ca** 40.1	21 **Sc** 45.0	22 **Ti** 47.9	23 **V** 50.9	24 **Cr** 52.0	25 **Mn** 54.9	26 **Fe** 55.8	27 **Co** 58.9	28 **Ni** 58.7	29 **Cu** 63.5	30 **Zn** 65.4	31 **Ga** 69.7	32 **Ge** 72.6	33 **As** 74.9	34 **Se** 79.0	35 **Br** 79.9	36 **Kr** 83.8
37 **Rb** 85.5	38 **Sr** 87.6	39 **Y** 88.9	40 **Zr** 91.2	41 **Nb** 92.9	42 **Mo** 95.9	43 **Tc** 98.0	44 **Ru** 101	45 **Rh** 102	46 **Pd** 106	47 **Ag** 108	48 **Cd** 112	49 **In** 115	50 **Sn** 119	51 **Sb** 122	52 **Te** 128	53 **I** 127	54 **Xe** 131
55 **Cs** 133	56 **Ba** 137	57 **La** 139	72 **Hf** 179	73 **Ta** 181	74 **W** 184	75 **Re** 186	76 **Os** 190	77 **Ir** 192	78 **Pt** 195	79 **Au** 197	80 **Hg** 201	81 **Tl** 204	82 **Pb** 207	83 **Bi** 208	84 **Po** 209	85 **At** 210	86 **Rn** 222
87 **Fr** 223	88 **Ra** 226	89 **Ac** 227															

58 **Ce** 140	59 **Pr** 141	60 **Nd** 144	61 **Pm** 145	62 **Sm** 150	63 **Eu** 152	64 **Gd** 157	65 **Tb** 159	66 **Dy** 163	67 **Ho** 165	68 **Er** 167	69 **Tm** 169	70 **Yb** 173	71 **Lu** 175
90 **Th** 232	91 **Pa** 231	92 **U** 238	93 **Np** 237	94 **Pu** 244	95 **Am** 243	96 **Cm** 247	97 **Bk** 247	98 **Cf** 251	99 **Es** 252	100 **Fm** 257	101 **Md** 258	102 **No** 259	103 **Lr** 260

GO ON TO THE NEXT PAGE.

The mechanism of vision is dependent on complex molecular interactions within light-sensitive cells of the retina. The main cells of the retina are rod cells and cone cells. Rod cells differentiate light intensities in white and black, but are insensitive to color. Rod cells are spread out over the surface of the retina and are most sensitive to dim light. Cone cells are color-sensitive and contain a slightly different photopigment than rod cells.

The mechanism of vision is complex, and was first studied in rod cells. Rods are the most light-sensitive cells in the retina, and contain excitable cell membranes with gated sodium channels. The rod-cell membrane is unique, however, in containing a binding site for cyclic GMP, in its sodium channel. When cyclic GMP is bound to this site, the gated sodium channels are kept open so that the cell is normally depolarized in the resting state. This resting state corresponds to dark conditions. The rod cell synapses directly to a sensory neuron and continuously releases a neurotransmitter which inhibits the sensory neuron. By this mechanism, the sensory neuron is maintained in a constant state of repressed activity until light strikes the rod cell.

In the presence of light, photons strike rhodopsin, a protein found within the rod cell. Rhodopsin contains a prosthetic group called retinal. Retinal is the primary visual pigment of the retina. When the retinal absorbs photon energy, it converts from an 11-cis form to an 11-trans form. This causes a conformational change in the rhodopsin molecule. When rhodopsin changes conformation, a G protein known as transducin is bound to the rod cell membrane. The transducin-G protein complex activates an enzyme which hydrolyzes cyclic GMP to GMP monophosphate. This hydrolysis and the resulting decrease in cyclic GMP concentration in the cytoplasm of the rod cell cause cyclic GMP to be released from its binding sites on the sodium channels. The sodium channels then close, changes in the cell membrane potential occur, and less inhibitory neurotransmitter is released. This causes activation of postsynaptic sensory neurons. Increasing numbers of action potentials reach the brain where they are interpreted as light. Figure 1 is a diagram of a rod cell and its adjacent connections.

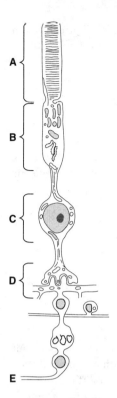

Figure 1. A rod cell and its adjacent connections.

143. Where are G-proteins most likely found in cells?

    A. Nucleus
    B. Golgi bodies
    C. Endoplasmic reticulum
    D. Plasma membrane

144. In which region of Figure 1 is rhodopsin found in the greatest concentration?

    A. Region A
    B. Region B
    C. Region C
    D. Region D

145. Based on information given in the passage, which is the best description of the state of the rod-cell membrane in the presence of light?

    A. The membrane is hyperpolarized.
    B. The membrane is depolarized.
    C. The membrane is at resting potential.
    D. The membrane has no electrical potential.

146. Which region in Figure 1 would be most senstive to a toxin which interferes with neurotransmission?

    A. Region A
    B. Region C
    C. Region D
    D. Region E

147. The prosthetic group retinal is dependent on the presence of which of the following nutrients?

    A. Vitamin C
    B. Vitamin D
    C. Vitamin E
    D. Vitamin A

148. Which of the hormone–receptor combinations listed below is dependent on a G protein–mediated mechanism?

    A. Epinephrine and its receptor
    B. Thyroid hormone and its receptor
    C. Cortisol and its receptor
    D. Estrogen and its receptor

149. The mechanism of vision can be characterized by a series of energy states and conversions leading to the perception of light. Which is the best order of energy states for vision?

    A. Physical energy, chemical energy, electrical energy
    B. Electrical energy, physical energy, chemical energy
    C. Electrical energy, chemical energy, physical energy
    D. Physical energy, electrical energy, chemical energy

Passage II (Questions 150–154)

It was discovered long ago that many substances with medicinal properties are naturally synthesized by plants. As organic chemistry has advanced and many compounds can now be synthesized in the laboratory, careful cost analysis is being performed to determine whether or not it is more cost-effective to extract useful drugs from plants, or to synthesize these drugs de novo in the laboratory.

A variety of therapeutic drugs may be extracted from plants and fungi. For example, some antibiotics including penicillin and other β-lactam drugs are formed naturally in specific species of fungi. The heart medication digoxin and the pain reliever morphine may be extracted from plants. Other drugs which serve as vasoconstrictors, such as cocaine, may also be purified and extracted from botanical sources. Although some of the drugs purified from plants may be abused, many of these have important medical uses. Cocaine is a common example of a drug with both medical uses and abuse potential.

Figure 1 shows part of the synthesis of cocaine (structure IV). Although it is not very difficult to make, similar to many other pharmaceutical agents, it is still cheaper to grow the cocoa plants and then isolate the drug from the leaves.

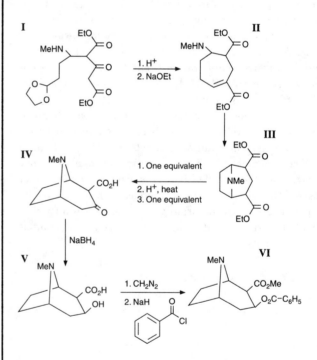

Figure 1. The synthesis of cocaine.

GO ON TO THE NEXT PAGE.

150. Consider the mechanism shown in Figure 1. In step 1 of the conversion of I to II, the purpose of the acid is to:

    A.   deprotonate the hydrogen α to the carbonyl.
    B.   protonate the amine.
    C.   remove the acetal protecting group.
    D.   hydrolyze the esters.

151. How many chiral centers are there in cocaine (structure VI)?

    A.   1
    B.   2
    C.   3
    D.   4

152. Consider the mechanism shown in Figure 1. Step 2 of the conversion of III to IV is the decarboxylation step. Why is the acid needed?

    A.   It is believed that the acid protonates the carboxylic acid and helps to create the six-member ring transition state for decarboxylation.
    B.   The amine must be protonated for this process to occur.
    C.   The other ester will hydrolyze unless it is protonated.
    D.   Acid is not necessary as the reaction will occur with a net negative charge on the carboxyl group.

153. A side-product formed in the conversion of III and IV is found to contain two chiral centers. How many possible stereoisomers would this molecule contain?

    A.   2
    B.   4
    C.   8
    D.   16

154. In the proton nuclear magnetic resonance (NMR) spectra of this molecule, the methyl group of the amine will be split into a:

    A.   doublet.
    B.   triplet.
    C.   quartet.
    D.   singlet.

Passage III (Questions 155–159)

The lysosome was the first organelle to have its biochemical properties described before it had ever been reported by microscopists. Discovery of the lysosome came about by chance in the laboratory of Christian de Duve in the 1950s. De Duve and colleagues realized that acid phosphatase, initially thought to be located in the mitochondrion, was associated with a class of particles not reported before. Because of its involvement in cellular lysis, the organelle was called the *lysosome*. All lysosomal enzymes are acid hydrolases—hydrolytic enzymes with an optimum pH around 5.

Experiments to confirm the function of lysosomes came from cytochemical staining reactions. These reactions were capable of localizing acid phosphatase to specific structures that could be visualized with electron microscopy.

The experiments were performed as follows: (1) Thin sections of tissue were fixed and incubated at a pH of 5 in a medium containing glycerophosphate (a substrate for acid phosphatase) and a soluble lead salt; (2) During incubation, the phosphatase cleaved the PO_4^-, which reacted with lead ions to form lead phosphate, an insoluble compound that precipitates at the site of enzymatic activity; and (3) Microscopy revealed the location of the acid phosphatase in the cell.

Once the functions of lysosomes were determined, a number of diseases were identified that appeared to be due to lysosomal dysfunction. One of these diseases, Tay-Sachs disease, was found to be due to a deficiency of one or more lysosomal enzymes. This results in the undesirable accumulation of excessive amounts of substances in lysosomes, which enlarge and impair host cell function.

In a series of experiments, tissue samples from four human subjects (samples A–D) were subjected to cytochemical staining reactions using a substrate for acid phosphatase. The results of the experiments are shown in Table 1.

Table 1. Results of Cytochemical Staining Experiments for Subjects A Through D

Sample	% of Unused Substrate	Size of Lysosome
A	20 = normal	+ (normal)
B	60	+
C	75	+ + +
D	0	+ + +

155. Which of the following does NOT describe the lysosome?

    A.   It is membrane bound.
    B.   It is involved in cellular lysis.
    C.   It is involved in the recycling of organic materials.
    D.   Visualization was key to its discovery.

156. Lysosomal enzymes can hydrolyze all classes of biological macromolecules. Why don't lysosomal enzymes digest the endoplasmic reticulum where they are made?

    A.   Biological pH is too acidic.
    B.   Biological pH is too alkaline.
    C.   There are too few hydrogen ions.
    D.   Both B and C

157. Why does electron microscopy reveal the location of acid phosphatase in the cell?

    A.   Light is blocked by lead phosphate.
    B.   Lead phosphate is electron dense.
    C.   Acid phosphatase has been modified.
    D.   Unused substrate is electron dense.

158. Which sample(s) might be from a patient suffering from a lysosomal storage disease?

    A.   Sample B
    B.   Sample C
    C.   Sample D
    D.   Samples C and D

159. What might explain the results with sample B?

    A.   Lysosomal storage disease
    B.   Normal results
    C.   Naturally low level of enzyme activity
    D.   Deficiency of enzyme for a common reaction

Passage IV (Questions 160–164)

One of the challenges in organic chemistry is to design reactions so as to minimize unwanted product. However, even in carefully designed reactions, a significant amount of unwanted product is formed. Techniques have been designed to help separate and purify the products of reactions so that desired products can be isolated.

Common techniques to separate, purify, and characterize organic compounds include extraction, crystallization, distillation, chromatography, infrared spectroscopy, and nuclear magnetic resonance (NMR) spectroscopy. Each of these techniques uses unique chemical properties of the molecules being studied to help with identification and purification.

The Experiment

A chemist runs an experimental reaction which produces five different products. The products form a mixture, and they are shown in Figure 1. The chemist uses techniques to separate the mixture. Answer the following questions based on the separation and purification sequence used by the chemist to evaluate the five reaction products.

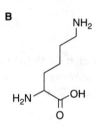

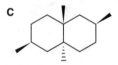

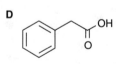

Figure 1. The products (A–E) of an organic chemical reaction.

GO ON TO THE NEXT PAGE.

160. The product mixture is dissolved in the polar organic solvent, ethyl acetate. After adding aqueous acid to this solution and shaking in a separatory flask, the organic phase will contain which of the following products?

A. Products A and B
B. Products C and D
C. Products D and E
D. Products C, D, and E

161. The ethyl acetate solution is then washed with an alkaline aqueous solution. The aqueous phase will contain which of the following products?

A. Products C and D
B. Product E
C. Product B
D. Product A

162. Ethyl acetate is then removed by distillation. Column chromatography is performed on the mixture to separate the compounds. The chromatography procedure elutes the compounds in order of polarity. In other words, the less polar compounds elute more quickly. Which of the compounds below will elute first?

A. Compound E
B. Compound C
C. Compound D
D. Compound B

163. Compounds E and D have been successfully isolated. A mass spectrum of each compound has been taken to confirm which compound is which. The mass spectrum of E will be easy to assign because:

A. Compound E is heavier than Compound D.
B. Each major peak, before bromine fragmentation, will have a prominent m + 2 peak.
C. Double ring systems do not break up in mass spectrometry.
D. The molecular ion is the only way to tell them apart.

164. Aromatic compounds will generally absorb ultraviolet (UV) light. Compounds A and C are placed on a thin-layer chromatography plate. Which compounds can be visualized on a thin-layer chromatography plate that reflects UV light (visualized by shining UV light on a developed plate)?

A. Compound A only
B. Compound C only
C. Both compounds A and C
D. Neither compound A nor C

Questions 165 through 168 are NOT based on a descriptive passage.

165. Which of the following regions contains a portal blood flow?

A. Thyroid gland
B. Adrenal cortex
C. Spleen
D. Intestine

166. Phenol is an *ortho-para* director because the hydroxy group:

A. donates electrons that increase electron density at *ortho* and *para* positions favoring nucleophilic attack.
B. donates electrons that increase electron density at *ortho* and *para* positions favoring electrophilic attack.
C. donates electrons to the *ortho* and *para* positions and attracts electrons away from meta positions favoring nucleophilic attack of the ring.
D. donates electrons to the *ortho* and *para* positions and attracts electrons away from meta positions favoring electrophilic attack of the ring.

167. Hemoglobin and myoglobin are two important respiratory pigments. Each molecule is able to bind molecular oxygen. When a plot is made of a percent of pigment bound versus oxygen tension, hemoglobin gives a sigmoidal curve while myoglobin gives a nonsigmoidal curve. The best explanation for the sigmoidal shape of the hemoglobin curve compared with myoglobin is that:

A. hemoglobin has a different cofactor than myoglobin.
B. hemoglobin is found in muscle tissue, while myoglobin is found in red blood cells (RBCs).
C. hemoglobin has fewer subunits than myoglobin.
D. hemoglobin shows positive cooperativity.

168. A research chemist wishes to synthesize a drug that competitively inhibits neurotransmitters at autonomic preganglionic synapses. To best accomplish this objective, the competitive inhibitor should be structurally similar to which neurotransmitter?

A. Acetylcholine
B. Norepinephrine
C. Epinephrine
D. Dopamine

Passage V (Questions 169–174)

Studies of prokaryotic transcription show that there is a direct correlation between the order of amino acids in a polypeptide and the contiguous sequence of nucleotide pairs in DNA. Experimental confirmation of this fact is shown when hybridization of an mRNA molecule to double-stranded DNA occurs. There is a direct, linear hydrogen bonding of complementary bases from DNA to mRNA.

Eukaryotic genes do not follow this pattern. Eukaryotic genes are interrupted by "extra" sequences of nucleotides that are not represented in either functional mRNA or functional protein products. When experiments are performed with mRNA and genes for eukaryotic proteins, multiple loops of DNA occur. These loops of double-stranded DNA are flanked by two loops of displaced single strands.

Eukaryotic genes are known to contain introns and exons. Introns are sequences of DNA which are excised during posttranscriptional processing. Exons are the sequences of DNA which are actually linked into the posttranscriptionally modified mRNA. Introns are found in almost all eukaryotic genes, and appear to be important in eukaryotic gene regulation. Although introns are not preserved in the functional message, they are transcribed along with exons. Thus, the initial transcript of a gene contains sequences that must be removed as the transcript is processed into the final mRNA product. The removal of these segments is known as gene processing. Figure 1 shows the structure and processing of a transcript from a eukaryotic cell gene.

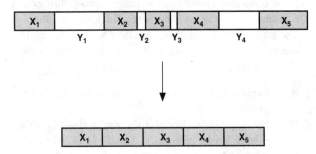

Figure 1. Structure and processing of a transcript from a eukaryotic cell gene.

There are several theories as to what introns and exons confer to eukaryotic organisms. One postulate suggests that RNA splicing mechanisms may provide flexibility of generating several different proteins from the same RNA transcript. This is possible if introns contain similar or identical junction sequences, allowing exons to be assembled in different combinations. The exon combinations may assemble due to the juxtaposition of different intron junctions. Examples of this postulate have already been documented in two different biological systems: animal virus RNA processing and antibody formation in animals.

242

169. The regions within the gene which are NOT present in the mRNA and do NOT become involved in hybrid formation are known as:

   A. RNA splices.
   B. exons.
   C. tRNA.
   D. intervening sequences.

170. Analysis of the nucleic acids (DNA and RNA) from a hybridization experiment is performed. Which of the following statements is correct?

   A. Both DNA and RNA contain the same sugar.
   B. Both DNA and RNA contain thymine.
   C. Both DNA and RNA are replicated from a DNA template.
   D. Both DNA and RNA contain guanine.

171. In eukaryotic hybridization experiments, the double-stranded DNA loops correspond to which of the following?

   A. RNA splices
   B. Introns
   C. Exons
   D. mRNA

172. An investigator studies the RNA splicing process with the aid of fluorescent stains and electron microscopy. With these techniques, the site of RNA splicing can be shown. Where is the investigator most likely to note RNA splicing taking place in eukaryotic cells?

   A. At the ribosome
   B. At the endoplasmic reticulum
   C. In the nucleus
   D. In the Golgi body

173. The shaded regions of the gene shown in Figure 1 correspond to which of the following?

   A. RNA splices
   B. Introns
   C. Exons
   D. mRNA

174. Which of the following processes are posttranscriptional modifications which protect the RNA transcript from degradation?

   A. The formation of intervening sequences
   B. The formation of introns
   C. Addition of a poly A tail
   D. Addition of exons

GO ON TO THE NEXT PAGE.

Passage VI (Questions 175–179)

Suicide inhibitors of enzymes are compounds that bind irreversibly to the active site of an enzyme by forming a covalent bond at the active site. Suicide inhibitors are all very effective in inhibiting enzymes. This enzyme inhibition property is potentially useful for the treatment of various diseases. However, these compounds have also been found to be somewhat toxic. Toxicity arises when the suicide inhibitor reacts with not only the target compound, but with other enzymes in the body and forms covalent bonds with them.

A drug company has found a compound that inhibits an enzyme which acts as a protease (hydrolyzer of protein amide bonds). The compound enters the enzyme active site and reacts with a free amine side chain of lysine, which is located in the active site. The drug company tests various forms of the enyzme inhibitor, each containing a different functional group. The basic structure of the enzyme inhibitor is shown in Figure 1. The position of various side chain options on the inhibitor molecule is indicated by the "X." The activity of the compound with a particular functional group (X) against the enzyme is shown in Table 1. By definition, the term IC_{50} refers to the concentration of the compound needed to inhibit the activity of an enzyme by 50%. The lower the IC_{50} more active the compound as an inhibitor.

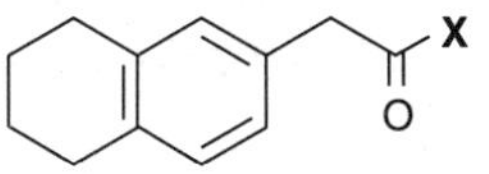

Figure 1. The basic structure of the enzyme inhibitor; X indicates the position of various side-chain groups.

Table 1. The Activity of a Protease Inhibitor with a Particular Functional Group (X) Against the Protease Enzyme.

X	IC_{50}	X	IC_{50}
MeO	0.05	F	0.002
EtO	0.02	Cl	0.005
n-Pr	0.09	I	0.015
i-Pr	0.29		
t-Bu	0.50	H	0.15
Y=H	0.14		
Y=NO$_2$	0.0008		
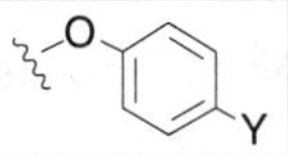			

175. Assume that NH_2 is the reactive group in the active site of the enzyme. By examining the data in Table 1, what do you think happens when the inhibitor enters the active site?

    A. Electrophilic attack of the nucleophilic carbon of C—O
    B. Electrophilic attack of the electrophilic carbon of C—O
    C. Nucleophilic attack of the electrophilic carbon of C—O
    D. Nucleophilic attack of the nucleophilic carbon of C—O

176. The reaction that occurs with the inhibitor described in question 175 can be best characterized as a(n):

    A. acylation.
    B. S_N2.
    C. E2.
    D. electrophilic addition.

177. Enzyme active sites have a definite limit in the size of compounds that can enter the active site. Based on the data presented in the passage, which compound would be expected to be just large enough *not* to fit into the active site?

    A. The t-butyl group
    B. Benzene
    C. The i-propyl group
    D. The ethyl group

178. Based on information presented in the passage, one can note that as the electronegativity of the halogens decreases, inhibitor activity:

    A. increases.
    B. decreases.
    C. remains the same.
    D. cannot be related.

179. For the compound X—phenoxy (Y—H), activity is not very high. When Y—NO$_2$, the activity increases markedly. This is due to:

    A. inductive effects.
    B. delocalizing effects.
    C. stereoelectronic effects.
    D. both inductive effects and delocalizing effects.

Recent outbreaks of mad cow disease have cast new interest on its human counterpart, known as Creutzfeldt-Jakob disease (CJD). CJD is an invariably fatal transmissible disorder of the central nervous system (CNS), and is characterized by rapidly progressing dementia and variable focal involvement of the cerebral cortex, basal ganglia, cerebellum, brain stem, and spinal cord. No treatment is currently available. A proteinaceous infectious particle, or prion, is hypothesized to be the etiologic agent. Prions contain no detectable nucleic acids.

Prion proteins have been demonstrated in the brains of patients with the disease. Familial, or heritable cases have been associated with mutations in a form of the prion protein (cellular isoform, or PrP^c), which is expressed by normal neurons but whose function is unknown. In sporadic, nonfamilial cases, an abnormal prion protein has been isolated (scrapie isoform, or PrP^{Sc}). This form differs from PrP^c in its secondary structure. In both circumstances, the result is accumulation of abnormal PrP^{Sc} prions in brain tissue.

Although transmission from humans to animals and animals to humans has been demonstrated, documented human-to-human transmission is rare. Prion particles are found in brain, cerebrospinal fluid (CSF), and other organs but not in bodily fluids. The notion of animal-to-human transmission is plausible and is of great potential impact to public health. Cases of animal-to-human transmission have been reported in Britain. These cases are believed to be due to the consumption of improperly cooked beef. Bovine spongiform encephalopathy, mad cow disease, is believed to be caused by a prion related to PrP^{Sc}.

Experiments designed to learn more about prions were conducted and the data are shown in Figure 1. A culture of nerve cells was inoculated with PrP^{Sc} in buffer (experiment A) or buffer alone (experiment B) and the levels of PrP^{Sc} as well as PrP^c were followed over a number of days.

A

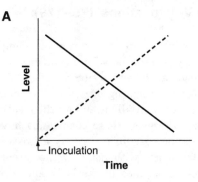

B

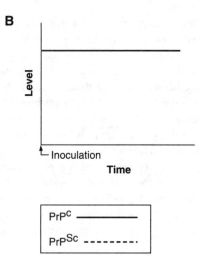

Figure 1. The levels of PrP^{Sc} and PrP^c for experiments A and B.

180. Which of the following best describes a prion?

    A.   A prion is a virus.
    B.   A prion is a lipid.
    C.   A prion is a protein.
    D.   A prion is a nucleic acid.

181. PrP^{Sc} and PrP^c differ in terms of secondary structure. Which of the following phrases best describes the difference between PrP^{Sc} and PrP^c?

    A.   Different amino acid sequence
    B.   Different arrangement of regular 3D arrays such as β-sheet and alpha-helix
    C.   Different number of disulfide bonds
    D.   Different electrostatic interaction between subunits

182. How might PrP^{Sc} replicate in sporadic cases of the disease?

    A.   By inducing a conversion of PrP^c to PrP^{Sc}
    B.   Using host machinery to copy its genome
    C.   By binary fission
    D.   Meiosis

GO ON TO THE NEXT PAGE.

183. How might a mutation of the gene encoding for PrP^c result in accumulation of PrP^{Sc} in familial cases of the disease?

    A.   Point mutation that generates stop codon
    B.   Deletion that alters secondary structure
    C.   Silent point mutation
    D.   Exon splicing

184. A CJD patient cannot maintain balance or touch her finger to her nose. What part of her CNS probably contains PrP^{Sc}?

    A.   Cerebral cortex
    B.   Thalamus
    C.   Spinal cord
    D.   Cerebellum

185. What conclusions can be drawn from looking at the graphs?

    A.   The normal isoform increases over time.
    B.   The abnormal isoform decreases over time.
    C.   Presence of PrP^{Sc} leads to loss of PrP^c.
    D.   The presence of PrP^c gives rise to PrP^{Sc}.

Passage VIII (Questions 186–190)

Identification of unknown compounds is important in organic chemistry. Techniques have been developed to aid in the determination of functional groups and active regions of organic molecules. The organic molecules which can be studied include a wide range of compounds including those of biological interest. These techniques are used extensively in pharmacology, toxicology, and pathology.

In an organic chemistry laboratory, a student was given an unknown compound to identify. Preliminary tests indicate that the compound is a disaccharide. At the student's disposal were additional tests and reagents, including the following:

1. Phenylhydrazine, which reacts with an aldehyde to yield osazone. This indicates that the sugar is reducible
2. Various enzymes for hydrolysis, including galactosidase enzymes
3. Bromine/water
4. Methylating agents

The results of the tests are:

1. When phenylhydrazine was added to the disaccharide, a phenylosazone is formed.
2. Hydrolysis of the disaccharide by β-galactosidase yielded L-galactose and L-glucose. Hydrolysis did not occur when the disaccharide was treated with α-galactosidase.
3. Treatment with bromine/water resulted in a disaccharide acid. Hydrolysis of this acid resulted in L-galactose and L-gluconic acid (acid of glucose).
4. Exhaustive methylation followed by hydrolysis yielded: 2,3,4,6-tetra-*O*-methyl-L galactose and 2,3,4-tri-*O*-methyl glucose.

186. The formation of the osazone indicates which of the following?

    A.   Mutarotation occurs in the disaccharide.
    B.   Mutarotation does not occur.
    C.   The sugars are identical.
    D.   The sugars are epimers.

187. Which of the following best describes the effect of acidic hydrolysis?

    A.   The bond connecting the sugars will be broken.
    B.   The cyclic hemiacetal will be cleaved.
    C.   The cyclic acetal will be cleaved.
    D.   All of the above.

188. Methylation followed by hydrolysis indicates that:

    A.   glucose is a six-membered ring in the disaccharide.
    B.   glucose is a five-membered ring in the disaccharide.
    C.   galactose is a five-membered ring in the disaccharide.
    D.   none of the above applies.

189. The enzymatic hydrolysis indicates that the disaccharide linkage is best described as a(n):

    A. α-linkage.
    B. β-linkage.
    C.   mixture of α and β forms.
    D.   mutarotated product.

190. What would be the reaction outcome of the disaccharide with the Tollen's reagent?

    A.   It would show that the disaccharide is non-reducing.
    B.   It would be negative for the presence of aldehyde.
    C.   It would be positive for the presence of aldehyde.
    D.   It would demonstrate an α-linkage.

Questions 191 to 195 are NOT based on a descriptive passage.

191. Radioactive substances may be used for diagnostic or therapeutic purposes in medicine. A sample of radioactive iodine is injected into a patient. In which region or organ of the body would the iodine collect in the highest concentration?

    A.   The brain
    B.   The bone marrow
    C.   The thymus gland
    D.   The thyroid gland

192. Which statement about the carbonyl group is NOT true?

    A.   The carbonyl carbon is sp^2 hybridized.
    B.   The bond angles among the three atoms attached to the carbonyl carbon are 120 degrees each.
    C.   The three atoms attached to the carbonyl form a nonplanar geometry.
    D.   The carbonyl group forms resonance structures.

193. Which of the following organelles are directly involved with the synthesis of RNA?

    A.   Golgi body
    B.   Ribosome
    C.   Endoplasmic reticulum
    D.   Nucleolus

194. Alanine is a nonpolar, neutral amino acid. The pK_a of its carboxyl group is 2.3, and the pK_a of its amino group is 9.7. At which pH does alanine NOT migrate in an electric field?

    A.   2.3
    B.   4.0
    C.   6.0
    D.   9.7

246

GO ON TO THE NEXT PAGE.

195. An unusual trait is known to afflict a particular family. Investigation of the family tree indicates that the trait is passed by a classic mode of inheritance. Evaluation of family members in each generation provides several clues. First, female children of afflicted fathers do not express the trait and tend to produce sons, of which one-half express the trait. Male children of afflicted fathers never express the trait. Which mode of inheritance is most likely?

A. Autosomal dominant
B. Autosomal recessive
C. Sex-linked recessive
D. Random mutation

Passage IX (Questions 196–202)

The human ABO blood group alleles afford an example of multiple alleleism. There are four alleles (or phenotypes) in the ABO system: A, B, AB, O. The allelic series includes three major alleles, which can present in any pairwise combinations in an individual. It is important to note that the series includes cases of both complete dominance and codominance. This gives rise to the fact that blood type AB shows codominance and type O is recessive. The ABO blood group is critical in determining the type of blood which can be transfused into a patient. Furthermore, the ABO blood group can often be used to assist in determining paternity or in reuniting a lost child with his or her biological parent(s).

Hemolytic anemia is a condition in which the red blood cells (RBCs) lyse while in circulation. This process is mediated by specific antibodies directed at RBC antigens. This was once a common medical problem caused by transfusion or pregnancy. One of the most common antigens responsible for hemolytic anemia is the Rh antigen of the RBC. A person is either Rh-positive or Rh-negative, depending on the presence or absence of the Rh antigen.

Life-threatening hemolytic anemia reactions can occur to a fetus in late development. This is most likely to happen when the mother of the fetus is Rh-negative and has an Rh-positive child in a prior pregancy. This can occur if the father of the child is Rh-positive. When the woman delivers her first baby, she is inoculated with a small amount of the fetal blood. If the woman is Rh-negative and the fetus is Rh-positive, the woman will make antibodies to the Rh antigen. When the woman has a subsequent pregnancy with an Rh-positive child, maternal antibodies can cross the placenta and cause a hemolytic anemia in the fetus. This may result in fetal demise. Special antibody treatments have been designed to minimize the risk of fetal hemolytic anemia due to Rh incompatibility.

196. A woman with blood type A marries a man with blood type B. They can have children with the following blood types except:

A. Type A
B. Type B
C. Type O
D. None of the above because types A, B, and O are all possible.

197. Which blood type is considered the universal blood recipient?

A. Type A
B. Type O
C. Type AB
D. Type B

198. If a man who is type B marries a woman who is type A, what is the chance of having a baby with type O blood?

    A. ¼
    B. 0
    C. ⅛
    D. ½

199. In a maternity ward, four babies become accidentally mixed up. The blood type of each baby is determined to be as follows:

Baby	Blood Type
1	O
2	A
3	AB
4	B

If the father is type O and the mother is type A, their baby is most likely:

    I. baby 2
    II. baby 3
    III. baby 1
    IV. baby 4

    A. Either I or II
    B. Either I or IV
    C. Either III or IV
    D. Either I or III

200. A type A woman who is Rh-negative has a child with a man who is type B and Rh-positive. What is the chance of their having a female child who is type O and Rh-negative?

    A. ⅛
    B. 0
    C. ¹⁄₁₆
    D. Cannot be determined

201. Special antibody treatments can be given to an Rh-negative mother to prevent Rh incompatibility reactions and hemolytic anemia in the fetus. Which of the following antibody treatments would best prevent hemolytic anemia of the fetus due to Rh incompatibility?

    A. Injecting the Rh-negative mother with antibodies against the fetal RBCs in her system
    B. Injecting the Rh-negative mother with antibodies against the Rh antigen of the RBC after delivery of an Rh-positive infant
    C. Injecting the Rh-positive fetus with antibodies directed against the Rh antigen
    D. Injecting the Rh-negative fetus with antibodies directed against the Rh antigen

202. Based on size alone, which class of antibody is most likely to cross the placenta and mediate fetal hemolytic anemia?

    A. Immunoglobulin G (IgG)
    B. IgA
    C. IgM
    D. IgE

GO ON TO THE NEXT PAGE.

Passage X (Questions 203–207)

Inborn errors of metabolism are commonly caused by mutant genes that generally result in a partial deficiency in enzyme function. Phenylketonuria (PKU), the most common clinically encountered inborn error of metabolism, is caused by a deficiency of phenylalanine hydroxylase (PAH). This enzyme converts the essential amino acid phenylalanine (Phe) to the nonessential amino acid tyrosine (Tyr). Tyrosine is used to synthesize catecholamines, neurotransmitters, and the pigment melanin.

Characteristics of PKU include increased Phe levels in tissues, plasma, and urine; mental retardation; failure to grow; and hypopigmentation. If detected before the first month of life, neurological damage can be greatly minimized by feeding a diet sufficiently low in Phe to maintain normal blood Phe levels. Despite dietary treatment, PKU patients show an increased incidence of behavioral difficulties. A genotypically normal fetus that is exposed to high maternal blood levels of Phe can show signs of PKU such as mental retardation.

Neonatal diagnosis of PKU involves restriction fragment polymorphism (RFLP) analysis. This technique uses restriction enzymes to cleave DNA into fragments whose length may be altered if a genetic mutation eliminates or creates a site of restriction enzyme cleavage. Gel electrophoresis is used to separate fragments by size, with the smaller fragments traveling further from the origin.

RFLP analysis of a family with one PKU child is shown in Figure 1. Two DNA fragments, A and B, are of interest. One of these contains a mutation PKU. Figure 1 shows both the pedigree for a family with one PKU child and the electrophoresis results of the DNA of each family member subjected to RFLP analysis. In the pedigree, squares are male, circles are female, diamonds are fetuses, individuals affected by PKU are stippled, and normal phenotypes are open.

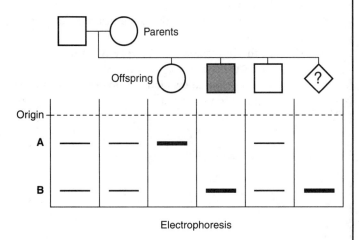

Figure 1. Pedigree and electrophoresis results for family members.

203. A reduced Phe diet would result in:

    A. death.
    B. Tyr becoming an essential amino acid.
    C. Phe becoming an essential amino acid.
    D. an exacerbation of PKU symptoms.

204. Which type of genetic mutation is unlikely to be responsible for PKU?

    A. Deletion
    B. Inversion
    C. Point mutation
    D. Crossing over

205. Which of the following statements is false?

    A. A PKU genotype is not required for a PKU phenotype.
    B. A Phe-restricted diet should not be devoid of Phe.
    C. Early detection and treatment guarantee a normal life.
    D. Certain neurotransmitters are derived from Phe.

206. Based on the RFLP analysis, what is the method of inheritance of PKU in this family?

    A. Sex-linked recessive
    B. Autosomal dominant
    C. Autosomal recessive
    D. Sex-linked dominant

207. What do the RFLP results reveal about this couple's baby?

    A. The baby will most likely be normal.
    B. The baby will most likely be a carrier for PKU.
    C. The baby will most likely have PKU.
    D. The baby will be retarded.

Reactions may produce different products depending on the presence or absence of light energy. The halogenation reactions are a prime example of this principle. For example, in the addition of bromine to carbon–carbon double bonds, there are two distinct mechanisms possible. In the presence of sunlight, a radical reaction often is the mechanism pathway. However, in the dark the reaction is different; in polar solvents, bromine adds to opposite faces of the alkene.

Figure 1 shows an example of the dark reaction. In this example, two ethylene 1,2-dicarboxylic acids are known. The *cis* acid is maleic acid and the *trans* is fumaric acid. When one adds Br_2 to fumaric acid, cold and in the dark, one obtains a symmetrical 1,2-dibromosuccinic acid that is optically inactive.

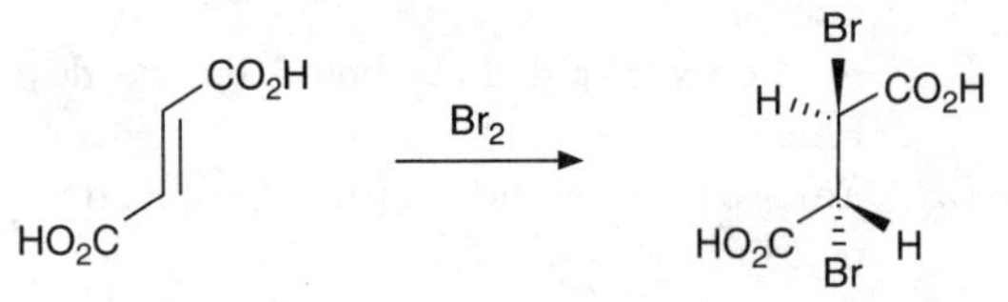

Figure 1. The addition of Br_2 to fumaric acid under specified conditions.

208. What is the relationship between the product(s) formed by the reaction of Br_2 with maleic acid and that of Br_2 with fumaric acid?

    A. They are enantiomers.
    B. They are homomers.
    C. They are diastereomers.
    D. They are regioisomers.

209. How many stereoisomers are theoretically possible from a compound that contains two chiral centers?

    A. 2
    B. 4
    C. 6
    D. 8

210. The addition of bromine to a double bond has been investigated thoroughly. If the reaction proceeded through a carbocation intermediate, how would you expect the products to be distributed?

    A. Both the maleic acid and the fumaric acid would yield three isomers in a 1:1:2 ratio.
    B. Both the maleic acid and the fumaric acid would yield three isomers in a 1:1:1 ratio.
    C. Both the maleic acid and the fumaric acid would yield the same two products.
    D. The maleic acid would yield one meso product while the the fumaric acid would yield two enantiomers.

211. If one added one equivalent of bromine to ethene (C_2H_4), how many isomers would be produced?

    A. 1
    B. 2
    C. 3
    D. 4

212. The *trans* isomer of an alkene is found to have a lower boiling point than the *cis* isomer. Which of the following best explains the mechanism for this finding?

    A. *Trans* isomers have better symmetry.
    B. *Cis* isomers have better symmetry.
    C. *Trans* isomers are less polar.
    D. *Cis* isomers are less polar.

213. In the presence of sunlight, a radical halogenation reaction occurs across a double bond. Why is this reaction often called a chain reaction?

    A. It occurs quickly.
    B. It occurs without the generation of intermediates.
    C. Each step generates the reactive intermediate that causes the next step to occur.
    D. The reaction allows long chains of halogenated alkanes to be formed.

214. An experiment is performed in which the differentiating notochord mesoderm from the dorsal surface of an amphibian embryo is transplanted to the ventral surface of the same animal. Which is the most likely result of this transplant?

    A. An intestine will develop in the overlying ventral ectoderm.
    B. Blood vessels and bone will develop in the overlying ventral ectoderm.
    C. Kidneys will form in the overlying ventral ectoderm.
    D. A neural tube will form in the overlying ventral ectoderm.

215. A chemist isolates (R)- and (S)-2-butanol. Which physical property distinguishes these two compounds?

    A. Melting point
    B. Solubility in common solvents
    C. Infrared spectrum
    D. Rotation of plane-polarized light

216. Consider a chromosomal map with five different allelic loci, A–E, as shown below. Which two loci can be expected to give the lowest crossover or recombination frequency?

```
A      B      C      D      E
_____

_____
A'     B'     C'     D'     E'
```

    A. A and C′
    B. B′ and E
    C. E′ and D
    D. A′ and E

217. The ability to produce a concentrated urine is primarily based on the presence of functional kidney nephrons. The most important structure involved in concentrating urine within the nephron is known as the:

    A. glomerulus.
    B. proximal convoluted tubule.
    C. loop of Henle.
    D. Bowman's capsule.

218. A mixture of amines in solution is shown to contain primary, secondary, and tertiary amines. All of these compounds have a similar molecular weight. To separate and purify this mixture, the solution temperature is slowly increased to the boiling point of the first amine of the mixure. Which amine is most likely to have the lowest boiling point?

    A. The primary amine
    B. The secondary amine
    C. The tertiary amine
    D. There is not enough information to determine

219. In humans, which of the following is not an appropriate physiological response to dehydration?

    A. Vasoconstriction
    B. Increased secretion of renin
    C. Decreased parasympathetic activation
    D. Decreased secretion of vasopressin

STOP. IF YOU FINISH BEFORE TIME IS CALLED, CHECK YOUR WORK. YOU MAY GO BACK TO ANY QUESTION IN THIS TEST BOOKLET.

ANSWERS AND EXPLANATIONS

Verbal Reasoning

1. D Evaluate each statement based on its own merit. Note that each statement is incorrect. Statement I is not supported because Lyell's religious beliefs are never mentioned. Statement II is untrue. Paragraph two states that Cuvier cited sudden freezes as evidence for his theories, but Lyell, the actualist, cited earthquake activity. Statement III is false. In the first paragraph, actualism is linked to Lyell. In paragraph two, volcanic activity is linked to Lyell.

2. A The bottom of paragraph one explains Lyell's theories as suggesting gradual and continuous change. The bottom of paragraph two mentions Darwin and emphasizes that Darwin's theory of coral reef formation, with its gradual uplifting of the earth, strongly supported Lyell's three principles of actualism.

3. B This answer is given directly in the passage. If you read question stems before reading the passage, it was easy to look for the answer to this question upon first reading the passage. The second sentence in paragraph two states that much of the catastrophists' evidence was based on what they believed was the result of the Great Flood described in Genesis.

4. D Use the process of elimination to answer this question. Note that choices A, B, and C can all be eliminated, because they apply to Lyell's theories. The third sentence in paragraph one supports choice D.

5. C Evaluate each choice based on its own merit. With careful analysis, you will see that choices A, B, and D all apply to catastrophism. Only choice C is true of uniformitarianism, and is supported in the first paragraph.

6. B Note the wording of the question stem: "gradual and continuous." The first paragraph emphasizes that uniformitarianism (Lyell) emphasized gradual and continuous change rather than sudden and catastrophic change. Choice A is somewhat alluring because the end of paragraph two states that Darwin's theories of earthquake activity and coral reel formation support Lyell's principles. However, choice B is best because the wording of the question stem closely links to Lyell's work.

7. D This essay describes both uniformitarianism and catastrophism and discusses each viewpoint with examples. The author does not take sides here. There is no obvious bias exhibited by the author. Choices A and B are incorrect because they imply that the author is taking sides. Choice D is best because it emphasizes the informational, non-biased nature of this passage.

8. C Choices I and III are found and supported in paragraphs one and two: the gorilla's actions are clearly those of an acrobat, and the orangutan's are those of an aerialist. And although the impala is referred to as "timid" in paragraph two, the description that ensues is more dominant and thorough, thus eliminating statement II. Therefore, statement II "might not be appropriate" (which is what the question asks for), thus making choice C correct.

9. D We have no reason to believe that the author would refer to herself, the reader, or the sea lion's trainer as "the swimmer." Such a generic, third-person reference, unless a particular swimmer has been discussed, would apply to "anyone who swims."

10. B Keep in mind that a writer chooses to use whatever information she wants. By choosing to discuss impalas in the same paragraph as reindeer (in two sequential sentences), we can infer that the author, Marianne Moore, sees some connection between the two. We do not know from the passage whether reindeer had ever been mentioned in the literature, which eliminates choice A; nor do we know whether reindeer are real or fictional (remember, we must rely on the information in paragraph two!), which invalidates choice C. Finally, the word "runway" is not enough of a "pointer" to lead us to compare impalas with airplanes, particularly because in the next sentences, impalas will be allied with reindeer.

11. B Statement I is supported in the first sentence of the paragraph. Although statement II might be true, we do not learn this in paragraph five. In the final sentence of the paragraph, the writer uses the words "tumbling, capsized, and capsizing" to describe the bear's actions; these terms often apply to boats, which makes statement III true. Therefore, statements I and III could be inferred.

12. C To answer this question, you must briefly review the passage, looking for tone and diction. The author talks about animals' physical feats, perseverance, patience, and muscular control, to name a few references. Her attitude would seem to be more positive and directed than "tolerant" or "carefree," and not quite as excessive as "adoring." The best choice would be "admiring."

13. C The author closely observed animals, and pointed out various skills and attitudes that human beings can learn or absorb from these observations. Choice A is unsupported in the passage: although the animals are observed at the zoo, the writer does not at length discuss the benefits of zoo living versus a natural habitat. As well, nowhere does the author assert that zoos mimic these natural habitats. Choice B is too specific: the author spends one short paragraph talking about privacy. Choice D is too "hyperbolic" or excessive. And although it is a direct quote from the final paragraph, it does not summarize the lessons we learn from the passage.

14. B The author does not judge the behavior of human beings in this paragraph (thus eliminating choice A); she simply describes the "concentrated. . . perseverance" of the duck, as well as the leopard spending 15 minutes to "wash a small patch of fur." She makes no comment on a "waterproofing mechanism" (choice C), and although she refers to the leopard's patch of fur that "is not sleek enough to satisfy it," she does not seem to find this behavior excessive. Rather, she seems to view it as admirable, which eliminates choice D.

PASSAGE III

15. D The first thing you should notice when reading this passage is the strong bias and position of the author. It is clear that the author resents the term "carrier" and wants to point out that heterosexual persons with the HIV virus appear to be treated differently than other groups. The author also emphasizes the "double standard" by which women with HIV are treated. To answer this question, note the author's statement in the last sentence of the first paragraph. The author explicitly uses HIV-positive in contrast to carrier.

16. B See paragraph two (statement I), and paragraph three (statement II). The author implies that words signify points of view and prejudices. Statement III is not supported; the author does not argue that words connote entire programs.

17. D Answer this question by inferring from the author's tone and message. The author wants to reorient HIV and AIDS discourse to the perspective of HIV-positive people or people with AIDS. This is emphasized in paragraphs two and three. Choices A, B, and C represent outside professionals who are not directly and personally involved with the day-to-day living with HIV.

18. C The author of this passage is fired up about this issue and takes it very seriously. The word "ardent" means impassioned or zealous. Although the author may be confident, the tone of the passage emphasizes more that the author's beliefs are strongly opinionated. The author is never flippant, and is rarely humorous.

19. **D**   See paragraph one. The author states that "perceived danger leads to real fear. . . ." The final sentence emphasizes that fear drives the reactionary conservatives to construct horrific plans for quarantining those with HIV. Choices A, B, and C are not mentioned, not implied, or not stated in the passage.

20. **D**   The answer to this question is not directly stated, yet it is implied throughout the passage, especially in paragraph two. Choices A and B are not discussed or supported. Choice C is incorrect because the author is arguing precisely for a non-prejudiced language.

21. **C**   Look carefully at the wording of the answer choices. Also refer to paragraph four. It is clear from the entire passage that the author does not like the use of the term "carrier." He especially points out that it is sad that the women who were partners of this basketball star were marked as "carriers" in this transmission. This supports choice C. Choice A is not as good as choice C because the author wants to do away with the word carrier altogether. Choices B and D do not make sense.

22. **A**   In paragraph four, the author clearly supports women, and claims that traditionally men have had more cultural power than women. "Heterosexual men" is the only exclusively male category offered in the four choices.

---

23. **D**   This passage has an argument, and it is expository. It explains one way of reading the Bible and the relationship between the Lord and Abraham, but because there are many ways of reading the Bible, this passage is attempting to convince readers to interpret the Bible in a particular way. This passage explicitly argues that the relationship of God to Abraham is a hierarchical one, in which Abraham is clearly permitted to question God, but he is never permitted to disobey him. Paragraph four clearly points out that in Genesis 22, Abraham demonstrates his understanding of the hierarchical relationship. In a complex passage like this, it is important to make a map of the coverage of each paragraph. Feel free to make small notations in the margins. If you can, a mental map is also useful. Mapping the paragraphs is as follows: paragraph one consists of the thesis. It presents the argument that a hierarchical relationship exists between God and Abraham, as shown in Genesis 18 and 22. Genesis 18 is a lesson in justice, and Genesis 22 is a lesson in faith. The rest of the paragraphs give evidence for this argument. Paragraph two discusses Genesis 18. Although Abraham questions God, he also does so respectfully and humbly. Paragraph three states that God invites questions of Abraham, but only out of a desire to have Abraham understand the Lord's justice. Paragraph four discusses Genesis 22, in which God asks Abraham to perform a task: sacrificing his innocent son. Paragraph five compares God's and Abraham's relationship as they are portrayed in Genesis 18 and 22.

24. **C**   Choice B is incorrect, because the passage states that Abraham may question God. However, in the second paragraph, the passage does imply that Abraham is careful not to arouse the wrath of God when questioning him. The passage does not specifically mention whether it is permitted for Abraham to displease or anger God, but it is clear that he is never permitted to disobey God. Choice C is well supported in paragraphs four and five.

25. **D**   Remember that thesis statements frequently are found at the end of the first paragraph. In this passage, this is also the case. Note that the last sentence of paragraph one emphasizes the consistency of Genesis 18 and Genesis 22. This is the author's primary underlying claim.

26. **A**   Check your margin notations or mental map to see which paragraph contains information on Genesis 22. See paragraph four. God is essentially training Abraham for his future role.

27. **B**   Paragraph two uses the phrase "wrath of God." This sets the tone for the rest of the passage and explains the care by which Abraham communicates and interacts with God. The other choices are not as well supported. Choice A implies friendli-

ness. There is no evidence of friendly interaction between Abraham and God mentioned in the passage. The passage does not give any indication that God is indecisive. No discussion is offered about the reasonableness of God. See especially paragraph two.

28. **C**   This is a relatively difficult question. Abraham can question God in matters concerning the nature of justice. He can also question God when God wants to be questioned. Note how Abraham carefully and humbly words all questions to remain subordinate. Choice D is incorrect, because it is not important whether or not Abraham likes God's actions. Choices A and B are not as good as choice C. Abraham is invited to question God. Abraham may not question God for lack of understanding.

29. **B**   This is an example of an application question. This question asks you to make an analogy of the relationship between God and Abraham and apply it to the answer choices. Notice that the passage makes a clear hierarchical relationship between God and Abraham. This relationship is most like a manager to an employee.

30. **A**   Be careful not to interject your feelings for God into answering this question! Just answer the question based on what you can support from the passage. See paragraph two. When Abraham does question God, it is clear that he fears God.

PASSAGE V

31. **D**   Paragraph four provides information that allies "Shout" in certain ways with traditional African music, and its characteristics are also described in paragraph one. Choice B can be eliminated because paragraph one asserts that rock and roll was "implicit in the music of the first Africans brought to North America," but goes on to say in paragraph three that "one shouldn't conclude that pure African music was somehow transformed into rock and roll." We can eliminate choice A simply because we do not know whether the musicians were influenced by traditional African music. Choice C is invalid because "Stagger Lee" and "Frankie and Johnnie" are cited in paragraph five as part of the ballad vogue in the European tradition, which was "very foreign to the mainstream of black tradition." Therefore, these songs are not logical outgrowths of African music's move to America.

32. **D**   Choice D is correct and supported in paragraph one, which mentions the high head voice ("considerable use of falsetto") of statement I, the "hoarse or grainy vocal quality" of statement II, and the participation of statement III.

33. **C**   Although this passage touches on the European musical tradition in paragraphs five and part of six (which might tempt us to choose B), it dwells on the influence of transplanted African music. Choice A's assertion that the task of discussing this influence is vast is no doubt true, but this passage certainly makes a go of it. And although choice D is asserted in paragraph three, it could not be determined to be an overall thesis statement for the passage.

34. **D**   In paragraph two, the passage states that all of the choices provided are parts of the singer's music. Paragraph five, however, provides us with a definition of the "objective performer": "one who comments on but does not become involved in the action." Choices A, B, and C in no way refer to the singer's relationship with the material or audience. Choice D—the participatory nature of the singer's "What'd I Say"—refers to his active role in the story being told through music. "What'd I Say," as described in this passage, could not be called a "narrative ballad," which we are told (in paragraph five) was "very foreign to the mainstream of black tradition."

35. **A**   The key to answering this question is to not be confused by the double negatives: "would not contribute" and "cannot conclude." To get around this, decide that they cancel each other out, and the question is: "Which of the following would contribute to why we can conclude. . . ." Then, work by the process of elimination. Choice B is invalid because this question has nothing to do with the European settlers or their songs. Choice C is related to the question, but the fact that African music was changing even before being transplanted to America makes this statement quite distant from rock and roll. Choice D asserts that certain "impon-

derables" of African music could not consciously change, which would contradict the assertion of "transformation" in the question.

36. **C**   Choice C is supported by information in paragraph four. We are given no evidence to support choice A, and although choice B may be true, the church's specific influence on these musicians does not respond to the more general nature of the question. Choice D may also have some truth, but it is not clearly supported in the passage, and is also too specific a response.

37. **D**   In the final paragraph, we learn that white country musicians played black-influenced minstrel tunes, blues-like ballads, and camp meet songs, which stem from the African tradition, thus eliminating choice A. In that paragraph, we are also told that these musicians developed a "tradition of virtuosity," and the instruments being discussed are specifically stringed instruments—fiddle, banjo, and guitar—which invalidates choice B. We also learned that English, Scotch, and Irish dance music survived in isolated rural areas, which was part of the European tradition, and became part of the repertoire of country musicians, thus eliminating choice C. What we were not told about these white country musicians is that they lived primarily in rural isolation. Plenty of the "country" where these musicians grew up and played is made up of city. If we inferred otherwise, it would be based sheerly on our own misinformation.

---

38. **D**   The "but" should give away some degree of contradiction, which eliminates choice A immediately. Now we must try to ascertain the "tone." To ridicule is to mock or make fun of in a derisive way. The second part of this sentence does not do anything so dramatic. Nor does the second part of the sentence totally invalidate (or "negate") the first. Although many other cultures survive the fiercest rays of the sun without aid, the Eskimos do employ slotted strips of bone to cut snow-reflected light, which eliminates choice C.

39. **C**   This is another question that asks us to read for "tone." We all know what a "tone of voice" sounds like when we hear it, but it is a little harder to determine upon reading. Although the judge may have been amused, his remark would seem a bit more critical than that (thus eliminating choice A). Although he is making fun of the driver in question, a parody would imply that he is mimicking her exact actions to show how foolish her behavior is, which invalidates choice B. And although he is judging her, the remark shows more humor—in the form of sarcasm, employing irony—than pure censure of her. The judge is making a point with tone as well as content.

40. **C**   The author plainly presents this fact at the beginning of paragraph three, and does not comment on it in any way. However, the author makes it plain by using the quotation in paragraph two and the last sentence of paragraph one (when he uses the word "capriciously") that he finds choice A ridiculous. He similarly seems to make fun of the options presented in choices B and D in the middle of paragraph 1.

41. **A**   Choice A is correct as supported by information in paragraph four. Nero looked through an emerald, and the Chinese used tourmaline. An emerald (being green) has "tint," which eliminates choice B. Nero was not Greek but Roman, which invalidates choice C. And nothing in the paragraph supports the assertion that these lenses were "awkward and handheld" (choice D).

42. **C**   The key to this question is recognizing the double negative, and restating the question in your mind: Which of the following may be true? In paragraph three, we are told that "the ophthalmic surgeon is often asked for advice by those living in countries where the sun is more evident than in northern climes." Therefore, statement I could be true. Paragraph four addresses statements II, which is false: we do not know that wavelengths above 7600 angstroms cause bright light. Once we know that statement I is correct and statement II is not, we can immediately opt for choice C.

43. **A**   Choice B is simply too vague, because the ancient Romans did many things.

Choice C is too flippant: earrings are also an accessory. And choice D is not a piece of advice; it is an opinion, with no suggestion directed toward an audience.

44. D This question is tricky. In paragraph five, the author mentions people who have had cataracts removed and cannot immediately tolerate increased intensity to light, or are sensitive to light. Statement I mentions these people being insensitive to light, and therefore it is false, which eliminates choice B as well as statement II. In paragraph 6, the author mentions "myopes in whom the pupil is habitually dilated," which fits with statement III. Thus, the best choice is D (statement III only).

PASSAGE VII

45. C Although this passage emphasizes Pasteur, significant discussion centers around Pasteur's interest in contradicting Pouchet and his beliefs. Paragraph two discusses Pasteur's religious convictions as motivating his experiments to disprove Pouchet's theory. Paragraph one sets up the religious footing of the conflict between Pouchet and Pasteur.

46. D Use the process of elimination to arrive at the best answer. Notice that choices A, B, and C all seem to be related. These three choices also appear reasonable at first glance, and emphasize evidence, data, and time. However, the passage states in the second to the last sentence of paragraph one: ". . .any 'germ theory'. . ." could not be firmly established as long as the belief in spontaneous generation persisted. This best supports choice D.

47. A Paragraph four overtly states that Pasteur's devotion to his work contributed to his productivity. Choice B is wrong because although Pasteur's conservative values are mentioned, they are not cited as a factor in his success. Choice C is incorrect because Koch and Lister came after Pasteur, as stated in the last paragraph. Choice D can be eliminated, because church support or lack thereof is not discussed in the passage.

48. D Look for evidence in the passage to support a personality description of Pasteur. What behavior did Pasteur exhibit in the Mont Blanc excursion? The answer is pretty clear; the fact that Pasteur endured a life-threatening situation to gather samples is evidence of compulsivity more than any of the other qualities. Choices A, B, and C are not accurate descriptions of Pasteur's personality based on the excursion. "Labile" means changeable.

49. D Statement I is supported in paragraphs one and two. Statement II is supported in paragraph six. Statement III is supported in paragraphs three and six. Thus, all three statements are true, and choice D is best.

50. A Use the process of elimination to arrive at the best answer. Beware that a statement may be true, yet it may not be the best true statement. Although choice B is true, it is likely that a friend of Pasteur would comment on his personality as well as his dedication. Choices C and D are contradicted in the passage.

51. B This question tests your understanding of the chronology of events and periods discussed in the passage. Immunology is mentioned in the last paragraph as being a result of Pasteur's work. Germ theory was Pasteur's own, and spontaneous generation was the theory already in existence that Pasteur set out to disprove. Thus, spontaneous generation was followed by germ theory, which was followed by immunology.

PASSAGE VIII

52. A Paragraph three discusses the Nebraska AMA delegation's request and its denial by the AMA. It can be inferred that the Nebraska delegation represented physicians who wanted more freedom in the way they could advertise. This supports choice A. Paragraph three contradicts choices B and C. Choice D is not discussed in the passage.

53. D Carefully evaluate the statement. Notice that it supports free-market principles. Now, evaluate the possible answer choices. Recall that paragraph 1 says that the FTC wants to allow physicians to advertise in order to align medicine with "fair trade" practices. This supports choice D. Choices A and B cannot be supported by

258

the information given in the passage. Do not use conjecture to answer this question and mistakenly choose choice A or B! Choice C is incorrect because the passage states that the AMA is against advertising, which is a common free-market practice.

54. D   Because there is no mention in the passage of how many physicians favor the right to advertise, statement I is not supported. The passage explicitly states that the AMA and the FTC are in disagreement on these issues, so statement II is also incorrect. This makes choice D best.

55. D   The Supreme Court decision did away with advertising restrictions and, therefore, was expansive. The use of the word "expansive" connotes wide-ranging and comprehensive. Encompassing means "around" or "on all sides." Divisive implies dishonesty. Confrontational suggests a conflict or showdown.

56. D   The author discusses the issues of untrained physicians performing aesthetic procedures, and the freedom of licensed physicians to perform any surgery they wish in a private surgical suite.

57. B   In the last paragraph, the author suggests irony. The author points out that physicians who are not trained properly in cosmetic surgery are free to perform any procedure they wish, and these are the doctors who are advertising heavily. On the other hand, plastic surgeons who are trained properly are discouraged from advertising by their professional board, the ASPRS. Choice A is not supported by the passage and is a broad overgeneralization. Choice C is incorrect, because the ASPRS affects only plastic surgeons and discourages but does not restrict advertising. Choice D can be eliminated because the final paragraph focuses on aesthetic or cosmetic surgery and its advertising, rather than on antitrust litigation and AMA issues.

58. A   The passage implies that all physicians can advertise and perform procedures because this allows "fair trade." Choice B is incorrect, because the ASPRS is an organization that plastic surgeons belong to. The ASPRS does not affect all physicians. Choice C can be eliminated because the passage does not indicate that the AMA supports advertising or cosmetic surgery. Choice D does not adequately address the scope of the question being asked.

59. C   The best way to answer this question is by the process of elimination. You must use inference here. Choice A can be eliminated because advertising disagrees with AMA philosophy, as stated in the passage. Choice B is not best because there is no mention or suggestion that the ASPRS has any link or interest in following FTC policy. Choice C is supported by the last paragraph of the passage. The ASPRS is mentioned in the context of being the professional board to which plastic surgeons belong. The last sentence of the passage links "rising above the unqualified" to the ASPRS's discouragement of advertising. Choice D can be eliminated because it is not mentioned or implied in the passage.

---

60. D   Statement I is supported in the third paragraph. Statement II is supported in paragraph six. Statement III is supported in paragraphs five and seven, respectively. Thus, choice D (statements I, II, and III) is best.

61. C   In paragraph two, the author calls infertility and having to care for parents "hurricanes" that blast the shores of marriage. According to the author of this passage, if these two potential difficulties could be avoided, marriage would have a more likely chance to succeed.

62. A   The passage supports the assertions of statements II and III. Statement I is not supported by the passage; there is no suggestion that the wronged partner is being cheated out of sex.

63. B   Choice B is supported in the fifth paragraph. The author emphasizes that communication is important. Paragraph eight specifically denies the advisability of choice A. The author asserts that marriage requires compromise, not dreadful self-sacrifice. Choices C and D are qualities never specifically discussed by the author.

64. **C** The author does not mention choice B. The author acknowledges choices A and D as problems, but paragraph seven is devoted to saying that modern couples expect everything to come about too easily. This paragraph clearly supplies the author's explanation for why divorce had become more prevalent.

65. **D** Paragraph one supports choice D. Note that the passage indicates that close to 50% of marriages end in divorce. Be careful to eliminate choice B. Note that choice B refers to the percentage of children growing up in single-parent homes, not the proportion of marriages ending in divorce. Choices A and C are not discussed or supported in the passage.

Physical Sciences

PASSAGE I

This passage contains elements of both a problem-solving passage and an information-presentation passage. You are told about fiberoptic scopes and are shown a diagram of a new experimental scope. The passage expects that you can apply your knowledge of optics to solve several calculation and conceptual questions. Although the passage may appear difficult at first glance, it is a relatively straightforward passage if you have reviewed refraction and total internal refection. Look at the diagram carefully and identify the refracting interface and the appropriate n values.

66. **B** This is a very important question. Fiberoptics and critical angle passages have been asked on the MCAT many times. Make sure that you understand how to solve this question! The angle that the incident ray makes with the normal is 25 degrees. The critical angle $= \sin^{-1} n_2/n_1 = \sin^{-1} \frac{1}{2} = 30$ degrees. Because the incidence angle is less than the critical angle, total internal reflection will not occur. This means that the experimental scope does not act as an endoscope. Choice C is incorrect because total internal reflection will either occur or not occur based on the n values of the media and the incidence angle. It does not depend on the intensity of the light source. Choice D can be eliminated because enough information (n values) is provided.

67. **C** Because the incident angle is less than the critical angle, light is refracted out of the scope at point P. In the region around section B of the scope, light is in the air outside the scope proper. Choices A and B are incorrect because the light is outside the scope in region B. Choice D is too vague and does not state as clearly as choice C where the light actually is.

68. **B** Refraction occurs if the angle of incidence is less than the critical angle. If the angle of incidence exceeds the critical angle, total internal reflection occurs. The light would be directed down the interface if the angle of incidence is equal to the critical angle. In this passage, the angle the incident ray makes with the normal is 25 degrees, and is less than the critical angle of 30 degrees. This means that the light ray is refracted.

69. **C** This question asks you to apply the formula for the critical angle to given values of n_1 and n_2. Make sure that you know this formula for the MCAT. The sine of the critical angle $= n_2/n_1 = 1.0/1.5 = 0.67$

70. **B** This is an example of an evaluation-type question. Although these questions are less common on the MCAT than many other question types, you need to feel comfortable with an approach for answering these questions. Carefully evaluate the statement and its tone. Then work through each answer choice to see which is most consistent with the statement. In this question, note that the statement is a strong, emphatic statement. If you can even think of one exception to the statement, it is likely incorrect. Theoretically, the image should be transmitted undiminished along the length of the scope by reflection. Thus, the physician is incorrect because the length of the fiberoptic scope does not affect image intensity. A long scope may be difficult to use and impractical. However, the lack of this physician's interest in using the fiberoptic scope in this clinical situation should not be blamed on physics.

260

This is a problem-solving passage (general chemistry) that tests your understanding of equilibrium expressions and equilibrium constants. The simple data table provided gives values for various types of equilibrium expressions. Several of the questions can be answered quickly by referring to data given directly in Table 1. Several other questions require data from the table, but require analysis and conceptual understanding to arrive at the best answer. From a science knowledge perspective, the passage expects that you understand the difference between dissolution reactions and ionization reactions.

71. C Equation 1 is the reaction representing the dissolution of carbon dioxide in water. You must decide which constant in the table best describes the dissolution constant for equation 1. Fortunately, the passage defines which constant is used for dissolution reactions. The constant which was defined to describe dissolution reactions is K_H. Looking on the table, the K_H corresponding to carbon dioxide is 0.045 mol/L·atm. The other choices are incorrect because they provide the values for ionization reactions.

72. A To solve this question, you have to compare the dissolution constants for carbon dioxide and sulfur dioxide. These are provided in the first column of the table. The dissolution constant for carbon dioxide is less than the dissolution constant for sulfur dioxide. This means that less carbon dioxide will dissolve in the water vapor than sulfur dioxide. Because the question asks about carbon-containing species as a group, the dissociation reactions can be ignored because they will not convert a carbon-containing species into a sulfur-containing species.

73. D Start your analysis of this question by looking carefully at the answer choices. You are expected to determine which equilibrium constants are important in explaining the effect of sulfur dioxide in decreasing the pH of rainwater. The important equilibria to consider for the pH of rainwater are the dissolution equation and the first ionization constant. The dissolution reaction is important because it produces acid. Ionization is important because it produces free hydrogen ions that decrease pH. Choice A is not the best choice because it does not consider the importance of acidic ionization on decreasing pH. Choice B is not the best choice because it does not consider the dissolution reaction for sulfur dioxide. Choice C shows the second ionization equilibrium constant. The second ionization constant can be disregarded because it is so much greater than the first ionization constant. Also, the negative log of the second ionization constant for sulfur dioxide would be 7, indicating that it is only important within about a pH unit of a pH of 7. The passage indicated that the pH of normal rainwater is 5.6, and polluted rainwater is 4.6. Neither of these pH values is in a range where the second ionization is important. Choice D is best because it considers the importance of both the dissolution and ionization constants.

74. B The dissolution reaction for carbon dioxide is reaction 1. The equilibrium constant for any reaction is always written with the product concentrations divided by the reactant concentrations. Remember that pure liquids such as water as well as solids are not included in equilibrium expressions.

75. B This difficult conceptual question requires that you understand the importance of the dissolution constants given in the data table. Refer to the table and analyze the K_H values for both ammonia and carbon dioxide. The K_H value for ammonia is greater than that for carbon dioxide. This indicates that the concentration of ammonia will be greater than the concentration of carbon dioxide. The second determinant of the pH is the first ionization constant. The passage states that the first ionization constant for ammonia is the reaction of ammonia with water to form ammonium hydroxide. This means that the K' for ammonia is really K_b whereas for carbon dioxide it is K_a. Remember that a high K_b means a strong base and a high K_a means a strong acid. Thus, not only is the concentration of ammonia higher, but it will dissociate more completely than carbon dioxide. This will result in a basic solution.

This is a great example of an information-presentation passage (physics). It has all the elements that are typically seen in information-presentation passages. First, it is wordy and descriptive. Second, quantitative relationships are given in both words and formulas throughout the passage. A diagram is also provided. If you are using the strategy of reading the question stems before reading the passage (as described in the *Columbia Review Intensive Preparation for the MCAT*), you will notice that you will find the answers to many of the questions as you read the passage for the first time. This approach is very strategic because it is efficient and timesaving. Also remember to rewrite all the formulas given in the passage in the margin of the passage. Write these formulas right next to each other. This will help you see the formulas in summary and help you brainstorm. You will also be able to see how to manipulate the formulas to answer questions in the passage.

76. A   This is an information-recall question. The answer to this question may be found in the second-to-last sentence of the first paragraph. The passage states in reference to a particle: "this increases their velocity and consequently their orbital radius." This passage statement implies that the orbital radius increases secondary to increasing velocity. This is choice A.

77. B   This question is asking you to manipulate variables that were discussed in the passage. The best approach for dealing with a question like this is to look at the summary of formulas that you made in the margin as you were reading the passage. You should have summarized the relationships described as follows: (1) T independent of v; (2) $vT = 2\pi R$; and (3) $R = mv/qB$. The question asks if B increases by a factor of 2, what happens to T if q and m are constant? Notice that you do not have a formula which relates B and T. However, you can substitute equation 3 for R in equation 2. This gives: $vT = 2\pi(mv/qB)$. Looking at this equation, it is possible to predict that if B increases by a factor of two, the denominator on the right-hand side of the equation increases. This in turn decreases the right-hand side of the equation by a factor of two, and the period on the left-hand side must decrease by a factor of two.

78. C   Some students spend a great deal of time rereading the passage to try to find a relationship between these variables. The passage gives you no information relating the period and frequency of a particle. If you write down the symbols for these variables as you read the question, it will be obvious that you actually know the relationship. You are only being asked to relate period and frequency. Recall that $T = 1/f$. If the period is found to progressively increase, the frequency must progressively decrease.

79. C   Start thinking about this question by writing down an equation that describes the energy associated with particle motion. This would be the equation for kinetic energy: $E = 1/2mv^2$. You would expect KE to increase if the mass or velocity of the particles increased. This helps you eliminate choices A and B. The passage indicates that the period of a particle is independent of the velocity of the particle. Based on the information given in the passage, it does not appear that altering the period would affect kinetic energy. This supports choice C.

80. B   The magnitude of the magnetic force (F_{mag}) can be determined using the expression: $F_{mag} = qvB\sin\theta$, where θ is the angle between the v and B vectors. In this question, the radii of the particle orbit and magnetic field are at right angles to each other. When $\sin\theta = 90$ degrees, note that F_{mag} is maximum ($\sin 90° = 1$). As θ decreases, F_{mag} decreases.

81. C   This is a conceptual question testing your understanding of nuclear particles. Alpha particles are helium nuclei that contain two protons and two neutrons. They have a positive two charge. Alpha particles will deflect in a magnetic field as given by the right-hand rule. Beta particles are electrons. They will deflect due to their negative charge. Gamma particles are photons. Photons will not be deflected in a magnetic field, as they have no mass or charge.

This is an information-presentation passage (general chemistry). It describes a breath analyzer and the basic chemical reaction by which the breath analyzer works. The passage emphasizes the color change that occurs, and the questions ask about the significance of this color change. Several of the questions are simple information recall questions whose answers are stated in the passage. Several questions also require that you arrive at conclusions based on information given or implied in the passage. The main chemistry topic tested is oxidation–reduction.

82. A There are two ways to arrive at the best answer. (1) The passage tells you that the breath analyzer uses a simple **redox** system. Redox means oxidation–reduction. (2) The reaction shows an alcohol reacting with a strong oxidizing agent (potassium dichromate) to produce an acid. This is a classic oxidation reaction. Choice A is the only choice which is supported by the passage.

83. C Remember that the reducing agent is the species in a redox reaction that donates electrons. A reducing agent donates electrons to become oxidized. This may be associated with an increase in oxidation number. In reaction 1, potassium does not appear to donate electrons or accept electrons. Eliminate choices A and B. The passage does not suggest that potassium is a preservative, so also eliminate choice D. The potassium ion is found in the same oxidation state on both sides of the equation. In fact, potassium is only written in to show all species present. It could be left out if only the net chemical reaction were needed. Ions or species that do not take part in a reaction are spectators. This supports choice C.

84. A The chromium in the potassium dichromate is in the +6 oxidation state. This is determined by using the atoms with known oxidation states (oxygen is normally −2, potassium is usually +1) and making the sum of all the oxidation states add up to the charge. $(2 \cdot 1) + (2 \cdot x) + (7 \cdot -2) = 0$; therefore x must be +6. The chromium in the chromic sulfate is in the +3 oxidation state. This change in oxidation state (from +6 to +3) involves the gain of electrons and is a reduction. The species reduced in a chemical reaction is the oxidizing agent.

85. C The best way to solve this question is to use the process of elimination to arrive at the best answer. Evaluate each choice and see which is true. Then choose the best true statement which addresses the question. Choices A and B are not supported by the passage. There is no information presented in the passage to suggest that potassium dichromate has any specific reaction with alcohol, or is very accurate. The exact nature of the color of potassium dichromate is likely not important. The passage does not mention the importance of color specificity. This passage does emphasize that the way the breath analyzer works is by measuring the degree of color change caused by a chemical reaction. The way that the alcohol is quantitated is by the magnitude of the color change. Thus, it makes sense that the reactant and the product must be different colors; this is true for potassium dichromate. Choice C best describes the importance of using potassium dichromate in this reaction.

86. B This question tests your ability to make conclusions from information presented in the passage. Although the passage did state that a breath analyzer is fast, it did not state that a blood test is slow. Although a breath analyzer may produce results faster than a blood test, you cannot emphatically conclude this from the passage. This eliminates choice A from consideration. The passage did state that an advantage of the breath analyzer is its portability. This makes choice B true. The passage also stated that blood tests are more reliable than breath analysis. This does not support the statement that a breath analyzer is more accurate than a blood test. Eliminate choice C. Because choices A and C are not supported, choice D cannot be correct.

87. C You have no information regarding a comparison of the reactivity of ethanol and dichromate. This means that either choice C or choice D must be the correct choice. Remember that a favorable reduction potential is a positive number. Because the dichromate is the reduced species in this reaction, it must have a higher reduction potential than ethanol. This makes choice C the best choice.

88. A   To solve this question, isolate horizontal and vertical components and think about using the kinematic equation which allows you to solve for time, given distance, and initial horizontal velocity. Note that the acceleration of gravity acts in the y-direction and does not affect purely horizontal travel. $x = v_{ox}t$; 50 m = (10 m/sec)(cos 60°)(t); 50 m = (5 m/sec)(t); and t = 10 sec. This is the time for the projectile to travel the entire 50 m. The projectile will be at its greatest height at the halfway point, or 5 sec into the trip.

89. A   Complete neutralization will occur when the number of equivalents of acid equals the number of equivalents of base. Remember for diprotic acids, each mole of acid will yield two moles of hydrogen ions.

Equivalents of acid = (molarity)(number of protons per mole acid)(volume acid) = (0.15)(2)(x)
Equivalents of base = (molarity)(number hydroxide ions per mole base) · (volume base) = (0.2)(1)(30)
Set the terms equal and solve for x: (0.15)(2)(x) = (0.2)(1)(30), x = 20 mL

90. C   This problem can be solved mathematically or conceptually. Mathematically, solve this problem in two steps.

Step 1: Find the volume of the block.

(The weight of the block in scenario 1) − (the tension in the string in scenario 2) = the buoyant force. Because the string tension is 8 N when submerged in the fluid, the buoyant force associated with submerging of the block is 2 N (10 N − 8 N = 2 N).

Buoyant force = $V\rho g$. Thus, 2 N = V(100 kg/m³)(10 m/sec²) V = 0.002 m³.

Step 2: Find the mass associated with the block.

If the block weighs 10 N when hanging in air, 10 N = mg. m = (10 N)/(10 m/sec²) m = 1 kg.
The density of the block = (mass in kg)/(volume in m³) = (1 kg)/(0.002 m³) = 500 kg/m³.

A quick way to find the answer: If you did not know how to solve this problem mathematically, there is a quick conceptual way to eliminate some choices. If the block is completely submerged in the fluid in scenario 2 and there is some tension remaining in the string, you know that the density of the block must be greater than the density of the fluid. This is because if the string were not there, the block would want to sit on the bottom of the container. The weight of the block is obviously greater than the buoyant force trying to lift the block. This allows you to eliminate choices A and B. If the density of the block were less than or equal to the density of the fluid, the block would tend to float rather than want to sink. Also note that the buoyant force of 2 N is fivefold less than the total string tension. This suggests that the density of the block is about fivefold greater than the fluid. This allows you to cancel choice D (it is 10-fold greater than the density of the fluid). By process of elimination, you have arrived at the correct answer, choice C.

91. A   This is a great conceptual question similar to several recent real MCAT questions. An electric field by definition is in a direction from positive charges towards negative charges. Determine the direction of an electric field by noting the direction of the force experienced by a small positive test charge (+q) when placed in the vicinity of the E-field. In this question, you are asked what would increase the potential energy the most if a positive charge is placed in the vicinity of an E-field. Because the E-field moves from positive charges towards negative charges, our positive charge of interest would feel opposition from the E-field if directed into the field. If placed in the path of the E-field, our positive charge of interest would tend to move in the direction of the E-field. To increase potential energy the most, you would want to move the positive charge against the E-field. This would be associated with charge repulsion and electrical potential energy storage.

This is a problem-solving passage (general chemistry) that contains some elements of information presentation. You are given two reactions to consider and are asked questions about reaction energetics, activation energies, and entropy changes. The passage also presents some information about how catalytic converters work (last paragraph), and you are asked some information-recall questions about the mechanism of catalytic converter function.

92. B   The reaction is endothermic. There are several clues given in the passage to support that reaction one is endothermic. (1) Reaction 1 is an equilibrium, and low temperatures favor the lower energy side of an equilibrium whereas high temperatures favor the higher energy side. Because the high temperatures inside the engine favor the forward reaction, it is probably endothermic (absorbing energy). (2) The passage indicates that the part of the catalytic converter which runs reaction 1 in reverse must be at a lower temperature. This is important because although a catalyst lowers the activation energy for a reaction, it does so in both directions. The lower temperature is needed to favor the lower energy side of the equation.

93. B   To answer this question, you have to read into what is implied by the passage. The passage does say that reaction 2 occurs very quickly. The need for a catalyst to run the reverse of reaction 1, as stated in the last sentence of the passage, indicates that reaction 1 probably has a high activation energy. This would make reaction 1 a slow reaction in the absence of a catalyst.

94. C   If you were able to solve question 93, this question should be easy. Remember that a catalyst speeds up a reaction by decreasing its activation energy. This allows the reactants to successfully produce products a greater percentage of the times the reactant molecules collide with one another. Catalysts are useful in both endothermic and exothermic reactions. The need for a catalyst gives no information as to whether a reaction requires energy or releases energy.

95. B   A change in entropy, or ΔS for a reaction is a measure of randomness or disorder. Reaction 2 involves 3 mol of gaseous reactants forming 2 mol of gaseous products. Remember that gases are in a higher entropy state than solids or liquids. A reaction that produces a greater number of moles of gas than it consumes has a positive entropy change, and a reaction which consumes more moles of gas than it produces (such as this one) has a negative entropy change. This makes choice B the best choice.

96. C   In the last paragraph, the passage states that a catalytic converter has two purposes. (1) It helps complete the combustion of carbon monoxide and other compounds. (2) It converts nitric oxide back to nitrogen and oxygen gases. Choices A and B are not supported by the passage. You must choose the best answer between choices C and D. Keep in mind that the conversion of nitric oxide to nitrogen and oxygen involves the removal of oxygen. This is a reduction of the compound even though the oxygen from the compound ends up being oxidized. Choice C best describes this reduction.

97. C   This question tests your understanding of oxidation–reduction. This is a commonly tested topic on the MCAT. In reaction 2, the nitrogen goes from the $+2$ to the zero oxidation state and the oxygen goes from the -2 to the zero oxidation state. This means that the nitrogen is reduced and the oxygen is oxidized.

This is an information-presentation passage (physics). The mechanism of human speech is discussed and the relationship between airflow and pressure is given. In addition, the passage provides a brief discussion of Bernoulli's equation and equates the nasal/oral cavities to a pipe model. Skimming the question stems of this passage is a useful strategy because you can answer at least two of the questions based on your first reading of the passage.

98. B The passage mentions in the second paragraph that the increase in air velocity has an effect on pressure. The pressure effects close the vocal cords. You have to infer whether closure of the vocal cords would involve increased or decreased pressure. First, the passage states that air moves between the cords. Pressure effects from this air would likely act between the cords, in the region that air was moving. If the vocal cords are in an open position, is it more likely that low pressure between the cords would draw them together, or high pressure outside of the cords would force them together? The former explanation is more likely and best supported by the passage.

99. C The passage does not provide frequency data. However, the passage does provide a speed of sound and the distance between the nose and mouth. The passage also indicates that an open-end/closed-end pipe system nicely models the nose–mouth resonant system. This is an important clue, because it allows you to consider the distance given for the nose–mouth system to equal the length of the pipe. What formula do you know for a pipe open at one end, which allows the calculation of frequency given a velocity and pipe length? The resonance frequencies for a pipe open at one end and closed at one end are found using the following:

$f = v/\lambda = (v)(n)/4L$, in which n is the set of positive odd integers (1,3,5. . .). Thus, $(344 \text{m/sec})(1)/(4)(0.17) = 500$ Hz. Note that for fundamental frequency, use n = 1. Additional overtones or resonant frequencies can be found if n = 3, 5, 7. . . are used.

100. D The first overtone is considered the second harmonic frequency. For a pipe open at one end and closed at the other end, the fundamental frequency is found when n = 1 is used. For the first overtone, use n = 3. $f = v/\lambda = (v)(n)/4L = (344 \text{ m/sec})(3)/(4)(0.17 \text{ m}) = 1{,}500$ Hz.

101. B This is a conceptual question that requires you to use logic and inference to answer the question. If the vocal cords are placed under increased tension, you would expect the frequency of sound produced to increase. This would be like tightening a guitar string. However, the question asks what effect there will be on the period of sound produced. Recall that the period is equal to the reciprocal of frequency: $T = 1/f$. Thus, if the frequency increases, the period decreases.

102. A Beat frequency = $|f_1 - f_2|$, where f_1 and f_2 are the respective frequencies of sound. If the subjects are stationary, you would not expect any changes in perceived frequencies based on the Doppler shift. Thus, beat frequency = $|250 \text{ Hz} - 300 \text{ Hz}| = 50$ Hz.

103. C Write down a relationship that allows you to find the wavelength given the frequency and velocity: $\lambda = v/f$. The question tells you that f = 300 Hz. The passage states that v = 344 m/sec. Thus, wavelength = $(344 \text{ m/sec})/(300 \text{ Hz}) = 1.1$ m.

This is a problem-solving passage (physics). To many students, this appears to be more like an information-presentation passage. However, when you preview the question stems, you quickly realize that the questions are relatively independent of the information being presented in the passage. The questions are problem-based, and the passage is superfluous. This type of passage is common on the MCAT.

Notice that the questions all ask independent tasks. Each question provides all of the information you need to solve that particular question. Question stem reading is a good strategy to use in this passage because it allows you to quickly realize that the questions are solvable independent of the passage. This means that the passage itself will be fairly unimportant in answering questions. This passage is an introduction to satellites, and is of little to no use in answering the questions. Quickly skim the passage, but do not waste too much time interpreting it.

104. B The equation relating velocity of electromagnetic radiation or light to frequency and wavelength is one of the most important relationships to know for the MCAT. To solve this simple calculation-type question, simply identify the two variables known and the variable you are looking for. Then, plug-in to the following formula:

$$v = c = (f)(\lambda); \text{ thus, wavelength} = (3 \times 10^8 \text{ m/sec})/(10^8 \text{ Hz from passage}) = 3 \text{ m}.$$

105. D The best way to solve this problem is to draw a diagram showing what the question stem is describing to you. On the MCAT, it is very strategic to use diagrams to help you arrive at a plan for the solution. In this question, the diagram for the described scenario is given below. Once drawn, you'll see that this question describes a Pythagorean relationship:

$$A^2 + R^2 = C^2$$

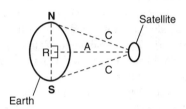

Thus, $A^2 + R^2 = C^2$ and $C = (A^2 + R^2)^{1/2}$. Because the beam travels 2C, the total linear distance that the beam travels is $2(A^2 + R^2)^{1/2}$.

106. C Unit problems are fairly common on the MCAT. These questions test if you can work with formulas containing constants. To solve these question types, start by writing down an equation that you know containing the constant desired. Then, plug-in the units of the variables in the equation. Finally, solve the equation in terms of the constant. This will give you the units of the constant desired. In this question, write down the equation describing the force between two bodies: $F = G/mm/r^2$. By rearranging, the units for G would be (Force)(radius)^2/(mass)(mass) = $N(m^2)/(kg^2)$.

107. B This is a fairly difficult question for most students to solve. Begin by writing the relationship for the acceleration of gravity on earth:

$$\text{At surface of earth: } g_s = GM/R^2 = 10$$

Next, look carefully at the above relationship and ask yourself how it should be modified to account for a distance above the earth's surface. Because R is the radius of the earth (distance of object to center of earth), it makes sense that the distance above the earth's surface should be added to R. This would give an equation which would take into account the total distance from an object above the earth's surface to the earth's center:

$$\text{At a distance H above the earth: } g_H = GM/(R + H)^2 = (g_s)R^2/(R + H)^2$$
$$= (10)R^2/(R + H)^2.$$

108. B This is a tricky, conceptual question. G, the universal constant, is universal. It never changes. This fact holds true for anywhere in the universe. Do not get confused between G and g. Lower case "g" refers to the acceleration of gravity on a given planet or body. Its value is variable, and depends on the radius and mass of the planet or body being considered. For your reference, a question very similar to this has appeared recently on the MCAT.

This passage is most similar to a research-study passage (general chemistry). Although the experiment was not part of a scientific research protocol, experimental data are presented and questions are posed about experimental design and method. Most of the questions test your understanding of the experiment performed. Questions also address potential sources of error in the experiments. The best way to begin an approach to this passage is to make a diagram of the procedure used in the experiment. Ask yourself why each step was performed. Pay attention to the data shown in Table 1. Note the differences between the compounds shown in this table. As with other passages, it is strategic to skim the question stems before attacking the passage. This will clue you in to what will be asked about and what is important.

109. D The only purpose of the ice bath is to condense the vaporized liquids. The temperature of the ice bath is never used in a calculation so its exact temperature is not important. To calculate the molecular weight of the liquids, you must be able to use the ideal gas law. To use the ideal gas law, you need a temperature and pressure. Because the temperature and pressure were not given in the passage, you need to assume that they are standard. Finally, because you are measuring the mass of each compound which vaporized to fill the flask, you do not want the vaporized liquid molecules to exchange with air.

110. A If you had the exact amount needed to fill the flask, some air would probably not be pushed out of the flask, and some of the vaporized liquid would probably escape instead. This would result in a lower mass than should be measured, resulting in a lower molecular weight.

111. D If some of the liquid had not condensed when the flask was weighed, the measured weight would be lower than if all of the gas had condensed. This would result in a lower calculated molecular weight.

112. B Working with units is very strategic on the MCAT. You know that molecular weight is in units of grams per mole. Look at the units of each of the possible answer choices and note which choice gives units in grams per mole:

Choice A: grams/(L/mol × L) = gram × mole/L²
Choice B: grams × (L/mol / L) = grams/mole
Choice C: grams × L/(L/mol) = gram × mole
Choice D: grams × L × L/mol = gram × L²/mole

The only choice resulting in the correct units is choice B.

113. A The molecules of butane occupy space. This means that the volume is not only the volume of the sample, but also includes the volume of molecules. This results in fewer molecules in the same volume. Fewer molecules have a lower weight which will provide a lower molecular weight than should be observed. The other choices are easy to eliminate. Choice B is false because the van der Waals equation has a term that corrects for the volume that molecules occupy in a gas sample. This indicates that the volume is significant. Choices C and D are incorrect because the attraction or repulsion of molecules should not affect their weight.

INDEPENDENT QUESTIONS

114. C Solve this problem by first calculating the total circuit resistance. For the parallel resistors: $1/R_T = 1/2 + 1/4$. $R_T = 4/3\ \Omega$.

For the total circuit resistance, add the series elements. Therefore, $R_{circuit} = 4/3\ \Omega + 3\ \Omega = 13/3\ \Omega$.

Now, find the total circuit current: $I = V/R = 13\ V/(13/3\ \Omega) = 3A$.

To find how much current flows through the $2\ \Omega$ resistor, set up a resistance/current table. This is a great conceptual way to solve circuit problems. Recall that current flows through resistors in parallel, in an inverse ratio to the resistances.

Resistance Ratio	Current Ratio
1	2
2	1

Therefore, the 3 A flows through the resistors in a 2:1 ratio inversely to their resistances; that is, 2 A flows though the 2-Ω resistor.

115. C Start by writing an equation for this reaction: $Al(s) + Fe_2O_3 \rightarrow Fe(s) + Al_2O_3$.

This reaction must be balanced. Balance atoms by adding appropriate coefficients: $2Al(s) + Fe_2O_3 \rightarrow 2Fe(s) + Al_2O_3$. Solve this problem by identifying which reagent is the limiting reagent. In this problem, A1 is the limiting reagent because two atoms of Al are needed to combine with 1 molecule of ferric oxide to produce products. If you start with equal numbers of moles of each reagent, the Al will be used up first. If 0.1 mol of it is used, 0.1 mol of Fe will be produced because the molar coefficient ratio for Al and Fe is the same (1:1).

116. C As an object rotates in a circular orbit with ever-increasing speed, there are two acceleration vectors which act on it. (1) There is a centripetal acceleration acting inwards (as shown by vector B), which helps hold the object in a circular orbit. (2) There is a tangential acceleration associated with circular motion, because the magnitude and direction of the velocity are changing. This tangential acceleration associated with counterclockwise motion is shown as vector D. The net acceleration vector is a combination of B and D, which is closest to choice C.

117. C A good way to solve this problem is to take the initial mass through half-life cycles in which the mass is halved. Count how many half-life cycles are required:

$$192\,g \rightarrow 96\,g \rightarrow 48\,g \rightarrow 24\,g \rightarrow 12\,g \rightarrow 6\,g \rightarrow 3\,g \rightarrow 1.5\,g \rightarrow 0.75\,g$$
$$\;\;\;1\quad\;\;\;2\quad\;\;\;3\quad\;\;\;\;4\quad\;\;\;5\quad\;6\quad\;7\quad\;\;\;8$$

Thus, eight half-life cycles have occurred in 120 days.

(120 days)/(8 half-lives) = 15 days per half-life.

118. D This question tests your understanding of refraction and Snell's law. Remember that when light moves from a lower to a higher n value (index of refraction), the light bends towards the normal. When light moves from a higher n value to a lower n value, as in this question, light bends away from the normal. Light bends away from the normal because it speeds up as it moves from a higher refractive index to a lower refractive index. Choice A shows total internal reflection. Although total internal reflection occurs when light moves from high n to low n media, this would be an unlikely event at a water/air interface. Choice B is incorrect because it does not show bending towards the normal. Choice C is incorrect because it shows the refraction causing bending towards the normal; this only occurs when going from lower n to higher n values.

This is a problem-solving passage (physics) that has elements of a research study passage. The passage describes an experimental apparatus and gives a simple data table. The questions test your understanding of fluid dynamics and basic mechanics. Most of the questions are simple calculations and conceptual questions rather than the more complex data interpretation, application, and evaluation questions normally stressed in research study passages. Spend some time studying the figure given in the passage. Note that the units are given in centimeters, rather than meters.

119. D Recall that the total pressure at some point under water is the sum of the pressure due to the stack of water above it (gravity effect) and outside atmospheric pressure supplying an extra little push:

$$P_y = P_{atm} + \rho gh = 10^5 + (0.4 \times 10^5) = 1.4 \times 10^5 \text{ N/m}^2.$$

120. B Because this question asks you to compare two different fluids, refer to the section of the passage that allows comparison. The data table provides you with a means to compare the two fluids of interest. Also, recall that the pressure at a point under the surface of a liquid sealed to the atmosphere is: $P = \rho gh$. You can ignore the effect of P_{atm} because the tank described in this problem is sealed to the atmosphere.

$$\text{Compare the } P_{glycerol} \text{ to the } P_{ethanol}: (\rho_g gh)/(\rho_e gh) = 1{,}200/800 = 3/2.$$

121. D Torricelli's theorem (which can be derived from the conservation of energy expression or Bernoulli's equation) says $v = (2gh)^{1/2}$. Notice that as the height of the water column in the tank decreases, the velocity decreases. This also makes intuitive sense. Curve D is best because it shows the nonlinear relationship and a decreasing velocity of fluid with time. Choices A, B, and C may be eliminated because one would expect the velocity to decrease rapidly as the weight of water overlying the drainage tube decreases. It is the weight of the overlying water column (above the drainage tube) that provides the force to drive the water out of the tube.

122. C Look for key words in this question. Notice that you are given mass and a velocity. The mass is then changed and you are asked for the new velocity. What relationship do you know which relates mass and velocity? Use conservation of momentum to answer this question: mv = mv; 100x = (1)(10); thus, x = 0.10 m/sec to the left (because fluid is to the right).

123. D The MCAT has repeatedly asked examinees about the direction of the acceleration of gravity vector. This question is just another way of asking if you know which way the acceleration of gravity (g) vector is directed! The only acceleration of g points downwards. This is true when there are no other forces acting on a unit of water other than gravity.

124. B You are asked how far the droplets travel in the horizontal direction. Be sensitive to the fact that the question is only asking you about horizontal motion. The x and y components of velocity are independent of one another in projectile problems. Recall that the horizontal movement of a projectile only depends on the velocity in the x-direction and the time traveled. The vertical component of velocity has nothing to do with the horizontal travel. The following kinematic equation is required:

$$x - x_o = v_{ox}(t) = (10 \text{ m/sec})(1 \text{ sec}) = 10 \text{ m}.$$

This is an information-presentation passage (general chemistry) that contains some elements of a problem-solving passage. You are given information on tooth enamel, hydroxyapatite, and the effect of fluoride on enamel solubility. The questions require that you find information in the passage and answer questions based on your chemistry knowledge. The concepts tested include acid–base and Lewis dot structures.

125. B   The passage states that a decrease in pH results in reaction 2, which is the reverse of reaction 1. A decrease in pH corresponds to an increase in hydronium ion concentration and a decrease in hydroxide ion concentration. Because a decrease in pH favors the forward direction of reaction 2, it would favor the reverse direction of reaction 1, or the equilibrium position of reaction 1 would be pulled to the left. This best supports choice B.

126. D   You are looking for the choice which is not at all supported by the passage. Choices which may be implied by the passage would not be the best answer to this question. The "quick" answer that might be chosen for this question is A because the passage never stated that fluoride prevents a decrease in pH. The passage does state, however, that fluoride prevents bacteria from metabolizing sugars, and that the metabolism of sugars results in a decrease in pH. Choices B and C are implied by the passage. Choice D is the best choice because it is neither stated nor implied.

127. B   The answer to this question is given in the passage. The passage indicates that a decrease in pH (or an acidic solution) leads to demineralization, which is the process of hydroxyapatite dissolving. This means that hydroxyapatite is soluble in acid.

128. D   Hydroxide is the strong base that you should remember for the MCAT. Just about anything else can be assumed to be a weaker base than hydroxide in the absence of information from the passage. This helps you eliminate choices A and B. Choice D is a better choice than C. Because fluoride is a weaker base, it will take a much larger decrease in pH to dissolve it. This means that fluoride would be less water soluble than hydroxide.

129. B   Determine how many valence electrons should be present in a correct Lewis dot structure. The phosphate ion, PO_4^{-3}, has a charge of -3. Phosphate has five valence electrons and oxygen has six valence electrons. Add three valence electrons to account for the -3 charge:

Total Valence Electrons for Phosphate $= 5 + 4(6) + 3 = 32$ valence electrons.

Of the choices, only A and B have the correct number of electrons. Thus, eliminate choices C and D. Recall that a single bond is worth two valence electrons while a double bond is worth four valence electrons. Choice A is correct in that all atoms have octets, but the formal charges are -1 on each oxygen and $+1$ on the phosphorus. Choice B has fewer formal charges, with -1 on each of the single-bonded oxygen atoms and 0 on the other atoms. Phosphorus is in the third period or below so it can have more than an octet of electrons because it can use empty d-orbitals. This makes choice B the best choice.

130. C   See answer to question 129 for the justification of the correct Lewis structure. The formal charges are calculated by the formula:

$$FC = \text{number of VE} - \text{number of bonds} - \text{number of LE}$$

where VE is the number of valence electrons and LE is the number of lone electrons. For the single-bonded oxygen atoms: $FC = 6 - 1 - 6 = -1$.

This is a problem-solving passage (physics) that tests the principles of pulleys and rope tensions. This is an area in basic mechanics in which many MCAT examinees have difficulty. The problem arises for many students because pulley diagrams can appear confusing. On the MCAT, it is very strategic to redraw any complex diagrams as simpler, easy-to-understand diagrams. Think about the forces acting on each pulley. Sketch a force diagram summarizing the opposing forces. This passage provides a good example of a typical problem which is easier to solve by redrawing the involved forces.

131. C This basic conceptual question tests your understanding of mechanical principles of pulleys. For conditions at equilibrium, the tension of ropes on two sides of a pulley is equal.

132. A This is also a conceptual question testing your understanding of the difference between single- and multiple-pulley systems. As you may recall, a single pulley is used to change the direction of a force while combinations of pulleys are used to reduce the force needed to lift a load. Choice B is incorrect because pulleys have no significant effect on system torque. Choice C accurately describes a single-pulley system, but incorrectly describes a multiple-pulley system. Choice D is inaccurate based on the discussion given above.

133. D Focus on the key word used in this question: "constant speed." This gives a clue on where to start your thinking. Constant speed should make you think of zero acceleration and no force. Equilibrium occurs at constant speed. Thus, you know that the sum of the upward forces (F + F) and downward forces (−W) equal zero. Because the rope is continuous, the tension on both sides of the pulley is the same. As mentioned earlier, it is very strategic to draw a simple force diagram to summarize the involved forces. See the following figure. (Note that 2F + (− W) = 0, thus, F = W/2.)

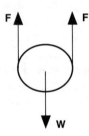

134. D The key to solving a complex problem like this is to try to diagram the net forces acting on the weight. See how the complex diagram is simplified in the diagram below. Always try to simplify difficult problems with pulleys. For this problem the equation describing the vertical components of forces acting on this system is derived by examining the diagram. The equation is 4F − W = 0. F = W/4.

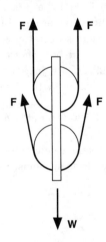

135. C The passage indicates that pulleys provide a mechanical advantage and act to redirect the direction of tension of strings which run over them. What the passage does not tell you, but what you are expected to know, is that the tension in a continuous string running over a single pulley is the same anywhere along the string. The pulley simply adjusts its position along the string to allow an even distribution of tension.

136. D The passage defines mechanical advantage. Notice that the diagram which was resolved for question 134 shows that there are four parallel ropes attached to pulleys, which support the weight. This means that the mechanical advantage is four.

137. A This question is easy if you know the definition of power. Power = work/time. Thus, choice A is the best choice. Choices B through D do not accurately describe power.

138. A A convex mirror acts to diverge light rays. Diverging (convex) mirrors create diminished, upright, virtual (DUV) images. The DUV mnemonic for convex mirrors is great to know for the MCAT because it saves you from having to do calculations with the thin-lens equation or drawing ray diagrams. The DUV rule holds for all convex mirrors, regardless of the focal length or object location.

139. C Charge X is positive, Y is neutral, and Z is negative. Use the right-hand rule to determine this solution. If the B-field is directed into the page (point fingers into plane of paper) and the direction of movement is up toward the reference point (point right thumb up), the palm gives the direction of the magnetic force on a positively charged particle (toward the right). The back of the right hand gives the direction of the magnetic force on a negatively charged particle (to the left).

140. D To solve this question, orient the half-reactions to show oxidation of magnesium and reduction of lead. Be sure to change the sign of the E^o value if you have to flip-around a half-reaction.

Oxidation of Mg(s): $Mg(s) \rightarrow Mg^{+2} + 2e^-$ $E^o = 2.37$ V
Reduction of Pb(s): $Pb^{+2} + 2e^- \rightarrow Pb(s)$ $E^o = -0.126$ V
Net Rxn: $Mg(s) + Pb^{+2} \rightarrow Mg^{+2} + Pb(s)$ $E^o = 2.244$ V

141. B Use the conservation of energy principle to solve this problem. The PE gained after bullet impact equals the KE of the bullet–block system at impact. The PE gained (vertical swing) = mgh, where m = total system mass and h = height gained by the system. Thus, PE = (x + y)gh = KE of the bullet–block system after impact.

142. A The elastic modulus is defined as: modulus = stress/strain = $Y_{(modulus)}$ = $(F/A)/(\Delta L/L_0)$. Force is in Newtons, area is in m^2, and both ΔL and L_0 are in meters. Therefore, $Y = (N/m^2)(m/m) = N/m^2$.

Biological Sciences

In this passage, the diagram of a rod cell is provided. Look carefully at the labeled regions of the cell and quickly think about what processes go on in each region. By previewing the question stems, it is clear that several questions test your understanding of cellular structure and function.

143. D The third paragraph of the passage indicates that G-proteins bind to the rod cell membrane. This best supports choice D. There is no information provided in the passage to support choices A, B, or C.

144. A The MCAT holds you responsible for understanding the basic mechanism for vision and the basic anatomy of rods and cones. In region A of the diagram, the stacked membrane disks of a rod cell are shown. These disks are a stack of tightly packed membrane structures. Embedded within these disks is the pigment rhodopsin. Region B of the rod cell contains mitochondria which act to supply adenosine triphosphate (ATP) for chemical reactions occurring in the rod cell. Region C is the nucleus. Region D is the rod cell–neuron synapse.

145. A In the second paragraph, the passage states that the rod cell is normally depolarized in the resting state. The paragraph goes on to say that this resting state corresponds to dark conditions. In the third paragraph, the passage indicates that in the presence of light, changes in the cell membrane occur. Use inference to answer the question being asked. In the presence of light, you should expect that the membrane would have the opposite state of polarity (hyperpolarization). This is the most reasonable choice. Resting membrane potential would be unlikely to lead to neuron activation. A state of no electrical potential would be extremely unlikely to lead to activation of postsynaptic sensory neurons.

146. C Region D is the location of rod cell to neuron synapse. Choice A is incorrect because region A is the region of the rod cell which contains membrane disks and cytoplasm. Region B contains mitochondria. Region E contains nerve fibers (optic nerve).

147. D This is a knowledge-based question. Vitamins have important functions in biological systems. Vitamin A is important in vision. Vitamin C is important to skin health and wound healing. Vitamin D is important in calcium and bone metabolism. Vitamin E has important antioxidant functions (preventing oxidation of important molecules in the body).

148. A The best way to answer this question is to look for similarities among the answer choices. Recall that there are two basic mechanisms for hormone function. Steroid hormones and thyroid hormone bind to intracellular receptors. Thus, choices B, C, and D have a similar mechanism of action. Choice A, epinephrine and its receptor, work by a G-protein–cyclic adenosine monophosphate (cAMP) mechanism. Generally speaking, epinephrine, norepinephrine, peptide, and glycopeptide hormones work via a G-protein–cAMP mechanism.

149. A Light energy enters the eye and strikes pigment molecules. These undergo a conformational change. The conformational change is associated with physical energy. The conformational change is linked to changes in ionic potentials. These potentials are associated with the conversion of physical energy to chemical energy. Finally, chemical energy is converted into electrical energy as action potentials are created. This question is easy to solve using the process of elimination. Only choice A shows that the last form of energy is electrical. Electrical energy is the form which is conducted down neuronal axons toward the brain.

PASSAGE II

This is a conceptual-understanding passage (organic chemistry). The passage describes the variety of useful drugs which can be extracted from plants. It also points out that for some drugs, including the vasoconstrictor cocaine, it is less costly to synthesize de novo. This passage provides the step-synthesis reactions for cocaine. The questions ask you to solve basic conceptual problems. It is important not to become overwhelmed when you see a complex mechanism on the MCAT. Remember that each step of the mechanism is relatively simple, and generally shows only one reaction taking place. Follow the synthesis carefully after previewing the passage and determine what is occurring in each step.

150. C This is a challenging question. In the conversion of I to II, note that there is a cycle. For this to occur, the acetyl protecting group needs to be removed from I. The purpose of the acid is to remove the acetal protecting group from I and expose the aldehyde for nucleophilic attack. Choice A is incorrect because the alpha carbon is not deprotonated. Choice B is incorrect because the amine on the upper portion of structure I is not protonated in the conversion of I to II. Acid does not hydrolyze esters in this reaction.

151. D Determining the number of chiral centers in a molecule is a common MCAT question. Chiral centers are found at carbons which are attached to four different substituents. There are four carbons in this structure, each bound to four different substituents. Recall that carbonyl carbons can never be chiral.

152. A This is a difficult question, best answered by the process of elimination. The question asks you why acid is needed in the second step of the conversion from III to IV. As you recall, acids commonly protonate compounds and help a reaction go forward. Choice A is reasonable because it suggests that hydrogen ion protonates the carboxylic acid group, allowing a transition state and decarboxylation to occur. This choice is consistent with the behavior of acids. Choice B states an absolute; the amine must be protonated for the reaction to occur. There is no evidence in the passage or reaction sequence supporting this choice. Choice C is also not supported in the passage. Choice D can be eliminated because it does not answer the question being posed; it explains why acid is not necessary, whereas the question asks why acid is needed.

153. B The number of stereoisomers in a compound = 2^n, where n = the number of chiral centers. If a molecule contains two chiral centers, there will be 2^2, or 4 possible stereoisomers.

154. D The MCAT requires that you understand the concepts of simple nuclear magnetic resonance (NMR). Remember that there are four important aspects of an NMR tracing. First, the number of signals gives information on how many different kinds of protons there are in a molecule. The positions of the signals on a tracing tells about the electron environment of each kind of proton. The intensities of the signals reveal the number of each kind of proton. The splitting of a signal into several peaks tells about the environment of a proton with respect to other, nearby protons. Always remember that equivalent protons do not split each other. For example, the protons of a methyl group are chemically and magnetically equivalent, and thus, no splitting occurs. In this question, the methyl group of the amine contains three protons equivalent to each another. These protons will produce a singlet. If seen on a tracing, expect this singlet to produce a tall peak, as all three protons contribute to the height of the peak.

This is a research-study passage (biology). In this passage, you are given a little background about the history of lysosomal discovery. The passage then presents an experimental protocol and describes the technique of the cytochemical reaction. Finally, the passage gives results of cytochemical reaction experiments for four patients. You are asked to evaluate the meaning of the experimental protocol and to interpret the results of the data presented.

155. D The lysosome is a membrane-bound organelle, so eliminate choice A. Choice B may be eliminated because the passage indicates that lysosomes are involved in cellular lysis. Choice C is incorrect because the lysosome contains hydrolytic enzymes and it is involved in recycling of organic materials within the cell. Look to the passage to identify the statement which is not true about lysosomes. In the first sentence of the passage, it is pointed out that the lysosome was described biochemically before it was found by microscopists. This supports that choice D best answers the question being asked.

156. D The passage indicates that lysosomal enzymes function best at a pH of 5. You should know that biological pH is around 7 (neutral). The cytoplasm bathes the endoplasmic reticulum and exposes it to normal, biological pH. A neutral pH is too alkaline for lysosomal enzymes to function properly. This is how lysosomal enzymes can function within the acidic environment of the membrane-bound lysosome without causing uncontrolled autodigestion of the cell. Excess alkalinity can also be thought of as insufficient protons (H^+).

157. B Electron microscopy (EM), as the name implies, is based on electron density. Areas of higher electron density visualize darker on EM. Light is not a factor (choice A). Choice C is incorrect; enzymes are catalysts and escape the reaction unchanged. Choice D is also incorrect because unused substrate is not localized to sites of acid phosphatase and is not electron dense. If substrate were electron dense, the experiment would be flawed.

158. D The critical issue here is lysosomal size. As long as the lysosomes are enlarged, we must consider a storage disease. Note that patients C and D show enlarged lysosomes. This suggests that these patients have lysosomal storage disease. Sample D shows no leftover substrate. This suggests an overactive acid phosphatase. However, based on the size of its lysosomes, some lysosomal enzyme is missing or dysfunctional. Sample B has leftover substrate, but the size of the lysosomes is normal.

159. C   Sample B showed lower than normal phosphatase activity (60% unreacted substrate) but the lysosomes were of normal size. This rules out storage disease (choice A), which by definition requires large lysosomes. The valid conclusion is that this lysosomal sample does not contain normal levels of acid phosphatase but its function does not require normal levels of this enzyme, as evidenced by the normal size of lysosomes. Thus, a naturally low level of the test enzyme may be at hand. Remember, there are many different lysosomal enzymes; each lysosome need not possess a complement of all lysosomal enzymes.

PASSAGE IV

This is a problem-solving passage (organic chemistry). The passage introduces you to the topic of separation and purification. Five different products of a chemical reaction are given and a series of questions test your understanding of various separation and purification techniques. The separation and purification of organic compounds is one of the most commonly asked organic chemistry topics on the MCAT. These questions may be particularly difficult because the answer to the first question is often required to answer subsequent questions. Make sure that you review this important topic!

160. D   The addition of aqueous acid will protonate any basic atoms (A and B) and place a charge on that atom if it started out neutral. The polar, charged species will dissolve in the water layer (compounds A and B), and the organic phase will contain C, D, and E.

161. C   Before the addition of an additional solvent, the aqueous phase contains A and B (see question 160). The addition of alkaline aqueous solution will deprotonate the carboxylic acid group in compound B and a negative charge will be placed on the compound. This charge and the polarity of the amine groups will allow compound B to stay in the aqueous phase. With the addition of base, compound A will be deprotonated and it will move into the organic layer. Note the aromatic, nonpolar, overall structure of compound A.

162. C   The question stem tells you that the least polar of the compounds will elute first. Of all the compounds shown in the figure, compound C is the least polar.

163. B   Use the process of elimination to arrive at the most likely answer. Choice A is unlikely because the mass of these two compounds is not all that different. You can estimate the molecular weight of each compound to determine this. Choice C is an emphatic statement which is false. Choice D is a nonsensical choice. Choice B is the best choice. The peaks associated with halogens show fragmentation. This is characteristic of both Br−, I−, and Cl−containing compounds. This is due to the natural abundance of the different isotopes of each of these halogens.

164. A   The question stem indicates that the aromatic compounds will generally absorb ultraviolet (UV) light when visualized on a thin-layer chromatography plate. Look at the structure of compounds A and C. Note that structure A is aromatic. Remember the 4n + 2 rule. A compound is considered aromatic if it has (4n + 2) π electrons (n = 0, 1, 2, etc) and is in a cyclic form. Double bonds contain 2 π electrons. Compound A is aromatic because is has 6 π electrons and is in cyclic form. Compound C has no π electrons, and is not aromatic.

INDEPENDENT QUESTIONS

165. D   A portal blood flow is defined as a circulatory pathway in which arterial blood flows into a capillary bed, veins, a second capillary bed, and a second set of veins (A → C → V → C → V). Thus, portal blood flow requires blood to flow through two sets of capillary beds separated by veins. Major portal systems are found in the intestine–liver and hypothalamus–pituitary.

276

166. B　Groups that are strong activators are ortho/para directors. This means that electrophilic additions take place at the ortho and para positions relative to the activating group. In the case of phenol, the activating group is the hydroxyl group attached to the ring. The hydroxyl group is a strong activator and ortho/para director. The hydroxyl group directs ortho/para because from these positions, the hydroxyl donates electrons into the ring to help stabilize the carbocation intermediate.

167. D　Hemoglobin is a respiratory pigment that contains four subunits. Each subunit contains a polypeptide chain and heme, which is an iron-containing prosthetic group. Each subunit can bind one molecule of oxygen. The binding of the first subunit with an oxygen molecule makes the binding of the second subunit with oxygen easier. The third oxygen molecule is bound easier than the second, and the fourth oxygen molecule is bound easiest. The progressive enhancement of oxygen binding with the binding of each hemoglobin subunit is known as positive cooperativity. This is possible because of the multisubunit structure of hemoglobin. Positive cooperativity gives the sigmoidal shape of the hemoglobin curve. Myoglobin contains only one subunit, and hence, can bind only one oxygen molecule. Myoglobin does not show positive cooperativity.

168. A　Competitive inhibitors have a structure similar to the molecule to be inhibited. This question is simply asking you if you know which neurotransmitter acts at preganglionic autonomic synapses. Recall that acetylcholine acts at autonomic, preganglionic synapses for both the parasympathetic and sympathetic nervous systems. Acetylcholine is the postganglionic, parasympathetic neurotransmitter. Norepinephrine is the postganglionic, sympathetic neurotransmitter.

This is a conceptual-understanding passage (biology). This passage emphasizes concepts in molecular biology. The concept of post-transcriptional modification, introns, and exons is discussed. The questions can be answered based on information given in the passage and a basic understanding of DNA, RNA, and eukaryotic gene regulation.

169. D　Although not discussed in the passage specifically, you should arrive at choice D as the best answer. The regions that are not present in the RNA are regions which have been spliced-out of the mRNA. The passage describes these as introns, yet introns is not a choice. RNA splices is an ambiguous term, making choice A unlikely. Choice B is incorrect, as exons are the coding sequences preserved in the mRNA. Choice C is incorrect; tRNA brings amino acids to the ribosome to translate proteins. Choice D is the best choice. Intervening sequences are those parts of the transcribed RNA which form loops during hybridization experiments (as described in the passage), and are not present in the final mRNA. Intervening sequences are the same as introns.

170. D　DNA contains deoxyribose, whereas RNA contains ribose. DNA contains thymine (which base pairs with adenine), whereas RNA contains uracil (which pairs with adenine). DNA is replicated from a DNA template, whereas RNA is transcribed from a DNA template. DNA and RNA both contain guanine.

171. B　When hybridization experiments are performed, mRNA is hybridized to DNA. The final mRNA is shorter than the region of DNA from which it was transcribed. This is due to the presence of intervening sequences or introns which have been "spliced-out" of the mRNA. When the mRNA is hybridized to the DNA, the regions of DNA which were ultimately "spliced-out" of the mRNA show as loops. These looped regions of DNA are unable to base-pair with the mRNA.

172. C　Post-transcriptional modification of RNA classically occurs in the nucleus. While a newly synthesized RNA molecule is still in the nucleus, the introns are removed and the exons are joined together. This process results in a continuous protein-coding sequence. A 5′ cap and a poly A tail are also added.

173. C　The shaded regions of Figure 1 are those portions of the RNA which are retained after the intervening sequences (introns) are removed. These shaded regions are known as exons.

174. C   The post-transcriptional modification of RNA, especially the addition of a 5′cap and a poly A tail, is important in protecting the RNA from degradation. Choices A and B (intervening sequences or introns) are cleaved to produce a functional mRNA; they have no distinct function in protection. Choice D is incorrect. Exons are not added to RNA and play no role in protection from degradation.

PASSAGE VI

This is a problem-solving passage (organic chemistry). In this passage, you are introduced to a group of inhibitors that binds irreversibly to enzyme active sites. A basic structure for the enzyme inhibitor is given, along with a table summarizing the activity of the inhibitor with different functional groups. The questions stress problem-solving ability, basic concepts from organic chemistry, and data interpretation from the table.

175. C   Notice that the inhibitor has a carbonyl group. The enzyme has an amino group. You should expect that the amine acts as a nucleophile and attacks the electrophilic carbon of the carbonyl. This allows a leaving group to be displaced from a tetrahedral intermediate. Notice that this mechanism is very similar to the formation of a peptide bond.

176. A   Answer this question by thinking about what the inhibitor does at the active site. Recall that the passage states that the inhibitor binds irreversibly at the active site by forming a covalent bond. Looking at the structure of the basic inhibitor, where do you think the covalent bond will form? On the hydrocarbon end or on the carbonyl end of the molecule? Certainly, you should expect that the reactivity is on the carbonyl end. Now look at the choices. There is no basis to expect that substitution or elimination reactions occur because the passage states that a covalent bond forms between the active site and the inhibitor. The passage does not mention whether any substitutions occur or whether double bonds form. The chemical reactivity of carbonyl groups (on inhibitor) and amine groups (in active site) best supports that an acylation reaction occurs. This occurs by the mechanism described in question 175. The active site is acylated by the inhibitor and renders the enzyme inactive by blocking the active site.

177. C   This is a data interpretation question. Use information given in the passage and the data table for reference. The passage states that the lower the IC_{50}, the more active the compound is as an inhibitor. Thus, the higher the IC_{50}, the less active the compound is as an inhibitor. If you wish to see where the size of the inhibitor may be interfering with its binding at the active site, look for where the IC_{50} markedly increases. Begin by evaluating the data table. Notice that at and above the i-propyl group, the IC_{50} increases significantly.

178. B   Your chemistry knowledge should tell you that the electronegativity of the halogens decreases from fluorine to chlorine to iodine. The data table shows that the IC_{50} increases from fluorine to iodine. Remember that the passage states that a lower IC_{50} corresponds to more inhibitor activity. Thus, as electronegativity decreases, inhibitor activity decreases.

179. D   Ask yourself what is special about the nitro group. Why does the nitro group increase activity? The nitro group brings into play both inductive effects and delocalizing effects. For the nitro group, one can draw resonance forms that "pull" electrons out of the ring of the inhibitor. Also, recall that the nitro group is electron withdrawing. A positive charge on nitrogen will inductively remove electron density from the ring. Stereoelectronic effects do not play a role in the activity of the nitro group.

PASSAGE VII

This challenging passage contains elements of an information-presentation and research-study passage (biology). The passage introduces the concept of infectious particles (prions), and discusses some disease entities that are believed to be related to infectious particles. The results of experiments are presented. Most of the questions require that you understand the meaning of the data presented. A few questions may be answered based on information given in the passage or your basic biology knowledge.

180. **C**   Prions are defined in the passage as proteinaceous, implying that they are proteins. No other conclusion is warranted. Comparisons between prions and viruses are made, but the key distinction is the absence of genomic material in the former.

181. **B**   Protein secondary structure refers to the formation of common three-dimensional structures like helices and sheets. Choice A is incorrect. The amino acid sequence comprises the primary structure. Choice C is incorrect because disulfide bonds are important interactions between cysteine residues; disulfide linkages are important interactions found in tertiary structure. Tertiary structure refers to the arrangement of secondary structure (helices and sheets) into a specific three-dimensional form. Choice D is incorrect because electrostatic interaction between subunits contributes to quaternary structure.

182. **A**   Replication of a prion is a good question given that they show no evidence of possessing nucleic acids. Choices B, C, and D all require that the particle possess a genome. Choice A is, by process of elimination as well as by looking at the experimental results, a valid hypothesis.

183. **B**   The two prion forms are stated to differ in terms of secondary structure. A stop codon would result in a truncated version of the protein. This answer would be acceptable were there no better alternative. Remember that on the MCAT, you should always look for the best answer. Understand that there are frequently two answers which are true statements, yet one statement is always better than the other. This is especially true in this question; choice B more specifically describes the desired change compared to choice A. Choice C is incorrect because a silent mutation does not alter the normal structure. Choice D can be eliminated because exon splicing is not relevant here.

184. **D**   This question simply tests your conceptual understanding of the function of central nervous system (CNS) regions. The cerebral cortex is reponsible for higher funtions, such as interpretation of sight, hearing, voluntary movement, and speech, memory, and higher level thinking. The thalamus is a relay station between the midbrain and the cerebral cortex. The spinal cord carries afferent and efferent nerve impulses to and from the brain. The cerebellum is responsible for maintaining balance, posture, and the coordination of smooth movements among other functions.

185. **C**   Answer this open-ended question by carefully evaluating each answer choice. Note that choices A and B are incorrect statements. Comparing the experimental from control results reveals primarily one thing: inoculation of the abnormal isoform is associated with a subsequent decrease of the normal isoform. This makes choice C correct and choice D incorrect.

This is a problem-solving passage (organic chemistry). This passage requires a basic understanding of carbohydrate chemistry. The concepts of monosaccharides, disaccharides, glycosidic linkages, and the Tollen's reagent are presented. The passage provides an unknown disaccharide which is evaluated with four different chemical tests. The results of these tests are given. You should take some time to evaluate the meaning of each test result. In addition, several terms are used in the passage that you may not be familiar with (e.g., osazone, phenylhydrazine). However, they are explained or used in a context that allows you to easily use the terminology to answer the questions being asked.

PASSAGE VIII

186. **A**   Disaccharides are molecules made from the linkage of two monosaccharides. The linkage is known as a glycosidic linkage, and forms when two hydroxyl groups from adjacent monosaccharide molecules combine in a dehydration reaction. Reducing sugars are those sugars that reduce Tollen's agent. Tollen's agent identifies aldehydes by reduction of a silver salt to silver metal. Recall that the process of mutarotation is one in which the optical rotation of a carbohydrate molecule changes between α and β forms during equilibration. All monosaccharides are reducing sugars because the process of mutarotation exposes the aldehyde group of the monosaccharide to Tollen's agent. Disaccharides can be reducing sugars if the free 1' OH-group mutarotates through its linear sugar form and exposes its

aldehyde group to Tollen's agent. This question requires that you refer back to the passage to see what formation of the osazone indicates. The passage states that the reagent phenylhydrazaine reacts with an aldehyde group to yield an osazone. This means that the sugar is reducible. This question asks you to determine what can be surmised based on formation of the osazone. Think about the structure of a disaccharide. What process will allow the disaccharide to become a reducing sugar? As already discussed, the process of mutarotation will allow the aldehyde group of the 1'OH-group to be exposed. This will allow the reduction of Tollen's agent. Choice B is incorrect. If mutarotation does not occur, the disaccharide will be in the cyclic hemiacetal form and will not reduce Tollen's agent. Choice C can be eliminated because there are no data to suggest that the monosaccharide units of the disaccharide molecule are identical. Choice D is also incorrect. Epimers are diastereomers that differ in the chirality about carbon 2. There are no data to support stereochemical structural differences of the disaccharide components.

187. D   The addition of acid to a disaccharide can have profound effects on the molecule. Extensive hydrolysis may occur. Generally speaking, the glycosidic bond linking the two sugars of the disaccharide will be broken. In addition, all of the acetal and hemiacetal linkages will be broken as well. This supports choices A, B, and C. Thus, choice D (A, B, and C) is best.

188. A   To solve this question, refer to the results of methylation reactions given in the passage. Note that exhaustive methylation followed by hydrolysis yielded monosaccharides with methyl groups in the 2,3,4 and 2,3,4,6 positions. Why is the 5'-OH group not methylated? The 5-OH position is not methylated because it must have been involved in some form of linkage, making it unable to participate in the methylation reaction. Look at the choices to see which best explains how the 5'-OH could have been involved in some form of linkage. Choice A is a correct statement (glucose is a six-membered ring), and explains the possible role of the 5'-OH group. If the 5'-OH group was involved in a ring linkage, it could not be methylated. Choice B is an incorrect statement. Glucose is a six-membered ring. In addition, if glucose was a five-membered ring, the 5'-OH group would be free to be methylated. Galactose is most likely a six-membered ring because it does not show methylation of its 5'-OH group.

189. A   This is a pretty easy question. The results of the enzymic hydrolysis reactions show that β-galactosidase hydrolyzed the disaccharide, while α-galactosidase did not hydrolyze the disaccharide. This suggests that the disaccharide contained a β-glycosidic linkage. Eliminate choices A and C; there is no evidence to suggest that α-linkages are found in the disaccharide. Choice D is a nonsensical term which does not address the question being asked.

190. C   This question is similar to question 186. Tollen's reagent identifies aldehydes by reduction of a silver salt to silver metal, producing a "positive result." The absence of an available aldehyde group to react with Tollen's reagent in a carbodydrate molecule gives a "negative" result. The reaction with the described disaccharide and Tollen's reagent would produce a positive result. This would indicate that the disaccharide would be a reducing sugar.

INDEPENDENT QUESTIONS

191. D   Iodine is an essential element contained in thyroid hormone. The two main thyroid hormones are T3 and T4. The hormones contain three iodine atoms and four iodine atoms, respectively. Radioactive iodine injected into a patient would be taken up by the thyroid gland. The radioactive iodine would then be used by the thyroid to make T3 and T4 hormones. Thyroid hormone, both T3 and T4, is important in controlling the metabolic rate of the body. The brain does not actively sequester iodine. The bone marrow is the site of blood cell and immune cell formation. The bone marrow does not actively collect iodine. The thymus gland is a structure located in the lower neck, overlying the trachea. The thymus gland is large in infants and progressively atrophies over time. The thymus is believed to be important in the maturation of T lymphocytes, a type of white blood cell

(WBC). Lymphocytes are produced in the bone marrow. Some lymphocytes leave the bone marrow after production and travel to the thymus gland. While in the thymus, these lymphocytes mature and develop the ability to function as competent immune cells known as T lymphocytes.

192. C Only choice C is false. The geometry of the carbonyl group and its substituents is trigonal planar (sp^2 hybridization), and the angle between the substituents is 120 degrees. The carbonyl group is resonance-stabilized and forms resonance structures.

193. D The nucleolus is active in synthesizing ribosomal RNA (rRNA). The nucleolus resides in the eukaryotic cell nucleus. The Golgi body functions include protein packaging and glycosylation. The endoplasmic reticulum has two forms: smooth and rough. The smooth endoplasmic reticulum functions in metabolic activities, including lipid synthesis. The rough endoplasmic reticulum contains many ribosomes and is an active site of protein synthesis.

194. C The isoelectric point is the pH at which an amino acid does not migrate in an electric field. The isoelectric point typically occurs where the concentration of the dipolar ion is greatest. For neutral amino acids, the isolectric can be found by averaging the pK_a values for the amino and carboxyl side groups. For alanine, $(2.3 + 9.7)/2 = 6.0$.

195. C This is a basic genetics question. Evaluate the clues carefully. The second clue is the easiest to start with. If male children of afflicted fathers never possess the trait, this suggests that the trait is linked to the X chromosome. An autosomal transmission would not always exclude transmission to sons. Recall that the father, with sex chromosomes XY, passes on the Y chromosome to his sons. The paternal X chromosome is never passed to sons. Daughters are produced when the paternal X chromosome is passed on. Now look at the first clue. The female children of afflicted fathers likely receive the genetic trait from their father. These females do not express the trait, suggesting recessive transmission. We also know that when these females produce sons, half of the sons are afflicted. This makes sense because mothers pass one of their two X chromosomes on to their sons. Note that the passage of this trait is linked to sex chromosomes. The most likely transmission is sex-linked recessive.

This is an information-presentation passage (biology). The topics of blood types, antibodies, and antigens are presented. Most of the information needed to answer the questions comes from the passage and your basic understanding of blood types. The questions that follow the passage focus on predicting the blood type of offspring, the probabilities of producing a particular blood type, and antibodies created to blood antigens. Use Punnett square analysis to evaluate the probabilities of producing offspring with a particular blood type.

196. D This question tests your understanding of blood genotypes versus phenotypes. The question stem and answer choices to this question give the phenotypic blood types (A,B,O), rather than the genotypic blood types. Recall that type A blood carries the AO genotype. Type B blood carries the BO genotype. Type O blood carries the OO genotype. Thus, if a woman with a genotype of BO produces a child with a man of blood genotype AO, the following genotypes can be produced: AO, BO, OO, AB. Thus, children with type A, B, AB, and O can be produced.

197. C A person with type A blood has type A antigens on RBCs and antibodies against type B antigens. A person with type B blood has type B antigens on RBCs and antibodies against type A antigens. A person with type O blood has antibodies against both type A and B antigens. However, a person with type AB blood has antibodies against neither type A nor type B antigens. Blood type AB is known as the universal recipient because the transfusion of any blood antigen into a patient with type AB blood will not generate antibody-mediated destruction of the transfused blood. Type O is the universal donor type because type O blood has neither type A nor type B antigens.

198. A As described in question 196, perform a cross between these two genotypes: BO × AO. The following progeny genotypes are formed: AO, BO, AB, OO. The chances of producing a baby with type O blood is 1/4. If you had been asked to find the chance of producing a baby boy (or girl) with type O blood specifically, the probability would have been $(1/4)(1/2) = 1/8$.

199. D Use blood type analysis to help identify which baby is which. A father who is type O has a genotype of OO. A mother with type A has a genotype of AO. A cross of these two genotypes produces 1/2 AO and 1/2 OO. This means that the babies have phenotypic blood types of either A or O. Babies 1 and 2 could be the sought-after baby. This corresponds to statements I and III, or choice D.

200. B The chance of a woman who is type B (genotype BO), and a man who is type A (genotype AO) having a baby of type O (genotype OO) is 1/4. A cross of the parental genotypes gives the following offspring genotypes: AB, AO, BO, OO. However, if the woman is Rh-negative and the man is Rh-positive, the offspring must be Rh-positive because the presence of the Rh factor (the term Rh-positive means presence of the Rh factor on RBCs) is dominant genetically to the absence of the Rh factor.

201. B This solution can be determined based on the description of hemolytic anemia and Rh incompatibility described in the passage. Choice B is the most reasonable choice. If antibodies against the fetal Rh-positive RBCs are injected into a mother shortly after delivery, any Rh-positive fetal RBCs will be destroyed. This will prevent the mother from forming her own antibodies against the Rh antigen. This is an effective technique to prevent hemolytic anemia of the fetus in future pregnancies. Choice A is not as good as choice B because it is too general. The key issue in avoiding hemolytic anemia as mentioned in the passage is to eliminate the fetal Rh antigen from the Rh- mother. Choices C and D are incorrect because these would likely damage the fetus.

202. A The immunoglobulin G (IgG) molecule is a monomer, and is the smallest of the major antibody classes and can cross the placenta. IgA is a dimer, consisting of two monomeric units connected together. IgA is an important antibody in secretions, and is found in saliva and breast milk. IgM is a pentamer, containing five monomeric units. IgM is found in highest concentration in blood, and is important in agglutinating bacteria. IgM is the first antibody type produced in an immune response. IgE is a monomer, and is usually found bound to cells of the body. For this reason, it is not able to cross the placenta. IgE is important in mediating allergic reactions and fighting parasitic infections.

PASSAGE X

This passage introduces the concept of enzyme deficiency, and discusses a clinical condition which is caused by the enzyme deficiency. An experimental technique known as restriction fragment length polymorphism (RFLP) is introduced, and a figure is provided which gives RFLP results. This is a problem-solving passage because you have to use the information provided in the passage and work through each question by applying your understanding of biology to new concepts and techniques.

203. B An essential amino acid is one that cannot be synthesized by the body at an adequate rate. Essential amino acids must be taken in through the diet. Phenylalanine (Phe) is an essential amino acid regardless of one's diet. Tyrosine (Tyr), on the other hand, is not essential because it can be synthesized by the body. Because Tyr is derived from Phe, it follows that once Phe is restricted, Tyr becomes essential. Choice B is therefore correct. Although it is true that the passage did not mention that Tyr is derived *only* from Phe, the other choices fortunately leave no room for this potential ambiguity. Choices D and A are incorrect because a reduced Phe diet would likely decrease phenylketonuria (PKU) symptoms in a patient with the enzyme deficiency. In addition, a diet low in Phe in a patient with PKU would protect the patient from illness and possible death.

204. D Choices A through C are all ways in which mutations are introduced into a genome. Crossing over, however, is the process by which recombination is accomplished. When homologous chromosomes are lined up during prophase I of meiosis, chromatids break at crossover sites and homologous segments are exchanged between the paired chromosomes. This process of recombination can serve to explain how new combinations of alleles arise on a chromosome. It can, of course, have a disruptive effect but this is not as likely as with the other three choices.

205. C The passage states that despite early detection and treatment, PKU patients often develop behavioral problems. Choice A is wrong because a PKU mother who does not maintain normal blood Phe levels can cause her genotypically normal fetus to manifest symptoms of PKU. Choice B is incorrect because nowhere was it stated that Phe should be eliminated from the diet of a PKU patient. In fact, an overly restrictive diet can result in abnormally low blood Phe levels which can lead to neurologic symptoms. Choice D can be eliminated because catecholamines, which include the neurotransmitters dopamine, epinephrine, and norepinephrine, are derived from Tyr, which is derived from Phe.

206. C The passage reveals that fragments A and B include the normal gene and the PKU gene. Three individuals (both parents and the unaffected son) in the RFLP analysis are not affected but carry both genes. Only affected individuals (stippled son and fetus) have no copies of fragment A. When a condition can only be expressed in the absence of a normal gene, that condition displays either an autosomal recessive or a sex-linked recessive pattern of inheritance. Choices B and D are therefore eliminated. The presence of any unaffected male with both fragments eliminates the possibility of a sex-linked recessive pattern of inheritance. This eliminates choice A, leaving only choice C. Many inborn errors of metabolism have an autosomal recessive pattern of inheritance.

207. C The RFLP analysis shows that the fetus has the PKU gene and no copy of the normal gene. Based on the genotype of its sibling with PKU, it is clear that the fetus will also have PKU. Choice B, although technically correct (all PKU patients carry the gene!), is not the best answer. *Carrier* describes an unaffected individual harboring a defective gene. Choice D is incorrect because early detection and treatment can greatly minimize neurologic symptoms.

---

208. C This challenging question requires that you have an understanding of basic stereochemical terms. Stereoisomers are isomers that have identical connectivity but different spatial configurations; two types are enantiomers and diastereomers. Enantiomers are stereoisomers that are nonsuperimposable mirror images of each other. Diastereomers are stereoisomers that are not enantiomers. In this question, the passage indicates that maleic acid and fumaric acid are cis/trans stereoisomers. The products formed by the reaction of bromine with these two acids would be diastereomers. Both enantiomers formed from the maleic acid/bromine reaction are diastereotopic with respect to the meso product formed from fumaric acid/bromine. Choices B and D are nonsensical terms.

PASSAGE XI

209. B This is a simple conceptual question. Recall that the maximum number of stereoisomers is given by 2^n, where n is the number of chiral centers. Therefore; $2^2 = 4$.

210. A Both the maleic acid and the fumaric acid would yield three isomers in a 1:1:2 ratio. Consider that both acids would give the same intermediates. Once the first bromine was attached, that would decide the stereochemistry at that site. The other carbon, as a planar carbocation, would contain no stereochemical "memory" of the type of acid from which it had been derived. Also, both faces of the carbocation would be accessible to attack by Br^-. Therefore, both starting acids would proceed through the same intermediate, and would give the same product ratio. The 1:1:2 ratio is an artifact of there being four possible orientations of attachment, two of which are identical.

211. A To answer this question, predict the product of the reaction described. Ethene is a symmetrical molecule. The product of the bromination reaction would be 1,2-dibromoethane. This molecule is achiral and has only one isomer.

212. C *Trans*-isomers are less polar than *cis* isomers. The net polarity vectors for *cis*-isomers are partially additive, whereas the polarity vectors for *trans*-isomers cancel. Molecule symmetry is not the primary reason why this trend exists; however, symmetry differences occur between *cis/trans*-isomers. This symmetry difference relates to the differences in *cis/trans* isomer polarity.

213. **C** Each propogation step of a free radical substitution reaction produces a product required for the next step to occur. This occurs in radical halogenation reactions, and is also known as a chain reaction. Adding halogens to alkanes tends to substitute halogens for hydrogens on alkyl groups. This substitution leads to a progressive halogenation of alkanes. The term *chain reaction* does not refer to reaction speed, so eliminate choice A. Choice B is incorrect because intermediates are formed in radical halogenation reactions. Choice D can be eliminated because radical halogenation reactions produce substituted, halogenated alkanes, not long chains or polymers.

INDEPENDENT QUESTIONS

214. **D** This question tests your understanding of tissue induction. Induction is a process by which a chemical mediator is released from one part of the embryo and causes a specific morphogenic effect in another part by inducing a particular developmental pathway. Notochord mesoderm usually induces the overlying ectoderm to form a neural tube. It is believed that the notochord mesoderm does this by releasing chemical mediators to the overlying ectoderm. By transplanting the notochord mesoderm to the ventral surface (stomach) of the animal, and assuming it is placed below ventral ectoderm, remnants of a neural tube will likely form. Choices A through C are incorrect because the mesoderm classically induces overlying ectoderm rather than other tissue types. Intestinal lining develops from endoderm. Kidney, blood vessels, and bone develop from mesoderm.

215. **D** Enantiomers have identical physical properties except for their behavior toward plane-polarized light. When a plane of polarized light is passed through a chiral compound, the plane is rotated. Pure enantiomers rotate the plane-polarized light in equal but opposite directions. Therefore, equal mixtures of two enantiomers provide no net rotation of plane-polarized light; in other words, the solution is optically inactive. In one molecule, they contain chiral centers with the same substituents but opposite configurations. Because they are always in solution at the same concentration, each cancels the optical activity of the other.

216. **C** Gene mapping can be performed when recombination frequencies are used to assign a gene a particular chromosome and to a region of the chromosome. Recombination frequencies can also be used to determine the distance between linked genes. The greater the distance between two genes on a chromosome, the greater the chances of a crossover between them, and the greater the recombination frequency. Of the gene combinations listed, E' and D are the closest together on the chromosome and would have the lowest recombination frequency.

217. **C** The loop of Henle plays an important role in helping produce a concentrated urine in the kidney nephrons. The loop of Henle is required to produce the high osmolarity of the interstitial space in the inner medulla regions of the kidney. This high osmolarity aids in maintaining the salinity of the interstitial space, which is needed for water reabsorption. The glomerulus is a tangled system of capillaries from which blood filtrate is produced. Blood enters the glomerulus under hydrostatic pressure. Small pores in the glomerular capillaries allow fluid and small molecules to filter out and enter an adjacent collecting structure, known as Bowman's capsule. From Bowman's capsule, filtrate enters the proximal convoluted tubule of the nephron.

218. **C** The tertiary amines do not form hydrogen bonds to one another. They can, however, form H-bonds to water; therefore, all low–molecular weight amines are soluble in water. The primary and secondary amines can form H-bonds to themselves and, therefore, have higher boiling points than tertiary amines.

219. **D** Normal physiologic responses to dehydration include sympathetic activation, parasympathetic deactivation, production of renin (leading to angiotensin II production), release of aldosterone, vasoconstriction, and increased secretion of vasopressin (also known as antidiuretic hormone [ADH]). All of these mechanisms either increase the blood pressure or decrease water loss from the body.

INTERPRETING SCORES ON THE MCAT PRACTICE TESTS

SCORING THE VERBAL REASONING, PHYSICAL SCIENCES, AND BIOLOGICAL SCIENCES SECTIONS

The scaled scores for Practice Tests 1, 2, and 3 are estimated based on the performance of Columbia Review MCAT students on these exams compared with their performance on the real MCAT. Each of these three tests is on an equal level of difficulty. However, an individual student may find one test more challenging than the other two based on that student's strengths and weaknesses.

Theses exams have been written to approximate recent MCAT testing trends. Most students should expect their results on these practice tests to predict actual MCAT scoring within 1 to 2 scaled points for each subject area. Therefore, these practice test scores do not necessarily reflect a student's *exact* MCAT performance. However, practice tests scores are useful for assessing performance range and guiding the student's study program.

For each section, count the number of questions that you answered correctly in the allotted time. This is your raw score. For each section, convert your raw score to a scaled score, using Table 1. The mean scaled score on each section (i.e., verbal reasoning, physical sciences, and biological sciences) is 8. The standard deviation for each test section is 2. For the two science sections, a score of 10 or higher is considered by many admissions committees to be the minimum score needed to be competitive for medical school admission. For the verbal reasoning section, you should aim for a score of 9 or higher. Good luck!

Table 1. Score Conversions for MCAT Practice Tests 1–3: Verbal Reasoning, Physical Sciences, and Biological Sciences Sections

Verbal Reasoning Raw Score	Physical Sciences Raw Score	Biological Sciences Raw Score	Scaled Score	Estimated Percentile Rank
64–65	70–77	71–77	14–15	99+
62–63	65–69	67–70	13	98–99
59–61	59–64	60–66	12	97
53–58	52–58	55–59	11	88–96
49–52	45–51	49–54	10	74–87
44–48	37–44	43–48	9	58–73
40–43	32–36	37–42	8	42–57
36–39	27–31	32–36	7	31–41
32–35	23–26	27–31	6	18–30
29–31	20–23	23–26	5	11–17
< 28	< 19	< 22	1–4	0–17

SCORING THE WRITING SAMPLE

The writing sample section of the MCAT is scored holistically, using a grading scale of 1 to 6, with a score of 1 being the lowest and 6 the highest. On the actual MCAT, two readers score the first essay and two different readers score the second essay. The final scores given to each of the two essays are summed. The numeric score, which may range from 4 to 24, is then converted to an alphabetic score, ranging from J (lowest) to T (highest). The letter score of N or O is usually the national mean. To be competitive on this section, you should strive to score at least two 4's on each of your two essays; this would correspond to a letter score of P or Q.

To score the essays, wait a few days before critiquing them. This will allow you to be more objective and critical. It is also helpful to have several friends or teachers read the essays. Use the real MCAT scoring criteria described below:

6   These papers show clarity, depth, and complexity of thought. The treatment of the writing assignment is focused and coherent. Major ideas are substantially developed. A facility with language is evident.

5   These essays show clarity of thought, with some depth and complexity. The treatment of the writing assignment is generally focused and coherent. Major ideas are well developed. A strong control of language is evident.

4   These essays show clarity of thought and may show evidence of depth and complexity. Generally, these essays present only a moderate treatment of the topic. The treatment of the writing assignment is coherent. Major ideas are well developed. An adequate control of language is evident.

3   These essays may show some problems with clarity or complexity of thought. The treatment of the writing assignment may show problems with integration or coherence. Major ideas may be underdeveloped. There may be some errors in mechanics, usage, or sentence structure. Generally, these essays neglect, distort, or minimally address one or more writing tasks.

2   These essays seriously neglect or distort one or more writing tasks. Frequently, there are problems with organization and analysis of the topic. There may be numerous errors in mechanics, usage, or sentence structure.

1   These essays may demonstrate the student's lack of understanding of the writing assignment. There may be serious problems with organization. Ideas may not be developed. Or, there may be so many errors in mechanics, usage, or sentence structure that the writer's ideas are difficult to follow.

Having your essays evaluated by multiple readers may not be practical during your MCAT preparation. If you have determined an approximate holistic numeric score from the scoring information above, you may estimate your alphabetical score.

Outstanding essays that have a score of 6 will earn you a letter score of S or T. Good essays that have a score of 5 earn you a letter score of Q or R. Better-than-average essays that have a score of 4 generally earn you a letter score of P or Q. Average essays with a score of 3 typically earn you a letter score of N or O. Essays that are below average, but still coherent, and that address at least two of the writing tasks are usually given a score of 2, which translates to a letter score of L or M. Poor essays that do not address the writing tasks are given a score of 1, which translates to a letter score of J or K.

GRAPHICAL ANALYSIS OF TEST RESULTS

The following figures show the distribution of students' scores on the *Columbia Review MCAT Practice Tests*. These distribution curves are similar to the percentile listing in Table 1. These distribution curves will give you a sense of how your performance on these tests compared with that of other premedical students. Best wishes, and good luck on the MCAT!

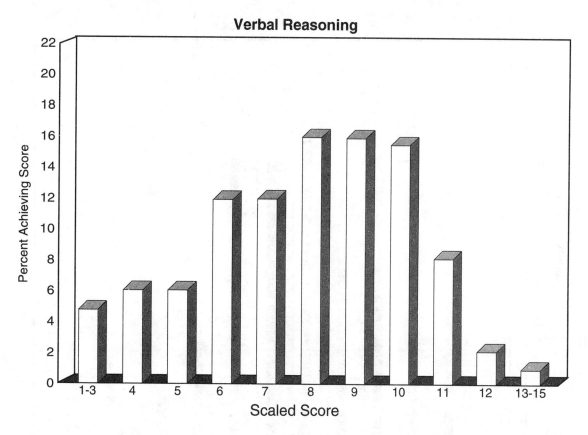

Figure 1. Distribution of scaled scores for the Verbal Reasoning sections of Practice Tests 1, 2, and 3.

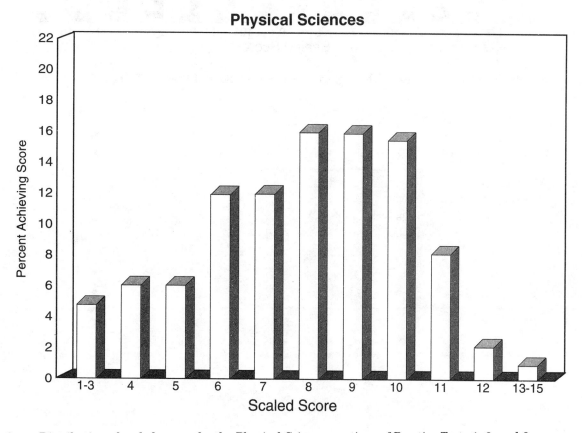

Figure 2. Distribution of scaled scores for the Physical Sciences sections of Practice Tests 1, 2, and 3.

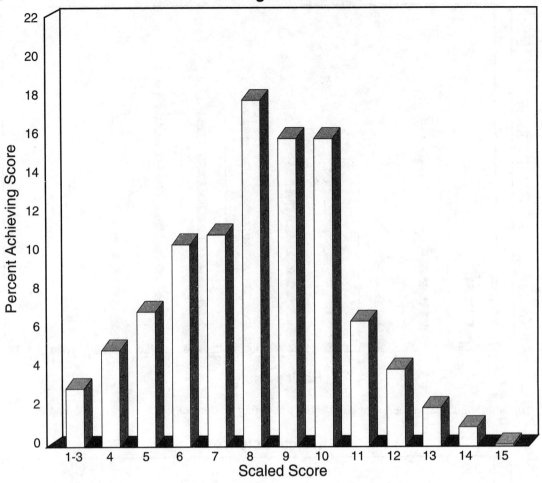

Figure 3. Distribution of scaled scores for the Biological Sciences sections of Practice Tests 1, 2, and 3.